Breaking the Bank

Breaking the Bank

The Decline of BankAmerica

BY

Gary Hector

Little, Brown and Company

BOSTON · TORONTO

FIRST EDITION

Library of Congress Cataloging-in-Publication Data

Hector, Gary, 1951–
  Breaking the bank.

  Includes index.
  1. BankAmerica — Management. I. Title.
HG2613.S54B334   1988   332.1'223'0973
ISBN 0-316-35392-2   88-8878

10 9 8 7 6 5 4 3 2 1

RRD-VA

*Published simultaneously in Canada
by Little, Brown & Company (Canada) Limited*

PRINTED IN THE UNITED STATES OF AMERICA

For Janice, Christopher, Colin,
Jaclyn, and Cameron

Acknowledgments

Many people contributed to the making of this book, not only those who gave generously of their time for interviews, but the scores who throughout my career helped educate me as a writer and taught me the mysteries of banking and the running of a large corporation.

In the course of writing this book, I spoke with nearly two hundred people. To those named and unnamed, I express my gratitude. They know how much their help has meant.

There are others, equally important, whose contribution I would like to acknowledge: Jennifer Josephy, my editor at Little, Brown and Company, without whose enthusiasm and careful editing this work would never have been completed; Kathi Paton, my agent and the instigator of this project; and Joseph and Miriam Gelband, whose advice and friendship helped me survive this process.

I would like also to thank Bruce Entin and Alison Rea, members of the Gang of Five, who read drafts of my manuscript and helped save me from myself.

This book would never have been started if not for my parents, who, by example, taught me the importance of honesty and morality.

And my thanks to the many colleagues at *Fortune* and former associates at *American Banker* and the *San Jose Mercury* whose aid and counsel have sustained and supported me during my career. In particular, I am indebted to Brad Henderson and William Zimmerman, who hired and trained me at *American Banker,* and Sanford Rose, whose challenging mind and friendship pushed me to understand how banks actually work.

I owe a special debt to Marshall Loeb, managing editor of *Fortune,* who not only granted without question my outlandish request for a leave of absence to write this book, but backed me enthusiastically.

The Hoover Institution also deserves special thanks. By accepting me as a visiting media fellow, it provided me with a home away from home, a stimulating environment in which to work, and generous support to ease all the mundane tasks of researching and writing a book. I cannot imagine a program better suited to the needs of a writer struggling to meet a deadline.

Through the long, difficult process of writing this book, no one played a more important role than my wife, Janice, whose skills as a researcher and reader were matched by her support and understanding through some very difficult moments. She survived the stress and strain despite being pregnant with our fourth child.

And finally, thanks to my children, Christopher, Colin, Jaclyn, and Cameron, who provide me with a constant reminder of what is important in the world.

Contents

When at some future date the high court of history sits in judgment on each of us, recording whether in our brief span of service we fulfilled our responsibilities . . . our success or failure, in whatever office we hold, will be measured by the answer to four questions: First, were we truly men of courage. . . . Second, were we truly men of judgment. . . . Third, were we truly men of integrity. . . . Finally, were we truly men of dedication?

John F. Kennedy, 1961
from a speech before
the Massachussetts
State Legislature

Prologue

On Monday, September 8, 1986, the directors of Bank-America Corp. faced the most daunting task that ever confronts a corporate board. Unlike other decisions made each month—the laying off of faceless employees or the wagering of millions on some bold strategem—this task was intensely personal, so personal that it had paralyzed the board for months.

Six years earlier, these men had chosen Samuel H. Armacost, a charismatic young lending officer, as chief executive of what was then the world's largest and most profitable banking company. Under his leadership, however, BankAmerica had fallen faster and further than any other bank in history, tumbling from record profits in 1980 to a loss of more than $1 billion for the latest twelve months. Now the board had to decide whether to fire Sam Armacost.

As BankAmerica's directors gathered in Los Angeles for their monthly meeting, the majority of the directors remained stubbornly committed to their young CEO. But by the end of the day their confidence would be shattered. Leland S. Prussia, the chairman of BankAmerica's board, would challenge Armacost's leadership, forcing the directors into action.

Prussia's move was unexpected and out of character. During thirty years at BankAmerica, Prussia had earned a reputation for being "too nice." Though he was a superb analyst and a solid economist, he had never openly challenged the chief executive, never displayed a strong, independent side. His job as chairman was a consolation prize, granted him in 1981 when the board chose Armacost, a man ten years younger than Prussia, as chief executive. Although he dined with heads of state, met regularly with the chairman of the Federal Reserve, spoke out on economic policy, and advised presidential candidates, within BankAmerica Lee Prussia had no real power.

For months, BankAmerica's decline had weighed heavily on Prussia. He had always looked years younger than his calendar age, erect, trim, with a broad forehead, thinning hair, and a quick, nervous smile that offered a glimpse of a warm, thoughtful human being. Now, at fifty-seven, Prussia looked worn, stooped. At business meetings he sometimes lapsed into long, awkward silences or launched into rambling monologues on the dismal state of the world economy. He avoided social settings where he might meet old friends and, at the office, regularly seemed submerged in gloom.

Intellectually and emotionally, Prussia was at war with himself. BankAmerica was taking desperate action. It was selling prized subsidiaries, closing offices around the world, and laying off staff—transforming itself into a smaller, more manageable firm.

But Prussia worried this might not be enough, that a major worldwide recession was coming, one that would capsize BankAmerica unless management found some way to raise billions of dollars of capital. Selling profitable subsidiaries and laying off people, Prussia was convinced, were not solutions, and might prove disastrous. In his darkest moments, Lee Prussia feared that BankAmerica was going to fail.

Never one to relish confrontation, Prussia now faced seemingly endless private battles with Sam Armacost. An unyielding optimist, Armacost believed—as he had for three years—that BankAmerica was on the verge of a turnaround. While others were worried about how to save BankAmerica, Armacost was on the golf course wooing customers, socializing with directors of the San Francisco Symphony or Safeway Stores, and spending weekends at the Bohemian Grove, a summer retreat north of San Francisco where busy corporate executives escape the pressure of their jobs.

In the last few weeks, the battles between Armacost and Prussia had taken a personal tone; Armacost had been urging Prussia to retire. Initially Prussia resisted, but when Armacost became insistent and an influential board member sided with him, Prussia conceded. Only those three knew that Lee Prussia had agreed to take early retirement later in the year.

With that choice something inside Lee Prussia snapped. For thirty years, he had played the good soldier, backing the chief executive whether he agreed with company policies or not. Now Prussia was prepared to break the habits of a lifetime. Pushed aside by Armacost, ignored by others in management, Lee Prussia was ready to take his policy dispute, his concern about the survival of BankAmerica, directly to the board. He was ready to confront Sam Armacost.

It was a typical fall day in southern California. A haze lingered over the valley, visibility was poor, and traffic crawled on the freeways. The weekend had passed uneventfully. The Los Angeles Raiders lost to Denver by two points, while the Rams beat St. Louis by a couple of field goals. News from the rest of the world sounded vaguely familiar. The Chilean government had cracked down on left-wing dissent, while in Russia, a U.S. reporter, Nicholas Daniloff, remained in custody for a second week, charged with spying.

BankAmerica's board had met informally, as it did each month, on Sunday, September 7. In the afternoon, board committees discussed policy questions, after which the full board sat down to dinner with Armacost. The only distressing event of the day was the appearance of a highly critical article in the *Los Angeles Times,* titled "BankAmerica Board: A Study in Inertia."

At 8:30 A.M. on Monday, committee meetings began again at BankAmerica's southern California headquarters. The building, an undistinguished rectangular solid of glass and steel, rose fifty-eight stories from the floor of the financial district in downtown Los Angeles. The committees and the full board met on the fifty-first floor in a huge conference room, with floor-to-ceiling windows that offered an uninspiring view of downtown. Heavy bronze double doors on either end of the room opened silently, automatically, as directors and staff passed in and out.

Shortly before 10:00 A.M., as the first committee meetings ended, Lee Prussia left the boardroom and approached a knot of men gathered in an adjacent executive suite. These were BankAmerica's outside advisers, some of the most talented counselors that money could buy.

Prussia headed toward John Gutfreund, the head of Salomon Brothers, one of Wall Street's largest, most influential investment banks, who had flown out from New York for this board meeting.

"I've got three scenarios that I want you to include in your presentation," Prussia said, clearly agitated.

Gutfreund was surprised. At the August board meeting, Salomon had been hired to review BankAmerica's financial position. For the last three weeks a team of investment bankers had been at work, meeting regularly with the company's top executives, including Prussia. They had spent days examining economic projections, financial statements, five-year forecasts, in the end accepting Armacost's optimistic vision of the world. Now the chairman of the board, one of the highest-ranking officers in the corporation, was telling them, ten minutes before they were to make their presentation to the board, that he disagreed with that forecast. He wanted Salomon to incorporate his views—three radically different sets of assumptions about the future—into its presentation.

Gutfreund explained that there wasn't time to make the changes, the directors already had Salomon's written report, and adding three new projections would only confuse them. "We just can't do it," he concluded.

Growing more agitated, Prussia asked a series of challenging questions, treating the forecast in the report as Salomon's assessment of the future, not management's. What about the possibility of a recession? What if the bank should shrink rather than grow? The questions implied that Salomon had failed in its job. Jay Higgins, a quick-tempered investment banker who was standing at Gutfreund's side, grew angry at Prussia's probing. Higgins, then head of Salomon's mergers and acquisitions department, began to defend the forecast, rebutting Prussia's charges, addressing him, tensely, as "sir."

Prussia kept pushing. He wanted the board to hear a complete analysis of these projections and he wanted Salomon Brothers to acknowledge that the economy could derail Armacost's plan. "You've got to do this," he urged. "This is important."

Gutfreund finally agreed to comment on Prussia's scenarios but refused to present them. Prussia turned and went back into the boardroom.

Normally, BankAmerica's board meetings run smoothly, unemotionally, dominated by a seriousness of place and of purpose. The size and importance of the boardroom itself discourages debate. Everything about it is solid, solemn, down to the massive board table, made of dark African bartiki wood, large enough to seat a dinner party of fifty, and the bronze bust of the company's founder, A. P. Giannini, watching over the proceedings.

Fifteen men sat on BankAmerica's board in September 1986. Four were members of management. The remaining eleven were outside directors, including the chief executives of three major corporations, retired executives from five more, a former president of the World Bank, and a former governor of the Federal Reserve. The youngest was sixty, prompting some in the bank to refer to them as "The Over-the-Hill Gang."

These were not emotional men, and, besides, decorum forbade shouting or table banging at board meetings, which were, traditionally, cordial affairs. Dissent, when voiced, came usually in the form of polite questioning normally preceded or followed by praise for management.

As Prussia returned for the start of the full board meeting, he took his accustomed seat with his back to the windows. Armacost was on his right. Seated on either side of the table were the other directors and behind them in a separate line of chairs sat a few other BankAmerica executives.

Many insiders expected the board to fire Armacost. With the morbid curiosity of bystanders at a serious accident, they watched and waited, trying to read the faces of the directors.

The board had already read the usual monthly reports, several dozen pages of financial and economic data. The drab, dun-colored briefing books, chockablock with computer printouts, described the state of the company in detail. There was a list of the bank's largest depositors, showing that the Bank of China had more on deposit than any other single entity. A few pages later, a director could review the monthly budget of any division or check the progress on major investments—anything from a branch parking lot to a computer system costing several hundred million dollars. And of course, there were lists of problem borrowers, economic forecasts, and tables full of information on financial markets and foreign currencies. "The board was given far more information than it could digest," one former BankAmerica executive observed.

The center of attention this month, though, was the special report from Salomon Brothers, a forty-six-page review of BankAmerica's finances. It was a typical Salomon study, slickly printed on 8 1/2-by-14-inch paper and bound in dark blue plastic with a clear acetate overlay. The title, chosen to conceal the identity of the client from prying eyes, was "Project Golden Gate."

As the investment bankers from Salomon Brothers entered, Lee Prussia began his presentation. A bank executive who had helped prepare Prussia's economic forecasts distributed them to the board.

Prussia discussed these projections, describing the major economic forces that worried him. He outlined his concerns about a recession, expressing his doubts about the profits predicted in the Salomon study. Their forecast was built on crucial assumptions about the economy, interest rates, loan demand, and the bank's ability to raise capital. Prussia emphasized that if these assumptions were overoptimistic—as he thought they were—the bank could not grow as fast as Armacost expected and would never report the profits he foresaw.

Within seconds, it was clear that Prussia was in trouble. To him, these economic forecasts revealed BankAmerica's true predicament. As an economist and financial analyst, he had spent thirty years preparing and reviewing such reports. But these weren't economists he was addressing. They were businessmen. They wanted a bottom line, a solution to problems. All Prussia had was questions.

To the board members, the tie between Prussia's economic scenarios and BankAmerica's health was unclear. And the relationship between his forecast and Salomon's report was infuriatingly muddy. What impact would these changes in the economy have on the bank's profits? Why was the chairman of the board introducing this material now? Why hadn't this been worked out before the meeting?

In another setting, Prussia's presentation might have played better. But in the boardroom, with its formal air, its icy rationality, Lee Prussia seemed emotional, nearly out of control. His voice rose, becoming shrill. Some board members grew angry, others seemed simply confused. More than one person felt "embarrassed." A witness described Prussia's tone as "whining, complaining," adding, "The only one who was in a panic was Lee."

Jay Higgins followed Prussia. Instead of the simple, calm presentation he had expected to make, Higgins faced a battery of questions. The meeting had grown tense, directors were on edge.

The first portion of the Salomon report was a grim recounting of Armacost's record. In 1981—Armacost's first year as chief executive—profits declined by 30 percent. They slid steadily for the next three years, and then, in 1985, BankAmerica posted its first loss since the Great Depression. The second quarter of 1986 brought even worse news, a loss of $640 million, which pushed the total red ink for twelve months to more than $1 billion. Only one other bank, Continental Illinois, had ever lost that much money. (Driven to the edge of collapse by panic-stricken depositors, it was then taken over by the U.S. government.)

Loan write-offs for the five and a half years totaled $4.6 billion—an amount then greater than the average annual income of the population of Sacramento, Louisville, or Tampa. At the end of June, BankAmerica still had more than $5 billion of bad loans on its books, as well as $10 billion of shaky loans to governments and businesses in underdeveloped countries. Even worse, the company was shrinking, which meant that the bad loans were becoming an ever-larger part of the company's total assets.

This was familiar information. Board members had heard it before, only each time they heard it, the figures seemed to grow worse. The only surprise in the Salomon study came in the report on expenses. In March the board had named Thomas A. Cooper president of the Bank of America, the principal subsidiary of BankAmerica, making him responsible for cutting costs, something Armacost had been unable to do. Salomon's report showed an embarrassing lack of progress. Management told the board in March that it would cut the company's total payroll by 6,800 people in 1986, yet in the twelve months ending June 30, only three hundred jobs—less than 5 percent of the cuts promised—had been eliminated.

Salomon had prepared charts comparing BankAmerica's performance with that of other banks. This simply converted the bleak statistics into even bleaker graphs. The line representing BankAmerica, in red, headed off the page in the wrong direction on almost every chart.

From this grim introduction, Higgins moved to the core of his presentation, the table labeled "management's projections of earnings for the next five years." This was the forecast on which everything else hinged. Any decision that BankAmerica's board made about Sam Armacost or the future of the company would depend on this forecast. And this was the material that had outraged Lee Prussia, forcing him to stand up. Salomon Brothers sensed how controversial the numbers were. "They called them 'management's projections,' " one insider pointed out, "and they seemed to hold them up at arm's length, like a dirty diaper."

Analyzed line by line, the projections looked reasonable. The company showed gradual progress through 1990. Loan problems dropped sharply in the first year, then slowly thereafter. In 1986, the company would set aside more than $2 billion to cover bad loans, but by 1990 the annual provision would drop to $600 million. Expenses would also drop sharply the first year and then rise gradually as the company began to expand rather than shrink. It seemed plausible, examined that way.

In total, though, the forecast read like a corporate reenactment of the resurrection of Lazarus. At the end of five years, BankAmerica would be earning $1 billion a year. That translated into a 1 percent return on assets ($1 of profit for every $100 of loans and investments), a state of perfection never before experienced by BankAmerica and not seen at any other large retail bank in decades. The forecast thus predicted the most dramatic turnaround in the history of American banking. Not only would the company turn losses into profits virtually overnight, it would end up more profitable than it had ever been in its history.

"It was simply unbelievable," says one individual who regularly attended board meetings.

Lee Prussia understood that. Salomon Brothers understood that. Whether the board—except for a few dissident directors—understood it is a matter of debate.

Throughout the Salomon presentation, Lee Prussia continued to ask questions. Higgins bristled at his combative, irritating tone. At one moment Higgins turned bright red as he attempted to control his temper. But Prussia was not deterred. Again and again he drove home the idea that the plan being presented by Salomon Brothers—Armacost's plan—was built on blind optimism.

"I know you've heard this before . . ." Prussia said at one point before launching into his speech again.

At that moment, John R. Beckett, head of the executive committee and former chief executive of Transamerica Corp., tried to silence him. Beckett was a powerful force on the board, and the only person in the room, other than Prussia and Armacost, who knew about Prussia's pending retirement. He was growing furious.

"We've heard that before, let's move on," he growled.

Prussia cut his answer short, only to resume his attack a few minutes later.

Board members turned to Armacost and Cooper for a rebuttal. In a less-charged session, Armacost might have quelled any rebellion on the board. He is a persuasive and quick-witted speaker, with the confident look of a chief executive. Just under six feet, with thinning black hair and dark features, he appears poised, self-assured, even under pressure. He has the build of a good golfer or tennis player, and he speaks in a rapid staccato, mixing pithy, personal asides with long, rambling, jargon-laden pronouncements, punctuated at moments with sports analogies. Occasionally, in his own expansiveness, his statements prove self-contradictory, but he casts such a spell with his rhetoric, speaking with such assurance and conviction, that a listener realizes only much later that Armacost's arguments might have been flawed.

The directors had long ago grown accustomed to Armacost's persuasiveness, and they expected to be swayed. His response to Prussia was predictable: the company's strategy was working, you could see it in the latest monthly financial reports. Management was cutting costs, progress was being made. If it weren't for the loan losses, the company would be right on target. Since the bank finally had the loan problems under control, profits would start rolling in soon. This had all sounded convincing in 1985 and in early 1986, but by now it had developed a hollow ring.

The board turned expectantly to Tom Cooper, the president of Bank of America and the company's chief cost-cutter. A blunt, plain-spoken executive, Cooper, then forty-nine, had a full head of close-cropped brown hair, square glasses, and the earnest look of someone who might have played the father in a 1950s situation comedy. Cooper had grown up in a lower-middle-class neighborhood in Philadelphia, worked his way through school, and spent a couple of years as a Methodist minister. He prides himself on his honesty and on his loyalty to his boss. Now these two elements of Tom Cooper's personality were in conflict.

Cooper knew BankAmerica was in serious trouble. At times

he doubted it would survive, or that it had a right to survive. He had no doubts, though, that the company needed to cut costs if it hoped to compete effectively in the future. Whether the profits that Armacost foresaw could be attained was impossible to predict. That depended on a host of factors outside Cooper's control: interest rates, the bank's competitors, the growth of the economy.

What Cooper knew, and what he told the board, was that he would trim expenses just as forecast. BankAmerica would reduce its overhead, lay off employees. He had drawn up a list months ago of what needed to be cut, and he knew which bodies had to be eliminated.

Out of loyalty to Armacost, Cooper did not go further. He stopped short of supporting management's predictions, but he also stopped short of expressing his doubts. Board members who were eager to hear a rebuttal of Prussia did not get it. Some observers sensed a Machiavellian motive in Cooper's silence. "He was making a play for Sam's job," one said later.

However anyone read it, Cooper's silence underscored the growing picture of a management at war. BankAmerica's three top executives were locked in a disagreement they could not resolve. Cooper's reticence confirmed the disarray, forcing the board to wonder whether Armacost should go. "We were watching a management team disassemble before our eyes," said one observer. "It was a historic moment in corporate America."

Now Salomon gave the board more reason for concern. After BankAmerica's huge losses, bank regulators had put intense pressure on the directors to raise capital. In March Salomon Brothers had told the board it could raise $1 billion from the public. Now that window had closed. After the $640 million loss in the second quarter, big investors no longer had any appetite for BankAmerica stock.

Private investors might inject capital, but they would offer low bids and in return would want seats on the board and a change in management. A merger with another bank was possible, but that would mean losing control of the company entirely.

The only palatable way to raise capital, it appeared, was to sell some of the bank's assets, to continue the slow process of liquidating the company. The bank had already disposed of $15 billion of assets in subsidiaries that were no longer essential to its strategy or in lines of business that were profitable but expendable. Salomon listed $16 billion more that could be sold, but this was a desperate strategy, one that might ultimately fail.

Throughout the meeting, Robert McNamara had remained surprisingly quiet. Over the past two years, McNamara had become Sam Armacost's sternest critic, voicing his doubts as he had throughout a long controversial career. He had been one of the original whiz kids at Ford Motor Co., rising from accountant to president of the company. He was an architect of America's war in Vietnam, serving as Secretary of Defense to John F. Kennedy and Lyndon B. Johnson. Under Johnson, McNamara had come to realize this was a war the United States could not win, but the public remembered him best for the blood-chilling statistics used to chart the war's progress, the kill ratios and projections of enemy dead.

By 1986, McNamara had grave concerns about the future of BankAmerica. In the waning minutes of the board meeting, as Jay Higgins wrapped up the Salomon presentation, McNamara found his voice.

For at least two years, he had spoken out regularly and strongly, with little effect. But at the end of the tense meeting, with the fate of the chief executive in doubt, he took the opportunity to raise the right questions, to voice the concern that all board members shared.

McNamara wondered whether management had properly weighed the risks facing it. Any number of changes could undercut the optimistic forecast presented by Armacost. He listed several.

Before joining the board in 1981, he had spent six years as president of the World Bank, grappling with the international debt crisis. He knew how a downturn in the world's economy could cripple countries like Argentina, Brazil, and Mexico. He knew what that would mean to BankAmerica, which had more than $10 billion in loans to major Latin American debtors. "Money center banks are going to take some big losses," he predicted.

Congress was finishing tax reform legislation; McNamara thought the changes might encourage consumers and businesses to cut back their borrowing. He worried that the bank's loan problems were not yet under control. Losses occurred erratically. "I have no confidence that the loan loss reserve is adequate," he said.

Bank regulators appeared ready to step up their demands

for capital, the benefits from cost-cutting were likely to come far more slowly than expected, and it was quite possible that the income on new loans would shrink over the next few years rather than increase. Everything else aside, the company faced growing competition in all its markets. And, most ominously, the bank was losing large depositors at a disturbing rate. McNamara estimated that the bank had lost $2 billion of deposits in recent months.

McNamara's speech provided a fitting coda to the session. "It was Bob McNamara at his best," says one observer. "He just let everybody have it."

John Gutfreund, from Salomon, followed McNamara. As investment adviser, his task was to pose the key questions remaining for the board. The directors, he said, had to balance the dark views of Lee Prussia with the optimism of Sam Armacost. If the board was comfortable with management's plan, it should stick with it. But Gutfreund's final comment reverberated like a judge's charge to a jury: "The board has to decide whether it has the management team that it wants."

The outside directors asked BankAmerica's management to leave the room. Then Philip Hawley, the chairman of Carter Hawley Hale Stores, Inc., an influential board member whose support for Armacost had been wavering, expressed alarm: "Have you ever seen anything like this in your life?"

After less than a half hour of discussion, the board voted on whether Sam Armacost should remain as chief executive. Hawley's defection split the board down the middle. Armacost retained his job by a single vote.

But with that decision, the support that had kept Sam Armacost at the helm of BankAmerica crumbled. The board was clearly so divided that a change in management was inevitable. Had one of the directors suggested a logical alternative, a replacement who could have rallied support, the vote might have gone the other way. But despite the record of Sam Armacost, the "Over-the-Hill-Gang" had not prepared itself for this moment. The lack of planning, the indecisiveness, the short-term thinking that had cost BankAmerica so much was as obvious in the boardroom as in management.

A month later, at its October meeting, the board would finally act. It would fire Sam Armacost and then stun the financial community by replacing him with Alden Winship "Tom" Clausen, Armacost's predecessor. Clausen, sixty-three, had spent six years at the World Bank, succeeding McNamara. His strongest asset was that he knew the company and the board well. He had appointed the majority of the directors. But he was also the person many insiders blamed for running BankAmerica into the ground.

BankAmerica's board was driven by panic. The members realized in September that the bank was adrift and that Armacost no longer had the support of his own management team. The board suspected that the company was in far worse shape than Armacost implied, and that under the circumstances anything was possible—a takeover, a run by depositors, some new management blunder. It was possible, just possible, that Bank-America, a powerful, swaggering institution five years before, might be dying.

Outside BankAmerica, especially among the alumni, the death of the company had been predicted long before 1985. It was, the old-timers said, "a tragedy." There had never been anything quite like Bank of America. Founded by a fruit peddler, opened in a converted saloon, run by a team of poorly educated children of immigrants, Bank of America in just forty years rose to become a bank so vibrant and self-assured that it terrified competitors and forced the rewriting of the nation's banking laws. For thirty years it was the biggest commercial bank in the United States, and for much of that period the biggest commercial bank in the world.

And then it had collapsed.

What had gone wrong? The world had changed: banks were allowed to compete more freely, the economy soured, and prices plunged for the first time in nearly fifty years. This took a horrible toll on BankAmerica. But in the end, it was a failure of management that cost the company most heavily. BankAmerica's management failed to foresee the changes that were coming, failed to prepare.

Some blame Armacost, others Clausen. But a few argue that the seeds of failure were sown in the company's earliest years and became part of the personality of the bank, a personality instilled by one of the legendary figures of American finance.

The Giannini
Years

Chapter One

I might never have gone into the banking game if I hadn't got so damn mad . . .

Amadeo Peter Giannini, Founder, Bank of America

Amadeo Peter Giannini founded the Bank of America in 1904. Within forty years it had become the largest commercial bank in the United States, but more than that it had redefined the way banking is done in America. A. P. Giannini's contribution to banking rivals that of J. Pierpont Morgan. While Morgan reshaped corporate America, building titanic competitors like U.S. Steel and the giant railroads, Giannini brought democracy to banking. He built a bank to serve "the little fellow," just as Henry Ford had built a company to produce automobiles for Everyman.

Giannini stood six feet two inches tall, weighed more than 240 pounds, had a booming voice, and a near-photographic memory for names and faces. He entered business at the age of twelve, buying and selling fruit on San Francisco's docks, and didn't become a banker until he was over thirty. When he did, he brought an unorthodox style to the profession. He advertised for customers, a practice his fellow bankers thought vulgar. He worked long hours, rising early, hitting the streets in time to solicit business from merchants, shopkeepers, workingmen. He coveted customers that other bankers wouldn't touch, the small businessmen and the working stiffs, many of them immigrants who could barely speak English.

In 1930, Giannini told Congress, "The little fellow is the best customer that a bank can have, because he is with you. He starts in with you and stays to the end. Whereas the big fellow is only with you so long as he can get something out of you; and when he cannot, he is not for you anymore."

Giannini despised most bankers, didn't trust big corporations or Wall Street, and worried constantly—often with justification—that his enemies were hatching plots against him.

He built the first statewide branch banking system in America. He diversified into insurance, investment banking, and mortgage banking. Fifty years before it became fashionable, Giannini was building a financial department store, a single, nationwide chain that would offer loans, investments, and insurance under one roof. He bought banks throughout the western United States, preparing for a march across the nation (a march that Congress would thwart with legislation passed in the 1930s and the 1950s).

Giannini championed nationwide banking. He sensed that it was inevitable that banks would operate coast to coast, just as department stores and drug stores did. As he told Congress in 1930, "It is coming gentlemen, and there is nothing that you can do to stop it."

Giannini was quotable, accessible, and independent, with a common touch that success never changed. He told the press that it was a constant battle for him not to build a large personal fortune. "Too much money spoils people, it always has, it always will," he said. At his death, Giannini's personal net worth totaled under $500,000, less than he had when he founded what is now BankAmerica. He could easily have amassed a fortune to rival that of the robber barons, but he chose not to. Under his contract with the company, he earned 5 percent of the company's annual profits—in some years nearly $2 million. He drew enough to live well, often traveling to Europe, but gave most of the rest away.

Giannini also built well. By the time of his death, in 1949, his family ran one of the largest financial empires in the world, for his son Mario was president of Transamerica, the holding company that owned Bank of America. The vestiges of that empire remain today in four companies: BankAmerica Corp., until 1980 the nation's largest commercial banking company; Transamerica Corp., one of the nation's largest insurance companies; First Interstate Bancorporation, the nation's seventh largest bank holding company; and Citicorp, the nation's largest bank holding company, in which the Gianninis were once the major single shareholders. These four companies in 1988 controlled over $400 billion in assets with stock worth more than $15 billion.

The shadow that A. P. Giannini cast still hovers over Bank-America. Almost forty years after his death, employees seek inspiration from him as they try to solve problems. A 118-page collection of quotations from A. P. circulates throughout the bank. The company quotes him faithfully in its publications, and, each May, celebrates his birthday with a ceremony that includes placing fresh flowers on the bust of A. P. in the lobby of the Bank-America world headquarters building.

A. P. Giannini was born in 1870, in San Jose, then a tiny agricultural community at the southern tip of the San Francisco Bay. In the late 1800s, San Francisco, and the surrounding area, was in its infancy. Ten years of prosperity had followed the great gold rush of '49. San Francisco grew almost overnight, from a small pueblo community into a boom town, complete with rickety wooden structures and festering slums. Its character was rough and vibrant, with more sin per square inch than any other city west of the Mississippi.

A portion of the city belonged to the immigrants, who began arriving en masse after the end of the Civil War. Most landed in New York and stayed there, but a small, hardy group found its way to California.

Among the immigrants were a vast number of Italians, largely peasants who had fled the poverty of their homeland for the promises of the new world. As have other immigrant groups, these Italians settled in their own neighborhood. In San Francisco, the section they claimed was North Beach, where they built a smaller, more affluent community than the corresponding settlements in New York and Chicago.

Prejudice against Italians ran strong as A. P. was growing up. In 1890, one writer captured the bias of the day, characterizing Italians as "dagos," who would stab one another just as readily as slice a pear, who played penny-ante games after dinner with their knives at their sides, quarreled over meals, slept in herds, and turned their backs on the violent brawls among their countrymen.

Many Italians settled south and east of San Francisco, where they began to farm. The area around San Jose was particularly attractive, recreating almost perfectly the warm, fertile agricultural climate that they had known in Italy. Into the valley flooded thousands of immigrants.

San Jose boasted some five thousand people by the 1860s, making it the largest city in the Santa Clara Valley at the time Luigi Giannini immigrated to California from Genoa. Giannini was the son of a well-to-do grape grower. Only twenty years old and accompanied by a new bride, Virginia, just fourteen, Luigi paid for their passage to America and took the new transcontinental railroad from New York. A family friend had moved to San Jose and had written home about its wonders. Luigi had decided to follow.

The couple brought enough money to lease the Swiss Hotel, a twenty-room, clapboard landmark in downtown San Jose, where, on May 6, 1870, Amadeo Peter Giannini was born. Within a year the Gianninis had saved enough to buy their own forty-acre farm, in Alviso, a town northeast of San Jose.

The farm prospered, and the Giannini family grew. Two brothers followed A. P.—Attilio, later known as "Doc," and George.

In 1877, as he rode his horse near the family orchard, Luigi Giannini was shot by a crazed farmhand in a dispute over a one-dollar debt. A. P., just seven years old, held his wounded father in his arms and watched him die. Biographers are tempted to view the circumstances of the shooting, and especially the role of that small debt, as powerful subconscious influences on Giannini that later led to his passionate commitment to build a bank for workers and small businesses.

Virginia Giannini, widowed at twenty-one, the mother of three small children, continued to run the farm, although she quickly married again, this time to Luigi Scatena, a teamster who worked for local merchants and produce farmers. In 1882, when A. P. was twelve, the family moved to San Francisco, where Scatena became a commission merchant, working midnight to noon buying and selling produce as it arrived at the docks.

Scatena's business fascinated young A. P., who would tag along when his stepfather rose at midnight to head for the docks, where river boats from the fertile inland valleys of California would appear, bearing fruits and vegetables. Under the glare of gaslights, the commission merchants would haggle and shout out orders until all the produce was sold, loaded onto horse-drawn wagons, and carted off to local merchants. Captivated by the excitement of this strange world, Giannini would steal out against his mother's orders, carrying his boots in his hands, rather than miss a night.

Giannini's grades scarcely suffered, for he was a good student, and would head right to school after a night on the docks. He attended Washington Grammar School in San Francisco, took six months of business courses at the Heald's Business College, and then, at age fifteen, left school to work full time for his stepfather.

Giannini's stepfather had opened his own firm, and A. P. helped out, wandering onto barges and other vessels to check the ship's manifests, making a mental list of the produce on board, which he reported back to Scatena. Armed with this inventory of the fruits and vegetables available on the docks, Scatena & Co. had an edge over its competitors.

A. P. also began to write letters to farmers in the region—without the consent of his stepfather—promising them a square deal and a fair price if they would do business with Scatena & Co. The sales program apparently worked, and Scatena started receiving shipments from farmers he had never called on before.

Selling fruits and vegetables was a volatile business, and A. P. quickly developed a sense of how markets operate. At midnight, the trading would begin, with boats arriving from all over the valley. Scatena would haggle with the other commission merchants to buy produce, then cart it to his offices for distribution to grocers in the city. Sales came either through auctions or in direct, one-on-one negotiations. Prices fluctuated sharply, depending on whether shipments arrived on time and on the quality of the day's produce. And since a company's profit margins were small—only a tiny percentage of the value of the produce— a single bad purchase could wipe out a day's profits. This was A. P.'s classroom, in which he learned many practical lessons about free markets and the laws of supply and demand.

A. P. also learned how to sell. One of his first challenges came before he was seventeen, as he began making calls on farmers in the delta region of the Sacramento Valley, northeast of San Francisco. Farmers along the islands in the delta grew a wide array of fruits and vegetables—everything from cantaloupes and grapes to beans and potatoes. Getting to the farmers was difficult by horse and buggy, but young Giannini quickly learned to work the countryside, hitting the road early and pushing himself as fast as possible. He pushed his rented horses, too; stable owners complained to one biographer that Giannini drove the rented horses so hard the owners eventually refused to rent to him.

The key to being successful was being first. A farmer was likely to sign with whoever showed up earliest. A. P. learned to eat his meals on the road, which helped him avoid the discomfort of arriving at a farm at mealtime and being forced to sit down with the family, an honor he couldn't refuse, no matter how far behind schedule it put him.

One story of Giannini's competitive spirit involved a literal race with another commission merchant to get an important agricultural account. Already behind, A. P. knew he couldn't win by staying on the road, but, remembering that it doubled back over a bridge, he decided to take a shortcut. A. P. undressed, tied his clothes in a bundle, swam across the river holding the bundle over his head, dressed, and walked to the farmer's house, arriving ahead of his competitor. He had a signed contract and was out the door before the other salesman arrived. The tale, its teller admitted, is likely apocryphal, but the spirit captured in the story is accurate.

An early biographer, Julian Dana, relates another story, which Giannini denied but others swore was true. At the time, A. P. was known as "Young Scatena" by many of the commission merchants. Dana says that Giannini carried neatly lettered signs with him in the back of his wagon that he would post at farms that had sold their produce to Scatena & Co. The signs read: "Drive on, boys. Young Scatena has been here."

A. P. enjoyed a good fight, having grown up in the physical, often violent world of the waterfront. By the age of seventeen he already stood six feet tall and weighed 170 pounds. He held his own on the docks and regularly backed up his words with his fists, proving that competing commission merchants could not push "Young Scatena" around and get away with it.

"Pop" Scatena made A. P. a junior partner in the firm at nineteen. For the next twelve years, Giannini applied his diligence to building Scatena & Co. into the most successful commission merchant on the West Coast.

"I kept on working hard, sticking to business, and not paying attention to anything else, like hanging around with the boys or going to parties or dances," Giannini told a reporter in 1949.

He traveled widely, soliciting business throughout the Sacramento and San Joaquin valleys. He even signed up orange growers in a community called Hollywood, four hundred miles south of San Francisco.

In 1892, A. P. ended his single-minded pursuit of business long enough to court and marry Clorinda Cuneo, the daughter of a prosperous merchant in San Francisco. A. P. had seen her at mass, singing in the choir, and though she was engaged to a young physician studying in Germany, A. P. began taking Clorinda to the theater and opera. He became a fixture of the San Francisco social community. With his size, well-waxed handlebar mustache, top hat, white gloves, and gold-headed cane, Giannini made a memorable suitor. One of the young women who lived in the Italian section later described him as "the handsomest man in North Beach."

The success of Scatena & Co. allowed A. P. to retire at age thirty-one. He had a son, Lawrence Mario, who would quickly be joined by a daughter, Claire, and a second son, Virgil. The young merchant had invested in San Francisco real estate, which produced an income of $250 a month—enough to live on. So A. P. sold his share in the firm to its young employees for about $100,000, and launched a second career.

Giannini may have been bored. "Nobody was fighting me anymore. I think that's why I quit," he told reporters. For several months, he worked with a real estate firm, where success came quickly. His investments, he would say later, brought him close to being a millionaire.

Less than a year after his retirement, Joseph Cuneo, A. P.'s father-in-law, died. After unsuccessfully working as a hydraulic miner and storekeeper, Cuneo had made a small fortune in real estate in San Francisco. The Cuneo family decided to keep the estate intact, with A. P. managing the portfolio. One of his responsibilities was to fill Joseph Cuneo's seat on the board of the Columbus Savings & Loan Association.

Banking in San Francisco at the turn of the century was wide open, competitive, but convention-bound. The banks of the community were largely unregulated and could engage in a host of businesses, including selling property insurance, buying and selling stocks, and advising on real estate investments. A few of San Francisco's banks, still flush with cash from the gold rush, had grown to rival in size the banks of New York and Chicago.

Bank of California, First National Bank of San Francisco, and Nevada National Bank of Reno ranked among the fifty largest commercial banks in the nation in 1900.

Like most successful banks of the era, they grew large and powerful by catering to businessmen, lending to only the most creditworthy citizens, and accepting only large deposits. If a bank couldn't find enough borrowers in San Francisco, it shipped money to banks in New York or Chicago, which paid a modest premium for the loan.

As immigrants pushed into the city, some smaller, ethnic banks opened, including Columbus Savings, which in 1893 became San Francisco's first Italian-owned bank. Opened in North Beach, Columbus Savings followed the policies of other conservative banks, loaning money to local businessmen, but considering the rest of the Italian immigrants who crowded North Beach "unbankable"—they left too little on deposit, borrowed only a few dollars at a time, and couldn't be trusted to pay back loans. So most of the Italians of North Beach kept their money in mattresses or stashed it under floorboards. If they borrowed, they turned to merchants or loan sharks, many of whom charged more than 20 percent interest, while businessmen paid 6 or 7 percent.

When A. P. Giannini joined the board of Columbus Savings he began urging the directors to expand rapidly by making loans to small businesses. A. P. had traveled throughout California and he knew that farmers, merchants, and workers needed money, not merely in North Beach, but outside as well. Scatena & Co. had, on occasion, acted as a banker to many of its clients, buying farmers' crops in advance, in effect making interest-free loans. So A. P. knew from experience they could be trusted to repay their debts.

But the management of Columbus Savings, which listened to Isaias W. Hellman, president of Nevada National Bank, saw no reason to change policy. Used to winning most battles, Giannini fought back. He tried to pack the board. Failing in that, he pushed for a vote on his policy recommendations—which he lost.

About this time A. P. discovered a banking practice common at the turn of the century. One of the Columbus directors was accepting commissions for arranging loans through the bank. In addition, he was selling fire insurance to bank custom-

ers and pocketing the premiums. Outraged by what he thought
was theft, A. P. confronted the board, arguing that the director
was taking money that should have gone to the shareholders of
the bank. When he demanded that the board fire the offending
party, the board refused.

This was too much for Giannini, who stormed off the board,
taking several other directors with him. Furious at being rebuffed, Giannini visited an old friend, James J. Fagan, an executive at the Crocker-Woolworth Bank. A. P. knew Fagan well
enough to call him "Giacomo" (Italian for James). "Giacomo,
I'm going to start my own bank," A. P. said. "Tell me how to do
it." Reminiscing later, Giannini admitted, "I might never have
gone into the banking game if I hadn't got so damn mad at those
Columbus directors."

A. P. found a home for his bank in the middle of Little Italy,
when the owner of a saloon decided to retire. He acquired the
lease and for just over $5,000 converted the saloon into the
headquarters of his bank, which he named, somewhat grandly,
the Bank of Italy. It opened on October 17, 1904, with A. P. taking the job of vice-president, without salary.

Then A. P. Giannini, one of the city's most successful fruit
merchants, with no experience as a banker, began banking his
own way. He knocked on doors to find customers, rising early to
solicit business on the docks and in the markets. He made loans
of as little as twenty-five dollars to workers who had no collateral
except the calluses on their hands. He advertised in newspapers,
passed out fliers. Other bankers complained that A. P.'s advertising was undignified, to which he replied, "How can people know
what a bank can and will do for them unless they're told?"

Giannini stumped not only for depositors and borrowers,
but for stockholders. He raised $300,000 from local business-
men by selling stock for $100 a share. By the time the bank
opened, it had 160 shareholders, dominated by local businessmen who knew North Beach.

From the beginning, Giannini's bank was successful. By the
end of twelve months it had $1 million in assets, and, one year
later, almost $1.9 million. By the standards of the city, it was still
a tiny, unknown commercial bank in the Italian section—that
"little dago bank in North Beach." But Giannini was about to
change that.

On April 18, 1906, just a little after 5:00 A.M., A. P.'s house,

Seven Oaks, in San Mateo, a suburb just south of San Francisco, shook with the reverberations of the worst earthquake in San Francisco's history. A. P. dressed quickly and headed for the commuter train. He hopped aboard and made his way north to within a few miles of the city, where the train stopped. Giannini could see smoke rising from downtown San Francisco, but didn't realize yet that the quake had broken gas mains and the city was in flames.

Whole sections of San Francisco lay in ruins. Worst hit was the area south of Market Street, which had been built on landfill. Whole blocks had been leveled. City Hall was in ruins, the roof of the Empire Theater had caved in. Although the business district still stood, it was in the path of the fire, which had started in the section south of Market and was spreading rapidly.

Giannini walked the last few miles to his bank. When he arrived, at around noon, the Bank of Italy was open for business. Two of his officers, Armando Pedrini, the assistant cashier, and Ettore Avenali, a clerk, had withdrawn the bank's gold, notes, and securities as usual from the Crocker Bank's vault (where they were stored each night) and were ready to serve the bank's customers.

But by now the fire was within a few blocks of the Bank of Italy headquarters. Giannini hurried to Scatena & Co. and grabbed two produce wagons, onto which he and his assistants loaded the bank's gold and other cash, heaping crates of oranges over it all to hide the valuables. They piled the bank's papers and records on top, but had no room for its new adding machine, which was left in the safe.

The city was in a state of anarchy. Gangs of thugs roamed the streets, breaking into stores and looting homes. At other, larger banks, employees stuffed papers and valuables into fire-proof safes. Refugees streamed out of the city, paying high prices for wagons or for ferries across the bay.

The roads were so crowded that it took all night to drive the eighteen miles to San Mateo. At Seven Oaks A. P. hid the bank's cash and gold in an opening under the fireplace.

Without sleep, he returned to San Francisco to assess the damage. The fire had destroyed much of the downtown business section, including Bank of Italy's headquarters and most of North Beach. About one third of the city, nearly 2,600 acres, was in ashes or rubble, with five hundred dead and damage estimated as high as $500 million.

A. P. attended an emergency meeting of business and city leaders near the waterfront. The merchants and bankers were desperate. Many had lost everything in the fire. Some had their records and cash stored in vaults that would be too hot to open for days, if not weeks. One banker proposed a moratorium of six months on all lending, admitting that it would be weeks before his bank could get its vault open.

Giannini decided this was incredibly wrongheaded. Normally quiet in such meetings, he rose to speak.

"Gentlemen, you are making a vital mistake. If you keep your banks closed until November, you might as well never open them, for there will be no city left. The time for doing business is right now.

"Tomorrow morning I am putting a desk on Washington Street wharf with a Bank of Italy sign over it. Any man who wants to rebuild San Francisco can come there and get as much cash as he needs to do it. I advise all of you bankers to beg, borrow or steal a desk and follow my example."

The next morning the bank opened for business, setting a plank across two barrels at one of the city's busiest piers. A. P. urged his customers to pull their money out of their mattresses, then lent them what they needed to start over. North Beach, devastated by the fire, was the first to rebuild. Hundreds of local residents saw their dreams restored from ashes by money from Giannini's bank. Their families would remember and remain loyal to the bank for generations.

Chapter Two

No one needs to defend branch banking. It was a proved success in England and Canada from the horse-and-buggy days, [and] is held back in America now by horse-and-buggy minds.

A. P. Giannini, undated

As the city of San Francisco emerged from the destruction of the Great Earthquake, A. P. Giannini watched with satisfaction. The young fruit merchant and real estate speculator had found a new calling: he had committed himself to banking.

Over the next two decades he would transform the little bank in North Beach into one of the largest in America, branching throughout California, picking fights with regulators and competitors alike, and imbuing the bank with his own growth-oriented, pugnacious personality, which it would retain on into the 1980s.

After the fire, Giannini broadened his efforts to find new business. Although "bankers' hours" was a common phrase by the turn of the century, A. P. continued to rise each day at 6:00 A.M., hopping into a carriage, or later, a chauffeured 1908 Packard, and hurrying through the streets of San Francisco and neighboring towns, looking for business and for possible branch sites. If he spotted a farmer whom he knew, he would offer him a ride, putting him in the rear seat with Mrs. Giannini (who usually accompanied him on weekend trips) while A. P. rode, as always, in the front seat beside his chauffeur.

Giannini's faith in the little fellow put him at the vanguard of a force that would transform the world's financial markets. During the next seventy years, the little guy would save more, spend more, and borrow more than anyone dreamed possible.

America's middle class would emerge as the most powerful force in the world economy. Giannini did not anticipate these changes. He simply saw a people with a need. By aiding them, he helped unleash the buying power of generations of consumers.

A. P.'s knack for self-promotion and his dockside training in market economics helped the fledgling bank survive in a turbulent economy. The lessons he learned in a business where the goods were perishable and where prices fluctuated widely gave him an understanding of market emotions and a respect for the ease with which a panic can wipe out the gains of a day, a week, or a lifetime.

His first chance to apply that education came in 1907. In January, after three years of work without a break, A. P. and his wife headed east on vacation. The United States was in the midst of an economic boom, complete with the normal excesses of speculation. Prices were soaring, the stock market was rising steadily. But as Giannini made his way through Chicago, Philadelphia, and New York, a minor panic struck. Interest rates soared briefly and the stock market plunged, but almost as rapidly as the panic started, calm was restored. Giannini found the bankers he met "down in the mouth," worried by the excessive speculation. When he returned to San Francisco in May, he had already decided that a crisis was coming. He prepared the Bank of Italy for the worst, stopped making real estate loans, started hoarding gold, and began a campaign to gather deposits. What Giannini expected was a credit squeeze, a period when deposits would be scarce, gold even scarcer.

Markets in the United States were particularly vulnerable to panics in the late 1800s and early 1900s because of the nation's system of issuing currency. The United States did not have a single, unified currency. Coins of gold, silver, copper, and nickel circulated along with currency issued by both the federal government and the national banks. The nation had ten thousand banks, or more, and any bank with a national charter could issue its own paper currency. But the paper was only as good as the bank that issued it. When a bank got into trouble, merchants discounted its currency, offering, say, ninety cents in coin, or less, for one dollar of paper money. Anyone stuck with paper from that bank lost out, and, if the bank failed, the paper would be worthless.

Another unstable element was the system for keeping reserves. Each of the nation's banks was required to set aside cash reserves to back its deposits. Small banks left reserves in interest-bearing accounts at larger banks, and the failure of a large bank in a major city usually meant losses for hundreds of smaller banks all around the country. As a result, when rumors of a credit squeeze began, small banks would quickly close their accounts at larger institutions. This left the larger banks and the stock market in a bind. The bigger banks, centered in New York, knew that country banks could panic at any moment, so they normally lent large amounts of money overnight. When the little banks got nervous, the big banks would pull money out of the overnight loan market and send it back to, for example, Des Moines or Poughkeepsie. The overnight loan market could virtually dry up, which invariably sent interest rates on overnight borrowings soaring. Since overnight loans were often used to support stock market purchases, a squeeze in the overnight market immediately affected the stock market, sending prices plunging, bankrupting speculators, and triggering a nationwide crisis.

Fearful of just such a panic, Giannini stockpiled hard currency. San Franciscans still preferred gold to paper, and in a crunch they withdrew their deposits in gold coin. The Bank of Italy was small enough that it could build its gold reserves without drawing much attention in the local market.

The crisis A. P. had foreseen began in midsummer in Egypt. After a run by depositors on several banks, one of Alexandria's largest collapsed. The panic rippled through Japan, Germany, and Chile, reaching the United States in the fall. By late summer, credit had already begun to tighten. Banks in the western United States began to pull their reserves out of New York banks. The mighty Knickerbocker Trust Company in New York City failed in October. Depositors panicked and a broader run began, bringing about the failure of six other banks and four trust companies. The stock market collapsed in shock. Not until J. P. Morgan, armed with $30 million from the U.S. government, stepped in to quell the uncertainties did the panic of 1907 end in New York.

Outside New York trouble spread quickly. Bank holidays were declared in Nevada, Washington, and Oregon, after banks there failed. On October 30, two weeks after the Knickerbocker Trust collapsed, the California Safe Deposit & Trust Company in San Francisco went down. The state banking superintendent declared a bank holiday in California that lasted until December 21.

(The holiday never forced the banks actually to close, but the superintendent used the holiday to delay collecting taxes, which reduced the demand for gold.)

Giannini had stockpiled more than $100,000 of gold in excess of what he needed for daily operations. Though a huge sum for his bank, it meant little in San Francisco's banking community. Crocker Bank, which suffered through a short run by depositors, had more than $40 million of deposits outstanding when the run struck. Giannini's stockpile would have vanished in an afternoon had Crocker accepted A. P.'s offer to use the gold.

San Francisco's banks responded to depositor runs by limiting withdrawals of gold and giving out Clearing House scrip—paper backed by not one, but all of the city's biggest banks, each of which belonged to the San Francisco Clearing House Association, an organization that oversaw the daily clearing of checks drawn on local banks.

The Bank of Italy was an exception. It paid all its claims in either gold or legal currency. When nervous depositors at other banks found this out, they flocked into the Bank of Italy, bringing their gold and strengthening the institution. At the end of the year, the Bank of Italy showed an increase of $300,000 in deposits to more than $1.6 million.

Giannini's bank was still tiny, but in the next decade that would change, for A. P. Giannini's romance with branch banking was about to begin. In 1907 he opened the first branch of the Bank of Italy, in San Francisco's Mission district, a neighborhood slightly wealthier than North Beach and with few Italians. Two other banks had already opened branches in the Mission district, so Giannini's decision was not particularly innovative. But Giannini would do more with branch banking than any other banker in America.

Branch banking was a controversial subject in the early 1900s. Most small bankers considered it a plot by the big bankers to drive them out of business. Giannini disagreed. He toured parts of Canada, which had nationwide branching, and saw that branches in small communities were offering services that independent banks in the United States could not afford to provide.

Giannini was filled with dreams, as he had been since his days as a boy writing letters to delta farmers. In August 1908, he fulfilled one of them when the Bank of Italy opened its new headquarters, a nine-story office at the corner of Clay and Montgom-

ery Streets. With Italian marble flooring, bronze doors, and a
ceiling patterned with inlaid gold, the bank was a monument to
Giannini's aspirations.

The entire ground floor was a banking office, and there, in
the open, was A. P.'s desk. (He refused to sit in a private office.
"That's one trouble with bankers. They shut themselves off away
from people and don't know what's going on. Why a banker
should do that I can't imagine," he said. "If I should drift into a
program like this—to my office in the morning dressed in silk hat
and cutaway coat; guarded behind closed doors while people
send in cards to gain an audience with me; golf on an afternoon
with new friends and my old friends shut out and no longer calling me 'Amadeo' or 'A. P.'—then, indeed, I would be broke, for
the first time in my life.")

On mornings when he was in the office, he sat at his desk
and greeted a steady stream of customers and friends, sometimes fifty or more in a single morning. They would pass by
Giannini's desk to conduct business or just say hello. Giannini
gossiped, asked about business, picked up news of the family and
the community. If a new father happened by, A. P. would pull out
a five-dollar gold piece for the little one, which invariably wound
up in a savings account at the Bank of Italy.

In early 1909, California's legislature passed banking laws
that permitted branch banking—clearing up the ambiguity of
past laws—and by October Giannini had opened his first branch
outside San Francisco. He bought a bank in trouble, the Commercial & Savings Bank in San Jose, which was saddled with bad
farm loans. This was the first step in building a statewide branch
system, and it created an unexpectedly important alliance. On
the board of the San Jose bank was Prentis C. Hale, a wealthy
merchant, whose stores would form the nucleus for Carter Hawley Hale Stores, Inc., a company still represented on Bank-
America's board of directors.

Giannini set a pattern with that first purchase that he would
follow for the next forty years. He would buy an existing bank,
rather than trying to open a branch from scratch. He would keep
the old employees and create an advisory board that included
prominent local businessmen and immigrant families. Wherever
possible, Giannini tried to retain ties to the community. He wanted the branches to be run by men who knew the local people,
not, as in Canada, by men straight from the head office.

In 1910 the Bank of Italy bought two banks in San Francisco. In 1912 it bought a bank in San Mateo. In 1913 Giannini jumped to Los Angeles, and in 1916 he moved into the state's rich agricultural heartland.

Giannini was bringing his brand of banking to more and more people. He was breaking the stranglehold of many local banks and in the process lowering the cost of borrowing. Very often local banks were controlled by a few wealthy citizens who made loans only to their friends, never extending credit to competitors or potential competitors. The Bank of Italy was different. Although each Bank of Italy branch kept its local staff, it was part of a statewide chain, with aspirations to expand rapidly and lend money broadly.

The bank's good intentions were backed by some ruthless muscle flexing. Critics argue that Giannini prospered by using predatory pricing. When the Bank of Italy entered a new community it would begin to build business by offering cut-rate loans to consumers and businessmen. In part, the bank was using its financial strength to put a strong arm on the competition. As the big guy on the block, the Bank of Italy (and later Bank of America) could afford to take a loss at a new branch if that meant more business in the long run.

This was an advantage and the bank used it well, but it was not a monopolistic practice. Giannini didn't drive others out of business and then later raise prices and gouge the public. Instead, he stuck with those loan rates, passing on to borrowers the benefits of a larger, more diversified bank. That diversification was one of the reasons Giannini could offer lower rates. Most small banks make loans only in their own community, which is often dependent on a single firm or industry. If a small town suffers in an economic downturn—say, cotton prices plunge in a town built around a cotton mill—the local bank can disappear, unless it has set aside huge reserves. In order to build prudent reserves, a small bank has to charge higher interest rates on loans and pay lower rates on savings accounts than it would otherwise.

The Bank of Italy didn't have that concentrated exposure. It had made thousands of loans all across the state, to cattlemen, cotton farmers, industrialists, and workingmen. If any one of those customers went bankrupt, or if any one small town took a beating, Bank of Italy could withstand the loss.

Though it took years for statisticians to discover the magic of this formula, Giannini had stumbled upon a powerful banking principle. Consumers and small businessmen turned out to be good customers, taken as a whole. Over time, a banker could expect to lose 1 or 2 percent of the amount he lent to consumers. Instead of setting aside a reserve equal to 5 or 10 percent of each loan, the Bank of Italy could get by with a much smaller reserve. That meant it could pay more than local banks on deposits, charge less on loans, and still make a reasonable profit.

By passing on this saving to the consumer, the Bank of Italy grew rapidly, taking away business from competitors who never ceased grumbling about predatory pricing, no matter what economists argued.

Not all of Giannini's ventures, however, were immediately successful. For example, his decision to invade Los Angeles was a near disaster. In 1913 Giannini bought the Park Bank, a troubled institution in the Los Angeles financial district with one branch and less than $2 million in assets. Los Angeles, with more than 400,000 people, had just passed San Francisco in population. It was growing feverishly, and speculation in real estate was a local pastime. The year after Giannini's arrival, the economy sagged and real estate values dropped.

Giannini saw the change as an opportunity. He began advertising that he would make mortgages of from under $1,000 to $3,000, when few others would. He advertised under the slogan "Why not build now when costs are cheaper?" The campaign failed. A few borrowers showed up, but not enough to generate profits for the branch. For two years, the Los Angeles economy remained in a slump. Bankers in the city, having trouble raising deposits, began a price war, paying 5 percent interest on savings accounts rather than 4 percent. Giannini refused to compete for accounts and his business suffered.

It was a rough period for the Bank of Italy. Giannini's rapid expansion seemed to be leading it into trouble. His branch in San Mateo was running at a loss. Some of his directors were losing faith. They wanted to close the branches in Los Angeles, give up the dream of branch banking in the state.

In 1914, A. P., who traveled frequently on vacations that usually ended up as business trips, left for three months in the West Indies, threatening to resign from the bank when he returned. He told the board that if it was getting cold feet, he was willing to buy back the Los Angeles and San Mateo offices of the

Bank of Italy. The board backed down, refused Giannini's resignation, and—though directors were not confident that Los Angeles would ever succeed—agreed to give A. P. another chance. Within a few months Los Angeles became profitable, thanks to World War I and the recovery that preparation for war brought the nation's economy.

With the boom produced by the war, the Bank of Italy grew more rapidly than ever before. Between 1916 and 1918, branches opened in Santa Rosa, Oakland, Redwood City, and Ventura. The bank spread south from San Jose, opened more offices in the state's rich farm country, and started a bank in Napa, in the heart of California's wine country.

By the end of 1918, the Bank of Italy was California's fourth largest bank. It had twenty-four branches in eighteen cities. Assets totaled $93 million. Crocker National Bank, which had loomed so large in 1907, was just half the size of the Bank of Italy, and the recently merged Wells Fargo Nevada National of San Francisco, run by Isaias Hellman—the man whose advice pushed A. P. Giannini off the Columbus Savings board—had $80 million in assets, lagging behind the Bank of Italy.

Giannini's admirers characterize this rapid expansion as a series of gentlemanly business transactions, with small-town bankers welcoming Giannini. Critics offer a less generous explanation. Giannini preferred to buy troubled banks at prices that didn't strain his pocketbook. The prospects facing the banker in a small community, especially one laden with bad loans, were never particularly good. Once Giannini expressed an interest in the community, the local banker had two choices: he could sell to Giannini or he could be driven out of business. While a healthy local bank might survive the invasion of the giant from San Francisco, a weak institution had no chance. Giannini had learned as a commission merchant that his competitors had their limits. In price wars on fruit and vegetables, Giannini had held out until his opponents were too weak to compete, and then had picked up additional business as they struggled to recover. He applied the same toughness to banking.

Giannini admitted as much in testimony before a Congressional hearing on May 8, 1930. Then sixty years old and retired from the company, A. P. said, "A country banker has a hard time making a profit in his limited field. Expenses run up and the banks are [hard put] to show earnings. Naturally the tendency is to charge as high a rate as possible on loans—10, 11, and 12 percent. And in some cases they even charged commissions. We are tickled to death to get good loans at 7 or 6 percent and in the big cities at 4.5 or 5 percent."

Giannini's juggernaut ran into its first real opposition as World War I ended. It was not trouble from other bankers, so much as his first serious confrontation with the government officials who regulated commercial banks.

For several years, California's bank regulators had criticized the Bank of Italy. It was growing too fast, it was not putting controls in place at its new branches. The criticisms stung Giannini, but did nothing to slow him down.

In late 1918 the state got a new banking superintendent, Charles F. Stern, who opposed branch banking. In his first few weeks on the job, Stern labeled Giannini's plans for statewide branching "un-American," sided with the owners of rural banks, who felt threatened by the Bank of Italy, and protested that Giannini would create a "money monopoly." Stern stopped approving Giannini's applications for new branches and began to lobby for changes in the California Bank Act that would curb branch banking.

Giannini met Stern's challenges indirectly. "If you can't do a thing in one way," Giannini said, "you do it in another way." Earlier Giannini had created the Shareholders Auxiliary Corporation, a holding company owned by the same shareholders that owned the Bank of Italy. The holding company had a specific purpose. Under California law it was illegal for a bank to buy shares in another bank. (A bank could buy the assets of another bank, but not the shares.) So James Bacigalupi, a young lawyer who would later become president of the Bank of Italy, designed the holding company. It acquired the shares of target banks, then turned around and sold the assets to the Bank of Italy.

With Stern refusing to let the Bank of Italy expand, Giannini decided to use the Stockholders Auxiliary Corporation as a warehouse. He kept buying banks, but instead of transferring them to the Bank of Italy, he left control of the banks with the holding company, just waiting for the superintendent's office to change its policies.

Between 1919 and 1921, the Bank of Italy grew from $85 million in deposits to $178 million with the acquisition of only a few small banks. The nation was in the midst of a period of deflation; declines in commodity prices ravaged the Midwest and the South. Banks throughout the Mississippi Valley failed in huge numbers. In California, the downturn was far less severe.

The new banking superintendent stepped up his attacks on Giannini. He sent letters to A. P. expressing his concern about "the safety and ultimate solvency" of the Bank of Italy, tough language for a regulator. Stern thought the company had grown too rapidly, failed to install proper safeguards and controls, and failed to integrate the many offices it had opened or acquired. It was the same criticism that had been leveled by Stern's predecessor, only now the language was inflammatory.

For two years, Stern bullied the Bank of Italy, refusing to allow it to open branches, sending threatening letters. But in April 1921 he was forced to back down. In Visalia, a farm community forty miles southeast of Fresno, the National Bank of Visalia was in serious trouble because of sharply lowered farm prices. It had too much of its money tied up in mortgages on farmland and it had lent generously on vineyard land, only to lose heavily when a killing virus struck the vineyards in late 1920. Depositors were slowly withdrawing their money, and the bank was on the verge of failure. Its management asked Stern for permission to merge with the Bank of Italy, the only institution willing to bid on the troubled bank.

Stern was caught. Although he hated branch banking, the Visalia bank was a major concern. If it closed, runs might begin at other rural banks, many of which were in weak condition. Stern spent a long weekend talking to the Visalia bankers and Giannini. They all knew that the Visalia bank might not reopen on Monday morning. Stern tried not to capitulate. He said Giannini could buy the bank, but only if it remained independent, rather than becoming a branch of the Bank of Italy.

Giannini, angered by the years of foot-dragging by the superintendent, refused to agree to anything but a conversion of the Visalia bank into a branch.

"That's my proposition," he said, and walked out.

Stern caved in. Giannini got the Visalia bank, on his terms. A few weeks later, Stern approved a series of other branch applications by the Bank of Italy.

Throughout the rest of his banking career, Giannini squabbled with bank regulators. His toughest opponent was to be the Federal Reserve System, which the Bank of Italy had joined in

1919 when the agency, created in 1913, was little more than a novel experiment in banking reform aimed at eliminating the excesses of 1907. Then, as now, the Federal Reserve regulated only those banks that chose to become members of the system. A. P. had hesitated to join because it was unclear how the Fed would view branch banking; not joining might have spared him some anguish. Examiners at the Fed received copies of Stern's examination reports criticizing the bank's frenzied growth. Throughout the 1920s its staff used those reports to hamstring the Bank of Italy. The Fed clamped tighter and tighter restrictions on branching by banks that it regulated, but the rules were aimed directly at Giannini.

A. P. had brought the problems on himself. In 1921 the Bank of Italy opened its third headquarters building, this time at One Powell Street, near the cable-car turnaround at Market Street. This seven-story granite building, the largest commercial banking office in the United States, was so big that it forced Giannini to close the Bank of Italy branch on Market Street, which was just a block away. A. P. thought the Powell Street location was such a terrific spot for a bank that he created a separate institution that would do business there, hoping to call it Liberty National.

But federal bank regulators didn't like Giannini's idea, which looked like yet another attempt to circumvent restrictions on branch banking. So Giannini went to the state banking regulators and opened the Liberty Bank—not Liberty National—as a state-chartered institution in August 1921.

That put the local representatives of the Federal Reserve in a snit. They didn't like the idea of Giannini's playing one regulator off against another and using competition among the Federal Reserve, the Comptroller of the Currency, and state regulators to get his way in opening branches. The Fed sent a letter to Giannini letting him know that if he wanted to buy any more banks, either through the Bank of Italy or any other affiliated company, he would have to get Fed approval first. The Fed wasn't amused by Giannini's newest wrinkle, and criticism of the Giannini "octopus" began to grow louder.

For the first time in his career, A. P. was stopped dead. He could use neither his state bank nor his federal bank to open branches. He was unable to move into Oakland, across the bay, and he was unable to expand in Los Angeles.

The impasse didn't last long. In 1926 the Republican party faced a close race for the governor's seat. Friend Richardson, the incumbent governor, who had chosen a superintendent of banking even less sympathetic to the Bank of Italy than Stern, was running against C. C. Young, the state's lieutenant governor. Giannini prepared to provide a little assistance to Young.

The bank sent telegrams to all its branch managers asking them to a conference in San Francisco, where they were told to prepare to campaign for a new governor. One week before the primary, Giannini's team began knocking on doors. They reached close to 100,000 stockholders, pointing out the problem that Giannini had had with the Richardson administration, and letting them know that A. P. had received word that Richardson planned to get even tougher if he were reelected. Whether the door-to-door campaign was decisive, no one knows, but Young won the nomination and in November was elected governor. The press quickly labeled him "Giannini's Governor."

Young appointed a superintendent of banking who was more to the Bank of Italy's liking; he permitted Giannini to merge his largest banks. Along with the Liberty Bank and the Bank of Italy, A. P. had acquired a bank in Los Angeles with a solid name, the Bank of America of Los Angeles, and when he merged it with the Bank of Italy, he transferred the name to a small bank the holding company owned in San Pedro. With the merger, the Bank of Italy now had 300 offices in 185 towns, stretching the length of California. Assets of the bank totaled $750 million, or about eight times what the Bank of Italy had claimed in assets at the end of World War I.

Giannini's empire now stood as a single, impressive entity in California. A. P. was at the helm of the largest commercial bank outside New York. He had carefully consolidated his banks before the passage of the McFadden Act, a new federal law that permitted branching by national banks, but with some restrictions. By consolidating the holdings before the law passed, the Bank of Italy was "grandfathered" under the act, permitted to keep its branch system intact, even though this violated some of the provisions of the new law.

The Bank of Italy's stock had risen as rapidly as the fortunes of the company. Between 1904 and 1920, the price of a share doubled from $100 to $200. By early 1928, as speculators began to discover the company and as the dividend increased to $30 annually, Bank of Italy stock reached the equivalent of $1500 per share.

A. P. Giannini was creating a second California "gold rush." He was a hero to thousands of Italian Americans, and he was prepared to try something new. Since the earliest days of the Bank of Italy, Giannini had been encouraged to come to New York. He had dreamed of building a bank that would span the continent. With the Bank of Italy an unquestioned success in California, A. P. was ready to make the rest of his dream a reality.

Chapter Three

When nationwide branch banking is an accomplished fact, America
will have come of age financially.

A. P. Giannini, 1935

A. P. Giannini's assault on New York began in earnest in
1927. Within two years, he would suffer the soundest defeats in
his business career at the hands of the men who controlled the
biggest institutions on Wall Street.

But his early forays into the city in 1927 brought success of
the type familiar to A. P. He won immediate public admiration,
or at least the support of the city's press. One journalist described the scene in Giannini's suite at the Ritz-Carlton, on
Forty-sixth Street:

> As in San Francisco, anybody could walk in and see him;
> there was no secretary or valet, and he would be banging
> away at a battleship-sized grand piano, singing opera airs in
> his mighty baritone, while Mrs. Giannini, in the bedroom
> next door yelled into a telephone above the din he made.
> Evenings [he] would dine at a good little Italian joint, with
> warm multilingual friends, then sit or stand at some movie
> for hours on end.

Others called him a "regular knockout for personality" with
"a titanic head, a face like a rock and a voice like a howitzer."

Newsmen marveled at his financial derring-do. In 1927 the
New York Times described Giannini's holding company, by now

41

called BancItaly Corporation, as the "world's largest investment trust." It owned shares in almost every major commercial bank in the country, had more than $1 million invested in each of fifty major industrial companies, and at one point owned more than one million shares of General Foods. The exploits of BancItaly—the rise of its stock price, and the performance of its banks—were front-page news. One article called Giannini "a veritable wizard of finance, a magician whose every move in the realm of the dollar produces a golden stream for his followers."

Giannini already had a beachhead in New York. Italian-American groups had convinced him to buy the East River National Bank in 1919, and in 1925 A. P. had added the Bowery National Bank, merging the two into the Bowery and East River National. A. P.'s brother "Doc" had earlier left medical practice to become a troubleshooter at the bank. With the expansion in New York, he moved east, became president of the bank, and slowly increased its assets to $106 million. A. P. also acquired the Commercial & Exchange Bank in New York, which had $45 million in assets.

In late 1927 Giannini learned that one of New York's oldest banks, the Bank of America of New York (completely unrelated to Giannini's bank in San Pedro), was in the midst of a struggle for control. Manufacturers Trust Co., a scrappy institution controlled by a banker who had risen from the streets of Brooklyn, was trying to seize ownership of this $167 million bank from a management led by Edward Delafield, a Long Island aristocrat. Delafield was backed by J. P. Morgan & Co.

Giannini at first hoped to buy Manufacturers Trust; he liked the bank's style. But advisers dissuaded him. It was obvious that the House of Morgan disapproved of Manufacturers. Buying it would probably provoke a battle with the most respected banking operation on Wall Street, one whose power reached throughout the banking world.

J. Pierpont Morgan, Sr., had died in 1913, but his legacy survived him. During his reign at Morgan, he had bailed out both the U.S. and British governments, and, at home, had pulled together the U.S. Steel Co. and countless major railroads. Many of the banks on Wall Street, including Bank of America and Bankers Trust, operated "within the Morgan sphere," which meant that Morgan influenced their management, even though it was not an owner. Morgan also appeared, at times, to act as an extension of the Federal Reserve Bank of New York, although no one knew who was dictating policy to whom.

Giannini decided to buy Bank of America of New York. As he had told journalists, anyone hoping to run a bank in New York City in the 1920s needed the support of the Morgan Bank. And so A. P. Giannini sought and won "the approval of the Morgans" before buying Bank of America. Faced with a choice between Giannini and Manufacturers Trust, Morgan sided with Giannini. A. P.'s son Mario, who had joined the bank after law school and was now a senior executive, observed: "[J. P.] Morgan [Jr.] chose us . . . because he felt he could dictate." In February 1928 Giannini paid $17 million for a controlling interest in Bank of America and prepared to merge it with his other banks.

Giannini's reputation rallied investors. In one month, the price of a single share of Bank of America of New York nearly tripled, from $510 to $1,520. But almost immediately Giannini faced other problems. When A. P. applied for a national bank charter, which was important to his goal of building a nationwide bank, the Federal Reserve Bank of New York demanded that BancItaly sell its Bank of America stock to the public. The Fed was uncomfortable with bank holding companies—especially those run by A. P. Giannini. It decided that if Giannini would not go along, he would be granted a charter but denied the permission to engage in the trust business. Since that was a major part of Bank of America's daily activities, and one of the reasons that Giannini wanted to buy the bank, the Fed got its wish.

Giannini agreed, but not for long. He sold shares of Bank of America to friends in San Francisco and then almost immediately hatched a plan to skirt the Fed's authority. He decided to replace BancItaly with a new holding company, Transamerica Corp., which would hold the shares of Bank of Italy, Bank of America, and the rest of the Giannini banks.

While Transamerica was being created, A. P. kept quiet. Doc wrote long, agonized letters about his mistreatment in New York. Delafield, Morgan's man at Bank of America, refused to let Doc, who was now chairman of the board of Bank of America, preside at board meetings (or at least that was the way Doc saw it). Delafield was using company funds to pay the golf-club dues of executives and was planning to pay salaries and bonuses far higher than the bank's profits justified. "Ingratiating methods will never do with these fellows," Doc fumed in one letter. "For many years they have been impossible and must be told where to head in. . . . The gang downtown never cared for our kind and never will. It is true we need them now, but it is not necessary to have them ride over us."

A. P. tried to calm his brother, counseling patience, while all the while working in secrecy to create Transamerica. In the fall and winter of 1928, he began to exchange Transamerica's shares for those of four companies: BancItaly Corp., the Bank of Italy, Bank of America of New York, and Bank of America of California, a new $400 million company created by combining several other banks owned by Giannini. He transferred money out of the Bank of Italy's accounts with Morgan. Then he closed Bank of America's accounts there.

Morgan's executives weren't pleased. A. P. headed to New York in the first week of February 1929 to explain his actions, then moved on to Washington for a session at the Federal Reserve. A. P. argued that he had a legal right to use a holding company to own Bank of America. His friends at Manufacturers Trust had recently acquired a bank with a trust department; why couldn't Bank of America?

A. P. felt he was being abused, but Jackson Reynolds, president of the First National Bank of New York (a forerunner of Citicorp) advised:

> You may be within your legal rights, and you may be within your moral rights. . . . You may have received the worst kind of treatment, but knowing the situation as I do, even if you were shanghaied, knocked down and jumped on, I would advise you to . . . divest Transamerica of all the stock it holds of Bank of America.

Giannini ignored that advice. He stuck with his plans and this time the Fed and Morgan capitulated. A. P. gained control of Bank of America, with Transamerica buying 63 percent of its stock.

Giannini took his victory in stride, though at moments he indulged in a little bragging. At one point, when asked about the brainpower in New York, he responded, "Shucks, I didn't find any people there could figure faster than I could."

Giannini may have been reading too many of his own press clippings. His entry into New York had created tremendous excitement. A San Francisco newspaper described his purchase of Bank of America as the opening gambit in "the most colossal financial plan ever projected." The writer said that "Giannini's three bases now are San Francisco, New York, and Los Angeles. Entrance of Chicago is anticipated within four months." And an invasion of "London, Paris and Berlin appears to set the stage for entrance of A. P. Giannini as the new colossus of world finance."

Giannini decided in May of 1928 to tour Europe, as he did regularly. On his way through Chicago, he stopped for lunch with a friend at the Union Trust Company. Union's stock soared 120 points that afternoon on the supposition that Giannini was buying. In Europe, Giannini visited the heads of the central banks in England and France. He was made a Knight of Malta by Italy's King Victor Emmanuel and received by Mussolini, and on a trip to Paris the stock exchange paid him an even higher compliment, as his mere visit caused the stock of Banque de Paris et de Pays Bas to rise 300 points.

For months, Giannini had been worried about the speculation in his stock. He had warned shareholders in BancItaly and Bank of America not to borrow to buy stock. He warned employees, "Our shares are too high. Don't gamble in them. Pay off your debts and sit tight. If you own your stock you have nothing to fear." But too many people didn't sit tight. In the speculative fever of the late 1920s, they borrowed heavily to own more and more shares.

Throughout the 1920s it was possible to buy stock entirely with borrowed money. If the stock rose, the buyer sold the shares and walked away happy. If they fell, he faced a "margin call" from his broker, which forced the shareholder to cough up cash or sell the shares at a loss.

In the first week of June 1928, A. P. was resting at a resort near Rome, suffering from pleurisy and neuritis, nervous disorders that can cause debilitating pain. He received urgent cablegrams from home: rumors of his illness had weakened the price of stock in his companies. A. P. was still working to create Transamerica, so it was the shares of BancItaly that were being pounded mercilessly, along with shares of the Bank of Italy, Bank of America (California), and Bank of America of New York, all of which traded on the stock exchange. A. P.'s companies were caught in what corporate executives of the 1920s feared most, a "bear raid," an attack on a stock by short-sellers—investors who had borrowed shares of stock from their brokers, sold the stock, and hoped to drive the price down so they could buy the shares back at a lower price. It was not uncommon in the 1920s for a group of investors, working in concert, to attempt to manipulate the price of a company's shares. Corporate executives responded with some manipulation of their own, buying back their own shares to prop up the price and foil the short-sellers.

Giannini had spent months putting together a war chest against just such an attack. In cables from Rome he told his executives to start buying shares. On Friday, June 8, the battle began. On Monday, June 11, BancItaly stock opened down $20, at $175. It hit a low of $109 early in the day, but Giannini's buying pushed it back to $153. Bank of Italy shares followed the same pattern. The pressure lasted for six days. BancItaly spent nearly $60 million to prop up its stock, suffering losses of perhaps $20 million.

Almost by itself, the BancItaly plunge cooled the bull market. The day after the BancItaly crash, the bulls retreated, and shares of some companies not even vaguely related to BancItaly dipped by 20 percent or more.

Giannini blamed the raid and the market drop on a group of speculators in the East, aided, he suspected, by Herbert Fleischacker, president of the Anglo California Bank in San Francisco and a man Giannini considered an enemy and an incompetent banker. Perhaps through Fleischacker, the speculators learned that West Coast investors in BancItaly stock had borrowed excessively to buy shares of Giannini companies. The raid caught these unsophisticated West Coast buyers unaware. As the stock dropped, they had to sell their stock and repay their debts, which pushed prices even lower, accomplishing exactly what the speculators desired.

When Giannini learned that his empire was under attack, legend has it, he pulled himself out of bed and caught the fastest boat home.

A. P. arrived in San Francisco in September 1928 to find his shares had recovered half their losses, but he still felt burned. He pushed ahead with the creation of Transamerica Corp., combining all of his companies into a single holding company early in 1929 and leaving him with one issue of stock, which would be easier to watch and defend.

As an additional safeguard, Giannini scoured New York to find a talented investment banker to help defend his empire. On a previous trip he had met Elisha Walker, president of the large investment banking firm of Blair & Co. A graduate of Yale and of the Massachusetts Institute of Technology, Walker was forty-nine, a native New Yorker, but one who didn't have the "cold aloofness" of so many on Wall Street. Now A. P. struck a deal. He bought Blair & Co., paying a hefty premium, and merged it into BancItaly, buying Walker's help in analyzing Wall Street and obtaining a toehold in the world of investment banking.

Walker was the first member of the eastern establishment to join what had been a large family business. A. P. Giannini, at fifty-nine, was near retirement, and it looked as though Walker would succeed him as chairman of Transamerica. Mario was president of BancItaly, and Doc was running the New York bank. Walker remained on the East Coast, but in May 1929 A. P. brought him west to introduce him to bank employees. At one banquet, A. P. described his new partner as the only man besides himself who could direct the big holding company. Walker promised, in turn, that he would continue Giannini's plans of expansion for Transamerica.

But Walker never got that chance. On Thursday, October 24, 1929, the market collapse began. Transamerica shares, with the firm support of A. P., who was at home in San Francisco, dropped by just one eighth of a point, while the rest of the market plunged. Stocks of major industrial companies declined $30 to $50 a share in a single day. A. P. bought furiously, propping up Transamerica shares for almost a week. Then, on the morning of the twenty-eighth, Black Monday on Wall Street, the stock, which had settled at 62-1/2, dropped to 20-1/4.

Two years later, Elisha Walker would announce that A. P. had spent $68 million in four weeks in a vain attempt to keep Transamerica's shares aloft. The company bought over one million shares at an average price of $62.50 a share. Walker concluded that Transamerica ended 1929 with few liquid assets and

a huge indebtedness. It was the beginning of the most turbulent
financial battle in A. P. Giannini's career—a battle that marks
Giannini as one of the few American entrepreneurs to win back
control of his company after losing it to Wall Street.

Chapter Four

The best fun I've had in life has been doing things that other people declared impossible. Perhaps, the folks who say I'd rather fight than eat aren't altogether wrong.

A. P. Giannini, 1921

At the end of 1929, worn out and in pain, A. P. Giannini retired as chairman and chief executive of Transamerica. Over the next two years, he would spend increasingly more time at spas in Germany and Austria seeking relief from polyneuritis—the crippling disease that now threatened his life. Giannini did not step aside in triumph. Like so many corporate executives caught by the crash of 1929, Giannini left behind a company weakened and struggling. Elisha Walker replaced A. P. as chief executive of Transamerica. A. P.'s son Mario became president.

Although incapacitated during much of the next few years, A. P. never lost track of the events at the bank. He cabled faithfully to Mario, who reported back on bank affairs. The news during 1929 and 1930 grew worse. In early 1929, before the market crash, Walker had promised to carry on Giannini's dream of expanding his banking empire across the country. After the crash, Walker examined Transamerica's books and found an institution in appalling shape.

America had entered the Great Depression. In 1930, the country's national income slumped from $94 billion to $88 billion. By the end of the year four million people were out of work. Soup kitchens, bread lines, street-corner apple sellers became fixtures of everyday life. Shanties at the edge of town grew almost overnight into little "Hoovervilles." More than one thousand banks failed in 1930, although only eight in California. Banks serving farmers in the Midwest suffered most.

Before the crash, Transamerica ranked as one of the nation's most potent financial institutions. Among its holdings were large blocks of stock in a score of major corporations. In the stock market debacle of 1929 these securities plunged in value. Transamerica's accountants, however, allowed it to list those securities at their purchase price, so when Walker dug in, he found a terrifying gap between the market value and the original prices. In order to reconcile the discrepancies he decided to write off more than $1 billion, a sum almost too large to conceive in 1930.

The extent of Transamerica's problems grew more visible during 1930, and Walker's pessimism deepened. By early 1931, bank examiners had delivered a scathing assessment of the quality of the bank's loans and Walker was furiously cutting staff, trying to keep the company afloat.

Neither A. P. nor Mario believed the disastrous numbers reported by the examiners. Mario fought the reduction of the dividend in mid-1930 and fought Walker's decision to publicize the drop in the company's value. The book value of Transamerica was $49.82 per share, but Walker gradually made public other prices reflecting the depressed state of the economy and the stock market, finally telling the public the company was worth $14.50 a share—an estimate presumably based on a very careful review of the value of all the company's assets. A. P. and Mario thought Walker was being overly pessimistic, perhaps trying to drive the price down so that investors on Wall Street could seize control of Transamerica.

On November 3, 1930, almost as a footnote to the company's financial condition, the Bank of Italy and Bank of America of California merged to become Bank of America National Trust and Savings Association. The Bank of Italy name disappeared.

Within two months of the fulfillment of one of A. P.'s dreams—the uniting of all of his California banks into one statewide branch system—Mario Giannini threatened to resign. Walker refused to fight the investors who were still attempting to drive down Transamerica's stock. He quarreled with A. P. and Mario over the reporting of the company's profits and over the cutting of the dividend—which A. P. had hoped to stall. Mario also felt slighted personally. Though he was the number two man in the organization, Walker arranged appointments with

Mario and then insulted him by letting Mario sit in his anteroom while other executives passed in and out. In December, Mario agreed to stay on until the annual meeting in March, but Walker's callous treatment got the better of him. In late January he quit, returning his paycheck for the month.

Mario kept in touch with the bank and in June 1931 cabled his father, who was resting at a spa in Badgastein in the Austrian Alps: Walker was preparing to liquidate the empire, selling off the largest of its banks to repay the company's debts and to provide for possible losses on its loans. A. P. had read previous cables with dismay. He stared at the decisions in disbelief. A. P. hadn't lost any faith in his company; he refused to believe that the only way to save it was to dismantle it.

A. P. responded with fury, calling the program a "plot" to rob the stockholders by selling their company's assets at bargain prices. He sent "violent" messages to Walker and others at the bank in a furious month-long battle of cablegrams that cost more than $10,000, in which A. P. tried to convince Walker to abandon his plans for selling any of the bank assets. Walker would not budge, and A. P. was still too ill to return to the United States. His wife and daughter, Claire, twenty-seven, had orders to keep him from getting excited, which proved impossible.

Mario kept A. P. abreast of changes. He sent word of a secret directors' meeting. Walker was planning to change the company's bylaws. He had a new slate of directors, dominated by cronies from the East. They planned to reorganize Transamerica, sell Bank of America of New York, and write down the company's assets. What worried A. P. most, however, was news that Walker would change the composition of the company's proxy committee, a group that voted the shares of more than 200,000 stockholders. It was through the proxy committee that Giannini had asserted control over Transamerica. His personal holdings, and those of his family, added up to less than 1 percent of the total stock.

A. P. fired off a cable on June 20, 1931, resigning from his post as chairman of the Advisory Committee of Transamerica. He told James Bacigalupi, who was now president of Transamerica, "Walker isn't on the square and I'll definitely prove all my charges. Have decided best give him absolutely free hand by tendering resignation. . . ."

The cable ended with a request that the company transfer

what remained in "Special Fund Number One" to Giannini's personal bank account. (In 1925 and 1926, the bank had paid A. P. no salary, just picking up his expenses, a total of $168,000 for the two years. Then, in 1927, the board had allocated him 5 percent of the company's profits—a typical arrangement in the 1920s. But in the first year, Giannini earned almost $1.8 million. At A. P.'s request, the bank donated $1.5 million to the University of California to establish the Giannini Foundation of Agricultural Economics. In 1927, Giannini drew $246,000 from the fund and in 1928 he drew $680,993, much of which went to support his medical treatments.)

In mid-1931, when A. P. sent his cable, Special Fund Number One contained $791,000. But Walker refused to pay, arguing that the compensation, 5 percent of the company's profits, was based on fictitious earnings reported in earlier years.

With that, the gloves came off. This was the final insult. A. P. cabled Bacigalupi, who was now in sympathy with Walker, and blasted him for changing sides:

> Does my retirement really preclude me from speaking my mind freely? . . . The plan to sell [the banks, etc.] is a deliberate steal, as you will soon discover. How many of our old stockholders have the ready cash necessary to exercise the suggested "rights"? Very few, I am certain. Of course, the New Yorkers [have] the money. . . . To think you fellows haven't seen through this scheme! How can you all stand for such a thing? The stockholders are entitled to the decision and should have the say in such matters. . . . [Do] I have no right to tell the [shareholders] why I have severed association with the scheming New Yorkers, for whose advent into the organization I frankly admit I am responsible? . . . I am not the man to stand by and see my "model child" put to death. . . . In my place you would pursue the rogues to the very end. . . . Well, that is exactly my conviction. I am going through with it. . . . Lawton [A. P.'s code name for Walker] will find in me one stockholder who can't be bought off. . . . No sir, Jim, never! . . . Now I have rambled enough. I really haven't any business exchanging cables with one of your ability, Jim, when—as the New Yorkers have it—I am only a peddler and a lowly one at that. Perhaps they are right. Well, let me say to you finally to consider my resignation in all-

around effect as of the 21st. . . . Good luck to you and to all. Regards, A. P.

A. P. had already cabled Mario that he was not well yet, but was "waiting only to recover health and strength to give the dirty gang a real stiff battle when the right moment to strike arrives." In September, Giannini began his trip home to California. Hoping to avoid publicity, he took an arduous journey by rail through Canada. Mario met him in Vancouver with news of the company's activities. They took a train to Lake Tahoe, rather than heading for San Francisco, where A. P. was likely to be immediately recognized.

The diversion failed. On September 11, after a barber finished shaving him, A. P. looked up to see Herbert Fleischacker, his archenemy, staring at him. Word spread immediately that A. P. was back, leaving Giannini free to return to San Francisco.

On September 22, he visited Transamerica's board meeting long enough to object to Walker's plans, though, as he had expected, the board ignored him and approved Walker's program. According to an official release, Transamerica would "dispose of the majority interest in each of the banks which the Corporation now controls." A new slate of directors took office, including ten members from the East Coast, two from the Midwest, two Europeans, and two Californians. Among the new directors were four executives from Lee, Higginson & Co., a Boston securities firm linked closely with Ivar Kreuger, the Swedish "match king." (Kreuger had built a massive business by obtaining monopolies in several European countries. Although no one knew it yet, his empire was in desperate financial trouble. Two months later he would rush to New York to arrange loans, making Bank of America one of his first stops. Unable to raise cash, Kreuger returned home and committed suicide.)

A. P.'s illness had taken a heavy toll. As one friend told a bank historian, "He looked like a man who did not have long to live." But the challenge to his bank was rejuvenating A. P., and he was preparing a counteroffensive. Over the next few months the nation witnessed a rare spectacle—a battle for control of one of the nation's largest companies waged like a campaign for political office.

A. P.'s decision when he founded the bank to sell shares to small businessmen in San Francisco would have a decisive role in the battle. By the mid-1920s, many of these early investors had made fortunes on Giannini's companies. The shares were spread widely, with a huge block in the hands of the bank's early customers.

Within days of the September board meeting, a committee of these small shareholders called on A. P., who said he was ready to fight, but wouldn't lead the challenge to Walker until he was sure the shareholders wanted him back. The head of this informal group, Charles W. Fay, a retired postmaster, told the press he opposed the Walker plan, and the stories prompted a torrent of telegrams. Encouraged, Fay established the Associated Transamerica Stockholders.

On October 1, 1931, Transamerica announced that it was selling control of Bank of America of New York to National City Bank, the only step ever completed in Walker's effort to liquidate Transamerica.

With the sale of the New York bank, the shareholder revolt began to build. Giannini attended meetings of shareholders. Four hundred showed up in Fresno, 150 in San Francisco. Slightly unnerved by the early success of his opponents, Walker sent a memo to employees threatening to fire anyone who supported the dissident shareholders.

In November, Fay's association addressed a mildly worded letter to shareholders asking them to oust Walker and vote the Gianninis back in. Walker responded by sending branch managers to talk with five thousand of the company's largest shareholders. The response was not promising for Walker; the big shareholders remained loyal to Giannini.

By the end of November, Fay's group controlled proxies from half of Transamerica's shareholders—not half the shares, just half the shareholders, but enough to convince A. P. to shed his reluctance.

A. P. was a natural politician. In the 1890s, he had helped oust two of San Francisco's most corrupt political bosses, Christopher ("Christ Himself") Buckley and Sam Rainey. A surge of good government sentiment was welling in San Francisco, and James Phelan, a friend of Giannini, was a leading candidate on the reform ticket. A. P. knew his district was one of the most tightly controlled in the city, that is, it always voted the way it was paid to vote. A. P. formed the "New Charter Democratic Club," and started ringing doorbells. On election day he brought the brawniest of his club members to the polls to protect voters against thugs, with stunning results. North Beach voted out the bosses by six to one. After the election, A. P. walked back over the territory, passing out cigars and "treats" to celebrate the victory. This was one politician who remembered the voters after the election was over.

He brought the same style to his campaign against Walker. His troops began a tour of the state. A. P. gave no speeches, but he answered questions, shook hands with the crowd, and displayed his phenomenal memory for names and faces. Mario and Fay gave short speeches, but the man who sold the crowds was A. J. Scampini, a San Francisco attorney who had worked in the bank's trust department. Four thousand shareholders attended a meeting in Stockton. Three thousand showed up in Sacramento.

A local speaker in Sacramento asked whether "we are to be dictated to by the golfers of Long Island or the cocktail sippers around some mahogany bar in the Bronx." Scampini revealed that Walker was earning $100,000 a year, then disclosed other salaries, fueling the indignation of this Depression-era crowd.

Walker countered with a charge that A. P. had earned $3.7 million in less than four years and had spent all but $792,000. The letter said Giannini demanded and had been denied the rest. Walker criticized A. P. for propping up the stock of Transamerica, and implied that he had resigned as president because the company was in sorry shape.

"Mudslinging," A. P. growled. Mario explained the board's decision to grant a share in the profits to A. P. and noted his special drawing fund, pointing out that most of the money drawn over five years had been spent aiding the corporation.

The campaign took on ominous overtones. Plainclothes policemen were brought in to guard the Transamerica headquarters. Walker ordered Bank of America's trust department to vote its shares in his favor. Borrowers from the bank who had Transamerica shares as security felt pressure to vote for Walker. And officers and employees, who owned 1.5 million shares, got warnings to fill out proxies for Walker.

A. P. advised old friends who called that they shouldn't fight Walker. "Fill out the Walker proxy if you have to," one remembered him saying. "Then later you may change your mind and want to fill out one for me. You don't have to take the bank into your confidence. It's the proxy you execute last that counts, remember." Worried by Walker's intimidation of his employees, though, Giannini obtained a temporary court injunction to restrain Transamerica from coercing votes from its employees.

During 1931, Walker had fired more than 1,500 employees and omitted the dividend, alienating the bank's customers and triggering a steady decline in deposits and loans. Business was leaving Transamerica faster than it was leaving competitors; the company's share of the California market dropped from 31 percent to just over 25 percent in eighteen months.

On January 9 and 11, John U. Calkins, a governor of the Federal Reserve, met with the feuding parties. He pointed out that in the first week of January, Bank of America had lost $20 million in deposits. He warned what might happen if the bank failed, and described its condition as "definitely precarious."

Calkins, who had once refused to work at the "dago bank" run by Giannini, was not sympathetic with A. P. and Mario. He accused Mario and Charles Fay of "insisting upon tearing down . . . [the] great [bank] of which they are directors." Without Walker, he contended, Transamerica would lose the support of Wall Street, which he was sure would doom the company to failure.

Mario ably countered the arguments, but A. P., who was campaigning in Los Angeles, expressed the problem most succinctly. In a cable to the meeting, A. P. said, "Restoration of public confidence is a condition prerequisite to success and future prosperity of institutions. This is impossible with Walker on board."

On February 15, 1932, Transamerica's annual meeting of shareholders convened in Wilmington, Delaware. (Transamerica was incorporated in Delaware.) A. P. Giannini received more than 15 million votes. He cabled home to a Fresno shareholder that his dissident group had won by 7 million votes.

A. P. stepped in as chairman of Transamerica and president of the bank, once again with no salary. The salary of the new president of the holding company was set at $20,000 a year, compared with Bacigalupi's $60,000.

"This is not the time to crow," he said after the victory. "The big work is ahead of us."

A. P. Giannini was back. But the company he built was still in serious trouble.

Chapter Five

In building up a great financial institution in the West we have met with every difficulty and every possible handicap has been put in our way, but with an honest purpose and public support we have surmounted them all.

A. P. Giannini, 1938

A. P. Giannini never again faced a threat to his control of Bank of America, but his battles with regulators and competitors continued, nearly endangering the company's survival.

John Calkins, the governor of the Federal Reserve Bank of San Francisco who had attempted to keep Elisha Walker in place, attacked Giannini after his return to office. Clearly the Transamerica empire was in trouble. Calkins believed it was at the edge of bankruptcy. He told others that, and shortly after Giannini returned to power, wrote him a note asking how Giannini planned to repay the loans outstanding from the government.

Calkins had reason for concern. The U.S. economy was in a tailspin in early 1932. The bread lines were getting longer and unemployment was increasing.

A. P. growled back, "Your letter . . . convinces me that you do not understand or sympathize with our problem. It appears to me that the bank is being harassed by those who should normally be . . . cooperating with us in the inherited task of reconstruction." He accused Calkins of plotting with Walker to liquidate Transamerica.

In spite of the economy, the company was slowly regaining its health. Instead of firing workers, A. P. had cut the salaries of all employees earning more than $100 a month by 5 percent and had cut the salaries of top executives by up to 20 percent. He forced everyone on staff to take a month off at half pay. With the depression at its worst, A. P. knew that jobs were just not available. By tightening its belt, Bank of America could afford to keep its people at work, but only if expenses stayed down.

Though he was sixty-two and ill, Giannini began work at 6:30 A.M. and stayed until ten at night. His decisiveness and drive seemed to pay off. Confidence increased and the steady drain of deposits reversed within days of his return. By mid-June 1932, Transamerica's California banks had added more than $50 million in deposits, while most other banks in the state were losing deposits.

Giannini used those deposits to support projects that put others back to work. The bank bought bonds to finance a high school in Vallejo, a highway in southern California, a host of projects in San Francisco. Giannini spent $6 million to buy the first bonds issued to support the construction of the Golden Gate Bridge.

But California, like the rest of the U.S. economy, continued to suffer. In February 1932, Herbert Hoover had created the Reconstruction Finance Corporation, lending money to prop up troubled companies and slow the failure of banks. But during 1932, bank failures rose. Nevada declared a bank holiday late in the year, the first of many around the country. Tiny runs by depositors began in various corners of the nation. Then, in St. Louis in January 1933, panic set in. Runs at suburban banks led to sixteen failures. A week later Sacramento depositors panicked after California National Bank failed to open. Five Bank of America branches lost deposits, forcing Giannini to ship $3 million to Sacramento by air, armored car, and limousine. By that evening, he had sent another $10 million. The run, which began on Saturday morning, ended Monday afternoon. Giannini's quick action restored confidence and Bank of America lost just $104,000 in deposits.

The failures spread to Detroit, parts of Maryland, and then Ohio, Indiana, Illinois, and Arkansas in quick succession. On March 2, the banks closed in California, and on the next day a nationwide bank holiday began. That Saturday, March 4, Franklin D. Roosevelt was sworn in as President of the United States.

Roosevelt faced a tremendous challenge. If he kept the banks closed, the nation's businesses would suffer. If he let the banks reopen too early, he could spark a second wave of panic.

Roosevelt approved a four-day bank holiday, which would allow the nation's banks to reopen on Monday, March 13.

A. P. Giannini—one of the banking industry's leading Democrats and a firm supporter of Roosevelt—attended the inauguration and Roosevelt sought his counsel before announcing the four-day holiday.

On Friday, March 10, A. P. returned to San Francisco. He expected a telegram from the Department of the Treasury authorizing him to reopen his bank, but it didn't come. On Sunday he went to the bank and telephoned Washington, asking one of his staff to talk with the Secretary of the Treasury. The aide called back shortly, saying the Secretary, William Woodin, had approved Bank of America's request to reopen.

At 3:00 P.M. Washington time, A. P. was still waiting for the telegram. He called California's senators and John Francis Neylan, counsel for newspaper publisher William Randolph Hearst. Hearst had supported Roosevelt. Neylan knew the members of the new administration. Neylan reported back that things were all right.

At 9:30 P.M. in Washington, Giannini got a call from California's senators informing him that Woodin had reversed his decision. Bank of America would not reopen with the rest of the nation's banks.

Giannini was furious. He knew that if Bank of America did not reopen on time, its depositors would panic. Then he learned the cause of the reversal. John Calkins of the Federal Reserve had sent a highly critical report to the Treasury, arguing that Bank of America was in such poor financial shape that it should not reopen. As Giannini listened, his outrage grew. Calkins based his recommendation on financial statements that were more than a year old, ignoring the recent reversal of Bank of America's slide and the steady increase in its deposits.

Giannini called Secretary Woodin, who listened politely, but refused to change his opinion.

At 10:00 P.M. in Washington, Franklin Roosevelt delivered the first of his many fireside chats. He discussed the bank holiday, legislation that he was preparing, and plans for issuing sound currency. He concluded by saying "I do not promise you that every bank will be reopened or that individual losses will not be suffered, but there will be no losses that possibly could be avoided; and there would have been more and greater losses had we continued to operate. I can even promise you salvation for some at least of the sorely pressed banks. We shall be engaged not merely in reopening sound banks but in the creation of sound banks through reorganization."

Giannini must have swallowed hard. Time was running out for the Bank of America. If that telegram did not arrive soon, Giannini's bank would make the list of institutions saved through reorganization. A. P. again called Neylan, who enlisted Hearst's support and then phoned Woodin at the White House. It was now 11:00 P.M. West Coast time, 2:00 A.M. in Washington.

Secretary Woodin said the report from Calkins showed the bank was "hopelessly insolvent" and "could not possibly stand up." Neylan explained Calkins's bias, mentioned the problem with the figures, and told him that the failure to reopen Bank of America would be a disaster. Woodin agreed to listen to Giannini's rebuttal.

Neylan called Giannini, got the new figures, and read them to Woodin, who called Calkins in San Francisco and asked him whether he would take the blame if keeping Bank of America closed turned out to be a mistake. When Calkins balked, Woodin decided to allow Bank of America to reopen. At 3:30 A.M. in California—after sunrise in Washington—Woodin called Neylan again. He wanted assurance that if something went wrong, Hearst and Neylan would step forward to explain how the decision was made. Neylan agreed. Woodin told him, "You can go to sleep. The bank will open."

A. P. Giannini's battles with regulators hadn't ended, but this was the last moment in his lifetime that the survival of Bank of America would be in doubt. The bank opened its doors the next morning, right on schedule.

Deposits flowed in more rapidly than many thought possible. By mid-1933 Bank of America repaid the last of the loans it had taken out from the government under Walker's tenure. In January of 1934 Transamerica restored its dividend to shareholders, paying twelve and a half cents a quarter on each share.

Between 1933 and June 1949, when A. P. Giannini died, Bank of America prospered. It was pushed, of course, by the California economy, which grew dynamically during World War II and into the next decade. Bank of America continued to operate according to its founder's ideals. The banks Giannini had bought operated as autonomous community organizations, with the head office watching carefully.

Under A. P. and Mario's guidance, Bank of America continued to serve small businessmen and consumers. Strange as it seems now, Bank of America was considered innovative when it began lending on automobiles, offering unsecured loans to help consumers buy appliances, and embracing government programs to lend money to farmers, home buyers, and returning servicemen. These programs, now commonplace, were controversial advances in banking in the 1940s and 1950s.

The bank worked and it worked well. After the scare of the late 1920s and the early 1930s, Bank of America stuck with a successful formula. The dream of a nationwide empire still endured, but the rush to expand and build was less pressing. Transamerica kept acquiring banks, but at a slower pace. Besides the stock ownership in National City Bank—acquired when Walker sold Bank of America of New York—Transamerica's holdings outside the western United States were minor.

Within California, Bank of America was building its power. During the Depression it had continued to underwrite the bonds of cities and counties in the state. Now it controlled that market. When cities and counties decided to sell bonds, Wall Street waited for Bank of America to set a price on the securities. In the automobile market, the bank captured close to 85 percent of all auto loans in the state. In other markets, it was just as dominant.

This brought challenges. In Washington in 1933 and 1935, Congress passed legislation curbing the powers of banks, limiting them to the staid business of commercial banking, putting investment banking, insurance, and other activities off-limits. Some of the anger of Congress was aimed at the scoundrels on Wall Street, but as much was aimed at A. P. Giannini and his vast empire. As part of that legislation, Congress put bank holding companies under the control of the Federal Reserve, a step to rein in Transamerica. Fear of Giannini also helped kill a series of bills designed to allow interstate branching. The sentiment lingered long after Giannini's death, encouraging such strong feelings about bank holding companies that Congress eventually limited them to owning banks in one state (except for a few "grandfathered" under the law) and restricted their nonbanking activities to a narrow list of acceptable businesses.

Until his death A. P. was never far away, but Mario ran the bank, bringing a different style to management. Mario was far less flamboyant than his father. Because he was a hemophiliac, he had spent his childhood as something of an invalid. While

A. P. ignored rule books, Mario wrote and revised the first standard operating manuals for the bank (which have since grown to more than seven volumes, each as thick as the Manhattan phone directory). While A. P. developed grand schemes, Mario paid attention to detail, shunning the limelight. While A. P. wandered through the bank, looking employees in the eye, Mario, who was unable to visit the bank for long stretches because of his illnesses, relied on others, "spies," one former employee called them. Like his father, Mario worried constantly about plots and cabals, displaying political intuition that a former executive likened to the sensibilities of the Medicis, the Florentine family whose political intrigues brought it wealth, power, and several papacies.

When he was ill, Mario often worked at his home atop Nob Hill, to which he summoned senior executives for meetings. He exerted control by scrutinizing expenses, salaries, and corporate policies. He grilled executives, asking tough questions and digging for details. He kept track of all promotions, from the most junior to the most senior employee. A. P. had a reputation for never yelling at anyone with a title lower than executive vice-president. ("After that though, watch out," one executive remembered. "He'd really take people apart. If he yelled at you that meant he respected you.") Mario regularly browbeat subordinates.

In October 1945, Bank of America became the largest commercial bank in the world, surpassing the Chase National Bank (now Chase Manhattan Bank). Bank of America had just over $5 billion in assets. In forty-one years it had helped transform the fertile, scarcely populated state of California into an economic power that rivaled many European nations. It had brought banking to millions of Californians, altering the way banking was done in the United States.

In 1949, A. P. Giannini died at seventy-nine. Two years earlier Doc had died, and in 1952 Mario's lifelong battle with illness brought his death at age fifty-seven. The only Giannini who remained in management was Claire Giannini Hoffman, A. P.'s daughter, who was forty-five. She took A. P.'s spot as a director, remaining on the board until 1985, when she resigned in outrage at the condition of the company her father had built.

The Clausen
Decade

Chapter Six

If our institutions have become great it is by the consent of the people we serve. We can endure only by continuing that type of service. This we always intend to do.

A. P. Giannini, 1944

The University of California at Santa Barbara rests on a narrow spit of land at the edge of the Pacific Ocean, just a three-hour drive south of Bank of America's headquarters in San Francisco. The campus is normally tranquil, a place to surf and relax, but in February 1970 students in neighboring Isla Vista erupted in violence. Demonstrators against the Vietnam War vented their frustration by burning the local branch of Bank of America to the ground. It was an attack on the insensitivity of corporate America that, like the shooting of students at Kent State and the battles over Berkeley's People's Park, became a symbol of the student protest movement.

The attack on the branch began on the evening of February 24, at about 8:30 P.M., when a small band of students set the contents of a garbage can on fire and rammed it through the front door of the branch. Then they and others ran through the building, destroying furniture and throwing chairs through windows.

By midnight a crowd of several hundred had gathered, piling tables and chairs against the walls of the branch and starting a blaze that eventually left the building a smoldering ruin.

In the twenty years since the death of A. P. Giannini, Bank of America had become a symbol of corporate arrogance and inhumanity to a generation of students. The United States had changed dramatically since 1949. The prosperity of the fifties and sixties had ended in social upheaval, leaving searing images of long-haired student demonstrators being clubbed and tear-gassed on the UC Berkeley campus and in the streets of Chicago during the 1968 Democratic National Convention. As the world's largest bank, with offices on seemingly every street corner in every town in California, Bank of America was an easy target for demonstrators, who picketed, disrupted business, and finally burned the bank's branches at Isla Vista and near UC Irvine.

Louis Lundborg, the graying, patrician chairman of the company, expressed the frustration of the bank's management. "When our branch at Isla Vista went up in smoke our first reaction was just plain amazement and anger that such a thing could happen to us." The bank roared in pain, lashing out with a full-page advertisement calling on then-governor Ronald Reagan to put down the forces of destruction and anarchy. Reagan responded by sending in the National Guard, and quoting George Washington: "Do not parley with sedition or lawlessness. Strike a blow that cannot be parried—and at once." When tempers cooled, Bank of America ran other ads that drew a distinction between violence and legitimate dissent.

In two decades, Bank of America had grown more distant from the people it served. The management that had led the bank under A. P. and Mario Giannini was largely gone. The remaining members of the old breed served as caretakers for the tradition. Some preserved the aspiration to, as Giannini put it, "be first in all things." But that spirit was dying rapidly.

A. P. Giannini's empire had been broken into pieces. In the late 1940s, the U.S. government had charged A. P.'s Transamerica holding company with antitrust violations. A lawsuit forced Transamerica to sell its stock in Bank of America. Congress then passed the Bank Holding Company Act of 1956, which forced Transamerica to shed most of its other banks. In mid-1958, it placed twenty-three banks in eleven western states into a new holding company, called First America Corp., which it spun off to Transamerica's stockholders. First America eventually became First Interstate Bancorporation, while Bank of America created its own holding company in the late 1960s, BankAmerica Corp.

Transamerica kept its nonbanking business, including a life insurance company, a couple of manufacturing companies, and the nation's fifth largest property insurer. It remained in San

Francisco, eventually building the now-famous Transamerica pyramid two blocks from Bank of America's headquarters.

Bank of America was by far the largest remnant of the empire. But unlike the Giannini days, when A. P. used his holding company to go where the bank couldn't, by 1970 the new Bank-America holding company was so restricted by law that it could do little besides owning Bank of America.

Since A. P.'s death, three men in succession had led Bank of America: Carl Wente, one of the family that founded Wente Brothers winery, who served for just two years; S. Clark Beise, a round-faced, bespectacled former national bank examiner who brought professional management to the company in nearly a decade on the job; and Rudolph Peterson, an urbane, thoughtful man with superb political skills, who ran the company for the last seven years of the sixties.

In 1970, Bank of America, with $25 billion in deposits, was five times larger than it had been in 1949. It was still a bank for the masses, serving two and a half million customers, and it was very profitable. But it had lost its single-minded devotion to "the little fellow," it was diversifying into new fields, including international lending, where it ranked third among all U. S. banks, and it had grown more and more bureaucratic.

The California branch system remained the heart of the company and clung to the Giannini traditions, but it too had changed, reflecting the growth of California. Now the largest state in the nation, rich, influential, and established, California had just under 20 million people. Immigrants continued to stream into the state, but they were less important to its economy and less important to Bank of America.

A. P.'s company still dominated banking in California, with nine hundred branches—nearly three times the number of its closest competitor—and as much as 85 percent of some aspects of the banking business. But though no single institution rivaled Bank of America, a host of smaller banks and savings institutions did battle on every corner, many of them hoping to emulate Giannini's success.

The symbol of the new Bank of America was its world headquarters. Finished in 1969, the new building rose fifty-two stories above California Street in the heart of San Francisco's financial district. A hulking, brown tower, built of carnelian marble, it was the model for the building in the movie *The Towering Inferno*. It was the tallest building in the western United States, dominating San Francisco's skyline, just as Bank of America dominated the city's financial community. It was also a cold and inhuman structure, an outward symbol of what was happening within the bank.

Much to the distress of Claire Giannini Hoffman, A. P.'s daughter, this new headquarters was not called the Giannini Tower. Bank of America's executives preferred the simpler World Headquarters, which had a more imposing sound and reminded them less of the bank's heritage as "the little dago bank" that Giannini had opened in North Beach. When Claire protested, management named the plaza on which the building sits after A. P.

By 1970, A. P.'s distrust of large corporations no longer restrained the company. Wooing the accounts of major corporations had become a pet project of the chief executive under both Beise and Peterson. Beise started the corporate finance group. Peterson made it grow, lending heavily to large corporations inside and outside California.

The bank also expanded rapidly outside the United States. Between 1950 and 1970, under Beise and Peterson, Bank of America bought interests in fifty-seven overseas operations, opening offices from Buenos Aires to Sydney. By 1970, 25 percent of the bank's assets were overseas, generating 19 percent of its profits.

This was an important break with tradition. A. P. and Mario had disliked making loans that were too large, with A. P. admonishing that the little fellow felt loyalty to a bank and stuck with it, while a large corporation only stayed as long as it could get the best deal. What had given Bank of America its special personality was A. P.'s devotion to providing every customer with the same high quality of service. With the move into corporate and international banking, the slow decline of the importance of the little fellow to Bank of America had begun.

But Beise and Peterson found running the California branch system boring. Built on plans laid by the Gianninis, the retail bank was rich and dull. There was no challenge to it. Not only did it generate huge profits, but the branches filled almost effortlessly with deposits. Each of the branches ran as an independent community bank, and day-to-day operations went smoothly. If disaster struck somewhere, the head office might change the branch manager. But that didn't happen very often.

"We don't change the rules, we change the man," Rudolph Peterson said. "It's much simpler, because the only way to change the rules is to write more and newer ones and that's bad. Banking has to be decentralized in a big organization. The manager, in the community has to be Mr. Banker in a very old-fashioned way. He makes the decisions. He comes to us for advice, not the answers." There wasn't much there to fix.

Beise and Peterson didn't ignore retail banking, but looked beyond the branch system for innovative ways to serve customers. Beise unearthed a novelty called a bank credit card. Although merchants had been using credit cards for years, only a few small banks had experimented with giving customers cards on which they could charge purchases. Beise liked the idea and ran with it, putting Bank of America's full marketing muscle behind the BankAmericard. Peterson pushed the idea even harder. "It got so bad we might as well have been dumping these things out of airplanes," a former executive says.

Eager to sell the innovation, Bank of America mailed the cards out by the thousands. What they discovered was the first law of finance: Making a loan is not the same thing as collecting it. Losses soared as some borrowers went on spending sprees. But the plastic card survived the early traumas. It became so potent, so quickly, that other banks felt threatened. Created in 1959, by 1970 BankAmericard had 29.5 million cardholders. Master Charge, which eventually became MasterCard, was a defensive response by other banks that banded together to create an alternative, worried that Bank of America might capture the entire market. BankAmericard eventually became so successful—and threatening—that Bank of America spun it off into a separate company, which later renamed the card Visa.

Beise also pushed Bank of America to the forefront in computers. It was the first commercial bank to use a computer to help process checks. The machine was designed by Stanford Research Institute and built by General Electric because the nation's computer companies, led by International Business Machines, saw little potential for large computers in banking.

Perhaps the bank's biggest challenge after the Gianninis died was managing its success. A. P. had built a company with very little need for a strong, central executive team. He and Mario, with a few trusted lieutenants, effectively ran the bank. But after Mario and A. P. died, the growth continued and the de-

mand for management talent grew exponentially. Even under
A. P. the thin upper ranks had worried regulators, who chided
him about what would happen if he were to die. They thought
the bank would expire, too. Giannini would respond by going on
six-month and year-long vacations to prove the bank could run
on its own (though, of course, he kept in constant touch by telegram, running the bank from overseas).

When Beise became president, he was surrounded by executives who had risen through the branch system, but were not up
to managing a modern bank. He increased salaries to attract
more talented bankers, weeded out the deadwood, but never
found the right successor. That's why he recruited Peterson, a
onetime officer of Bank of America, who had jumped to Transamerica, where he eventually headed its bank in Hawaii.

When Beise chose Peterson as his successor, it sent shud-
ders through the organization. Peterson was not one of the old
guard, but an outsider. The board's message to insiders was that
they were not quite good enough to run A. P.'s bank, a message
reinforced by the board's instruction to Peterson to make sure he
had a successor when he got ready to retire. Peterson quickly
identified talented young officers, moving many to the corporate
finance division, which called on large businesses. He wanted to
watch these men develop without interference from the old
guard in the branches, who still dominated Bank of America and
liked to see employees make slow, steady progress through the
ranks. Peterson was creating his own team, a new political force
within the bank, which would provide the next generation of
leaders for the company.

This unit turned out to be a huge success. Lending money
to large corporations in the 1960s proved almost too easy. American companies were growing, expanding overseas, and hungry
for cash. The commercial paper market, in which companies borrow directly from other companies, was new, unfamiliar, and not
very practical. Foreign banks, which would flood the United
States with money in the 1970s, rarely lent to U.S. corporations
in the 1960s. That left U.S. banks in a safe, protected world, in
which they grew fat. Big corporations paid high rates of interest,
the prime rate or better, and left huge balances in accounts earning no interest. The average deposit was equal to about 20 percent of the money borrowed.

Bank of America stepped into this market with deep, deep

pockets and expertise in some industries. Though it had never aggressively courted large corporations, many of its small clients had prospered, allowing Bank of America to finance some spectacular operations. Bank of America had backed Henry Kaiser as he expanded from heavy construction work into the making of steel, aluminum, cement, automobiles, and ships. It had financed the construction of huge dams throughout the West, and it knew the industries that were important to California—aerospace, fashion, agriculture, real estate, construction, and moviemaking.

Doc Giannini, A. P.'s brother, had been one of the first bankers to lend to the movie business. Giannini's New York bank, which Doc led, had its headquarters in a section of the city that spawned the movie industry. In 1909 the Bank of Italy was financing nickelodeons in San Francisco, and by 1918 it was backing the biggest movie producers in the industry. Doc approved what appears to be the first secured loan in the movie business, taking the prints of one of Charlie Chaplin's hit films, *The Kid,* as collateral for a $250,000 loan, then the largest bank loan ever made to a film producer. Bank of America financed Walt Disney's filming of *Snow White* in the midst of the Depression and in the 1950s backed his creation of Disneyland. For a time Cecil B. deMille worked for A. P. at one of the banks he owned in Hollywood. Later Bank of America supported deMille's making of classics such as *The Ten Commandments*. Doc even served for a short while as chief executive of United Artists, the film company started by Mary Pickford, Douglas Fairbanks, and Charlie Chaplin.

As the 1960s ended, BankAmerica also dominated lending to the high-technology companies that were starting up throughout California, including Memorex and Teledyne, two of the glamour companies of the 1960s.

By the time Peterson was ready to retire, his corporate lenders were ready to inherit control of Bank of America. Most had never worked in the California branches, or not for very long. They were talented, presentable, and knew how to wine and dine a corporate customer, how to write a solid loan. As one observant BankAmerican noted, "They all tended to be six feet tall and look good in a suit."

In 1969, before the shock of the Isla Vista conflagration, Rudolph Peterson reached down into the ranks of the company, past a generation of older managers, to tap Alden Winship "Tom" Clausen, a forty-six-year-old credit specialist, to run the company. Tom Clausen was perhaps the brightest of Peterson's team of corporate lenders.

Though he was only the fourth man to lead the bank since Mario's death, he worked in a different world from that of his predecessors. The executive suite had moved steadily higher, from the docks of San Francisco to the fortieth floor of the new world headquarters. While A. P. refused to use a private office, Clausen got a huge, northeast corner suite with a large attached conference room, oriental rugs, and floor-to-ceiling windows that offered a sweeping panorama of the San Francisco Bay from the Golden Gate to the Bay Bridge. The fortieth-floor lobby for visitors ran three-quarters the length of the building, with the same spellbinding view as a backdrop. Nowhere in the banking world was there a more opulent setting for an executive suite, nor a headquarters built to radiate so little concern for human beings—this was the center of a vast empire, the icy heart of a modern corporation.

In the late 1920s A. P. had admonished that "an important executive should not have to keep himself hidden. He should not have to bolster up his personality with private offices, secretaries, a lot of superfluous paraphernalia. He should be strong enough to be able to protect himself from bores and cranks— and to make the direct human contacts that real business thrives upon." But by 1970 the executives of Bank of America lived in an isolated world. Appointments were essential just to reach the executive floor of the bank and two armed private security guards protected Tom Clausen and his team from unwanted intruders.

From this sanctuary, Tom Clausen presided over the growth of Bank of America from 1970 to 1981. In the turbulence of the 1970s, he quadrupled the company's size and profits. He pushed the company more heavily into international lending, especially in the farthest corners of the developing world. He was not a charismatic leader, nor a popular globe-trotting figure. Clausen was Mr. Inside. The battles he fought hardest were battles to reorganize Bank of America, wars fought over accounting systems, corporate structures, and financial statements.

Chapter Seven

This bank must and will be run solely for the benefit of the stockholders and the depositors. No man will be permitted to acquire
power enough to dominate its policies unwisely.

A. P. Giannini, 1904

T om Clausen was a demanding and humorless boss. He intimidated subordinates, many of whom found his decisions ma-
nipulative and hypocritical. Those who admired Clausen praised
his drive to succeed, his intelligence, and his high standards, but
even they recognized his insensitivity. Clausen's fits of temper
became legendary and tales of his callous disregard for junior officers spread so extensively through the company that it is hard
to separate myths and half-truths from reality. But there is no
doubt that Tom Clausen's personality and the myths he built
played a dominant role in the transformation of Bank of America
in the 1970s.

Tom Clausen had a typical middle-American upbringing.
He grew up in Hamilton, Illinois, just across the Mississippi River from Keokuk, Iowa. Hamilton had a population of about two
thousand and its only real commercial success was a company
that then, as now, manufactured beekeeping equipment.

As Clausen was growing up, the Depression rolled through
the Midwest. Clausen's father, Morton, an immigrant from Nor-
way, owned the local paper, the *Hamilton Press*, and the family
survived in relative comfort, living in an apartment above the
newspaper. Morton was a fixture at the Kiwanis club and active in
social affairs, a man, one Hamiltonian later told a journalist,
"who could talk on any subject and give it authority whether he
knew anything about it or not." His wife, Elsie, tall and stately,

73

watched over the family and took the children to the Presbyterian church every Sunday.

Clausen's childhood seems to have been untroubled. He joined the rest of the children ice skating on the frozen ponds and rivers around town, fished with his father and grandfather, and swam in a local creek or in the Mississippi at the Lakeview Club, a small riverside club with a sandy beach.

Tom and his sister, Jocelyn, attended public schools in Hamilton, where he was a serious, dependable student, valedictorian of his high school class, editor of the school newspaper. He played the flute in the band, sang in the chorus, and after school ran a linotype for his father, earning scars from the hot lead that provide lasting reminders of his apprenticeship. He went on double and triple dates, to Friday night dances at the Lakeview Club, and spent weekends at picnics or the movies.

Clausen attended Carthage College, a small liberal arts school a few miles away, changing his major from philosophy to mathematics. He worked his way through school as a linotype operator in a couple of small print shops, then served as a flying meteorological officer in the Army Air Corps from 1943–1946, spending part of his time in the Azores making flights over Europe and Africa. After the war he went back to school, earning a law degree from the University of Minnesota.

Before taking bar examinations, Clausen followed Mary Margaret "Peggy" Crassweller to Los Angeles. Clausen hoped to convince Peggy, whom he had met on a blind date, to marry him. She balked, but Clausen was persistent. He settled in Los Angeles, began studying for the California bar exam, and continued to court her. "In order to eat," he took a job at the Bank of America counting cash in the vault of the main Los Angeles branch.

The next year Peggy Crassweller gave in to Clausen's persistence. In 1950, they married. The same year he passed the California bar, but instead of charging into the legal profession, he waited in vain for the bank to offer him a position as a lawyer. "I didn't get any offers, so I had to make do with what I was doing," he recalled later. "Up to that point I had been progressing through the ranks of branch management. After four or five years, I realized that banking involved many different things and that maybe it was more interesting than practicing law."

Clausen was a compulsive employee. On the Saturday of his

wedding, he worked two hours late at the bank trying to track down a ten-dollar bookkeeping error. He suffered miserably after his first major loan loss. Years later he still remembered the exact amount, $546,312.13. "I started to second guess myself and I lost a lot of sleep," he said later. "Then one of our senior officers said 'You know you can only do your best, and if you've done your best, who could do better?' That made a lot of sense to me; it was what got me through a very tough period of self-doubt."

Once committed to banking, Clausen transferred to Bank-America's corporate lending area. He spent the rest of his career clambering up "a tall, skinny ladder." The ladder took him through a series of positions as a lender, credit officer, and executive, with no stops in the branches, the back office, finance, or overseas.

In the history of most chief executives, it is possible to find one or two moments when, through luck or diligence, they excel, catching the eye of senior executives. Clausen's colleagues remember no specific event in his rise at BankAmerica. One former colleague contends that when he stepped into the executive suite, "he had an unblemished record, no pluses and no minuses."

What Clausen offered was diligence and dependability. He worked hard, minimized big mistakes, and developed a reputation as a solid corporate lender and a decent judge of credit. He had also done well lending money to small electronics companies such as Teledyne in southern California.

That was enough to set him apart from the rest of the executives at BankAmerica. In 1963, after reorganizing the corporate finance group, Rudolph Peterson selected Clausen as its new boss. The unit, which had slowly been emerging as a special department within the bank, was large enough to stand alone now. Clausen moved to San Francisco, bought a house in the rich suburb of Hillsborough, and got a big raise.

In 1965 Clausen became a senior vice-president, the next year he headed to Harvard University to attend the advanced management program at its Graduate School of Business. When he returned to the bank, he was promoted again to executive vice-president, joined the managing committee—the bank's top policy body—and moved into an office next to Peterson. A year later Peterson gave him worldwide responsibility for the bank's lending activities. As executive vice-president, Clausen reviewed and often became involved with the largest and most complex loans that the bank was making. One of these had special importance. Bank of America had been trying for years to win the business of many of the largest mining companies, which were expanding rapidly during the 1960s. Rio Tinto Zinc, Ltd. (RTZ), a large British company, was actively exploring in and around Australia for copper and other minerals. Bank of America wanted its business.

In 1968, the bank hit paydirt. RTZ selected Bank of America to arrange two loans to raise $250 million for the development of open-pit copper mines on the South Pacific island of Bougainville. It was one of the largest loans of the day and being the lead bank was a little like striking the mother lode.

Bank of America bragged about this loan. It had been chosen over a host of other international banks to serve a major-league client, a big multinational company, a company with stature. It was a complex transaction, marshaling lenders from all over the world and providing $250 million to the Australian subsidiary of a British company. The paperwork alone took nine months to complete, as lawyers struggled through the intricacies of Australian, U.S., and British law. Tom Clausen got credit for landing the big one. One associate later told *Fortune* that Clausen had a way "not just of seeing something that should be done, but working out the way it can be done."

One junior officer also enjoyed new celebrity as the result of the Bougainville loan. The rank and file gave credit for the Bougainville deal to Samuel H. Armacost, an assistant vice-president, fresh out of Stanford business school. Poised, articulate, a little brash, Armacost got Bank of America's foot in the door. When the deal went through, Armacost took his first giant step down a road that would eventually lead all the way to the presidency of Bank of America.

As executive vice-president, Clausen displayed a zeal for decentralization. Under Beise and Peterson, the head office had grown powerful and bureaucratic. Lending officers complained that they were shackled by loan committees and operating manuals. Tom Clausen sympathized, and made noise about transferring more power to the field. He set up regional offices throughout California to which he delegated responsibility for loan decisions. Later, as president, he would reorganize the bank and send more and more people out into offices away from San Francisco, giving the bank the appearance of being decentralized.

But in practice, Clausen was a centralizer. He liked to make decisions himself, so even after shipping people into the field, he would meddle in the most minute details and second-guess senior executives—even those several thousand miles away. Parts of the bank functioned like a decentralized organization. In some disciplines, such as making loans overseas, power shifted dramatically away from the head office. But Clausen simultaneously built a huge bureaucracy in San Francisco that slowed decision making. In some outposts of the bank, which supposedly ran with autonomy, junior executives would carefully watch Clausen's schedule, knowing that if he left on a business trip their bosses would hesitate to make any major decisions. The executives learned to make their important requests when Clausen could be reached in San Francisco.

On January 1, 1970, the day he became president of Bank-America, Tom Clausen was almost totally unknown outside the bank. A friend described him to the *Wall Street Journal* as "a reserved, shy person with almost a little boy character."

Rudolph Peterson's choice of Tom Clausen as Bank-America's new president surprised many in the company. Peterson had attempted to infuse outside blood into BankAmerica's senior management. He had brought in Walter Hoadley, the well-regarded chief financial officer of Armstrong World Industries, and hired Robert Truex, a solid manager from Irving Trust Co. But when it came time to select a president, he ignored both men.

"Clausen was obviously intellectual," says Joseph J. Pinola, a former executive who worked with Clausen for more than a decade. "He was probably the brightest guy around."

But the ability to motivate people, rallying them to tackle a tough task, the natural stuff of leadership, was lacking. Years later a longtime client of the bank would quip that "Tom Clausen is the only person I've ever met with a charisma by-pass." Bank-America's board had chosen a driven, extraordinarily hard-working, but colorless man to head the bank during the decade of the 1970s.

The choice ended an era at BankAmerica. Clausen became the first chief executive not hired and trained by either A. P. or Mario Giannini. He was also the first commercial lender to head the company.

Clausen pulled around him a cadre of managers who specialized in lending money to big corporations. They brought a new spirit to the executive suite. These specialists saw themselves as the Prussian guard of BankAmerica, an elite group. They were arrogant, at times insufferable, showing disdain for the retail bankers who served the little fellow. The new managers measured themselves against the best of the world's biggest: First National City Bank and Morgan Guaranty, the premier corporate lenders in America. And BankAmerica's new management wanted to beat those banks at their own game.

As commander-in-chief, Tom Clausen was neither innovative nor a visionary, but he was a keen student of how to produce profits. During his ten years at the helm of BankAmerica, the company made more money than any bank in history. It bristled with a sense of direction and purpose. The purpose, however, was shortsighted. Tom Clausen's goal was to increase profits each quarter, with little regard for the long-term costs.

Clausen grasped for power, growing autocratic and imperious. Claire Giannini Hoffman labeled him "Der Führer." He ignored the existence of secretaries on the fortieth floor and found it hard to carry on anything other than the most cursory conversations with the rank and file. He scheduled his personal calendar so tightly that he did not have time for impromptu, relaxed meetings with other executives. He barked when executives dropped by unannounced, and even disliked people passing by his door.

One unsuspecting lending officer, on a visit to the fortieth floor, started to walk past Clausen's door on his way to a meeting in another office. As he approached, Clausen's secretary jumped up, almost in horror, and ushered him around the other way, admonishing that "Mr. Clausen doesn't like people walking in front of his door." Clausen eventually installed a seven-foot Japanese screen to shield the door, which remains in place today.

Clausen's brusque manner emerged most often during management meetings. As one of his supporters put it, "When you presented an idea, he always asked the one question that you wished he wouldn't ask." Others described this same trait as more like a little boy gleefully pulling the wings off a butterfly. A former top bank officer, who worked closely with Clausen for three years, said, "He made his attacks personal. If you came in with an idea that he didn't like, he'd attack you." Disagreeing with Clausen was painful. "You didn't challenge him very often," says Walter Hoadley, who became Clausen's chief economist. "It wasn't worth the fight."

What unnerved staff people was that Clausen was both thorough and unpredictable. He did his homework for almost all presentations and had a memory for figures that was prodigious. He could rattle off the bank's financial ratios from memory, even though he was drowning in reports laden with numbers of all kinds. (Other numbers were harder to remember. He kept his home and office telephone numbers written down in his wallet.) Clausen backed up his own recall by relying on staff people who knew the numbers better than he did. Before any important presentation, Clausen wanted a memo outlining the issues. No matter how thick, he read it, understood it, and asked tough questions.

"He didn't suffer fools—period," says another executive who worked closely with him. He almost always found some weakness in a presentation. And when he found it, he would bore in, asking more and more detailed questions, until he forced the person presenting the report—whether it was a junior staff member or vice-chairman—to admit he didn't know some specific detail. If it was a junior staffer, Clausen would dispatch him to find the answer. If it was a senior executive, he'd belittle the man. "He loved to show people up," says Hoadley.

His message, says one victim, usually went something like this: "How come I know that and you don't? You're the expert, I'm the chief executive. You should know those things. How can you manage your department if you don't?"

Those who watched him closely swear that one-upmanship was often Clausen's only goal. On occasion, when nothing else seemed to be working, Clausen resorted to a technique that a former high-ranking executive calls "the unanswerable question." No matter what an executive answered, Clausen would criticize the response. An example was a meeting in the mid-1970s with Joe Pinola, who had worked as Clausen's lieutenant in the National Division before succeeding to the top post in that division. Pinola was responsible for all corporate lending in the United States outside California. He also ran all activities in Mexico and Canada. For this session, Pinola flew from Los Angeles to San Francisco to make a presentation on his division.

It was clear, recalls the former executive, that "Clausen was out to get him. You could feel the tension in the room." There was a bit of parrying, and then, after Pinola finished his presentation, Clausen began to ask questions. At one point, he asked, with seeming innocence, "What do you think of the prospects for Mexico?" Pinola paused. He knew Clausen well enough to suspect what was coming. "You could see the wheels turning," the executive remembers. "He knew that either way he went, he was doomed." Pinola responded cautiously. He was concerned about Mexico. Over half the population was under eighteen. The debt was growing too fast. It was best to proceed cautiously.

Clausen closed the trap.

"That shows what you know," Clausen said. "I've just been to Mexico and I'm very impressed with the progress there." Had Pinola said exactly that, he would have fared no better: Clausen would have still disagreed.

Clausen's most insensitive comments were usually reserved for junior staff members. One former Bank of America recruit still remembers a Clausen rebuke delivered a decade earlier. The young MBA had spent days preparing for his first presentation to the managing committee. Like all newcomers, he anguished over his report, presenting it to other workers, making sure that he had it down pat. This was a minor event for Clausen, who heard reports like this every day, but it was a big day for the junior officer. Clausen arrived late and sounded out of sorts. He interrupted a few times with questions, then dismissed the report with a wave, saying, "Well, we already know all that"—a crushing summary.

A former credit officer remembers Clausen leaning over in the midst of another talk, by a short, junior executive, and saying, "Get the dwarf out of here and let's get back to business."

The most dangerous time to see Clausen was early in the day. "You never wanted to have a meeting with him before ten A.M.," a senior executive of the bank observed. Joseph Carrera, a vice-chairman, once admitted to a journalist that he told his secretary not to accept any calls from Clausen earlier than ten. "All my life it's been difficult for me to say 'hello' or 'good morning' until ten o'clock coffee. But I get stronger as the day goes on," Clausen told the same journalist. By late afternoon, "I'm very mellow."

Clausen's tough demeanor never extended much beyond verbal abuse. He didn't fire senior executives, just moved them into backwaters of the bank and hoped they would resign. He never actually forced cost-cutting, just complained as costs rose each year. The most notable result of Clausen's tyrannical behavior was that executives hid bad news from him and hoped they could fix a problem before Clausen discovered it on his own.

And not all memories of Clausen are caustic. A former executive assistant remembers early evening chats in Clausen's office. "He seemed to need someone to talk with." On a few occasions, Clausen asked for help while preparing for meetings the next day. He was "genuinely concerned that he send the right message to visiting branch managers." This man remembers sitting with Clausen for up to half an hour as he pondered what to say to a branch manager visiting from overseas. A pat on the back? A few words of caution? Clausen realized that his comments would remain with the officer throughout the year and agonized about saying the right thing—in total contrast to his performances at early morning management meetings.

Clausen displayed a wry sense of humor, but not often. "He'd smile once a month or so," said one executive. And not everyone thought him funny. On one occasion, a crank threatened one of Clausen's executive assistants. The man wrote letters and telephoned the bank. Now the security staff reported that he was in the building, apparently armed, and riding up in the elevator. The executive assistant, panic-stricken, told Clausen that an armed man was in the building and was probably on his way up to the executive suite. He added that it would probably be all right because the man was coming after him, not Clausen. Sensing the discomfort of the young officer and realizing how little danger either was in, Clausen's face spread with a huge grin. "Better you than me," he said, and went back to work, leaving his young aide slightly nonplussed.

In eleven years as president, Clausen's personality, as much as his actions, changed Bank of America. Tom Clausen inherited a company still dominated by the spirit of A. P. Giannini. The company was changing, but it remained at heart a regional, California bank. Two thirds of the company's profits still came from its California division. Despite the growing international operation and the new team at the top of the bank, Bank of America remained an overgrown savings bank, a servant of the mom-and-pop grocer, the local Rotarian, the little fellow in rumpled denims and muddy boots. Clausen, like Peterson, wanted that changed.

    In the Clausen decade, the transformation begun by Peterson and Beise accelerated. Bank of America was bent on becoming a world-class competitor in corporate and international finance, leaving its roots behind. Under Clausen it would grow from $25 billion in assets to more than $100 billion, expanding into new businesses, opening offices throughout the United States, and pushing its expansion overseas at a breathtaking pace. Profits from overseas would nearly double to around 40 percent of total profits. When Tom Clausen stepped down as president of BankAmerica, international and corporate lending produced two thirds of BankAmerica's total assets. The retail bank, though still the major source of the company's profits, was dwindling in importance and in influence.

Chapter Eight

The time to go ahead in business is when the other fellows aren't doing much.

A. P. Giannini, 1927

Tom Clausen turned out to be the wrong man to head Bank-America in the seventies. In a decade that saw more innovation and upheaval in the financial markets than at any time in the past, Clausen stuck doggedly to a strategy inherited from his predecessors, pushing for growth, but milking the company for profits and investing little for the future.

The bank bullied its way into more and more markets around the world when prudent contraction would have worked better. It wooed corporate customers shamelessly while profits in that business shriveled. Infatuated by its own success, it clung to the old ways in California, while other banks moved ahead, modernizing and upgrading their business.

The seventies demanded more. The decade that began in social upheaval quickly sank into economic chaos. Twice during the decade oil embargoes left angry drivers waiting in long lines at gas pumps. The U.S. dollar plunged, causing America to worry that it was becoming a second-rate economic power. Slow economic growth, steadily increasing inflation, and high unemployment frustrated economists. Richard Nixon resigned in disgrace. Political revolt spread in countries served by Bank of America.

The safe, profitable world that commercial banks had known since the 1930s was torn apart. In 1974, for the first time in decades, two large commercial banks failed—Franklin National in New York and A. G. Herstatt in Austria. Huge corporations—Penn Central and later Lockheed—collapsed or nearly collapsed.

The turbulence of the seventies altered the role that commercial banks played in financing American business. Stung by inflation and high interest rates, corporations thought long and hard about the cost of borrowing. Many turned away from their banks, borrowing instead from pension funds, other corporations, and institutional investors by selling them commercial paper. Corporations like General Motors could borrow in the commercial paper market for less than the prime rate, the best interest rate available from a bank.

Foreign banks, trying to buy their way into the U.S. market, stole business by offering cut-rate loans, putting pressure on U.S. banks to respond. By the end of the decade, major corporations that still borrowed from banks could virtually dictate their own terms. Gone were the sweet days of the sixties. Instead of paying the prime rate plus 1 percent, corporations paid 1 percent below prime. Gone also were the big deposits that companies had once left at banks whenever they borrowed.

The relationship between banks and their small depositors also changed. Under federal regulations, consumers had been able to earn only 4 to 5 percent on money left in savings accounts, while depositors with $100,000 or more earned whatever the market dictated. When inflation pushed the rates on those big deposits to more than 10 percent, innovation became inevitable. Money market mutual funds were born. Small savers pulled money out of the bank, sent it to the funds, and the funds put the money right back in the same banks. Only instead of putting it in small accounts, the money funds opened deposits that paid market rates. The cheap, reliable core of small deposits dwindled away. By the end of the decade, more than $70 billion had poured out of banks and into the money funds.

The California market sheltered Bank of America from the turmoil of the seventies. The bank's small business customers couldn't issue commercial paper, so they kept borrowing at rates well above the prime. Many Bank of America depositors found it too much of a nuisance to switch to money funds, so they kept their deposits open. Until 1980 those deposits kept Bank of America rich and fat.

Bank of America's prosperity allowed Tom Clausen to make the biggest mistake of his career. He stuck with a strategy that was fatally flawed, tinkering with Bank of America's direction, adjusting knobs, changing organization charts, but never allowing his vision of the company as a major international and corporate lender to evolve. He acted as though those cheap deposits would never disappear and misread the steady decline in profits from corporate and international lending. The world began to pass his company by.

Clausen's overconfidence was born in 1974, as the U.S. economy struggled through the first Arab oil embargo. Throughout the nation, major banks suffered their worst loan losses since the Great Depression, with real estate loans inflicting the greatest pain. But not Bank of America.

Banks had created Real Estate Investment Trusts (REITs), special companies that borrowed heavily to buy commercial real estate—often borrowing even the downpayment on buildings such as office towers and downtown hotels, a high-risk strategy. When the oil embargo hit and the U.S. economy plummeted, commercial real estate values sank, leaving the REITs of Chase Manhattan, Citicorp, and other banks with losses of hundreds of millions of dollars. Bankers Trust Co., a bank whose debts were then rated triple-A, a hallmark of safety, was so badly hurt that some worried about its survival.

Bank of America emerged virtually unscathed. At the peak of the REIT problems, large New York banks reported loan losses equal to 3 to 5 percent of their loan portfolio. Bank of America, which had loaned relatively little to the REITs, had losses of less than one half of 1 percent. This was conservative banking. In a decision that appears ironic now, the Office of the Comptroller of the Currency grew so impressed with Bank of America's system for managing loans that the agency encouraged other banks to model their approach after it.

The truth about Bank of America may not have been that attractive. E. A. "Ive" Iverson, one of Bank of America's toughest credit specialists, observed to a colleague that the reason the bank escaped the REIT debacle wasn't that it was too smart, but that it was too slow. Bank of America's lenders took so long to figure out what an REIT was, that they were just getting ready to lend when the bubble burst.

Clausen buttressed the bank's image as a prudent lender in 1974 when he slammed the brakes on Bank of America's growth. He won praise from the press for limiting the bank to a "sustainable" 10 percent increase in loans each year. Corporations were banging on Bank of America's door, begging to borrow, the collapse of the commercial paper market after Penn Central having left them desperate for cash. In the six months before Clausen limited growth, Bank of America's loans had grown at an annual rate of 30 percent. For a conservative bank, that was just too much, too soon, especially with inflation soaring and the finances of many large companies looking shaky.

Within the bank, the record of the early 1970s was a source of pride, but also the focal point of a furious debate. Bank of America's lenders saw opportunities in the wake of the 1974 recession. Major banks were shell-shocked, spending much of their time digging out from under bad loans. The biggest of them tightened their credit standards, virtually pulling out of key markets, such as lending to the shipping industry and trading foreign exchange. Bank of America saw an opportunity to grab new business and its loan officers wanted the freedom to go after it.

The problem was the head office. Through the early 1970s, the bank's credit staff in San Francisco—still dominated by the spirit of Giannini—worried about lending too much to big corporations, especially those outside California. It kept a phalanx of committees busy reviewing large loans, just to make sure nothing went wrong. On these committees sat some of the most cautious lenders in the bank. These men, like Iverson, remembered the disasters of the 1930s. Though often in the minority, they argued for prudence.

The REIT debacle proved just how prudent they were. Too prudent, Bank of America's deal makers argued. The credit people were standing in the way of making good loans. It took too long to get a loan approved by San Francisco. The lenders in the field needed more authority. It was time for a change.

Clausen sided with the branch officers. He had always appeared to champion decentralization, the process of pushing authority out closer to the customer. Changing the loan review system appealed to him. In 1974, he combined the old National Division and the International Division, calling them the World Banking Division. He moved the top officers for Europe, Asia, and Latin America from San Francisco to London, Tokyo, and Caracas.

Without changing his 10 percent growth target for the whole bank, he increased the size of loans that could be made in the field from $5 million to $20 million. Then he transferred many of the curmudgeons in the central credit staff out into these new divisions, removing the bottleneck in San Francisco. The committees still met, but with different people and reviewing only larger loans.

Tom Clausen was tinkering with success. He was taking a carefully balanced system, a ponderous, centrally controlled system, and trying to make it more agile, more responsive to the needs of customers. The objective was right, but underlying Clausen's decision was a more disturbing motive, an emphasis on size and market share over loan quality.

The emphasis on growth was part of the legacy of A. P. Giannini. Throughout his tenure Bank of America grew faster than was safe. It was always testing the limits of prudence, growing, expanding, entering new markets at a breakneck pace. That is what worried bank regulators. They saw the disorder of the empire. They cited it again and again in bank examinations. They had cautioned Giannini about the lack of controls at branches, the slow incorporation of new branches into the system. When John U. Calkins of the San Francisco Fed panicked in the 1930s and tried to keep Bank of America from reopening, he was expressing the dark fears many regulators harbored about Bank of America. It was out of control, perilously out of control, but still growing larger every day.

Giannini kept order by having the right people in place in his branches. These were the bankers he had hired after buying their banks. They knew their communities. And they kept Bank of America from making loans to local deadbeats. Even if the control systems in San Francisco failed, these men provided a final line of protection. They knew how to make loans and how to collect them.

Clausen wanted the same rapid growth overseas, but he didn't have the same controls. Bank of America expanded overseas by pulling officers out of Fresno and Tule Lake and shipping them off to Frankfurt or Cairo. They didn't understand the markets, they didn't speak the language, and they were usually underpaid. The best of these officers, after being trained by Bank of America, found they could double their salaries by joining a competitor.

This was a change from the bank's early expansion overseas. Rudolph Peterson had relied on joint ventures for much of the bank's international growth. He had also acquired a team of Dutch bankers, referred to within Bank of America as "The

Dutch Mafia," seasoned international lenders who served as the final line of defense in international lending. When Clausen created the World Banking Division in the mid-1970s, he forced out the Dutch Mafia, replacing them with former colleagues from his National Division days.

This new team brought a different emphasis to international banking. These men wanted to make larger loans, and hired executives away from other banks—Citibank, Chase Manhattan—as well as large foreign institutions. These officers wrote manuals, created training programs, bought computers. But the growth continued so rapidly that the control systems always seemed at the point of exhaustion and the senior hands were always surrounded by a crew of undertrained, underpaid junior officers.

By 1977, as Clausen strove to keep quarterly profits climbing, the 10 percent a year growth limit fell to demands from the head office. Tom Clausen wanted to restore Bank of America to its rightful place as the nation's most profitable bank. He pushed lenders to increase loans rapidly, even though Bank of America was running at the limits of its ability to control its growth.

In a prescient analysis in 1977, Paul Albrecht, a professor of management at Pomona College, explained the potential weaknesses of Clausen's program of decentralization. He told a seminar of the bank's top executives that in order for a decentralized system to work, the bank needed to measure carefully the profits and performance of its branches and other offices. Otherwise the entire system might lurch out of control. However, the bank had no apparatus for measuring performance and Clausen never built one that worked.

Albrecht said the branches would get caught up in making deals and handling this week's problem. They would resist major structural changes, creating a rigid and inflexible organization. Unless tightly controlled from above, the size of these branches and offices would increase and costs would rise "in a rather startling manner." Different units would begin to perceive one another as "the enemy." "The internal competition may become more fierce and deadly than competition with other organizations," Albrecht warned.

The central point, though, was the one that Giannini had realized and mastered. According to Albrecht, "Organizations moving from the centralized or functional form [the old Bank of

America system] frequently underestimate the demands on persons. The talent pool must have enough quality to meet needs. Care, courage, even a certain harshness must be present in selecting and replacing managers." Bank of America was working to upgrade its people, but the changes were not coming fast enough. The expansion overseas produced new demands, required new skills. In the outposts of the empire, these skills were rare.

The problem grew worse thanks to another Clausen innovation, a process of budgeting that eventually became a painful charade for many managers. In the early 1970s, Clausen grew frustrated with the bank's financial systems. When a branch or subsidiary calculated its budget, it could juggle its numbers. Two branches might claim the profits from the same loan, because each had helped make it originally. But if the loan went bad, each unit denied ownership, saying the loan belonged in the other guy's budget. It was not unusual for the profits reported in division budgets to add up to 200 percent or more of the bank's actual profit.

This needed to stop. Clausen created a tighter budgeting process by which each unit developed its budget for the year, sent the budget to headquarters, negotiated changes in its targets, and then tried like hell to meet those goals.

Managers learned quickly that headquarters always wanted more growth than they could supply. Clausen used the budgeting process to force his line units to produce. He eliminated the double-counting of profits, but his cure had equally bad side-effects. One difficulty was that the budgets ignored loan quality. Because the bank had been so cautious in the past, it assumed that the quality of the loans being written was high. Even though two signatures were on every loan—a loan officer's and a credit administrator's—quality became the responsibility of the credit administrator, growth the responsibility of the loan officer. Credit administrators, overburdened by the bank's rapid growth, began to rely more heavily on reports from their loan officers. At the same time, the loan officers realized they were better off adding a pile of new loans of dubious quality than adding too few loans. The head office didn't differentiate between the good and bad loans in its budget reviews, and a loan officer's salary increases and promotions depended on only two variables: the size of his loan portfolio and the number of people working for his unit.

Rarely was any manager fired for missing his budget or for taking on too many bad loans. With the company's rapid growth and its family atmosphere, such penalties seemed too harsh, especially since everyone knew the budgets were always too aggressive.

By the late 1970s, Clausen had a serious, structural problem. Inexperienced lenders had been sent out to offices all over the globe. Credit administrators, once a tough roadblock in San Francisco, now worked in the field and proved more accommodative. Under unrelenting pressure from the head office, these inexperienced officers increased their loan totals by 10 to 20 percent a year, sacrificing quality in their desire to meet targets.

The loans didn't go bad immediately. They never do. Bankers usually discover their bad loans after a recession strikes. Thus, until the recession of 1982, Bank of America's weak loans remained largely hidden. (In the late seventies inflation drove prices and profits up, made dollars cheaper, and kept borrowers solvent.)

Few banks foresaw the extent of the risks they were taking in the seventies. Big banks everywhere were rushing into international lending. It was a heady time to be overseas. The Euromarket, an unregulated financial market outside the United States, was emerging as a new source of money for corporations and governments. Dollars once trapped in U.S. bank accounts were now circulating freely offshore, looking for investments. Bank of America was swept along in the enthusiasm, joining the huge syndicated loans to corporations and national governments. It rushed to lend in Iran, Poland, Mexico, and Brazil, throwing dollars at governments with shaky balance sheets and even shakier prospects for repaying those loans.

This was part of a global mania. The best lenders—Citibank, Morgan, Deutsche Bank, Bank of Tokyo—all succumbed, convincing themselves that governments in Latin America and eastern Europe were good risks, that inflation would last forever, that lending to governments was an attractive, profitable business.

The growth overseas made the World Banking Division the darling of the company. Bank of America was able to attract hundreds of talented young executives. "It was an exciting time to be at B of A," say executives who passed through the bank in the mid-1970s. Bank of America was on the move. An influx of young MBAs joined the bank, hopscotching through jobs, never staying in one place more than two years. "If you stayed in one job longer, you took it as a sign that it was time to look for work at another company," says a graduate of the Bank of America program. Responsibility came fast, enough responsibility to make up for low pay.

The division's top executives gave World Banking a special energy. Al Rice, a Stanford MBA with a charismatic style, had a flair for making big deals and a knack for resuscitating troubled companies. He displayed those skills while helping create success stories such as Hiller Aircraft and Memorex. He generated a spirit of enthusiasm in the people who worked with him. So did Joe Pinola, the son of a Pennsylvania mine-worker, who wore hand-tailored, three-piece suits and still came across as a working-class guy. Pinola headed the newly created North America Division under Clausen. Around them these men collected a young, dynamic team of executives.

The rise of the World Banking Division paralleled the slow decline of the California system. Though it was still the biggest profit producer at Bank of America, it was no longer an exciting place to work. People on the fast track wanted out, they wanted to move overseas. A sullen, mutinous spirit spread in the California branches. Its managers still considered the operation the heart and soul of A. P. Giannini's bank, but they were treated like second-class citizens.

What forestalled any serious revolt was the presence of a strong, independent leader in California, where Joe Carrera ran the retail bank like a personal fiefdom. A big, rough-hewn Italian, Carrera was sometimes affectionately called "The Godfather." He seemed to know everyone and to have, at one time or another, done them a favor. His enemies suspected him of plots to eliminate rivals and disrespectful junior executives, but the rest of the bank admired him. "He was a real corporate hero," said one former executive.

Carrera had spent his entire career at Bank of America. He had grown up in the orchards of the Santa Clara Valley, never graduating from high school. As a young man, he worked in the canneries and the packing houses in the valley, later telling fellow officers a story of how growers made money selling prunes, one of the valley's major crops. (He explained that after loading prunes onto carts, workers would take them to a weighing station. The trick was to put water on the prunes first. That added weight. The toughest part was making sure that there wasn't so much water on the prunes that the guy running the scales would notice.)

Joe Carrera was a practical man. He took a few courses at a business college and landed a job at the Bank of America in 1937 as a messenger at the main branch in San Jose. He never left the bank, spending the next twenty-seven years in the California branch system, before a six-year stint as chief administrative officer of the international bank.

Carrera was a trusted adviser to Clausen because he knew Bank of America's people. As an administrative officer for the California branch system and then as the chief administrator for the international branches, Carrera had followed the careers of the bank's executives closely. He made it his business to review each promotion, check every increase in salary. When he moved overseas, he handpicked branch managers and watched their progress just as carefully.

Carrera also had his own style. He had a reputation within the bank "for being crude before it was fashionable to be crude." He had a vocabulary of four-letter words for every occasion and used them to shock, and, on occasion, to lighten a tense atmosphere.

Carrera's job included revising the branch operating manuals first drafted by Mario Giannini, by this time swollen to several volumes. Carrera understood how important these policy books were, but he didn't relish making revisions. He would listen restlessly to the arguments over the arcane language required in job descriptions or consumer information circulars. When staff members turned to him for advice in the midst of these debates, Carrera would respond, "Fuck 'em all," invariably drawing a laugh, before he made his contribution.

As he rose at the bank, the rough edges of the manual laborer from San Jose rubbed smooth. He acquired a taste for the good things in life: theater, opera, fine wine. He dressed stylishly, tending to shirts with French cuffs and large gold rings, to which he would draw attention by cracking his knuckles as he talked.

Throughout Tom Clausen's tenure at BankAmerica, Joe Carrera served as a buffer for the retail bank. He deflected the pressure for change and coddled his staff as best he could. Executives on the corporate side blame Carrera for permitting the retail bank to run down, falling far behind in applying computer technology and moving too slowly in improving service and lowering costs. But what Carrera brought was stability and profitability, which is what Clausen demanded. As a result, Carrera stood almost alone among Clausen's top executives, an independent power within the corporation, free to run the retail bank without needed changes, even when they were long overdue.

One other key executive helped hold Bank of America together during the 1970s: Clarence Baumhefner, Bank of America's tall, slender, "icy-eyed" financial czar. Baumhefner was the numbers man at Bank of America. Hired out of high school to play basketball on the company team, he started as a messenger in a San Francisco branch, but rose quickly, becoming one of the youngest men on the managing committee, known to everyone as "Baum."

Baum's title was "head cashier," which translated roughly into chief financial officer. His job was to make sure that Bank of America's profits went up, quarter after quarter, year after year. Baumhefner's position made him the high priest of an occult order. No one in the organization except Baumhefner and a small group of lieutenants knew how to compile the financial statements of Bank of America. With a labyrinthine collection of tax and accounting items, Baumhefner controlled the profits of Bank of America, smoothing them, polishing them, adjusting them. He ran the bank conservatively, kept the financial ratios in proper alignment, and told virtually no one what he knew. "He carried around the financial position of the bank on a slip of paper that he kept in his pocket," says a former executive.

One night a year was Baumhefner's night at Bank of America. On December 31, he presided over a unique ritual, the year-end closing of the books. Under A. P., Bank of America had developed a tradition of being the first bank to report its profits each year. Baumhefner continued the tradition.

On the last night of the year, Bank of America employees all over the globe worked late. At the headquarters in San Francisco, Baum and his lieutenants ran an administrative three-ring circus, more like an election-night ballot count than anything else. Staff people manned telexes and telephones. After the close of business, the phones began to ring, the telex machines to clatter. From each branch in California, from every subsidiary anywhere in the world, the reports would begin to pour in: year-end loans and investments, year-end deposits, and the profits for each branch or subsidiary. The staff would begin to sift and collate, totaling the results.

As midnight approached, the bulk of the statements would already be collected. Now it was time to get on the phones and bully or cajole numbers from the late branches. Hours after the New Year had begun, with the numbers all in, Baum and his lieutenants would slip into a private room. A hush would fall over the staff who had been working so diligently. For a half hour, or perhaps more, the door would remain closed, the stillness unbroken. Then, finally, Baumhefner would emerge with the year-end figures. It was a dramatic moment. In the privacy of a closed room, Baum had usually worked some magic.

The mysterious arts of calculating loan loss reserves, adjusting for international accounting differences, declaring dividends from foreign subsidiaries, and the like were closely guarded secrets. A few executives, and some on Wall Street, called these dark corners of Bank of America "Baum's cookie jars." If the bank's profits at the end of the year didn't quite live up to expectations, Baumhefner would raid a cookie jar, grab some profits from an overseas subsidiary, or utilize some accounting nuance. Suddenly the profits would look fine. No other major commercial bank had a pattern of quarter-to-quarter changes in profit like Bank of America. Analysts didn't exactly know why Bank of America's profits rose and fell differently from most other banks, but they were sure Baum did.

One cookie jar the analysts found was the company's wholly owned overseas subsidiaries. Each of these subsidiaries had the authority to pay, or not to pay, a dividend. Baum made the decision. If Bank of America was having a good year, the subsidiary would pay no dividends, and Baum would leave the money overseas, stuffed in a safe place, waiting for a later day. If the bank was having a rough year, Baumhefner would declare a dividend, bringing the profits home. There was nothing illegal in all this, but it wasn't exactly kosher either. Baum hid many of his financial maneuvers by arguing that they weren't "material events," which meant they were too small to divulge to the public. He reported the bank's international profits as a single item on the income statement, vexing analysts who sought, and obtained, more detail from other banks. Ernst & Whinney, Baum's accountants, tended to go along with the practices, even when others in the industry looked askance. What kept critics at bay was the solidity of Bank of America's finances, which Baumhefner guarded with the ardor of a religious fanatic.

Within Bank of America Baumhefner was known for his secrecy. He told no one more than they needed to know, not even Clausen. One executive at a financial institution in San Francisco remembers Clausen quipping, a few years into his presidency, "I'm finally getting somewhere, Baumhefner's starting to talk to me." A few years later Clausen chortled to an executive assistant, "I figured it out. I finally figured it out. Now I know how we calculate our loan loss reserve."

Baumhefner's impatience and gruffness with subordinates were legendary. "He was Darth Vader in a blue suit," said one staff member who regularly prepared reports for Baumhefner. In later years, key lieutenants carried beepers. When the beep sounded, the aide would get up, say "Baum needs me," and rush to his side. Like Mario Giannini and Clausen, Baumhefner would grill subordinates, especially those who were not yet in his small circle of confidants. Though Clausen got the rap for skinning people with his criticisms, a former aide to Baumhefner said Clausen was a pushover. "I'd been worked over lots worse by Baumhefner." In at least one instance Baumhefner's attack was so menacing that a junior officer, trying to back out of Baumhefner's office to escape the torture of his questions, backed over an end table and fell flat, making a memorable exit.

Baumhefner and Carrera helped maintain the stability of Bank of America while it rushed to expand internationally and in corporate lending. Neither was an innovator, neither chose a bold new path for Bank of America. They were typical of the men that Tom Clausen surrounded himself with, typical of the men who ran A. P.'s bank in the seventies.

Chapter Nine

The reason that our bank has become one of the world's greatest
financial institutions and is still going ahead is because we have
never been satisfied with things as they are.

A. P. Giannini, 1923

In the early weeks of 1978, Tom Clausen took a rare moment
to brag. "You might say that conservatism has become a virtue,"
he told *Forbes* magazine. At the end of 1977, seven years into the
Clausen decade, BankAmerica had passed Citicorp in the race to
be number one in banking. "We have regained our rightful position as the world's most profitable bank," Clausen concluded.

The gap was modest in 1977. BankAmerica earned $395
million, just $14 million more than Citicorp. But it was enough.
Clausen had bested Citicorp. He had bested Walter Wriston, Citicorp's chief executive. BankAmerica's money machine was
pumping out profits. Between 1975 and 1979, the company's
earnings increased at a phenomenal rate—just under 19 percent
a year, or around twice the rate that Clausen had considered
"sustainable" back in 1974.

Not everyone shared Clausen's enthusiasm. Some executives worried that the bank was changing fundamentally, losing
its special character. Tom Clausen had focused everyone's attention on profits. In the process, the character of the institution
changed. As old-timers looked around for vestiges of the spirit of
A. P., they saw few.

Before the Clausen regime, the list of BankAmerica's inno-
vations was long and impressive: BankAmericard, the first large
bank computer, a host of consumer loan programs, innovative
real estate lending.

96

Under Clausen, however, innovation virtually stopped. He boasted about the budgeting process and decentralized decision making. Nothing that Clausen attempted during the 1970s came close to catching the public's imagination, or changing the industry.

BankAmerica's eclipse of Citicorp came more because of the New York bank's huge bet on the future than because of BankAmerica's strong performance. Citicorp was investing— recklessly it appeared—in a scheme to put two automated teller machines in each of its retail branches. The company had decided that ATMs were the wave of the future, the only way to provide good, twenty-four-hour-a-day service to consumers at a reasonable price. The investment was massive, hundreds of millions of dollars, and the common wisdom in the industry was that Citicorp was betting big on a system that would never pay off. In the late 1970s, the investment depressed Citicorp's profits while inflation was buoying BankAmerica's.

BankAmerica had decided against investing heavily in ATMs. As Citicorp was finding, ATMs were expensive. Bank of America's studies concluded they would never pay for themselves. Instead of jumping into ATMs, Clausen decided to wait. Bank of America would install machines after the prices dropped, after someone else made the initial mistakes. This was prudent, cautious banking, although not at all in the Giannini tradition. "Be first in everything," A. P. had admonished in 1923, and a few bank executives still tried to live by that slogan. A former senior officer in Europe once asked Carrera why the bank was being so cautious. Carrera told him that customers didn't like ATMs, the machines broke down regularly, and then repeated the concern about profit. The former executive thought it was crazy. "This was not our style. We were innovators, leaders, that was the Giannini tradition."

Some managers sensed a more ominous problem: the lack of innovation was a symptom of Clausen's short-sighted preoccupation with profits—monthly increases, quarterly increases, annual increases. It was also a symptom of his desire to run Bank of America with numbers, rather than the sense of the marketplace that had guided A. P.

By the mid-1970s some senior executives wondered aloud what this would mean for the long term. One critic was William Hurst, a banker who retired for health reasons in the mid-1970s.

At his retirement party, Hurst, who had been a senior strategist in the international banking division, blasted management for focusing blindly on short-term profits. The same message came from another source, one that management preferred to ignore. Claire ˙Giannini Hoffman, A. P.'s daughter, complained each time the bank altered one of her father's cherished programs. She railed when the bank canceled the school savings program, although she knew it was an expensive, time-consuming service. But Claire remembered why it was begun: to teach children thrift. The children were better off for it and so was Bank of America. The program personalized the bank, children brought in their parents, and they remained customers for life.

Clausen heeded the cries of shareholders for profits today. He delayed investing in computers. He scrimped on bank control systems, whether by delaying the purchase of sophisticated telecommunications equipment or spending too little on hiring and training qualified auditors and credit specialists. The reasons were always the same. Improvements cost too much and drove profits down.

Tom Clausen milked Bank of America's franchise. In his obsession with Citicorp, in his desire to restore Bank of America to its rightful place, he was taking more out of the bank than he was putting back in. He made shareholders happy, he delighted analysts, but he never laid the foundations for the future.

Evidence of the underinvestment was everywhere by the late 1970s, although disguised by the bank's soaring profits. The bank had fallen years behind other California institutions in modernizing its branch system. It had failed to reorganize the humdrum routines of check processing and lending to make them more efficient and cheaper. Management gathered critical information by hand, without aid of computers. National bank examiners, normally timid about criticizing Bank of America, admonished the bank to upgrade its archaic systems for collecting data. Bank of America, which had been the first bank to use computers, was now years behind other institutions.

Clausen didn't completely ignore the criticisms. After 1977 he expanded the bank's planning activities. He hired a young executive to modernize the bank's data processing system. Bank of America began to tackle its problems, cautiously and deliberately. But the new planning process took several years to install. The bank refused to pay the $100,000 or more needed to hire a top computer expert, turning instead to an executive from a bank subsidiary who was willing to work for close to half that amount. His computer systems helped solve the problem of processing checks, but didn't satisfy the company's other needs.

Managers got some help from a sophisticated analytical tool called "building blocks," designed by the Cashiers Division. It looked at each unit of the bank, from the smallest branch to the largest division, as a profit center—satisfying Tom Clausen's desire to know where the bank's profits came from. But even it had flaws. Building blocks allocated profits among individual units in the bank, a tough task. Many of the system's choices were arbitrary and confusing. The most notable glitch was a decision to assign the profits and losses associated with any bets on interest rates to the Cashiers Division. When short-term interest rates rose in the late 1970s, the bank lost heavily on fixed-rate loans, many of which earned no more than 8 percent interest, while deposits cost the bank 10 percent or more. This "mismatch" created horrendous losses for the Cashiers Division, but didn't affect numbers for the building block profits of the branches. Branch managers watched their profits and salaries rise steadily, which encouraged them to keep making fixed-rate loans as late as 1981, though losses on those mortgages were soaring.

Clausen also attacked the steady rise in expenses that came from decentralization. He excelled at understanding figures, the numbers spewed out by building blocks and the budgeting process. He studied them, used them to set targets, burrowed into them to gain control of BankAmerica, to maintain a grasp on the empire.

Just as Mario Giannini had pored over salary data, keeping tabs on raises down to the level of tellers and messengers, so did Clausen. He sat on a committee that reviewed the salary increase of every person in the bank earning $20,000 or above. "I remember that he spent an inordinate amount of time looking at proposed salary increases," says a former aide. "He thought long and hard about salary increases. It's one thing to think about how to reach out and motivate people, but he worried about whether a raise should be 7.4 percent rather than 7.5 percent. It struck all of us as incredible that Tom would take the time to dip that far down in the ranks. How could he really know the guy to begin with?"

As the seventies drew to a close and inflation soared, Clausen became ever more vigilant about salaries. In 1980, the last year of his presidency, Clausen vowed to keep the average wage increase to 9 percent—in a year when inflation was heading toward 15 percent. Though the salary review committee normally handed out raises ranging from well below 9 percent to well over, on occasion Clausen stormed into these sessions and announced, "No one we're going to review today will get a raise of more than 9 percent. No one. We've got to hold the line." The employees up for review that day ended up with 9 percent or less, no matter what they might have deserved, or what their boss had promised.

Despite Clausen's efforts, costs soared during his last years on the job, rising by more than 15 percent in some years.

By focusing on expenses in such detail, Tom Clausen thrust himself into the most minute decisions in every unit of the bank. The man who bragged about the decentralization of authority meddled constantly, and his interference at one inopportune moment would lead to an embarrassing public scandal.

Chapter Ten

From the day of its founding it has been an undeviating policy of
Bank of America that no employee should seek to feather his own
nest by taking advantage of his position. . . . Because we have stuck
firmly to our policies, we stand with clear conscience. . . . Our skirts
are clean.

A. P. Giannini, 1939

No other event brought Tom Clausen more notoriety than
"The Rice Affair." It began on Friday afternoon, August 18,
1978, shortly after 4:00 P.M., when BankAmerica issued a terse,
four-line statement to the press. Alvin C. Rice, vice-chairman of
the board, had resigned.

The statement said Rice had "informed the bank of his intention to pursue personal business opportunities, which pre-
clude his ability to continue as a principal officer and director of
the bank."

The statement fascinated the press and the local business
community. Al Rice ran the World Banking Division, which generated more than 50 percent of BankAmerica's profits. Rice was
the heir apparent, a Clausen protégé. He had followed Clausen
up the ranks toward the executive suite. Now, as he approached
the pinnacle of American corporate success, Rice had pulled out
of the race.

Why? The press release gave no answer, Bank of America
refused to comment, and Rice remained mum. At a hurriedly
called press conference shortly after the announcement, Rice
said he was going off to run a small company, a start-up that
would design automobiles to run on organic matter. It didn't
ring true.

Had Rice been pushed? With Clausen's peculiar personality, it seemed likely. Not only was he a rough boss, but others who had seemed too close to "The Corner Office" had left. Robert Truex, at one time a contender for the presidency, was forced into a corporate backwater, to head social policy. He left. Joe Pinola, Clausen's former aide in Los Angeles, got the message that he wasn't in the running to replace Clausen, that Rice was the front-runner. So he left. If Rice had not been pushed, then why did he end up in obscurity? He moved to a desk at Hambrecht & Quist, the San Francisco investment banking company, where he spent a few months working on big deals, but in a short while became president of a small, fast-growing Los Angeles bank, Imperial Bank.

The Office of the Comptroller of the Currency asked for an explanation of the firing. Unsatisfied by the bank's response, the agency launched its own investigation. A federal grand jury convened, interviewed key executives, and then announced that there was nothing illegal.

The press was furious with the lack of detail. In 1977, Clausen had received a torrent of favorable attention when the company adopted a policy on "full disclosure" of corporate activities. It had been a superb public relations gimmick. Aerospace giant Lockheed had just been slapped for paying bribes overseas. The Watergate scandal that led to Richard Nixon's resignation remained fresh in people's memories. Corporate and political ethics were on trial. Clausen, colorless as he was, ended up in *People* magazine. In an interview accompanied by a full-page photo, Clausen challenged the notion that "payoffs, bribes, influence peddling, book juggling, falsification of records and miscellaneous hanky-panky are somehow a normal part of doing business."

But he had also added that BankAmerica had never faced any serious scandals. Al Rice's departure—a minor event in comparison—was the bank's first misstep. Clausen chose to use his disclosure policy as a shield. He stonewalled. This was a personnel matter, at least that's how the bank's public relations staff put it. In the fine print of the disclosure policy, the bank had left itself a gaping loophole. Personnel problems would remain confidential.

It took six months for the press to unearth key details. In the spring of 1979, a column by Dan Dorfman in *Esquire* and articles in the *Los Angeles Times* described Rice's ouster. Early in 1978 the bank had begun an audit of Rice's finances. The reason for the investigation was unclear, but the team spent months ferreting through Rice's personal records. The examination was run by the audit staff, known without any affection in the bank as "The Secret Police" or "The Gestapo." They struck fear in the hearts of branch managers and executives. A little infraction, a $4 overcharge on an expense receipt, was just as serious as a $4 million blunder.

The audit department had sweeping police powers. It could review any document in the bank, down to checks written on an officer's personal account.

Al Rice got a complete audit. The team rummaged through his checkbook, reviewed his savings account balances. The investigation went back nearly a decade. It is still not clear what triggered the audit, but what they found was eye-opening— nothing illegal, but enough to challenge Rice's judgment.

Rice had approved loans to a real estate developer with whom he was investing outside the bank. He had also pocketed a refund from a private club even though the bank, not Rice, had paid the fee originally. That was the substance of the grievance.

Rice denied any wrongdoing. He said he listed the investments, as required by law, in annual disclosure statements. And he claimed he was planning to open a new membership at a different country club and had put the money in his checking account until the transfer was complete. Rice said Clausen never allowed him to see the audit report, so he didn't know exactly what the auditors had found. Then he told *Business Week* that his investments were no more questionable than others made by bank executives, including a few real estate investments by other senior bank officers with the same developer.

Rice acknowledged that he had long, profitable relationships with Joseph Duffel, a major borrower from the bank. In the early seventies, he had approved loans for Duffel, sometimes over the objections of his subordinates. Though this suggested favorable treatment, Rice denied it, pointing out that Duffel paid back the loans he approved, unlike later loans made by others.

In 1970, the same year that Duffel borrowed $8 million from Bank of America, Rice invested in a limited partnership organized by the real estate developer. Rice was one of several dozen investors who made a large profit. Rice invested $25,000 on which he made $150,000. It was a legitimate investment, a legitimate profit. A few years later, Duffel and Rice built condominiums together near Lake Tahoe. Rice says he bought the property and as a concession to Duffel agreed to develop it jointly, which meant they would end up as neighbors during the summer. They built four buildings. Rice kept one, Duffel another, and a third partner got one. They sold the fourth, splitting the profit.

Improper or not, the deals created the appearance of a conflict of interest. Clausen had high standards, standards laid down by A. P. Giannini. "He wanted the bank to be whiter than white," says a retired executive.

The issue of the country club membership looks more innocuous, but it was apparently given almost equal weight. Rice had joined the Claremont Country Club in Oakland. The bank bought a membership for him in 1969, then in 1976 Rice decided to switch clubs. He sold the membership and put the $4,350 fee in his own bank account. The amount was peanuts compared with Rice's salary, but it was a big amount to the audit department. Rice failed to buy a membership in the new club and did not return the cash to the bank. Other companies might have treated it as an oversight. Not BankAmerica.

Since the days of A. P., Bank of America had functioned on a basic premise: If you'll steal $1 from the bank, you'll steal $1 million. There was no code of strict morality at Bank of America. Bank folklore relates that senior executives used to lunch at a local bordello. When A. P. learned about the practice, he was furious, not because of the location, but because no one stayed behind at the bank to help customers. One former resident of North Beach remembers interrupting lunchtime poker games at a bank branch to deposit money from illegal gambling operations. And stories of sexual indiscretion abound. A former senior executive related an anecdote about a chairman of the board in the seventies who grew so disgusted by the amorous adventures of another executive, that he thundered, "If he has to fuck the secretaries, why doesn't he fuck the secretaries at Wells."

A. P.'s distaste was for bankers who pocketed fees for arranging loans or opened property insurance businesses as a sideline and used their relationships at the bank to increase their personal wealth. His outrage grew into a crusade. Expense accounts drew painstaking reviews. "They'd spend $120 to find a twenty-cent error," one former executive said. An expense account watcher in southern California in the 1950s regularly returned expense vouchers on which executives had misstated the mileage for driving from one town to another, say, Pasadena to Los Angeles. In the mid-1960s a junior officer who chose to take an early morning flight rather than charge the company for a hotel, put a $4 breakfast charge on his expense account. The expense control clerks found it and refused to pay it.

The penalty for larger violations was dismissal. One oft-repeated story relates that the entire audio-visual department was once fired when the auditors found the staff had been collecting receipt stubs from local restaurants and putting them in a fishbowl in the office. When an employee worked late and ate out, but forgot to get a stub, he could grab one from the bowl to submit with his expense account. According to another story the bank fired a trust executive for exchanging a first-class airplane ticket for a coach ticket and pocketing the difference. Clausen reportedly fired the man himself.

The bank treated Al Rice no differently than the audio-visual staff or the trust executive. He had flouted the rules, put personal gain ahead of bank procedures. The lesson was obvious: No one breaks the rules.

What remains in doubt is who decided to teach Al Rice that lesson. "It's clear that someone wanted to get Al Rice," says a former colleague. "And they got him."

The "someone" is not Tom Clausen, or at least not necessarily. Al Rice had a way of making enemies. He overrode decisions of lower-level executives, took credit for others' successes, blamed subordinates for failures. Within the World Banking Division he was widely liked and admired. Outside it, he was distrusted.

Rice was one of the first MBAs ever hired by BankAmerica. In the 1950s, fresh out of Stanford, Rice signed up for a new program along with eight other young MBAs. The other eight left the bank, most in a hurry. Even Rice quit once, spending six years at a real estate construction company. "The salaries at the bank were so bad you couldn't raise a family on them," he says.

Rice didn't fit in with the Bank of America family. Bank of America was still run by people who were a little rough around the edges. Rice was polished, suave. He would impress the men who ran large corporations. Polite and soft-spoken, Rice sprinkled his conversation with quaint expressions of outrage, such as "goodness me" and "good gracious" where others might throw in four-letter words. Even when he was being savagely critical, he delivered his lines with a lightness that suggested idle cocktail chatter.

A fellow loan officer who sat next to Rice for a few years remembered his inscrutable character. "He would laugh and smile when he was happy and he would laugh and smile in exactly the same manner when you knew he must be angry. It was impossible to tell what he was thinking."

Beneath the laughter was a demanding executive. Rice's first management post came in the branch system. After joining the bank, he rose quickly to loan supervisor, a powerful job in middle management. Although each branch manager reported directly to the president in theory, in practice the loan supervisors exerted strong control over the branches. The branch manager had responsibility for profits, but the loan supervisor made sure the branch's loans were high-quality.

Rice was young, confident. He applied higher standards than other loan supervisors. When branch managers objected, as they invariably did, that this customer or that one had been with the bank for years and deserved special consideration, Rice could prove inflexible. If the branch manager stuck by his customer, Rice bullied. He developed a reputation for harshness. When one branch manager under Rice's supervision committed suicide, some paranoid branch managers who worked for Rice fantasized that Rice must have been at fault.

When Rudolph Peterson established the corporate finance division, Al Rice was one of the promising young officers drawn into the unit. Rice had just rejoined the bank, and he was quickly recognized as a skillful deal maker, and as an even more skillful specialist in "work-outs," taking troubled loans and making them pay off. "We'd give him a company. We knew it was dead, there was no way we could ever collect. And Al would go to work. He would sweat over it, he would work on it, and pretty soon the loan would be paid off," a former colleague says.

As with others in corporate finance, Rice moved up rapidly. He transferred overseas, then came back to succeed Clausen as head of the National Division. In the early seventies he went back to London to patch up the bank's ailing European operations, then headed home to San Francisco to run the World Banking Division.

In London, Rice fought to keep the business under control,

arriving just after the explosive growth under Peterson. He found traders in the bank's securities area drowning in paperwork. "We literally opened traders' desk drawers and found them stuffed with orders that had never been reported to anyone," he said. "It was an absolute mess."

Rice, with the help of a young Dutchman named Paul Verburgt, put the systems in place for controlling the trading area. By then it was 1974, with its oil shocks, bank failures, and soaring inflation. Rice saw the disaster as an opportunity for BankAmerica. The shock wave from the failure of A. G. Herstatt, a respected Austrian bank, forced many of the largest players in the currency business into hiding. If Herstatt could fail, they asked, who was immune? Rice didn't spend time worrying, he charged into the open market. Within a year, the bank had become the single largest trader in key foreign currencies, a dominant, deep-pocketed newcomer in a sophisticated market. Verburgt proved skillful as a trader, using Bank of America's now dominant position to gather information and move prices, to the benefit of Bank of America.

Rice saw a similar opportunity in shipping. A glut in oil tankers, thanks to the high price of oil, had stung the shipping industry. Many banks had bailed out, leaving high-quality shipping companies with no one to lend them money. Bank of America stepped up. The bank won key accounts, adding new loans, though under Rice the expansion was carefully watched.

Rice also struggled with operating problems. He installed a computer system to handle much of the division's data processing needs. He brought in qualified senior staff from other banks and fought for increases in salaries to keep them on board. When he left London in 1977 to return to San Francisco, the business was under control, but growing so rapidly that it would soon be nearly out of control once more.

In his new post as head of the World Banking Division, Rice was in line to run BankAmerica. He began, for the first time, to think about leading the institution and to act like the heir apparent.

Rice was running a risk. Throughout his career, Tom Clausen had pushed aside people who threatened his authority. Clausen surrounded himself with men who were either much younger than him, or who were willing to serve as tank commanders rather than four-star generals. In Europe, six thousand miles away, Al Rice could get away with playing the supreme commander. In San Francisco, the only boss was Tom Clausen. Those who challenged him seemed to end up working elsewhere.

Rice was not always discreet about his ambitions. He thought the retail bank was run by marginally competent people and expressed disdain for Joe Carrera, The Godfather. Rice also criticized the management information systems.

Rice challenged powerful forces in the bank. More than anything else that he did, perhaps even more than his cozy relationships with any real estate developer, picking those fights undermined his position at BankAmerica.

While the top man in London, Al Rice confronted the audit department, "The Secret Police." Despite their fear of the auditors, most executives considered the department one of the backwaters of the bank. Giannini and his followers dismissed auditors as killjoys. When Bank of America matured, grew into a $50 billion company, then a $70 billion company, the control group, the auditors, should have gained increasing power. But they didn't. The bright young men, those with talent, wanted to be in the field making loans, not in San Francisco reviewing other people's work. The audit staff became a ragtag collection of officers who hadn't made the grade elsewhere, sprinkled with a few solid executives who enjoyed swooping in on a branch, scrutinizing financial reports, and striking fear into the hearts of managers.

Rice considered the audit teams incompetent. Though they might be adequate to analyze the books of a U.S. branch, in London they were out of their league. Rice had a point. The Eurocurrency markets are huge and complex, with transactions conducted in dozens of currencies. The systems needed to control those activities were foreign to an auditor who had spent his life working in retail California branches.

Rice tried to oust the auditors reviewing his division. He began an open, aggressive battle, pushing Clausen to get these people out of his hair. "It wasn't that I didn't want London to be audited," Rice says. "But they weren't up to the job."

The conflict continued when Rice returned to San Francisco. His contempt for the audit division showed and he hinted that if he were to succeed Clausen as president he would bring in a whole new team of specialists. As head of the World Banking

Division, Rice fought to reduce the role the audit staff played in World Banking. This time he challenged Ken Martin, the bank's controller, the head of the Secret Police. Martin understood his own powers and his ability to fight back. At one point in mid-battle, Martin turned to a vice-president and said, "You tell Rice there isn't a single piece of paper in this bank that we can't examine." By that time the audit of Al Rice had already begun in secret in the back rooms of Bank of America.

Rice also had begun to challenge Clausen. His clash with Martin implied a criticism of Clausen. But more important was Rice's determination to run his business with autonomy. The opening salvo, as Rice remembers it, came before he returned to San Francisco from London. As head of Europe, Middle East, and Africa (EMEA), Rice was one of those executives in the field who benefited from "decentralization" of decision-making power. Like many of those executives, he disliked Clausen's meddling. The decision he remembers most vividly involved a raise for the bank's senior officer in Germany. Rice knew the man well and wanted to reward him. Bank of America's operation in Germany had passed Citicorp's to become the largest foreign bank in the country. Rice authorized a raise, around $4,000, designed to achieve one goal: to make Bank of America's senior man in Germany the highest paid foreign banker in the country. The raise put him just a few dollars ahead of his rival at Citicorp. "This was really important to the guy. I knew we'd have him for life if I did this," Rice says. As head of the company's most profitable international operation, Rice thought he should have no trouble getting the raise approved, so he informed the banker in Germany that the increase was coming. Then he sent the paperwork back to headquarters for approval.

The request came back with Clausen's approval, the single letter "A" that he invariably scrawled to grant permission to go ahead, but the amount he approved, instead of $4,000, dropped to $3,500. Instead of being the highest paid foreign banker in Germany, Bank of America's man remained number two. Rice phoned San Francisco. He was furious. "How do you know, from six thousand miles away, what this guy is worth, when I'm right here, watching over him and I don't know whether the right figure is $5,000 or $3,000?" Al Rice was pushing Tom Clausen, who didn't like to be pushed.

The audit of Al Rice was made during the first half of 1978. In June, Rice says, Tom Clausen met with him privately and asked him to resign, explaining that the audit had uncovered improprieties. Clausen refused to let him see the audit report. At first Rice thought Clausen wasn't serious. He couldn't believe he would be ousted over such minor infractions. Clausen didn't immediately force the issue, giving Rice time to talk with directors, to argue his case. But the directors didn't want to challenge Clausen.

The situation stayed quiet for weeks, though it weighed heavily on Clausen. Peter Nelson, formerly an executive of Bank of America, remembers sitting with Clausen on a weekend in July at the Bohemian Grove. The two were dressed as soldiers for one of the plays put on by the Bohemian Club. Clausen seemed disturbed and when Nelson asked him what was wrong, he said, "I'm facing the toughest decision of my life." A few days later, the bank announced Al Rice's departure. The heir apparent was gone. The race for the presidency was wide open.

At fifty-five, Tom Clausen was too young to retire and was unlikely to just give up his $600,000-a-year job, but he had been courted by the Carter administration to come to Washington for various government posts. Within eighteen months he would accept one of those jobs, forcing the board to select a new chief executive from a very thin field of candidates.

Chapter Eleven

[This bank] will keep clean, keep clear and attend solely to the business of banking. There will be no speculative exploits with bank money.

A. P. Giannini, 1928

Within hours of the resignation of Al Rice, Leland Prussia began receiving calls of congratulation. Rice's departure appeared to clear the way for Prussia to become the next chief executive of BankAmerica. Of the senior executives in San Francisco, he was the only obvious contender.

Prussia, fifty, had succeeded Clarence Baumhefner as head cashier in 1974, building the unit into a brain trust for Clausen after shedding much of Baumhefner's secrecy. Prussia had a vulnerable, human quality. He rode the bus to work, voted as a Democrat, seemed comfortable at staff Christmas parties. Unlike Clausen, he encouraged debate with key aides. He surrounded himself with bright, challenging minds, some of whom called him "The Professor." If Lee Prussia had a flaw, they agreed, it was that he was probably too nice to become chief executive.

Though he had been an executive of BankAmerica for more than twenty years, no one ever described Lee Prussia as a businessman. He was an economist, a financial executive, the quintessential staff guy. Prussia had never made a loan, never managed a branch, never worked overseas. He had spent his entire career at world headquarters.

Outside San Francisco few thought Prussia had a chance. They were betting on Samuel Armacost, who succeeded Rice as head of Europe, Middle East, and Africa. The young assistant vice-president who had helped cement the Bougainville mine

111

transaction was now the head of the largest, most profitable off-shore division. Armacost had spent his career lending money to large corporations or managing those who did. In London, everyone knew that Sam was among the anointed.

Armacost was a textbook manager. Liked by almost everyone, he remained a friendly, but distant figure, never allowing others to get too close. He excelled at meeting and wooing customers. He did his homework, made cogent remarks about banking, and remained unflaggingly upbeat. His salesmanship enthralled people, but his dedication and standoffishness caused some to dub him "Clausen's clone."

Armacost had spent half his career overseas, much of it in London. He had approved billions of dollars in loans, but he had spent almost no time on the retail side. He had never worked on the fortieth floor in San Francisco. And he was young, only thirty-eight years old.

At first the competition between Prussia and Armacost remained low-key. Armacost was in London, Prussia in San Francisco. Only once did they disagree at a meeting of top executives. In late 1979, the Federal Reserve put pressure on banks to curb their lending. Prussia, as head cashier, championed the Fed's cause. Armacost, as head of EMEA, argued that his operation couldn't live with slow growth. The two clashed at a management meeting in San Francisco, where Armacost convinced Clausen that he needed more room to grow than other units.

The real race for the presidency began in earnest in November of 1979 when Clausen shuffled top executives. Although Clausen was only fifty-seven, he had promised to leave before the mandatory retirement age of sixty-five. "If I don't," he said, "an awful lot of these bright young fellows will get tired of waiting and go somewhere else." He knew that both Prussia and Armacost had weaknesses. So he moved Prussia to head the World Banking Division, giving him his first chance to oversee a lending operation. He brought Armacost to San Francisco to take Prussia's spot as head cashier, watching over the bank's finances. Armacost objected, preferring the top spot in the retail bank, which was held by Joe Carrera. But Clausen had a different plan. He needed to test and broaden both men, to give each more experience.

It proved an expensive experiment.

In the recent history of BankAmerica, 1980 stands out as a critical year. The economy turned hostile. Pressure built on

BankAmerica's profits for the first time in a decade and a half. Congress passed landmark legislation that removed the ceiling on the rates paid on small savings accounts, virtually ensuring a drop in BankAmerica's profits of $100–200 million a year—at a time when the bank was earning around $600 million a year. Worse yet, the two men vying for the presidency—Prussia and Armacost—made decisions that would cost the bank billions of dollars.

Financial markets turned brutal in 1980 thanks to Paul Volcker, a six-foot-seven, cigar-smoking career bureaucrat, who was Jimmy Carter's choice as chairman of the Federal Reserve Board of Governors. In October 1979, Volcker announced a dramatic change in Federal Reserve policy. He was going to rely on tight money to beat inflation. Six months later, with interest rates soaring and an election campaign under way, Volcker and Carter slapped credit restraints on the nation's banks. Using emergency economic powers, they limited the growth of bank loans to 9 percent for the year. They put curbs on consumer credit, and placed restrictions on how much banks could borrow. At the time, interest rates on many loans were running between 15 and 18 percent.

Within weeks, Congress passed the most sweeping revision of the nation's banking laws since the 1930s. The government had come under tremendous pressure from banks and savings and loans, for whom money market mutual funds were making life miserable. So Congress passed a bill designed to allow banks and S&Ls to compete with the funds. A six-year timetable was set for eliminating Regulation Q, the Federal Reserve guideline that set the maximum interest that banks could pay small savers. It was a major step in the process of deregulating banks, starting in motion forces similar to those that had rolled through the airline industry, generating fare wars that drove many companies out of business. The changes were set to begin on January 1, 1981, when banks and S&Ls anywhere in the United States could pay interest on checking accounts for the first time in almost fifty years.

Cheap consumer deposits, the main source of Bank-America's profits for seventy-six years, were on their way out. More than any other bank in the United States, Bank of America faced a crisis. Without Regulation Q, profits from Bank of America's network of branches in California would shrink if consumers demanded high interest rates on their savings.

Even before 1980 began, Bank of America was finding profits harder to come by. One of the industry's major problems was the steady rise in short-term interest rates, which seemed stuck above 10 percent. Savings accounts were pouring out of the bank and flooding into money funds, forcing it to pay high rates to lure money back into large deposits.

Adding to this was the crimp in earnings from long-term fixed-rate mortgages. Many of the mortgages that Bank of America had made in the past were at rates of 6 to 9 percent. Now they were losing money—the bank earning less on the mortgages than it paid out on high-interest deposits.

Bank of America faced conflicting loyalties. Demand for mortgages was strong. Speculation that home prices would continue to go up sent investors flocking into the real estate market despite the high interest rates. Buyers stood in line to acquire homes, but had trouble finding lenders willing to gamble that rates would not go even higher.

Bank of America felt a responsibility to the millions of consumers in California who hoped to buy homes. It knew that it was taking a risk if it made more mortgages, but decided to keep the loan window open. Throughout 1979, it not only made mortgages, it made them in record amounts. And throughout the year, interest rates rose.

Bank of America felt pinched, but less than its competitors. It still had more low-rate savings accounts than any other bank. In addition, it had discovered the magic of "front-end fees." Every time an individual borrowed, Bank of America charged a fee, equal to around 2 percent of the value of the loan. That gave the bank a big cushion against rising interest rates.

But when interest rates continued to rise during early 1980, Bank of America was left with a throbbing headache. The mortgages made in 1979 were still on the books, earning around 9 percent, but short-term interest rates now topped 14 percent.

Bankers call Bank of America's problem a "mismatch." Its expenses—what it paid out on deposits—changed every day. Its income—what it earned on loans—changed less often. Internal bank documents show the mismatch cost $150 million in 1979, a year in which the bank had profits of just over $600 million.

As head cashier, Sam Armacost chaired meetings of the money and loan policy committee. This was a panel of the most senior executives in the retail, corporate, and international banking units. It decided what loans the bank would make.

Shortly after Armacost became cashier, the money and loan policy committee set the bank's policy for mortgage lending in 1980. If interest rates rose fast enough, making more mortgages would be a disaster. If, instead, interest rates tumbled, any new mortgages would produce huge profits—a 12 percent mortgage might be matched with a large deposit costing the bank 6 percent instead of 12 percent. If rates stayed flat or rose slightly, new mortgages would turn a modest profit, thanks to the front-end fees.

Would rates continue to go up? In early 1980, short-term interest rates had already passed 15 percent. Many economists believed that the country simply could not bear higher interest rates—if rates rose higher the economy would tumble, after which rates would have to drop. Since the only way Bank of America would lose money on new loans was if interest rates rose by 4 percent or more, the chances of sustaining big losses looked minimal.

What if the bank slowed its lending? The mortgages made in 1979 and before were losing money in a big way. At least by making more loans the bank could hope to generate enough fee income to make 1980 a good year.

Lee Prussia, as head of the World Banking Division, was also a member of the money and loan policy committee. As he had before, Prussia advocated making more mortgages. He believed a recession was coming and that rates would tumble. Others within the committee, such as Lloyd Sugaski, the bank's top credit specialist, disagreed.

Sam Armacost did not vote. He remained silent during the debate, never attempting to sway the group. It was a tough question, the kind on which any decision might come back to haunt the bank in the future. Sam Armacost, head of the committee and candidate for the presidency of BankAmerica, abdicated his role as a leader. He let a consensus develop. When the committee decided to keep the spigot open, Armacost went along, but then observed, "I hope the bank can live with this decision."

The bank had lost on a massive bet in 1979. Its decision in 1980, despite all the sound reasons for making more mortgages, amounted to doubling the bet in hopes of winning everything back. But the bank would lose again. Interest rates soared in

1980. The mismatch cost the bank more than $500 million, according to the bank's own studies. In 1981 the losses continued, reaching $850 million. Lee Prussia and Sam Armacost, the two men destined to lead BankAmerica in the 1980s, had bet the bank and been wrong. It was the most damaging of a string of poor decisions in 1980 that would haunt the bank.

The first year of the 1980s is one Lee Prussia would like to forget. Throughout his career, he worked in the bank's ivory tower, beginning as a business economist, then buying and selling tax-exempt bonds. He finally rose to become head cashier, the bank's top financial officer. He was nurtured and protected by Clarence Baumhefner, BankAmerica's imperious money man. In this insulated world, where theory and debate were an essential part of making decisions, Prussia was at home.

As head of World Banking, he had jumped from a cloistered corner of the bank into perhaps the toughest job at Bank-America. World Banking consisted of four separate fiefdoms, all operating independently of the home office. In one of his attempts to decentralize decision making, Clausen sent teams of lenders, credit specialists, and the like all over the globe. The overseas offices—London, Tokyo, and Caracas—ran like independent kingdoms, when Clausen wasn't meddling with their decisions. The North America Division, based in Los Angeles, was only slightly less freewheeling. The men chosen to run these divisions had a strong, independent streak. They believed Clausen had given them the right to ignore the home office—everybody but the CEO, that is—as long as they kept the deals flowing.

Prussia faced a rough baptism. Many of the line officers in the field distrusted him, as for years he had been one of the cautious nay-sayers in the head office. In the cashiers department, Prussia had surrounded himself with a cadre of bright, trusted lieutenants who analyzed decisions, and on whom Prussia had depended. Now, as head of World Banking, Prussia left behind that team. He had a new staff and faced battles with the division heads, a tough challenge even in the best of circumstances. "I thought at the time that the change was made," says a former lender, "that Tom was giving Lee enough rope to hang himself."

Prussia's instincts were superb. Inflation was soaring and the economy appeared headed toward a recession. Prussia ordered studies on how best to survive the downturn. Back from

Amadeo Peter Giannini, 1904 (Courtesy BankAmerica Archives)

Great San Francisco Earthquake and Fire, 1906 (Courtesy the Bancroft Library)

Bank of Italy in ruins after San Francisco Earthquake.
(Courtesy BankAmerica Archives)

Little Italy after the earthquake and fire
(Courtesy the Bancroft Library)

A. P. Giannini at retirement in 1927 (Courtesy BankAmerica Archives)

A. P. and Mario Giannini (Courtesy BankAmerica Archives)

*A. P. Giannini in 1949
(Courtesy BankAmerica
Archives)*

*Claire Giannini Hoffman
(Courtesy BankAmerica Archives)*

Rudolph Peterson

Alden Winship Clausen, chief executive, BankAmerica Corp.
(1970–81, 1986–   )

Clarence H. Baumhefner, chief financial officer of BankAmerica Corp. under Clausen

Joseph Carrera, vice-chairman, head of the retail bank under Clausen

the credit staff came a list of loans to avoid. It included all the industries dependent on inflation and ranked the companies most vulnerable to an economic downturn: shipping, mining and other extractive industries, and agriculture.

Lee Prussia had a blueprint for reducing the damage a recession might inflict. With that list, he could have begun to extricate Bank of America from a dozen areas that proved troublesome over the next seven years. But he didn't.

As Prussia read this list, BankAmerica's profits were shrinking. In the first quarter of 1980, Tom Clausen handed out marching orders. He wanted every unit to increase revenues or lower costs. Lee Prussia's concerns about a recession appeared to evaporate. Though his instincts had been good—1982 brought the deepest recession since the 1930s—as head of the World Banking Division it was his job to generate the loans that would create the profits that would sustain Tom Clausen's unbroken record of rising earnings.

For 1980, World Banking Division's loans increased by 10 percent, in compliance with Federal Reserve guidelines, which provided the flexibility for some parts of a bank to grow more rapidly than others. The division's profits increased 20 percent.

As head of World Banking, Lee Prussia made two other critically important decisions, championing investments that may have cost the bank as much as $200 million.

The first of these was announced in early 1981, when the company disclosed it had acquired Banco Internacional SA, an Argentine bank. Lee Prussia had played a central role in its purchase.

Argentina, like many countries in Latin America, tightly controls the ownership of commercial banks by foreigners. Though foreign banks can have branches and representative offices, the number that own local banks is very small, and profits can be huge. BankAmerica had watched enviously as Citicorp reaped profits from local banks in Brazil and Mexico, and as others bought banks elsewhere in Latin America.

Some executives in the Latin American division were still smarting from an attempt to buy a bank in Puerto Rico. A Puerto Rican bank had nearly failed, was taken over by bank regulators, and then put up for sale. BankAmerica analyzed what the bank was worth, using all the standard techniques. The figures pointed to a price of $15–20 million. So the bank put in a bid, coming in second. The highest bidder, a Spanish bank, paid nearly twice what BankAmerica offered, leaving executives in San Francisco to wonder whether the Spanish bank had overpaid or they had been too timid.

In the fall of 1980, BankAmerica's Argentine staff, headed by Bill Wilson, a young vice-president, sent its analysis of Banco Internacional to the head office. As in Puerto Rico, this was a troubled bank with a respectable retail branch system. Wilson's group argued the bank was worth $25–30 million, but acknowledged BankAmerica might need to bid $40 million or slightly more to get it.

Wilson flew to Washington for a presentation before the executive council of the World Banking Division in October of 1980. He repeated his analysis, but as the group discussed the decision, it became clear that Lee Prussia and Bill Bolin, the head of the Latin American unit, wanted the Argentine bank enough to pay much more than $40 million.

In a later meeting in San Francisco three key people—Bolin, Prussia, and Dick Puz, a senior credit analyst—dominated the debate. Once again they reviewed the material from the Argentine staff. They discussed a $40 million bid, then quickly shifted to the premium needed to ensure a winning offer. As the staff from Argentina had made clear, this was a rare opportunity to buy a bank in Latin America.

Prussia, Bolin, and Puz had heard rumors that the bidding would be fierce. Several major U.S. and foreign banks had paid a large fee to obtain financial information on Banco Internacional.

They wrestled with these facts. As they did, the price began to creep up, then soar, until halfway through the session it reached more than $125 million. Somehow, in their enthusiasm to acquire what might be the last commercial bank available in Argentina, the key staff members in San Francisco had created their own bidding war. Not sure how to put a premium on the bank, they convinced each other that more was better than less.

Goaded by executives who remembered the failure in Puerto Rico, Prussia led the push to a higher price. A more skeptical boss, one not in the running to succeed Clausen, might have asked other questions: why do we need to be in retail banking in Argentina, a country with inflation running well over 600 percent a year? What happens if the peso is devalued? Others were asking the questions, but Prussia, Bolin, and their aides quickly identified the counterarguments: retail banking in Latin America could be extremely profitable and the failure of this bank provided a rare opportunity to enter a major market. Not everyone thought those responses were sound. "It was a crazy idea at any price. Bank of America had no business being in retail banking in Argentina. No business whatsoever," says one former international credit specialist.

By the time the bidding war reached the managing committee, Prussia and Bolin had raised their offer to more than $200 million, or about eight times what the Argentine staff figured the bank was worth. A few skeptics remained, among them Martin Elenbaas and John Mickel, the two most senior executives in the retail bank under Carrera. Although new to the managing committee, both expressed skepticism, but didn't push the point. Tom Clausen had already decided to buy the bank.

Though BankAmerica chose, finally, to tone down its bid to $150 million, it offered $100 million more than the next highest bidder. Within the next few weeks, Argentina announced a major devaluation of its currency, which, in effect, made the Argentine bank nearly worthless.

Prussia also helped acquire an office building in Hong Kong in 1980 with such disastrous timing that it may have cost the bank as much as $50 to $100 million. BankAmerica spent $124 million to acquire fifteen floors of a twenty-four-story office building in the financial district in Hong Kong. They bought in at the height of the real estate boom.

The impetus came from top executives in Hong Kong. Over the years, most of BankAmerica's major competitors had acquired space in the city, a sign of confidence in Hong Kong. The treaty between the British and the Chinese that allowed Hong Kong to remain a British protectorate was set to expire after 1990, and the Hong Kong Chinese who worked for BankAmerica wondered whether it might desert the colony.

BankAmerica also had plans to consolidate its Asian headquarters in Hong Kong, moving staff from Manila and Tokyo, where costs were high. It wanted to buy enough space to handle this consolidation.

Some executives opposed the bid. Since World War II, Hong Kong's real estate market had soared and plummeted in regular succession. Some BankAmerica executives realized that real estate prices were near an all-time high. So the bank hired an outside consultant to study the real estate market and its report encouraged the bank to buy.

The purchase closed in early 1981. Hong Kong's real estate market abruptly plunged, leaving BankAmerica executives red-faced. Making matters worse, the bank decided it was too expensive to consolidate staff in Hong Kong, and shortly thereafter dropped plans to expand rapidly in Asia, leaving the bank with a monument to the dubious quality of its decisions.

Sam Armacost's sins as head cashier proved no less grievous. Armacost moved from London, with its sprawling empire of independent sales and marketing executives, into the tightly knit unit of bright, specialized money men in the Cashiers Division in San Francisco. He brought a new style of management. Unlike Prussia, who wanted to review several drafts of each report, Armacost wanted only the final copy. He liked short, concise memos and preferred no debate. Staff members used to arguing with Prussia felt a chill descend when they disagreed with Armacost. He even removed the extra chairs from his office, so they had to stand, discouraging the intimacy that Prussia had encouraged.

Within the Bank of America hierarchy, the office of the head cashier was an unusual post. The money makers in the company, the people who could get things done, were the heads of corporate lending or retail banking, men who made loans and collected deposits. The cashiers department filled two important functions: it aided the people who really made money and it ensured the growth of the bank's profits. The head cashier's power came from his knowledge of the intricacies of accounting and finance. Clarence Baumhefner understood how to use and protect that power. He had turned accounting and auditing into a dark science, attended with the ceremony and wonder of a magician's art. Lee Prussia opened the books and allowed others to peer inside, dispelling some of the magic. But Prussia retained influence by hiring the best and brightest people he could find and training them to speak a language that few in the bank had mastered. They knew how the bank made money. They knew how to analyze balance sheets and income statements and how to detect which branches were hiding expenses or overstating profits. They knew how to use accounting and financial sleight-of-hand to create profits out of thin air.

Sam Armacost was not an initiate of this world. Some staff

members intimidated him, displaying more knowledge of the inner workings of the bank than anyone Armacost had worked with before.

Armacost didn't have the luxury of time to learn the secrets of the department. In late 1979, just as Armacost became head cashier, Fed chairman Paul Volcker's experiment with monetary policy threw the financial markets into chaos. Interest rates soared and then plunged and then soared again. It was possible to lose millions of dollars in a single morning. In early 1980, the Fed put credit controls in place that slowed loan growth and crimped profits, while the bank's interest rate mismatch inflicted ever more pain.

In the spring of 1980, head cashier Sam Armacost took control of a remarkable exercise. Earnings had slumped, in large part as a result of rising short-term interest rates. Tom Clausen's record of ten years of increasing profits was in jeopardy. So Armacost sent out the message that each division needed either to increase revenues by 5 percent or lower costs by that much.

BankAmerica's basic problems were daunting. With the gradual elimination of the cap on interest rates that banks paid small depositors, the bank needed to revamp the retail branch system or face lower profits as it paid higher interest rates to consumers. The cost of the overseas network, thanks to the decentralization of decision making, had swollen. It had a huge bureaucracy and was opening offices too rapidly, in far too many locations. The interest rate mismatch was huge and growing bigger. The bank's computer systems needed replacing—the bank expected to spend hundreds of millions of dollars to bring them up to date.

Yet Clausen and Armacost focused on how to make profits rise in 1980—not on how to fix the bigger problems that were causing the decline. The divisions sent back suggestions that ignored the larger concerns. Cut staff here, trim investments there, delay setting aside a few provisions for loan losses and profits would revive. Despite the bank's problems and the obvious challenges of the new environment, management assumed that it only needed to tinker with the system. Nowhere was there a sense of urgency or panic. This was, after all, BankAmerica.

Sam Armacost, and most of management, knew the world was changing. They simply did not realize how much Bank-America would suffer. The great forward march of A. P.'s bank had continued undisturbed since the 1930s. How could a bank with more than $100 billion in assets, which earned more than $600 million in 1979, be in serious trouble?

Tom Clausen had a choice between fixing tomorrow's problems or producing profits today. Sam Armacost was in a race for the presidency. His job was to find a way to make Bank-America's profits rise.

He did.

As hard and scientific as the profits of commercial banks look on paper, they are often spun from gossamer. Clarence Baumhefner used this knowledge to build BankAmerica's strength. Sam Armacost was learning this lesson, but he would use it to disguise the company's weaknesses.

By 1980, some of the pockets of profit that Baumhefner had stashed for the future were gone, either because of accounting changes or prior use. But there was still ample room to maneuver.

The largest cushion in a bank income statement is the "provision against possible loan losses." Each quarter management sets aside a little cash to cover bad loans. Accountants call it a provision. It is added to the reserve against loan losses, a pool of cash that sits on the balance sheet. The provision brings the money in, loan charge-offs take the money out.

In theory, managers review their loan portfolio each quarter, see how many loans are going bad, scratch their heads about what the economy might do, and make various projections and statistical forecasts that predict how much the bank will lose on its loans in the future. Then it sets aside enough to cover those expected loan losses.

In practice, the statistics give management a range of options. Management gets to pick the amount it likes best, as long as the reserve doesn't fall dangerously below industry standards. In 1980, the job of determining the loan loss provision each quarter fell to the head cashier, Sam Armacost. He increased the provision, but only slightly. Since the bank's loans grew more rapidly, the reserve against losses actually slipped from 0.88 percent of loans to 0.86 percent. This occurred even though the bank's actual losses increased and the number of problem loans still on its books rose.

This may look like an inconsequential change, but that 0.02 percentage point difference increased the bank's profits by

$12.5 million. By letting the reserve decline just that much, instead of holding it steady, Armacost contributed about 30 percent of the bank's $43 million increase in profits in 1980. Cautious bankers might have actually increased the reserve, but Tom Clausen and Sam Armacost put a stronger emphasis on short-term profits.

And that was only the beginning. In the fourth quarter, the bank took its most controversial step, adopting a new method for putting a value on the bank's investments in venture capital companies. BankAmerica had been buying small stakes, here and there, in private companies since the 1950s. During that period it had chosen to carry the value of the investments at their original cost even after the companies went public. In 1980, Armacost proposed a change in accounting, undoubtedly with Clausen's blessing. The company decided to report the value of all publicly traded stock in the venture capital portfolio at market value.

This was not a widely used practice, and it shocked a few bankers in New York. "I asked my accountant if I could do that," says a former chief executive of a major New York bank, "and he said that if I tried it he'd shoot me." The weakness in this accounting approach is that the publicly traded portion of the portfolio is the successful portion. The remaining assets, those that have not gone public, include all the companies that have dropped in value or may never go public. Putting a value on the public shares let BankAmerica count its gains before it wrote off its losses.

The change came in the final quarter, adding $45 million to 1980 earnings. Armacost's position on the decision is ambiguous. Although he was the architect of the venture capital accounting proposal, when the managing committee voted on the decision, Armacost voted against it. Other executives wondered later whether he saw controversy ahead and stepped aside to protect himself from criticism. Whatever the reason for Armacost's decision, his unit had provided the weapon for Tom Clausen to keep profits up.

With those two decisions, Armacost had added $59 million to profits—an amount greater than the company's increase in profits for the year.

And he wasn't done.

The Cashiers Division reversed a decision by the European group to set up a $5 million reserve against possible losses on an investment in a Nigerian bank. It was a judgment call. Cashiers decided that the reserve wasn't necessary, but three years later BankAmerica wrote off its entire investment.

Cashiers also bought back $200 million of outstanding debt. The bank had borrowed the money in the past, when long-term interest rates were under 7 percent. As rates soared in 1980, the market value of that debt had plummeted, allowing the bank to buy back the debt at far less than one hundred cents on the dollar. Bank of America bought it back in the fourth quarter, posting a gain of $23 million.

In just those four transactions, Armacost generated $85 million of profit—the difference between an up year and a down year for Tom Clausen. The annual report for 1980 hints at other actions, sales of ownership in overseas subsidiaries, sales of assets that the company had acquired through leases, such as aircraft and automobiles.

None of this was illegal, even immoral. But it helped to overstate the strength of BankAmerica. In a year when profits should have dropped, when the operations of BankAmerica were feeling the stress of a new, deregulated world, Sam Armacost helped soften the bad news.

He helped put a gloss on BankAmerica's profits. Sophisticated readers of annual reports, stock analysts and the like, could discern that Bank of America inflated its profits. The little fellow, the general reader of the annual report, the person that A. P. Giannini had courted for his bank, would never have figured it out. The troops in the field, busy making loans, got the same message that the little investor got: even in this difficult year, BankAmerica increased its profits.

Management had sent the wrong message. Its margin for error was shrinking because of deregulation. The easy profits from those cheap deposits were disappearing. Management should have let profits decline, sending a different signal, a signal of just how tough the coming decade would be.

The Armacost
Years
1981–1983

Chapter Twelve

You've got to give youthful men authority and responsibility if you're going to build up an organization.

A. P. Giannini, 1939

On October 31, 1980, Tom Clausen announced he would step down as president of BankAmerica. He had accepted the presidency of the World Bank, an international agency created to support the growth of the less-developed world. Clausen had previously passed up offers for other government posts, including chairman of the Federal Reserve. But after ten years as the boss at BankAmerica and with the election of Ronald Reagan imminent, Clausen chose to accept a new challenge.

At its November meeting the board of BankAmerica named Samuel H. Armacost president and chief executive. In April, when he was to take office, he would be forty-one—the youngest man to run the company since the bank's earliest days. And although few realized it, he was stepping into the most difficult job in American banking, taking the helm of the world's largest and most profitable commercial bank at one of the most difficult moments in its history. Lee Prussia was named chairman, a far less powerful job at BankAmerica and clearly a consolation prize.

Bank employees greeted Armacost's appointment with elation. Many of BankAmerica's senior executives had grown weary of Clausen and his focus on short-term profits. Armacost's role in 1980 had been obscured by Clausen's domineering presence. The troops knew Armacost only as a charismatic, personable executive, a sharp contrast to the autocratic, aloof Clausen. Says a former executive, "I thought, at the time, it was a brilliant choice."

How could anyone have argued otherwise? Here was the

all-American boy. Bright, articulate, tall, and good-looking, Armacost had the ability to become a star in an industry of otherwise drab, gray men.

Everything about him seemed perfect for the role, from his childhood to his marriage to his brief, meteoric career. He grew up in a stimulating, intellectually spirited world. His father headed the University of Redlands, a small, well-regarded liberal arts college in a suburb southeast of Los Angeles. The family moved to Redlands when Sam was six, and for the next twenty-five years lived in an elegant two-story stucco home on the campus, surrounded by campus athletic fields.

Redlands was a Baptist school, but under Sam's father, George, it shed the tight constraints of the church to offer a broad curriculum. George Armacost is a big man with a long, oval face and a prominent nose. He and his wife, Verda, attended an endless string of meetings, convocations, and parties, raising money for the local symphony, fulfilling responsibilities to the church, serving as presidents and board members in dozens of organizations. Verda spoke regularly on everything from the woman's role in the home to the breakdown of morality in society. "She was the much better speaker of the two," says a family friend.

The two had met while studying for doctorates in education at Columbia University in New York; George got his, Verda never finished her thesis. They both taught school in Virginia, then George became a professor and dean of men at William and Mary College. In 1945, Redlands asked him to become president.

When the family arrived in Redlands, the couple had four children, three boys and a girl, ranging in age from four to twelve. They drove to their home on campus after dark and the boys, including Sam, the youngest, "cased the joint," discovering the kidney-shaped fish pond on the lawn and an avocado tree that looked great for climbing.

George Armacost's career at Redlands was long and successful. When he retired in 1970 after twenty-five years he had the longest tenure of any university president in California. The only blot on his record was a distasteful feud with the dean of the campus experimental college. George had expelled one student because she kept a cat in her dormitory room, but then couldn't enforce the expulsion.

At home George Armacost pushed his children to succeed, while Verda admonished them not to dwell on past mistakes. The home served as an introduction to the world of culture, as prominent people, including poet Robert Frost, stopped in for dinner or cocktails on their way through campus.

George and Verda emphasized the positive. "Our parents were constantly dwelling on the things we did well. They didn't nail us too hard for our shortcomings," Peter Armacost told the *Los Angeles Times* in 1986.

On weekends the family would head to church for youth group meetings, stopping for lunch afterwards at the original McDonald's, in San Bernardino, which may help explain why Sam and his associates often stepped out for fast-food lunches during his presidency.

The Armacost home produced a remarkable family. Peter, the oldest, followed his father into education, serving as president of Eckerd College in St. Petersburg, Florida. He was both a Woodrow Wilson and Danforth Fellow.

Michael, the second son, distinguished himself in the State Department, serving as ambassador to the Philippines in 1983 during the turbulent period after the assassination of Benigno Aquino and then as undersecretary for political affairs in the Reagan administration. Michael was a Fulbright Fellow and, later, a White House Fellow during the Nixon years. He excelled at basketball and baseball and fantasized about playing professional baseball.

Mary, now Mary Hulst, became a leader in the Calvary Baptist church in Denver and, in 1985, an ordained minister. Both Peter and Michael graduated Phi Beta Kappa.

As a youth, Sam faced stiff competition from his bigger brothers. Though as bright as his siblings, they remembered him mostly as "a bit of a ham," mugging for the cameras, doing voice imitations, and making crazy sounds.

Popular and athletic, Sam swam on the high school team and played water polo, working in the summer as a lifeguard at the Redlands municipal pool. He was elected class president in his senior year.

But in college he didn't earn the same honors as his brothers. He attended Denison University in Granville, Ohio, but spent more time his freshman year chasing girls and attending fraternity parties than knuckling down to study. His father began

to wonder about pulling him out of school. Sam joined Beta The-
ta Pi, "a jock house," as one fraternity brother put it, and played
lacrosse. In his sophomore year he switched from pre-med to
economics and his grades improved, though not enough to make
him a Phi Beta Kappa member.

A year after graduating from Denison, Sam married his college sweetheart, Mary Jane Levan. They had met while he was a
sophomore and she a freshman. Over the course of his career,
Mary Jane would become his closest confidante and strongest
supporter. Other bank executives described her as "the last of
the corporate wives," devoted, supportive, and just as resilient
as her husband.

BankAmerica hired Armacost as a credit trainee immediately after graduation in 1961. He stayed only a year before enroll-
ing at the Graduate School of Business at Stanford University,
but returned to the bank in 1964 with his MBA, landing a job in
the National Division calling on large corporate customers.

Armacost stood out even as a trainee. Thorough and polished, he had an innate ability to sell, a smooth, impressive patter
and the skill to push a deal to a close.

Notice came with the loan for the Bougainville open-pit
copper mine. BankAmerica had assigned their new assistant
vice-president to the Kaiser companies. He arranged a loan to finance work they were doing on Hamersley iron mine with Rio
Tinto Zinc, the British mining company, then was asked to bid on
the loan to RTZ for Bougainville. Swept up in the excitement of
this new deal, Sam reveled in his sudden prominence. "Sam
didn't step out of the spotlight if it passed his way," a former executive who worked in London remembers.

What Armacost lacked in experience, he made up in brass.
The Bougainville credit was one of the most complex that Bank-
America had ever attempted. The international loan market was
in its infancy and this deal presented a host of difficult legal issues. But Sam didn't hesitate. In the fall of 1968, he promised executives at RTZ that they could sign the loan agreement by January. Then he went to BankAmerica's legal staff to get the
paperwork moving, meeting Thorne Corse, a young vice-
president. Armacost told Corse the deal had to be done by January, and Corse told Armacost he was crazy. "No way," he recalls
saying. "This will take months to complete." The transaction involved the legal systems of three countries; banks in Australia,

England, and the United States; and subsidiaries of RTZ in all three countries. The banks and the subsidiaries each had to approve the contract. Bristling with importance, Armacost said, "Well, this is what I've committed to do and this is what you are going to do."

The battle never escalated. When Rio Tinto Zinc's attorneys took a look at the legal problems, they yelled just as loudly as Corse. Instead of January, the deal closed in July. And even then the attorneys had to work round the clock to get the transaction completed.

Sam received enthusiastic reviews from executives at Kaiser, which helped his career immeasurably. The Kaiser group had a long, close association with BankAmerica. In the 1920s, Henry Kaiser had run a small construction company that did industrial projects in the western United States, but he quickly graduated to massive public works projects, including the Hoover Dam. When World War II started, Kaiser diversified into shipbuilding, steel and aluminum production, and automobile manufacturing. Bank of America financed Kaiser's growth.

In the late 1960s, one of Kaiser's executives sat on BankAmerica's board, but the Kaiser group was in decline. Many of the key business units faced foreign competition and the auto company had long since disappeared.

Although Sam impressed Kaiser executives by backing their projects, he may have suffered an early bout of overoptimism. His successor as account officer at Kaiser, Jim Kearney, a tough, street-smart lender who had started at Citicorp, found deep problems at Kaiser, including a string of appallingly bad investments by its managers. Kearney's report to the bank precipitated the long process of dismantling the Kaiser empire. Kearney took a year to spot Kaiser's problems and doubts Armacost missed anything obvious. But Peter Nelson, who supervised both men, saw Armacost's oversight as a symptom of weak credit skills. Nelson remembers rejecting one of Sam's loan proposals as amateurish. When Nelson told him to rework it, Sam got angry. But before the two could settle their score, Armacost left for London, spirited away by the international division.

On his first tour in London, Sam helped create a local multinational lending unit, which catered to the biggest companies in the world. Sam was on the fast track. He would never stay longer than two years in any one job. Not only Armacost, but a battalion of other bank officers job-hopped through BankAmerica at a breakneck pace, never pausing long enough in one place to learn the intricacies of a job, but rushing through position after position—producing more loans, bigger loans, bigger profits at each stop.

In 1971, the bank sent Armacost to Washington as its first participant in an executive exchange program with the federal government. Armacost spent a year in the Office of Monetary Affairs in the Department of State.

When he returned to the bank in 1972, Sam ended up in London again, this time running the London branch. By now Armacost had the assurance of one destined for bigger things. He dispatched his duties at the London office with aplomb, then was off to the United States for a new job and a new title.

He moved to Chicago and another choice assignment. The bank had just begun to open corporate lending offices outside California. Joe Pinola, head of the North America Division, handpicked the team for Chicago, choosing some of the bank's best and brightest. It was a great time to be a banker in Chicago. Robert Abboud, a feisty Lebanese American, led First National Bank of Chicago, the city's second largest bank. Abboud thought banks didn't earn enough to cover the risks they were taking on loans, so he launched a one-man campaign to tighten the market, demanding higher rates on risky business. Bank of America's lenders ignored Abboud's lead, kept prices down, and picked off attractive corporate accounts.

Sam Armacost, now a senior vice-president and the team leader in Chicago, proved distant but likable. He ran the office almost by the textbook, introducing a system of management by objectives, getting his officers to draft their own goals for the year. In this small office, staff meetings proved effective, professional. At one, Armacost announced a pop quiz. He tested his officers on their knowledge of the bank; after all, they were selling not just the bank's money, but its services around the world. Armacost asked detailed questions, such as how many offices the bank had, the names of subsidiaries in various countries, and the like. The questions weren't arbitrary. A client might need help overseas or ask for general information. A lending officer could duck the question or have the answer at his fingertips. Armacost wanted his officers prepared. After letting his officers sweat through the exam, Armacost tossed the answers in the wastebasket. "This one doesn't count," he said. "But we'll have another one in a month and that one will count." A month later, they knew more about the bank.

Within two years, Armacost moved back to San Francisco as head of the San Francisco Corporate Service Office, and, more important, as the liaison between president Tom Clausen and the international division.

He obviously impressed Clausen, for he was quickly promoted to executive vice-president and sent back to London as head of EMEA—Europe, Middle East, and Africa, the most profitable of the bank's three international divisions.

The Sam Armacost who arrived in London to head EMEA was thirty-seven years old. In thirteen years he had climbed through the ranks of a giant American corporation to one of the most influential posts in its international empire. Reporting directly to him were the heads of operations in more than eighty countries. London alone had the largest single branch in the BankAmerica system, with assets of more than $10 billion. It was heady stuff for a young executive. He had a large personal staff, rode to work in a chauffeured limousine, traveled on three continents reviewing his troops and calling on customers. He lunched with sheiks in the Middle East, dined with billionaire shipowners in Greece, and met some of the richest and most famous business executives in the world.

Armacost inherited a money-making but disorganized operation. In the early 1970s, under the leadership of Al Rice, the unit had prospered. The bank ranked as one of the largest dealers in the foreign currency markets. It traded actively in the Eurodollar and Eurobond markets, financing major corporations in Europe and the United States.

But no supply lines existed to support that activity. In the rush to expand, management systems lagged far behind. The unit had a decent team of managers and lenders, who had pushed BankAmerica into larger and larger transactions. But the computer system cobbled together by Rice was dangerously overburdened and outmoded. The basics of banking, the credit manuals, the histories of corporations and industries, the general lore of international lending, all of the control systems were missing or outmoded. Training of lenders was barely adequate.

Armacost needed to repair the European organization. So he took action. He hired a specialist to fix the computer system.

He brought in a new personnel chief from Ford Motor Co. of London to instill professionalism in hiring and promotion. He beefed up other staff positions, and used them to ride herd on the lenders and country managers. Armacost completed the sale of several branches in provincial France. He also sold the company's minority stake in the Bank of Credit and Commerce International, an Arab-owned bank that Clausen and Rice, now back in San Francisco as head of the World Banking Division, had decided to unload.

None of these were tough decisions; they were obvious and not particularly controversial. Other decisions, the more controversial ones, never got made.

Armacost had moved so far, so fast that criticism was inevitable. But the weaknesses that worried critics in London would prove Armacost's undoing as president.

Close aides in London saw firsthand his reluctance to make tough decisions about people. Trying to fire someone, Armacost agonized for months before acting. And weak performers, people in over their heads, drew only a mild rebuke.

Though Armacost talked about strategic issues, he passed up his one small opportunity to alter EMEA's strategy. The senior executive in Africa wanted to expand, but others within the bank urged Armacost to pull out of the continent entirely. BankAmerica owned part of a consortium bank in Africa with major French and Dutch banks. Some of the offices of the bank were in former colonies, and the reasons for owning them were more political than economic. Those offices were losing money, making African profits anemic. A decision needed to be made. Should the bank get out of Africa altogether? Should it sell the part ownership in the consortium bank? Should it embark on an independent course in Africa? Armacost didn't find the answer. He left it to his successor, Mont McMillen, who sold BankAmerica's interest in the consortium bank and began to pull the company out of Africa.

Sam revealed other blind spots. He had no gift for reading financial markets. In preparing for one speech, Sam decided that interest rates were likely to rise. He attempted to convince Paul Verburgt, the head of the trading desk, to borrow $500 million for sixty to ninety days, a long time in the London money market. If Armacost had guessed right, he would have made millions for

BankAmerica. But Verburgt, who had spent years in the markets, balked. Rates might rise, but they could just as easily fall. When Armacost pushed him, Verburgt said he would certainly borrow the money if Armacost ordered him to. At that Armacost's enthusiasm wilted, and he let the matter drop. But Verburgt kept a running tally of "The Armacost Position," regaling his troops with the details of just how much the bank would have lost if he had listened to Sam.

The critics even faulted Sam's personal habits. Visitors to London marveled at Armacost's ability as a communicator. He sounded like a walking textbook and appeared accessible and open, working in shirtsleeves and charming visitors. But his aides never knew where Armacost stood. "He was like a sponge with detail," says a former officer who served under Armacost in London. "You would go in and sit with him for an hour and you would come out feeling drained. He would drill you with questions, always digging for more detail, but he never really told you anything about what he thought."

Armacost called regular monthly staff meetings in London, requiring his senior officers to fly in for a few days. The meetings tended to have no set agenda. "It was Sam talking about whatever he found interesting. They were very unproductive," says a frequent participant. What had worked effectively in Chicago, didn't seem to work in Europe, a bigger, more demanding post.

Some rank and file lenders felt ignored. Jim Nelson, head of a unit that specialized in construction lending, spent two years working for Armacost in London. Though he occupied an office on the floor below him, Nelson saw him only once or twice. "I never saw him come and I never saw him leave," he says. "We called him 'Sam Who?' "

Armacost socialized with a few bank officers, playing tennis on the weekend or meeting them for dinner. But one of his tennis partners didn't learn until years later that Armacost was a superb golfer, a seven-handicap. Says another London officer, "I think he decided early on that if you are going to be the president of Bank of America you can't afford to have friends."

Despite the criticism, most who met Armacost in London came away impressed. He sounded brilliant, seeming to understand the weaknesses of BankAmerica. Later they remembered that the shortcomings he saw in BankAmerica were those that slowed or inhibited the company's expansion. In a church that worshipped at the altar of growth, Armacost was an acolyte of rapt devotion.

Sam Armacost's commitment to growth and his weaknesses as a judge of credit created a potentially destructive flaw in the man. The best commercial lenders and executives sense changes in markets; their intuition keeps them out of bad loans. A. P. Giannini had that intuition, Sam Armacost did not. Only the advice of a savvy London credit officer, George Selby, saved Armacost from jumping into the London real estate market at the wrong moment. Armacost wanted desperately to approve a loan to Iran Air in 1979, after the fall of the shah Mohammad Reza Pahlavi, even though Iran's parliament had never agreed to the credit. He approved loans to Poland and other eastern European countries and tried to intervene when BankAmerica refused to lend money to Itel Corp., a fast-growing leasing company in San Francisco that shortly ran into serious financial problems.

In his extraordinary rise to the top of BankAmerica, Sam Armacost led a charmed life. He had never suffered through a major economic downturn, never managed in adversity. The bank had pushed him to the top too fast, never allowing him to stay in one job through an entire economic cycle. In that way his management skills and his credit judgment remained untested.

Chapter Thirteen

Banking is not a secretive enterprise. . . . The public has a right to know everything about it and the more the public knows the more support the banks will get.

A. P. Giannini, 1928

Although Sam Armacost had been tapped to become president of BankAmerica in November 1980, he had not yet taken office on the morning of February 16, 1981, when Tom Clausen brought his top executives together in a conference room on the fortieth floor for a hardheaded session on the 1981 budget. Although a lame-duck president, Clausen remained in charge.

"There's some good news and some bad news," Clausen began. "I'll start with the bad news. We have to cut $200 million from expenses." He never made it to the good news.

Since the beginning of the year, profits had been falling short of expectations. Six months earlier, management had predicted that 1981 would be a record year, with a profit of $645 million. By the end of January, that forecast looked ridiculously high. The company had lowered the official estimate to $435 million, nearly 30 percent below 1980.

To make the 1980 profits robust, Sam Armacost had raided the cookie jars in the cashiers department. The jars weren't empty, but the store of major items had been depleted. Cashiers would not be able to contribute as much in 1981.

In the weeks preceding this meeting, Clausen had asked his managers for lists of ways to improve profits for the year. The suggestions had flooded back. Now Tom Clausen wanted action. In the next few hours, Clausen would demand commitments to cut costs or raise revenues enough to make 1981 more respectable.

He would get promises, but not action. Tom Clausen's executives had never suffered through such a severe downturn—nor had Clausen, and they would do little to make the year better.

"This is a disaster, totally unsatisfactory," he said, referring to the poor profits in January. "Our job is to shape 1981."

Clausen's aides explained how bad the drop in profits was, and how bad it might be for the year as a whole. Clearly management had no control over interest rates. Rates had soared to more than 20 percent in 1980 and were still high. This was cutting hell out of earnings because of the bank's interest rate mismatch—the bet it had made on interest rates by financing thirty-year fixed-rate mortgages with short-term deposits.

In 1980, the mismatch had reduced net income by more than $500 million; this year could be much worse thanks to the "Wellenkamp decision." BankAmerica had lost a case on appeal to the Wellenkamp family in California's highest court. A bank could no longer demand repayment of a mortgage when a person sold a home. That meant a low-rate mortgage would probably never be completely repaid until it was due, but passed from owner to owner of a home. Before Wellenkamp, homeowners moved and repaid their mortgages often enough that the average mortgage lasted only five years. After Wellenkamp, who could guess the average life?

Overhead was running out of control. Costs were up 16 percent in 1980, thanks to Clausen's decision to build big staffs outside San Francisco. High interest rates and inflation made the economic outlook dicey. And deregulation of the interest rates banks could pay on savings accounts would put even more pressure on earnings.

"Does anyone disagree with the idea we have to do something?" Clausen asked.

"No," came the response.

"I'll take the blame. In the last couple of years we've become lax. The economy has made it more difficult to plan. We permitted empire builders and prima donnas. The record of the seventies has lulled us to sleep. We always do better than our plan. Maybe, because of our record, there's been a bit of reluctance to surface the problems this year. But it's here, we have to deal with it. Maybe we can start by agreeing on obvious, simple things."

Over the next hour, the senior management of Bank-

America discussed possible budget cuts. BankAmerica's expenses in 1980 totaled $2.3 billion, with easily enough fat to slice $200 million from the total. Some decisions looked easy. Slash the advertising budget by $10 million; reduce contributions by $9 million to the BankAmerica Foundation, a charitable organization financed by the bank; bring home expatriate employees; sell some buildings; put a curb on travel; eliminate a few employee newsletters; cut out merit increases for lower-level executives; and eliminate overtime for clerical and other staff.

Other suggestions drew an emotional response: they would signal a permanent change in the bank's stature rather than a response to a short-term earnings problem. This included items such as cutting club dues, selling excess furniture, and stopping all purchases of art. More basic were decisions that would be irreversible, such as cutting research and development spending for new products, changing the structure of joint ventures, and selectively freezing hiring. But the most painful, to many, were the proposals to raise revenue, for they invariably meant a further drift from the principles of A. P. Giannini. Eliminating all waivers of service charges for corporate customers (a multimillion dollar change) worried some lenders, but raising other fees—for bounced checks or small savings and checking accounts—meant ushering more "little fellows" out the door.

Some of the proposals were nickel-and-dime stuff, others meant big dollars, but Clausen wanted to hear everything. As the executives tossed out suggestions, it was easy to imagine the cuts had already been made, but in fact, the exercise turned out to be largely futile. Expenses would rise 15 percent in 1981 and profits for the year would be just about as forecast, a sharp drop. But the meeting sounded impressive, with Clausen hammering away forcefully at his managers.

At one point, Marty Elenbaas, the head of the branch system in California, raised a traditional objection to cutting budgets. Every change inflicted pain, either on employees or customers. The costs had to be weighed. It would take a while to review the proposed changes, he told Clausen; there were social issues at stake.

"How long will it take?" Clausen asked.

"We can have it within a month," Elenbaas answered.

"Before the ninth?" (less than two weeks away).

"We'll try."

"You can."

"Probably."

"You will."

Minutes later, after extracting that commitment and others from Elenbaas, Clausen moved on. "Okay," he said, with a note of sarcasm, "we thank you for that 'voluntary' action."

Lee Prussia, head of the World Banking Division, offered to sell property, including a building on the Place Vendôme in Paris and the residence of the Tokyo manager, which had been acquired for $50,000 and now appeared to be worth around $4 million. Clausen decided to sell the Paris building, but kept the Tokyo residence, which was not sold until mid-1986, when it fetched more than $58 million.

Clausen moved through each major division with his expected thoroughness. He prodded and poked. He goaded managers to make deeper cuts by referring to "the Stockman approach," the process used by David Stockman, the Reagan administration's new director of the Office of Management and Budget. He had tried to develop U.S. budgets from scratch, as though funding to all programs had been eliminated, a process called zero-based budgeting.

At one point, after the discussion of cost-cutting stalled, Clausen leveled a humorous threat, "We're not going to have a down year. If we are, I'm leaving."

Clausen obviously enjoyed the task. At another point, as the head of the electronic banking system, John Mickel, prepared to defend his budget, Clausen almost salivated. "Let's go to Mickel," he said, "I've kinda been waiting for this one."

The message throughout was simple and straightforward. Although a few items might be sacred, the bank couldn't afford runaway budgets, a social conscience, or investments for the long term. Only essential items, installing automated tellers, upgrading the back office, hiring good people, and soliciting new business, would get support. Whether anyone believed the message or not, spending scarcely slowed in 1981. New investments were delayed, buildings were sold, but costs rose just as they had in every year of the Clausen reign. With the cashiers department's ability to create profits depleted by the strain of making 1980 a good year, profits in 1981 shrank just as predicted before the cost-cutting exercise began.

But the meeting was vintage Clausen and allowed him to tersely summarize the message he had been sending for much of his ten years. After one executive defended an investment as being for the company's long-term good, Clausen snapped back, "You're talking about tomorrow, I'm talking about this afternoon."

In the second week of April, BankAmerica reported that its profit for the first quarter of 1981 had dropped 19 percent from the same quarter a year before. For the first time in fourteen years, BankAmerica's profits had declined. Perhaps on Wall Street a few securities analysts sensed major problems, but very few. Within the bank, however, at least among those who understood the bank's finances, concern grew rapidly. Clausen had exhausted the hoard of reserves and special accounting items stored up during the early part of the 1970s. The bank could not hide problems as it had in the past.

In private, Tom Clausen sounded alarmed. In public, he wore a tight-lipped smile. In his letter to shareholders in the company's annual report—dated March 2, 1981, but released shortly after the first-quarter profits were announced—he allowed no hint of the difficult first quarter to disturb his positive tone. "We extended to 18 years our record of full year earnings gains, a rare achievement for a corporation with the size and scope of BankAmerica . . . we take heart in the fact that the 1980 advance concludes a 10-year period in which our . . . per share earnings have increased at annual growth rates of . . . 14.8 percent."

Clausen mentioned the U.S. government's credit restraint program, which had made it harder to increase loans in 1980. He pointed out that the interest rate mismatch had cost the company a bundle. He fretted about the increasing competition from financial institutions unfettered by the regulations that governed commercial banks. But all in largely boilerplate language.

Clausen apparently saw no reason to share with stockholders the sentiments he had expressed to his senior executives. His sense that the company faced "a disaster" never surfaced.

The upbeat tone continued at the annual meeting, where Clausen added an ironically prophetic note to his departure. After discussing his successes in the decade of the 1970s, Clausen acknowledged the importance of what had been done by his predecessors, the Gianninis, Carl F. Wente, S. Clark Beise, Rudolph

A. Peterson: "If I have been fortunate enough to guide this institution to further achievements and stature, it is because of the groundwork laid and the momentum built by these men and their associates."

What had Sam Armacost inherited? What groundwork had Tom Clausen laid, and what momentum had he established? How seriously had Armacost, the heir apparent, hurt his own presidency by going along with the boss in 1980?

"I made some mistakes as president," Armacost says now. "If I had it to do over again, I would walk in on the first day and declare a major crisis."

That is not what Sam Armacost did on his first day in the $400,000-a-year job, April 22, 1981. That would have required tremendous courage. "It would have been like spitting in Tom Clausen's face," says a former member of Armacost's managing committee.

Young and untested, Armacost felt insecure. He confided to close associates that he didn't have enough support from the board to take the tough steps needed. He admitted to reporters that being chief executive had come earlier than he expected. "In my private moments, sure, it's a little awesome and it has got to be a scary prospect, but it's a thrilling one. I'm not going to shrink from it."

Like the rest of management, Armacost knew the problems ran deep. "We knew we were passing him a hot baton," says Walter Hoadley, BankAmerica's chief economist under Clausen. "We just didn't know how hot it was."

A special team from Boston Consulting Group had described the problems in depressing detail at a managing committee session the previous October. For nearly a year prior to that session, BCG, one of the nation's best-known management consulting firms, had been working with the corporate planning staff, reviewing its strategy.

BCG's analysis amounted to a condemnation of Tom Clausen's last five years in office. The report concluded that the California banking business was the company's most profitable operation by far—lending to small businesses in California was nearly three times as profitable as lending done anywhere else in the bank. Yet Clausen milked the California division for profits, rather than expanding it. BankAmerica had invested hugely, but not particularly wisely, outside the United States. While Citicorp, BankAmerica's main competitor, appeared to be investing where profits were highest, Bank of America invested without clear targets. Wherever a glib executive operated, he seemed to get money to expand.

Deregulation might slice up to $200 million off annual profits. The interest rate mismatch would pare away $500 million or more. In order to stay competitive, the bank needed to invest heavily in computer systems. And the bill would run to hundreds of millions of dollars. Just installing a network of automated teller machines, which every other major bank already had in place, would require $100 million or more.

Boston Consulting Group could measure that damage. But others dismissed BCG's analysis as a list of symptoms. The cause, they argued, was a decade of mismanagement. Says one executive who has worked with both Clausen and Armacost, "For ten years the bank was not at the cutting edge. The institution just drifted." Clausen did not build strong managers. The team he left in place for Armacost "wasn't fit to shine the shoes of its counterparts at Citicorp," said another disaffected former executive. Said the former chief executive of a major commercial bank, a contemporary of Clausen's, "The bank paid low salaries and it retained mediocre people. You can't do that and win."

No one disagrees that management was thin. While at a well-run major commercial bank, a Citicorp or a Morgan Guaranty, three or four young executives might vie for any top job, Bank of America felt lucky to have one well-qualified candidate. Part of the problem was salary, part was a twisted interpretation of the Giannini tradition. The policy of lifetime employment adopted during the Great Depression lingered at BankAmerica. People were not fired, salaries were kept as low as possible. When a fast-rising young executive quit to join another institution at a higher salary, the bank let him go. "We did not want to become an elitist institution," says a former personnel executive.

The officers running the retail branch system represented a special challenge. As deposit takers, they had done a superb job in the 1960s and 1970s. But they had been trained in a world that was about to disappear. Instead of taking orders, as they had since the 1950s, they had to learn to sell. Instead of offering a simple list of products, they had to offer a mind-boggling array of options, which might change daily. No one could be sure that the branch staff was up to the task. Whether anyone could successfully change the culture—turn order-takers into salespeople—was debatable.

Profits on international and corporate activities were abysmal. The loss of key executives—top lenders and talented credit officers—had hurt. Surveys of corporate treasurers suggested that Bank of America's lenders compared poorly with their counterparts at Citicorp, Chase, and Morgan. They didn't have the skills, the knowledge, or the insights of their competitors.

Faced with these overwhelming problems, what could a new chief executive do?

Armacost rejected any bold steps. Two young officers from the cashiers department advised a draconian change, but not because they felt the company lurching out of control. They wanted Armacost to report sharply lower profits in his first year in order to make later years look better. Studies done by Cashiers justified beefing up the loan loss reserves, laying off up to 15,000 employees, and closing hundreds of branches. "We did comparison studies with other major banks. Every study we did showed that Bank of America had one-third more people than competing banks," the former executive said.

Their suggestion drew a puzzling response. "That would be dishonest," Armacost said. The man who had emptied the larder for Clausen refused to restock the shelves. One fear may have paralyzed Armacost: how would the public react to such an announcement? Could a bank slash earnings and still maintain public confidence? As chief executive of the world's largest bank, Sam Armacost had to worry about the effect of his actions on the world financial markets. The responsibility made the young executive timid.

Even before Sam Armacost took the presidency, he made decisions that sent disturbing messages. Between Armacost's selection as president by the board and Clausen's actual departure, Armacost and Clausen filled key spots in management. George Skoglund, Clausen's head of personnel, retired and was replaced by Verone Gibb, a solid corporate lender with no background in personnel. Robert Frick, another corporate lender, became chief financial officer, though he, like Sam, had no experience in finance. Martin Elenbaas and John Mickel, Carrera's henchmen in the retail bank, joined the managing committee, replacing Carrera, who retired. None of these men was a strong manager.

None was likely to instill new, thoughtful leadership at the company.

But no decision caused more consternation than the appointment of the new head of the World Banking Division. In early February 1981, three months after Armacost was named president, Clausen announced that Bill Bolin, the fifty-eight-year-old head of the Latin American division, would succeed Lee Prussia as head of the World Banking Division. Throughout the company, jaws dropped. Bolin had led the Latin American division for fifteen years. The hard-chargers in the banking division dismissed him as a thoughtful person, better suited for teaching school than being an executive. Clausen thought differently.

Bolin first gained notice at BankAmerica making loans to farmers in Guatemala in the mid-1950s. That led to a transfer to the Middle East before his return to run the Latin American division. Under his guidance, the Latin American division produced mediocre results. While at other big banks profits poured in from Latin America before the debt crisis, BankAmerica's division there lagged far behind Europe and Asia in profitability. Bolin's strategy was to build banks to serve both consumers and businesses in major Latin American countries, an expensive and controversial exercise that never panned out. He told one executive that he lent money to governments in Latin America, at very narrow spreads, in order to get the opportunity to make more lucrative loans to businesses there.

The crowning event in his tenure, though, was the company's embarrassing purchase of Banco Internacional in Argentina, at a price $100 million above the next highest bidder. Although Lee Prussia pushed the purchase, those who knew Prussia decided the real culprit was Bolin, who desperately wanted a banking charter in Argentina. When Clausen—apparently in consultation with Armacost—promoted Bolin instead of firing him, the criticism began. The idea that the bank ran as a "meritocracy" lost credibility.

Word quickly spread that Armacost didn't actually agree with the choice. Sure it upset him, but he didn't want to rock the boat. As a newcomer he was unsure of his support from the board of directors. This wasn't the time to push them. Some remember Armacost describing the Bolin appointment as part of Clausen's theory of "weak generals, strong lieutenants." If you chose a strong executive to head the World Banking Division, his competitors might leave the company. But if you chose a weaker officer, one who might take early retirement in a few years, the stronger executives would stay, believing their turn would come next.

Armacost's supporters wondered what Armacost was doing. Why didn't he step in and select his own team? Why accept Bolin? "Sam obviously preferred to do things gradually," says a member of his managing committee. "He was worried about how the employees would respond, how the public would respond."

Once Armacost became president, he made another, quieter personnel decision that upset a few well-informed executives even more than the choice of Bolin. Paul Verburgt, the Dutchman who ran the money market operation in London under Rice and Armacost, was a talented, though difficult, executive. He flaunted his freewheeling lifestyle, bragging to other executives in London about vacations with bank customers or potential customers aboard yachts in the Mediterranean, showing snapshots of attractive young female companions on board.

Verburgt also had business relationships with some clients of the bank, similar to those that got Al Rice fired—nothing illegal, just a question of debatable judgment. At about the time that Sam Armacost became president, Bank of America's auditors were investigating Verburgt's business dealings. What they found, says one former senior executive in London, "Made Al Rice look like Snow White."

The results of the audit, bank officers say, were shown to Armacost, who responded much differently than Clausen had in a similar situation a few years before. In 1982, Armacost named Verburgt to head Europe, Middle East, and Africa. Those who knew about the audit realize that Armacost was probably justified in not firing Verburgt, perhaps even in not reprimanding him, but his promotion left them uneasy. The appearance of impropriety that had led Clausen to fire Rice was just as obvious with Verburgt, but the new chief executive had different standards.

While supporters wondered about Armacost's decisions regarding people, those in the California branches worried about his enthusiasm for change. With a vigor that surprised them, Armacost rushed to install automated teller machines, like those installed in the late 1970s by Citicorp, which would allow consumers to bank twenty-four hours a day. Worried that Bank of America was too far behind, Armacost ordered the bank to install more than one machine a day during 1981, catapulting Bank of America from dead last among the major banks in the state in number of ATMs to first in the nation.

This shored up the defenses in the California market. Bank of America had a preeminent position in the market, with more branches than any other financial institution. Armacost pushed the installation of ATMs to ensure consumers would keep coming to those branches. By spending more than $100 million in a single year, he was raising the stakes for his competitors. If they wanted to grab market share from Bank of America, they would have to match its investments in technology.

Armacost also had to wring costs out of the system. Boston Consulting Group's study confirmed the bank could eliminate perhaps three hundred of its eleven hundred branches, without losing ground to its competitors. Instead of closing the branches rapidly, though, Boston Consulting recommended a series of steps to organize the system differently. Not every branch needed to offer every service. If a branch made very few business loans, why not transfer the commercial lending operation to a nearby branch with more demand for such loans? It sounded logical. Other banks had done it successfully.

Armacost believed in his consultants. "Whatever BCG said, that was the word," says a former senior executive in the retail branch system.

Pilot programs were begun. The bank closed two dozen branches and grouped others into clusters, with several small branches reporting to a single, larger branch. Lending was centralized in fewer branches and small "convenience banking centers" opened, each with an ATM and a couple of tellers.

On top of these changes came the new products. As a result of deregulation, Bank of America had the freedom to offer a panoply of new loans and deposits. In 1981, Armacost bragged, "We introduced more major products than in any year in recent memory." Bank of America began making mortgage loans with adjustable interest rates. It offered banking by phone and through cable television. It began marketing a string of new, high-interest deposits, and simultaneously raised the fees customers paid on items like bounced checks and overdrawn accounts.

Armacost's intensity brought a struggle with Martin Elenbaas, head of the retail branch system. Elenbaas was from the old school, a Carrera lieutenant who understood the virtues of the retail network and the risks of asking a thousand branch managers to change overnight. He had risen through the branches and then spent a few years working under Pinola in the North America Division. He even looked conservative, bearing a faint resemblance to the farmer in Grant Wood's *American Gothic*. Elenbaas had absorbed the Giannini values, tempered with the cautious desire not to change the character of the retail bank. "Marty and Sam disagreed on how fast Sam was moving to change the distribution system," said a former executive in the retail division. "Marty is a people-person. He was concerned that if you moved too fast, you might lose control."

Elenbaas felt the tugging of power politics. "Instead of one CEO, we had two," he said. Both Armacost and Prussia were trying to change the retail system. "There was always a power struggle there," he said. Before Carrera's departure, he shielded the California branches from any pulling and tugging from the chief executive. Now, the division was open game. The only guardian was Elenbaas.

"Sam took over in April of 1981," Elenbaas pointed out. "Our offices were a hundred feet apart. If I'd been in that job, I'd have walked down the hall to the California guy and said, 'I want to learn as much as I can about the retail bank.' He never did that. He never had a feel for the people in the division. He just didn't understand them."

Elenbaas resisted Armacost by cautiously opening pilot programs. One legacy of the Giannini days was that each branch sent out checking statements to its local customers. Elenbaas opened a regional office in Walnut Creek, east of San Francisco, that handled the statements for several branches, testing an approach used successfully by most other banks. Another process called proofing—in which an employee typed the amount of each check onto the bottom of it in computer-readable code—had also been done in each branch. Elenbaas opened one regional center to study the merits and risks of centralized proofing, though a decade earlier most banks had adopted a similar approach.

Armacost wanted more, and he wanted it faster. His slogan, embraced to encourage experimentation, was "Think it, try it, fix it." But he was either too timid or too polite to shove Elenbaas, who knew Armacost wanted more, but stuck to his cautious ways.

Armacost seemed to be getting tough in early December, when he sent a "Sam-O-Gram," a one-page memorandum saying, "I know you are working on further refining the retail banking strategy. . . . It seems to me these issues have to be brought to a head soon, if only to get them behind us as an issue and then to start coping with the implementation of the strategy. Therefore I need from you, by January 15, a comprehensive strategy document which pulls together all of the various strategy elements that have been considered over several years and which need to be crystallized now, if only to obtain another opinion concerning them."

The order from "The Corner Office" sounded tough, implying Elenbaas and his staff should spend the Christmas holidays working on that strategy document, but that's not the message Elenbaas got, as he stuck to his own pace, finishing the document early in the year. By then Armacost had mentioned he would like Elenbaas to move into a new post—but never decided which one. Elenbaas finally announced his decision to retire in April 1982, five months after the Sam-O-Gram.

Armacost's supporters grumbled on, hoping for something more decisive. They wanted a bold assertion of the Armacost presidency, a sign that Armacost was ready to put his own stamp on the company. On November 22, 1981, only seven months after Armacost became president of BankAmerica, they got that sign.

Chapter Fourteen

The bank of tomorrow is going to be a sort of department store, handling every service the people may want in the way of banking, investment and trust services.

A. P. Giannini, 1929

Chuck Schwab looked and sounded like a politician searching for votes. A self-made millionaire, with fresh-scrubbed good looks, gleaming teeth, a full head of impeccably blown-dry hair, stylish eyeglasses, and a face known by millions of Americans, Schwab smiled out like a matinee idol from advertisements in newspapers, on television, and at subway and bus stops in Manhattan and other large cities.

But Schwab wasn't running for office, just running his company. As the president of the nation's largest discount stock broker, Schwab had become an asset as powerful and recognizable as Morris the Cat or Mr. Speedy the Alka-Seltzer relief man. That face had given a human quality to Charles Schwab & Co., a link to customers who often talked of doing business with "Chuck," rather than some faceless corporation.

On November 22, 1981, Chuck Schwab agreed to become part of the BankAmerica family for a price of $53 million.

Within BankAmerica, the response was euphoric. "We broke out the champagne," one officer wrote. Said another, "Everything stopped when we heard about it, as everyone was talking about the bank moving forward."

This was the bold step BankAmerica's troops had wanted. Even the newspapers sounded excited, describing the deal in heroic terms. The emotion was more than Armacost or any of his colleagues had expected. This was not a big purchase, $53 mil-

150

lion was peanuts to a company with $120 billion in assets. Bank of America spent more installing ATMs in six months than it spent to buy Schwab & Co. But the public, the employees, and the press realized this was a purchase that Tom Clausen would not have made. It reflected a new, assertive spirit at Bank-America and echoed, however faintly, the energetic leadership of A. P. Giannini.

Buying Schwab threatened to chop a huge hole in the Glass-Steagall Act, a law adopted in the 1930s while the country was still reeling from the 1929 stock market crash, that separated the commercial banking activity of lending money to consumers and businesses from the investment banking activity of underwriting securities of corporations. The line between the two industries was never precisely drawn and both sides claimed frequent, unfair incursions by the other. But by 1981 the securities industry was so terrified of competition from commercial banks that it was certain to challenge the Schwab purchase in court. (Which it did, eventually losing in 1983 when the U.S. Supreme Court upheld lower court rulings approving the acquisition.)

Armacost was thumbing his nose at Wall Street, something A. P. had loved to do. The big boys in the securities houses hated Schwab & Co. and all the other low-budget, low-overhead companies that were stealing their business. In May 1973, the Securities and Exchange Commission had broken the Wall Street club, forcing an end to fixed commissions on stock and bond sales. Schwab & Co., like other discount brokers, offered commissions 70 to 80 percent below those of full-service brokerage houses. Old-line brokers justified their commissions by offering research and advice on what stocks to buy and stressing personal service. They disparaged discounters as fly-by-night outfits with little capital. The public seemed to agree. By 1981, discount brokers had captured only a small slice of the securities business, around 10 percent. But by buying Schwab, BankAmerica would give the discounters credibility. No longer could Wall Street point to the shaky finances of its cut-rate competitors.

More important to BankAmerica, Armacost was breaking out of the stodgy world of banking. Giannini's idea of a financial department store now captivated many firms on and off Wall Street, including Sears, Merrill Lynch, and Prudential. With his purchase of Schwab, Armacost threatened to join the battle.

He had also embraced an entrepreneur with a reputation

for innovation. Armacost saw the executives at Schwab as a model for others at BankAmerica, decisive, fast-moving, not afraid to take chances. It was not a problem that Chuck Schwab and his executives lived in style, driving Porsches and Mercedes Benzes, living in expensive homes or townhouses, and earning millions of dollars—that part of the message was important too. It paid to innovate.

Sam Armacost's decision to purchase Schwab & Co. had begun innocently, with a telephone call between Stephen McLin, BankAmerica's thirty-four-year-old strategic planner, and Peter Moss, thirty-three, his acerbic, at moments brilliant, counterpart at Charles Schwab.

Moss had called McLin, whom he had never met, in May, seeking his help. He was organizing a luncheon group for strategic planners and had thought immediately of McLin, who had taught planning courses at a local university. McLin, aware of possible antitrust problems if BankAmerica sponsored any such organization, begged off, but he suggested names of planners at other companies.

The conversation seemed innocent, but both men saw the chat as the first step in a campaign leading toward well-defined objectives.

Charles Schwab & Co. had a chronic problem: it grew too fast and, as a result, was always short of capital. In the five years ending in 1980, Schwab & Co.'s sales had grown an average of 70 percent a year. Like most entrepreneurs, Schwab relished growth, but worried that if he grew too fast he might have to sell a big chunk of his company to raise capital. He had already done that once, selling 20 percent of Schwab & Co. to outsiders in 1979.

As 1981 began, Schwab expected even faster growth for the next few years. The company planned to double its branches and quadruple revenues by 1985. Yet for all this growth, competitors were breathing down its neck, threatening to dislodge it from first place in the industry. Remaining number one was important enough to Chuck Schwab that he was willing to consider taking on a new partner.

When Moss called McLin, Schwab & Co.'s investment banker, First Boston Corp., had just tried and failed to raise $7.5 million of new capital—an amount BankAmerica could easily provide. Years earlier Schwab had applied twice for loans from Bank of America and had been turned down. The bank didn't lend to discount brokers, not so much because they were a bad risk, but because Bank of America was selective about making "subordinated" loans to brokerage houses. Subordination meant that if the brokerage house ever went bankrupt, other investors would be standing in front of Bank of America when the time came to get cash from the bankruptcy judge.

Schwab & Co. didn't require capital immediately. But by the end of 1981 or early 1982 it would need that injection. As a strategic planner, Moss was not normally involved in trying to raise capital, but after First Boston's failure, Schwab & Co. was considering joint business operations or other strategic alliances that might bring in money. One of his reasons for calling McLin was to get better acquainted with a possible investor.

Steve McLin would rise rapidly under Sam Armacost and would play such an important role in his presidency that at times he would seem the young president's alter ego. Though at moments contemplative, engrossed by basic questions of strategy, McLin thrived on the combat and the adrenalin high that comes with buying and selling companies. He was balding, with eyes that reflected a nervous energy, constantly darting about the room even in moments of calm.

In 1981, when Sam Armacost became president, McLin had strong opinions about BankAmerica's strategy. But he was not the clear choice to lead the planning division. In Clausen's effort to decentralize, he put planners in each of the major divisions of the bank, many of whom aspired to head planning for the whole company.

Smart and ambitious, McLin had the instincts of a survivor, developed perhaps while bouncing among U.S. Air Force bases with his family as he was growing up. McLin began his business career as a chemical engineer, working for Atlantic Richfield, but quickly grew bored, left to earn an MBA in finance from Stanford, and landed a job in strategic planning with First National Bank of Chicago, before moving to Bank of America. He worked in the Cashiers Division, then joined Bank of America's fledgling strategic planning group, where he directed the work done by Boston Consulting Group.

Once Armacost was named cashier, McLin worked at getting to know him, building on their mutual interest in golf and sports cars (both men drove Datsun 240Zs). McLin volunteered to do special projects for Armacost. This improved their relationship, but on the day the board selected Armacost as president, the two were still distant. So McLin asserted his claim on the planning job. He called the new president, grabbed some of his staff members, and trotted up to Armacost's office for a brief presentation on what strategic planning could do for the chief executive-to-be.

It was a gutsy tactical maneuver, one that might have backfired. But Armacost liked the brass McLin displayed. He listened attentively and seemed impressed. Over the next few months, McLin fed Armacost a steady diet of ideas, and in June 1981 was named the head of strategic planning, with the title of senior vice-president, on his way to earning more than $250,000 a year as one of the company's highest paid executives.

McLin believed Armacost could transform BankAmerica through a series of acquisitions. He saw himself as Armacost's deal maker. In May, when Moss called, McLin was already assured of the new post. But he realized that Sam Armacost, the professional salesman, was an impatient man who liked people who produced. McLin needed a project.

The brokerage business offered an opportunity for BankAmerica. Earlier in the year, investment bankers had offered McLin a chance to buy Dean Witter & Co., one of the nation's largest stock brokers. Sears, Roebuck and Co., the giant retailer, was chasing Dean Witter, but the securities firm's top executives didn't like the idea. It seemed undignified, selling securities in a Sears store a few aisles over from shirts and socks.

BankAmerica was a logical alternative. It sold financial services, it was big, and both BankAmerica and Dean Witter had begun in San Francisco, though Dean Witter had moved to New York after a series of mergers in the 1960s. What stood in the way was the line drawn by the Glass-Steagall Act after the stock market crash of 1929. BankAmerica was on one side and Dean Witter was on the other.

For days, McLin struggled to find or create a bid. In other instances where regulations were likely to change, some companies had arranged "stake-outs." One firm invested in another with the proviso that when regulations permitted, the two would merge. Both Armacost and McLin sought a way to hurdle Glass-Steagall, but in the end, the prize went to Sears, which was free to own an investment bank.

With Moss's call in May, McLin saw another possible road

into the brokerage business. Even though Glass-Steagall apparently forbade a merger with a broker, Schwab and BankAmerica might work together in other ways. Many banks had recently begun renting space in their lobbies to insurance companies and travel agencies, which then sold their wares to bank customers.

The first phone call led nowhere, but in late June, Moss called again. This time, he mentioned Schwab's need for capital and Bank of America's past reluctance to lend money. McLin sounded surprised, in part because he thought that an investment by BankAmerica in Schwab's subordinated capital might be illegal. It wasn't, Moss assured him. First Interstate, a rival of Bank of America, had lent money to Schwab in the past. Then Moss mentioned that another San Francisco bank, Crocker National, was rumored to be seeking a seat on the New York Stock Exchange, taking advantage of a loophole in Glass-Steagall. (Crocker later applied for and got a seat on the exchange.)

After the phone call, McLin began to study discount brokerage, spending much of the summer on the work. In mid-August, McLin called Moss. The company's legal department had decided BankAmerica might be able to buy Schwab thanks to the loophole in the Glass-Steagall Act that allowed banks to buy and sell securities for their customers, as long as they were not selling newly issued securities—a process called underwriting. The two arranged to meet for lunch.

They met on September 11 at the Bankers Club on the top floor of the BankAmerica building, twelve floors above Sam Armacost's office. The restaurant commands the same sweeping panorama of the city and the bay. A haunt for business executives, especially those with offices in the building, it seems an unlikely setting for delicate negotiations. The risk of eavesdropping by a competitor would appear too high.

The conversation began amicably. McLin said BankAmerica would reconsider Schwab's request for a loan, but McLin wasn't particularly impressed with Schwab's profits. Though the company was much larger than its competitors, its return on investment was dismal, and that was the number that lenders and investors focused on first.

Moss explained the basic economics of discount brokerage. The profits, he said, are all in the scale of the operation. The investments needed to capture a large market share are high. A discounter needs a string of offices, a sophisticated computer system, and banks of telephones. Every time the company buys or sells stock for a customer, it earns a tiny commission. Put enough of those trades together, and you cover the overhead— the phones, computers, and office rent. Put together a few more trades, and profits build. Once the company gets large enough, and handles enough volume, the costs per trade drop and the profits soar.

Moss was telling McLin exactly what he wanted to hear. Schwab & Co. fit the profile of the kind of businesses McLin wanted to acquire: it was profitable, growing rapidly, and already had a large share of its market. With the money invested by Schwab, the company had become a leader. Backed by the deep pockets of BankAmerica, it could build an almost unassailable position.

McLin had been evasive about his intentions, but Moss began to press. He wanted some assurance that McLin would pony up part of the $7.5 million subordinated capital. McLin avoided the question. Exasperated, Moss finally asked, point-blank, "What are you really interested in here?"

"I think we can find a way to get together," McLin responded.

"You mean some kind of joint venture, a minority interest?" Moss asked.

"We haven't been too happy with joint ventures," McLin said. "It's been especially difficult where we were a minority partner, but even when we hold a majority interest, it has been difficult."

"What would you like to do?"

"We'd like to buy you."

Now it was Moss's turn to grow flustered and evasive.

"Are you sure you understand our business?" he asked. "Chuck wouldn't be interested. He's independent-minded, aggressive. He's really so much of a maverick that it would be hard to see him in a large company."

McLin was undeterred.

A few days later, the two began what Moss described as "shuttle diplomacy." Worried about meeting publicly, Moss and McLin arranged to talk on the way to work. Moss lived in Lafayette, just across the bay from San Francisco, and McLin lived a few miles farther out, driving to the city with his fiancée, Cathy, while Moss rode the Bay Area Rapid Transit (BART).

Three times over the course of the month, McLin, his fiancée, and Moss met and rode together to the city. Moss would leave his car at the BART station, then walk to a bus stop, where McLin would pick him up.

By September 21, Moss was convinced that McLin was serious. "Don't you think I should talk to Chuck?" he asked. With that the discussions escalated. Both men thought a merger was attractive. All they had to do was convince Chuck Schwab and Sam Armacost.

Schwab was skeptical. Why would a company that had refused to lend him money now want to buy his firm? How much would BankAmerica pay? He doubted that the bank would ever pay enough.

Armacost was equally concerned. McLin asked the company's lawyers whether BankAmerica could buy Schwab. They saw huge obstacles. Why waste time on a merger that wouldn't be approved? Why would Schwab want to sell his company to Bank-America anyway?

On September 25, 1981, McLin and Moss brought their bosses together for a two-hour lunch in Armacost's private dining room on the fifty-second floor near the Bankers Club. It was a get-acquainted meeting. Both men had attended the Stanford Graduate School of Business and both were products of California's warm, open climate. They were salesmen and marketers, and, as expected, they hit it off.

Three days later, McLin briefed BankAmerica's managing committee on the pending talks. The idea went over well. On Thursday, October 1, McLin and Armacost toured Schwab's offices, four blocks from the Bank of America headquarters, coming away impressed with its efficiency. In all the early conversations about the company, one of the points they had largely overlooked was Schwab & Co.'s computer system, perhaps its main strength. Schwab & Co. had developed software that allowed low-paid clerks to take orders to buy and sell securities over the phone. It was similar to the systems that BankAmerica needed, but didn't have, to make its branch system more efficient. On the walk back to the head office, Armacost told McLin to buy Schwab.

In the first week of November, negotiations began. Bank-America was offering about $40 million, Schwab wanted $80 million—twice the company's annual revenues. Two weeks of negotiations followed, with pressure building on Schwab. Other efforts to raise $7.5 million of capital had failed. Schwab's investment banker, First Boston Corp., had been unable to interest investors in buying securities at a reasonable price. Schwab's profits had evaporated. A venture into insurance sales cost the broker $500,000 in 1980. The stock market was also in the doldrums, leaving Schwab & Co. with little trading volume. By preparing for a surge in volume and diversifying, Schwab had created so much overhead that his firm was no longer profitable.

Schwab sent officers out to find other candidates to buy Schwab, but no other company showed interest at the price BankAmerica was offering. One bank suggested it might offer $25 million.

As negotiations continued, the price range narrowed with BankAmerica staying firm at about $40 million, while Schwab's asking price slipped to $60 million. On November 17, Armacost agreed to nominate Schwab for a position on BankAmerica's board. Then McLin offered a compromise. The bank would pay $53 million in stock. Since it would take months for regulators to approve the deal—it faced a review by the Federal Reserve, and probably a long court fight—McLin gave Schwab an option. He could fix the price at $53 million, no matter how many shares of BankAmerica stock that might be. Or he could fix the price at 2.2 million shares, which meant a windfall if BankAmerica's stock price rose. Schwab chose the 2.2 million shares.

In a brief ceremony in Armacost's fortieth-floor office, the two signed the papers. They shook hands. Sam Armacost had taken his first bold step.

Chapter Fifteen

I have never believed in beating about the bush. When you have a purpose in hand, go after it and achieve it as promptly and efficiently as you can. Don't dawdle.

A. P. Giannini, 1923

The public enthusiasm for the Schwab & Co. purchase represented a bright spot in a string of tough years for Sam Armacost. Two months after he and Schwab agreed on the merger, Bank-America formally announced a 31 percent drop in profits for Armacost's first year on the job. "With all the pressures we faced in 1981, there is a renewed sense of dedication and direction to meet the challenges that lie ahead," Armacost said.

The most immediate challenge was the interest rate mismatch. According to internal bank documents, the bet on interest rates cost BankAmerica $850 million in 1981—using a calculation that assumes all those fixed-rate loans were financed with high-cost deposits. What saved the company from horrendous losses was its rich core of low-cost savings accounts, but as Armacost knew, with the deregulation of banking, those accounts would not last forever.

During 1981, Armacost reduced the mismatch. The bank borrowed money for longer terms and started making mortgages with adjustable interest rates instead of rates fixed for thirty years. Progress came, but not fast enough. By year's end, the mismatch had dropped from $7 billion to under $6 billion.

The next challenge was the retail bank—the source of much of the bank's profits, but the division that would be hardest hit by deregulation. After Elenbaas retired, Armacost brought in executives who had worked with him overseas to slash expenses in the California branch system and prepare it for the fierce competition of a deregulated world.

He asked James Wiesler, fifty-four, a tall, rawboned veteran of more than thirty years, to head the retail bank. A graduate of the University of Colorado, Wiesler had risen through the California branch system, lending money to farmers in the Imperial Valley, managing the San Diego branch, and running the San Jose region. He knew the California bank and understood its people. But he had also experienced the wide-open competition overseas. He had run the company's operations in Germany, run all of Asia, and, in 1980, moved to the North America Division, which included Mexico and Canada. In each of these jobs, from the branches through the Asian division, Wiesler had "produced." Each unit had grown, its profits had increased.

Wiesler never lost the small-town spirit of the California division. He wasn't as polished as Al Rice or Sam Armacost. "He had a 'hi-ya-bub' style and a tendency to pull you forward when he shook hands, pulling you off balance, something he must have picked up in a Dale Carnegie course," says one former colleague. Armacost bought his suits in Hong Kong or London, had his shirts tailor-made, always looking the part of a worldly banker. Wiesler could dress well, but he was comfortable in something less fashionable. On a visit to New York as head of the North America Division, Wiesler arrived for a staff meeting wearing a tan suit with dark brown piping on the chest and brown half-boots with zippers on the side. Executives in the New York division nearly went into shock. One began referring to Wiesler as "The Cowboy." Another pulled aside his boss later and joked about Wiesler's attire, asking, "You expect me to work for this guy?"

Those who regularly saw Wiesler knew a different man, a determined, dedicated, and honest individual who inspired tremendous loyalty. "If the bank needed it, he'd get off a twelve-hour flight from overseas, dog-tired, and work another twelve hours," says a former executive who reported to Wiesler. "He was an old war horse. You had to admire him."

To run the branches for Wiesler, Armacost brought in James Miscoll from Asia. Jesuit-trained, with a brusque manner, Miscoll got things done. His career paralleled Wiesler's, but he was different, energetic and active, yet pretentious and prone to opaque observations on the relationship between the bank's problems and the writings of St. Augustine and other philosophers.

These were Armacost's storm troopers. Their job was to bring new order to the retail bank, to carry out the missions dictated by Boston Consulting Group, reorganizing and trimming branches, as well as installing expensive computer systems. Armacost was on the attack.

Armacost's other preoccupation was with "the culture of the bank." He wanted to change the way the bank operated, to shake it to its foundations, redefine what he referred to as its "visions, values, and strategies." This meant casting aside many of the principles inherited from (or at least attributed to) Giannini, including the bank's reluctance to fire incompetent executives, the tendency of senior executives to avoid criticizing one another's programs, and the emphasis on size rather than profit.

The stress on culture was also a blast at the bank's appalling lack of talented managers. Shortly after becoming president, Armacost mentioned that the company, "doesn't have a very deep bench." Since the days of Giannini, the bank's policies on paying for talent had changed. A. P. had paid his employees modest salaries, but he encouraged them to buy stock and profit as the company grew. Many branch managers owned large blocks of stock and Giannini occasionally bragged about making them rich. In 1927 the Bank of Italy was the first bank to adopt an employee stock ownership plan, which helped put hundreds of thousands of shares of the company in the hands of employees. Giannini had also brought in new people continuously—either by buying their banks or hiring them.

In the seventies, the hubris of BankAmerica led it to look inside for senior executives almost exclusively. Pay for most jobs was kept well below the industry average and stock options were miserly. Insiders viewed working for BankAmerica as a privilege.

Armacost began to reach outside the bank for senior executives. He hired Max Hopper from American Airlines to oversee investments in technology, and Robert Beck, an experienced personnel executive from IBM. Beck's job was to create new incentives for executives, and find better ways to train managers. In other positions, Armacost hired officers from Citicorp, Chase, and other big banks, trying to bring new ideas to the bank.

All this Armacost did with enthusiasm. But he balked at making some more controversial decisions. Internal studies showed BankAmerica needed to eliminate 15,000 jobs just to have an average work force for a commercial bank. The bank needed to close hundreds of branches to lower its costs. It needed to upgrade the skills of thousands of employees—not to pass the competition, just to catch up. And time was running short.

But when executives pushed Armacost to go faster, he warned that "the place is likely to blow up." Sam Armacost was a product of his culture. After nearly twenty years at BankAmerica, deep inside Armacost did not believe that big bonuses and high salaries motivated people. And like Clausen, he found it hard to fire people. He preferred to push them into make-work jobs and hope they would resign.

He failed to get open discussion among the eight men on the managing committee. It remained a one-man show, as it had under Clausen. Armacost blamed his executives for being too timid to speak up; they blamed him for being just as tough, enigmatic, and off-putting as Clausen. "He had a personality that was like the brightest kid in class. You'd say three words and he would know what your point was and where you were going with the rest of your sentence. He'd want to cut right to the end," says a BankAmerica senior vice-president. As positive as that characteristic might sound, it stifled debate.

At first senior executives occasionally spoke up at committee meetings, but by mid-1982, they waited for Sam to speak first, wanting his view before they expressed their own opinions. Armacost set the agenda, only "there usually wasn't one," says a former member of the managing committee.

What undermined the process further was Armacost's habit of reaching decisions while walking down the hall between meetings. Members of the managing committee learned quickly that they could circumvent opposition in the managing committee— or kill a project they didn't like—if they could get Sam's ear. They struggled to build direct links with Armacost. If they could get to him directly, they could play on the salesman in him, which wanted to please everyone. As long as a decision was not too controversial, Armacost could be convinced to take a position and to sway the managing committee.

The economy didn't help Armacost. The soaring interest rates of 1981 turned into a murderous recession in 1982. The world economy slumped worse than it had in 1974. California's economy, which had weathered the seventies with little stress, sank under the weight of the new recession. Inflation turned to deflation, major industries—including oil, agriculture, and real estate—went into free-fall. Crisis followed crisis, bringing new woes to BankAmerica.

The nation's savings and loans suffered so much that half the industry ended up technically bankrupt. Farmers failed in record numbers, unable to repay loans now that land and crop prices had tumbled. Throughout Colorado, Louisiana, Oklahoma, and Texas, companies disappeared as oil prices plunged from $40 a barrel to under $10 a barrel. Farm banks, oil banks, and S&Ls all slouched toward insolvency. Failures reached levels not seen since the Great Depression.

One spectacular failure came in Oklahoma City, in July 1982, when officers of the Federal Deposit Insurance Corp. swarmed into the tiny, shopping-center headquarters of Penn Square Bank. In the oil boom of the late 1970s, Penn Square had transformed itself into a boiler-room operation, creating and selling loans to large commercial banks. As regulators sorted through the debris in the Penn Square collapse, they came away shocked. Continental Illinois Bank in Chicago had acquired more than $1 billion of oil and gas loans from Penn Square, mostly bad. Seafirst Corp., owner of Seattle's largest bank, had acquired $366 million of the loans. Both companies would almost fail. Seafirst would eventually be rescued by BankAmerica. Continental Illinois would be taken over by the U.S. government.

A month after Penn Square, Mexico announced more bad news: it could no longer pay its interest. The sudden slump in the price of oil—followed by a sharp devaluation in the Mexican peso—left the country without enough hard currency to keep up payments. In September, Jose Lopez Portillo, Mexico's president, dramatized the nation's plight by nationalizing Mexico's banks and freezing all bank accounts denominated in U.S. dollars. Within months, the crisis spread from Mexico throughout the less-developed world. The fuse of the international debt bomb had been lit.

The economic shocks sent tremors through BankAmerica. It had $6.8 billion outstanding to the three largest troubled countries: Mexico, Brazil, and Venezuela. It had lent more to farmers than any other bank in America. It had one of the largest portfolios of real estate loans in the country. And it had lent heavily to all the ancillary businesses that were being hit by falling prices: shipping, oil and gas, and small businesses in Latin America. A little over one third of the bank's loans in those three Latin American countries—Brazil, Mexico, and Venezuela—had gone to private companies.

BankAmerica's loan losses in 1982 rose to $433 million, a 66 percent increase from 1979, high though not yet a disaster. More ominous was the increase in troubled loans—those not paying interest, ninety days past due, or on which the bank had agreed to lower the interest rate. They doubled to more than $3 billion.

Against the backdrop of a global recession, however, Bank-America's problems seemed almost modest. Although large commercial banks such as Chase Manhattan, Citicorp, and Bankers Trust had lost heavily in the past, they rarely failed. Small banks might disappear in droves, but it took a special brand of stupidity or bad luck to kill a big bank. (In 1974, Franklin National Bank had failed. It grew too rapidly, moving from Long Island to a new headquarters in Manhattan. It lost big on loans, and then tried to cover the losses by speculating in foreign currencies. A few years later, First Pennsylvania Bank, Philadelphia's largest, nearly failed when its strategy of "go-go" growth ended in the recession of 1979. Bad real estate loans almost killed others, such as Citizens & Southern of Atlanta and Union Bank of California.)

No one at the helm of BankAmerica saw reason to panic. Armacost had proclaimed at the annual meeting—in a language perhaps best described as BankAmerispeak, "I think we'll see that 1981 marked a watershed year in which we took the bull of change by the horns and prepared for the challenges and opportunities of the new era of a deregulated, technology-driven, market-responsive, modern-day banking and financial services." No one knew exactly what he meant, but it sounded upbeat.

Armacost had once compared BankAmerica to an ocean liner. The captain may try to change direction, setting all the controls accordingly, but the boat has so much momentum that it travels for miles in the wrong direction before changing course. One of the jokes circulating in the bank was that Armacost had gone to the bridge, set all the levers in the right place, and now he was waiting for the ship to turn. The trouble was that none of the levers were connected.

Chapter Sixteen

Failure usually comes from doing things that shouldn't have been done . . . often things of questionable ethics.

A. P. Giannini, 1923

On the day before Christmas in 1982, Sam Armacost and Steve McLin took time off for a round of golf. Armacost had little reason to smile or relax with 1982 turning out to be another miserable year. Profits were off by 13 percent, problem loans had doubled, Latin America's debt was turning into a nightmare. "Sometimes I wake up in the middle of the night in a cold sweat worrying about Mexico," he said in late 1982.

McLin was continuing to look for acquisitions. As the company's in-house investment banker, and as the architect of Armacost's strategic plan, he wanted to find the right pieces to make the strategy work. He thought he had one.

While Armacost and McLin played, McLin asked whether Sam wanted to pursue Seafirst Corp. "You've got to be kidding," Armacost responded.

Seafirst was the parent of Seattle-First National Bank, the premier bank in the state of Washington. It was also one of the biggest buyers of loans from Penn Square Bank, the little Oklahoma bank that had collapsed in mid-1982. Seafirst was in trouble.

McLin realized there were huge risks, but he also saw an opportunity. Rarely did big commercial banks come up for sale. Thanks to laws passed in the 1930s and 1950s to constrain A. P. Giannini, almost the only time one big bank could buy another in a different state was when it was ready to fail. Seafirst was that sick.

165

Seafirst offered BankAmerica a dominant position in Washington, with a solid consumer banking business, similar to its own in California. Seafirst had a reputation as an innovative, well-run bank—except for the oil and gas lending. That was an aberration, or so it appeared.

A few days after the golf game, Seafirst announced that it had a new chief executive, Richard P. Cooley, one of the best-known bankers on the West Coast. Cooley had headed Wells Fargo Bank for nearly a decade before deciding to take early retirement. As he prepared to retire, Seafirst's board, which had ousted its CEO in a shakeup following the Penn Square disaster, asked Cooley to come to Seattle to clean things up. He jumped at the opportunity.

Dick Cooley thought he could turn Seafirst around quickly, all he needed was a little time and better management. When he arrived in Seattle, he found more damage than he had expected. "It's hard to believe that one man could do all this damage," he told *Fortune* in early 1983.

The one man was John Boyd, an ambitious young lending officer, who had discovered Penn Square Bank.

Seafirst was one of the companies bank securities analysts loved in the 1970s. It seemed to do no wrong. Profits soared, competitors seethed, and the stock price rose briskly. But by the mid-1970s, the growth in Seafirst's profits, just as at Bank-America, slowed. Needing ways to expand further, it began lending more aggressively outside the Pacific Northwest, mostly to corporations large and small. One of the sexiest businesses in America in the late 1970s was the oil business. The boom in oil prices, the success of the Organization of Petroleum Exporting Countries, brought a renaissance to the oil patch. Some of the glamour of "the oilies" came to Seattle as they passed through town on their way to drill in Alaska. So while BankAmerica was pressuring its loan officers around the world to make more and more loans, gambling on inflation, Seafirst was prospecting for business in Texas and Oklahoma, betting that the oil boom would last forever.

John Boyd was the man Seafirst sent to Oklahoma City, where he met Bill Patterson, the head of Penn Square's oil and gas division. Patterson had a style all his own. He drank beer out of cowboy boots, showed up for work in a Nazi uniform, and when he traveled to the Middle East, came back dressed in the robes of a sheik. He also had a way of losing paperwork, doing deals before he investigated the value of collateral, and writing loans to nearly bankrupt companies. (Despite this, Patterson had not been convicted of any crimes and an Oklahoma court had acquitted him on twenty-four separate counts of illegal activity.)

Boyd was new to the oil business, but he was eager to learn. At first Bill Patterson ignored him, but soon Seafirst became one of Penn Square's special friends, putting together a collection of credits arranged by Penn Square that other clients of the Oklahoma bank had rejected as too risky.

In a two-month burst of optimism in late 1981, Boyd doubled the size of Seafirst's loan portfolio by buying $350 million of loans from Penn Square. By the end of 1982, when Dick Cooley came to Seafirst, the company had nearly $1.2 billion of oil loans, not all from Penn Square, but most of which nevertheless might never be repaid.

As 1983 began, the price of oil wilted once again, as the OPEC cartel continued to lose power. By the end of January, worried about a run that might cripple his bank, Cooley arranged a $1.5 billion safety net from the nation's largest banks. He flew to New York and talked with Lee Kimmel, one of the top investment bankers at Salomon Brothers, a powerful Wall Street firm that would be hired in 1986 to review BankAmerica's financial outlook. Cooley figured he needed about $200 million of capital to keep Seafirst afloat. Kimmel's conclusion was not optimistic.

"You may have to sell Seafirst to raise that rescue money," Kimmel told him. "Two hundred million is close to the market price of Seafirst stock."

Cooley didn't have many options. The only other large commercial bank in Washington was Rainier National. It wasn't large enough to swallow Seafirst, even if the board of directors approved a deal, which wasn't likely.

It was illegal for an out-of-state bank to acquire Seafirst. State law forbade it, as did federal law, unless Seafirst failed. In that unhappy event, an emergency provision in federal law allowed an out-of-state bank to step in to rescue depositors. That was something Cooley hoped to avoid.

Salomon's Kimmel began to search for a buyer. It was legal for a foreign bank to acquire Seafirst, but with all those bad oil loans, none was interested. Desperate, Kimmel began to call on other large U.S. banks. Perhaps a bridge could be built over the legal barriers. Kimmel eventually reached McLin, who feigned disinterest. "Seafirst is a black hole," he told Kimmel.

When McLin mentioned the idea to Armacost a second time, Sam growled, "My God, we've got enough to do here in California. We don't need to buy someone else's problems." But McLin pressed and Armacost gave him permission to investigate further.

McLin brought Kimmel to San Francisco to talk with Armacost, and Kimmel argued that Seafirst comprised two banks. One was in lousy shape, saddled with $1 billion of bad energy loans. The other was in terrific shape. All that BankAmerica had to do was figure out a way to buy the good bank and minimize the losses related to the bad bank. But Armacost seemed unimpressed.

In mid-April Dick Cooley flew to Washington, D.C. to discuss a federal bailout of Seafirst, then on to New York to talk with the banks that had provided the safety net. Seafirst's annual shareholders meeting was coming at the end of the month and he would soon have to announce the results for the quarter. They looked bad enough to spark a run by depositors, which meant Cooley was just about out of time.

In New York he got a call from Sam Armacost. McLin had come up with a gimmick that convinced Armacost to bid.

Bank of America offered $250 million, a little more than Seafirst's market value. Only Bank of America's bid was not all it seemed. It consisted of $125 million in cash, and $125 million of a special preferred stock.

What had finally swayed Armacost was the preferred stock, a "shrink-to-fit" security. BankAmerica could buy the preferred shares back in 1990 or afterwards at a price determined by Seafirst's loan losses. Since Seafirst was still sorting out its problems and didn't know how much it would lose, this represented McLin's insurance policy. If the losses exceeded $350 million, Bank of America would begin to reduce the total value of the preferred by $1 for every $1 of loan losses. If the losses rose high enough, the preferred stock holders would end up with paper worth $2 a share instead of $25—or a total of $9 million, not $125 million. By 1987, the maneuver would prove good for BankAmerica. It would announce that the redemption price of the preferred had slumped to $2.

But Seafirst had no choice. There were no other bidders.

On the Saturday before Seafirst's annual shareholders meeting Cooley announced the deal.

Sam Armacost, who rightly thought he had enough to worry about in California, now had an outpost in Washington State. Just as with the Schwab purchase, Armacost won praise for his boldness. Only now the praise rang hollow. The acquisitions weren't solving BankAmerica's problems. Those seemed to be getting worse all the time.

Chapter Seventeen

The organization has always been very much like a large family. . . .
People often comment on what they call "the spirit" of the place.

A. P. Giannini, 1926

The acquisitions of Seafirst and Schwab drew public attention away from the company's decline. But as the loan losses mounted in 1982 and 1983, as the bank struggled under the conflicting demands of Armacost's plans for a new bank and the recession's toll on daily activities, management splintered.

Prussia and Armacost drifted toward opposite ends of the spectrum on almost all issues. Prussia was the pessimist, Armacost the optimist. Armacost was in control, as he had been since the first day he stepped into the corner office. The major divisions—the retail and wholesale bank—reported to him, and Prussia soon lost control of the staff departments he supervised. Most of the disagreements he should have solved ended up on Armacost's desk, as Prussia's staff circumvented him.

Prussia didn't openly challenge Armacost, but he expressed differing views and fought his loss of power. "It was obvious that Lee had not recognized Sam as the leader," says a former executive vice-president. Prussia presented his own ideas as a counterbalance to Armacost. As early as the fall of 1981, Prussia had differed sharply with Armacost over the course of the economy. Prussia correctly predicted the coming recession. He argued for the bank to batten down, prepare for the worst. It was not the first time he predicted bad times, nor was it the first time he was ignored.

Friction developed as well between James Wiesler and Armacost, who were probably destined to clash. Armacost preferred to keep his distance from subordinates, while Wiesler, who was eleven years older than Armacost, wanted a close, personal relationship. He offered Sam advice, based on his own, longer experience, and Armacost bristled. When Wiesler deserved credit, a pat on the back for doing well, Armacost refused to give it.

One of those moments came in early 1983, when banks first were permitted to offer checking accounts that paid market interest rates. Armacost gave Wiesler specific, and quite contradictory, instructions. He told him to increase the bank's market share. Then he told him not to buy market share by paying high rates. Since every bank and S&L would begin offering the new deposits on the same day, about the only way to gain market share would be to pay a high rate, which Armacost realized. But Sam had scheduled a trip to Europe and so he jumped on a jet and left the country. Wiesler instinctively put market share ahead of price and charged into the market with a rate one percentage point higher than the competition. He snared 55 percent of the market for the new accounts. But when Armacost returned from Europe, Wiesler later told aides, he said, "You've just bankrupted this company." Wiesler's decision squeezed profits slightly for about six months, but as general interest rates fell, the cost of the accounts dropped. The bank began to brag about its bold stroke as a major victory, but Armacost never conceded credit to Wiesler.

The disagreement between the two grew most strained over the need for a chief operating officer. Having worked with Armacost in Europe, Wiesler realized that Sam didn't have the temperament to run day-to-day operations. When Armacost asked Weisler to head the retail bank, Wiesler suggested that Sam create a number two spot in the company, a chief operating officer. That was the job Wiesler wanted.

Armacost dismissed the idea, pointing out that Clausen never used one and most major banks don't require a COO. Armacost viewed Wiesler's aspiration to that post as a threat. He began to bludgeon Wiesler in budget meetings, displaying the same impatience and curtness that had marked Clausen's tenure. "In quarterly reviews, Sam would beat up on him almost every time," says a former executive vice-president.

Wiesler struggled to improve the relationship. As a manager, he believed in building a close, tight-knit team of people who could talk comfortably with him. When he failed to develop that rapport with Armacost he let his frustration spill out in comments to his staff, which always seemed to funnel back to Armacost. Over the years, Armacost had learned to use his executive assistants to tap into corporate gossip. With that conduit and other sources in the company, Armacost had an effective spy network, and he heard quickly about Wiesler's gripes. "Armacost thought Jim wanted his job," says Ichak Adizes, a consultant who began working with the bank in 1983. "The more Jim complained, the less Sam would talk to him. The less Sam talked the more frustrated Jim became."

The real lightning rods in management, however, were John Mickel and Max Hopper, the two men with responsibility for technology and operations. Mickel, the youngest member of the managing committee, had soared to prominence under Joe Carrera. He ran the company's first major public test of automated teller machines and installed the bank's first software for managing all the information in its huge data bases, a system called IMS, or Information Management System, from IBM. Mickel also spawned an empire. Nearly ten thousand people worked under him at one point and his budgets always seemed to call for even more bodies. As his bureaucracy grew, it fostered ill will, becoming less and less responsive to the needs of other managers.

While Clausen was in office, Mickel was protected. Joe Carrera searched for nine months for a computer specialist before hiring Mickel away from Decimus Corp., a subsidiary of BankAmerica. The outside specialists had wanted more than $100,000 a year; Mickel accepted something close to half that. Carrera was Mickel's guardian, watching over the young, opinionated executive and protecting him when he stepped on toes. One of the toes he stepped on belonged to Steve McLin. In the late 1970s, as McLin's unit—then headed by Peter Nelson, Armacost's onetime boss—began working with Boston Consulting Group, Mickel hired his own strategic planning staff and consultants from Stanford Research Institute. Nelson and McLin felt threatened.

After Carrera left, BCG's reports grew sharply critical of the bank's strategy for computers and technology. Mickel's star fell quickly. Stories circulated that he had spent $200 million without authorization, a tale that seemed unlikely, given Bank-

America's tightfisted budget reviews. In mid-1982, Armacost pushed Mickel into a job as the head of marketing for the retail division. Within a few months, criticism began to build about his activities there. In early 1985, Armacost pushed Mickel off the managing committee. A few months later, he demoted Mickel again and Mickel finally resigned.

Mickel's replacement fared better with Armacost, but ended up as an equally controversial figure. Max Hopper had built one of the most sophisticated reservation systems in the airline industry for American Airlines. A tough executive, with a touch of a Texas accent, Hopper normally spoke his mind. At Bank of America, Hopper initially reported to Wiesler, joining a small group of executives that formed the equivalent of a managing committee for the retail bank. Hopper brought to these sessions the directness expected at American Airlines. "After a few meetings," Hopper says, "I was pulled aside by Jim Miscoll and told that wasn't the way things were done here. I thought my job was to raise objections, get things out in the open, so that we could go on to the next decision. The bank didn't work that way."

Hopper tempered his outspokenness. "I began to phrase my questions more delicately," he says.

His tough reviews of budgets, though, didn't change, winning him the nickname "Hopper the Chopper," and word spread that he was an intimidating boss.

Armacost liked Hopper. "The two developed a very close relationship," says another member of Armacost's managing committee.

That bond helped Hopper get money for projects when others couldn't, making him unpopular. His largest and most controversial undertaking was a system called Transaction Processing Facility (TPF), an improved version of the software around which he had built the reservation system for American Airlines. Hopper planned to collect information for BankAmerica with TPF, then use the data base management software installed by Mickel to massage the information once it was in the computer. TPF was a fast, expensive system, built to handle massive volume, something like a thousand transactions a second.

BankAmerica didn't need this sort of computing muscle—its volumes were a fraction of that total. But then, the systems were in disarray. This was one side of the bank where decentralization of decisions was in effect. Seemingly every unit in the bank bought its own system. The result was a computer system that was out of date and poorly organized. While the California branches relied on IMS, the computers that handled other consumer products—such as credit cards, traveler's checks, and even savings accounts—ran on incompatible systems. The World Banking Division had installed computers in various parts of the globe that couldn't "talk" with the California system or other computers in the World Banking Division. As a result, Bank of America had no easy way to know what services its customers were using.

Hopper planned to slowly combine all the computers into one or two central systems. Mickel had already spent millions of dollars on the same general idea—siphoning off money for repairing existing systems to help build a bankwide system. Hopper scrapped most of Mickel's plans and started over. He organized a team to review the bank's computing needs for the next five years. After talking with marketing officers throughout the bank, the team discovered a phenomenal demand for computing power by the early 1990s—enough to justify investments in TPF.

Hopper started to install TPF, even though it had a few weaknesses. The airline industry created TPF to handle thousands of standard transactions. Every airline ticket contains the same information, in the same format, which makes it relatively easy to handle by computer. Banks are different. They handle a variety of services—checking accounts, traveler's checks, credit card authorizations—with varying information requirements. When Hopper suggested TPF, some specialists at IBM thought it was the wrong solution, as did some of Bank of America's top technologists.

But Max Hopper liked it. He had always worked on systems at the frontiers of applying technology, fighting skeptics. He convinced Armacost that the company could leapfrog the rest of the nation's banks by installing TPF, which was exactly what Armacost wanted to hear. Hopper received the go-ahead to build his system.

It was an impractical choice. In order to justify TPF, the bank had to reach the goals set by its marketing staff. If it missed, the investment in TPF was wasted. But those projections, developed in large part by Mickel's staff, turned out to be seriously inflated. Plans for a host of snazzy new products fizzled, including banking by phone, banking by computer, and installing computer terminals in stores to verify credit card purchases. The reality never measured up to the promise.

Resentment of Hopper deepened as Armacost continued to spend on technology while cutting staff elsewhere. "We'd go into budget meetings, where Hopper would ask for $200 million for some project. Sam wouldn't know what questions to ask next," says one former senior vice-president.

As BankAmerica's fortunes sank, top management grew increasingly frustrated. Although a couple of executives, particularly McLin and Hopper, appeared to have a good working relationship with Armacost, not even they felt close to him. Throughout management people wondered whom Armacost turned to for advice. Though he listened to everyone, he had no confidants, or at least none that anyone could identify with assurance.

The friction between senior executives grew as Armacost refused to settle critical issues. Although a superb salesman, Armacost was not comfortable with confrontation and conflict. "I don't remember him ever stepping into a conflict to resolve it," one former senior executive said. Executives who were in the middle of feuds, including those who took sides in battles over technology, soon found that Sam put them in isolation.

Other tough decisions were never made. Instead of firing people, Armacost shuffled them. He proved unable to cut overhead. This only increased the contention that Armacost was not a man of action, for while some units, including the retail bank, met their annual targets for profits, others, including the World Banking Division, consistently missed their goals. Armacost threatened to invest only in businesses that made money, but the retail bank, which made profits, had to fight for investment dollars, while Armacost poured money into computers for use overseas.

Sam Armacost was failing to build a team, to create the sort of cohesive unit needed to run a major corporation. Though his staff worked long hours, pushing hard to carry out his orders, profits still skidded. By the end of 1983, as clashes between executives grew more frequent, as profits continued to drop, Armacost embarked on one of the most controversial, time-consuming efforts of his presidency. Some executives argue that he turned over control of BankAmerica to an obscure management consultant from southern California.

The Armacost
Years
1984–1985

Chapter Eighteen

When you have ideas that are different from others, you are never broke, so long as the ideas are good . . .

A. P. Giannini, 1921

When I was in high school," said Ichak Adizes, the management consultant whom Sam Armacost relied on for two and a half years, "twenty of us kids took a train from Biarritz to Paris. You travel all night long. Like kids do, we all try to sleep in one compartment, which can accommodate only eight people. It took us two hours to fall asleep.

"In my lap I had a head, another head is here, a hand is there. We just fell asleep. One kid says, I want to go to the bathroom. A tremendous commotion. Watch out you don't step on my toe! Watch out! Don't step on my toe! Goddam! You are stepping on my hand! Watch out! Move here, move there. The whole compartment had to wake up because one guy went to the bathroom. And nobody liked him.

"Some organizations are structured the same way. The structure is so badly interwoven that any change that anyone wants to make in one compartment requires a full involvement of the total system and thus is not very popular. The change agents, the innovators, are known by the arrows in their backs. It is easier to sit in a compartment, piss in your pants, and act like everything is fine, rather than get everybody mad at you. You are wet, but you are acting like everything was fine.

"BankAmerica was in that situation."

In December 1982, Sam Armacost met Adizes, a rumpled management consultant from Santa Monica, who speaks with the passionate intensity of an Israeli tank commander. If there is a

179

holy land for management consultants, or perhaps more properly a land of milk and honey, Ichak Adizes had just found it. Sam Armacost was looking for someone to help him change BankAmerica's culture, and it appeared that he had found his prophet.

Ichak Adizes was a virtual unknown in consulting. There were others, such as best-selling author Thomas Peters or well-known firms like McKinsey & Co., with better track records and far higher visibility. But Adizes had worked with dozens of clients, including Coca-Cola Bottling in New Orleans, Domino's Pizza, several government agencies, and corporations in Brazil and elsewhere outside the United States. Former clients considered him brilliant and perceptive. But the feedback on his process was less inspiring. It was painstaking, time-consuming, too detailed.

Everyone agreed, though, that Adizes was a great performer. The Yugoslavian-born consultant made speeches regularly to the Young President's Organization, a group for corporate presidents under forty. He made people laugh with stories and jokes, but used them to make serious points. By the time his speeches were over, the listeners felt they had learned something.

When Armacost and Adizes first met, just a few weeks before Adizes was scheduled to speak at BankAmerica's management retreat, they hit it off. Armacost understood what Adizes was selling: a way to reorganize BankAmerica and build a management team—without firing people. This was what Sam Armacost wanted.

In February 1983, Adizes spoke during the three-day retreat for BankAmerica's top executives at the Silverado Hotel, a corporate resort in the wine country north of San Francisco. He was a hit. He spent more than three hours with BankAmerica's senior management, telling some of his jokes and explaining his theory of management. Then he had them write down criticisms of the bank on index cards, pass them around, and read them aloud. "Even Lloyd Sugaski was excited about the guy," marveled a former senior executive, explaining that Sugaski, the bank's senior credit officer, was by temperament and position a skeptic.

Sam Armacost had his man. Adizes would help him unite executives behind his vision of Bank of America. Adizes would help them face the tough, divisive issues. With this consultant,

Armacost would finally build a team and unite warring factions.

These men were going to hate the process, hate the changes. Adizes knew that. He had been through the process dozens of times. His job was to bear the criticism, take the heat for the chief executive, using his process to move toward the CEO's vision of the company, while the CEO sat quietly in the background. "I volunteered to take the pain," Adizes says.

For more than two years, until early 1985, Ichak Adizes would work with BankAmerica. In the process he undoubtedly opened lines of communication within the company and helped solve some problems, but it cost Sam Armacost dearly. Adizes tied up Armacost's top executives—including Armacost, Prussia, McLin, and others—in sessions that required up to 20 percent of their time, or one full day a week. The process wounded morale and eventually became a symbol of what was wrong with the Armacost presidency.

Ichak Adizes describes himself alternately as a professional "insultant" and a corporate psychotherapist. In long, painful sessions, similar to psychoanalysis, Adizes asks questions of corporate executives, drawing out the weaknesses in an institution, defining them, categorizing them, and developing strategies to solve them.

Adizes builds his process around a view of man as manager—nothing revolutionary, just a simple framework for analyzing people. He defines four skills that a manager, or any business person, can have. The acronymn, one of many that Adizes uses, is PAEI. *P* is for producers, executives who can get things done, whether it's selling toothpaste or manufacturing widgets. *A* is for administrators: the organizers, controllers, and schedulers. *E* is for entrepreneurs. They build businesses, spot new ideas, identify trends, and exploit them. And then there is *I*, which Adizes counts as the ability to integrate others, to get producers, administrators, and entrepreneurs to work together. A perfectly balanced manager has all these skills, while a perfectly balanced management team might consist of four people, each displaying one dominant trait.

He uses those letters to reduce managers and issues to basic, almost humorous, dimensions. "He's the biggest *P* you've ever seen," Adizes will argue with animation, or "He wanted to *P*, while the other guy wanted to *I*."

The other foundation of the Adizes process is his vision of

the corporation as a living, growing entity, with a life cycle similar to that of a human. In infancy, the company is innovative, fast growing. As it matures, it needs more administrators and more producers. At some point in the cycle it becomes a go-go company, run by salesmen who want market share and growth. As that stage passes, the company may enter the prime stage, where growth continues, but with better controls provided by administrators. As the administrators seize more control, however, the company begins to decline. It loses its vitality, passes through a stable period, then becomes bureaucratic. Finally, as it nears the end of the cycle, even the good administrators leave and the company operates with fewer skilled people, on its way to bankruptcy or extinction.

Looking just at BankAmerica's size, Adizes says, "I was expecting a bureaucracy." But once inside he found BankAmerica was dominated by salesmen. Instead of sitting around, drawing up manuals, thinking about details, BankAmerica's team was writing loans, making deals, aspiring to grow. "What I really found was a go-go company, only instead of a $40 million company, it was a $120 billion company." What worried Adizes was that in his studies of go-go companies he found they invariably ran into trouble by growing too rapidly and not installing sufficient controls. In a $40 million company, these excesses can lead to bankruptcy. With a $120 billion bank, confidence in the world financial system was at stake.

Adizes thought Armacost was a terrific manager, brilliant, thoughtful, decisive, courageous. As others pointed out, though, "He was the wrong general for the wrong war." Armacost was not an autocrat. He rarely gave specific directions, preferring instead to develop a broad consensus for action among his top executives. That was the wrong style for BankAmerica. The troops at a go-go company want to march; point to a hill and they will charge it; they don't appreciate subtlety. "Sam would create an environment in which the decision would be made, then he would manipulate the situation until the people made the decision by themselves," Adizes says.

BankAmerica's executives found Armacost's consensus building a frustrating, time-wasting effort. This was nothing compared to the feelings they would develop about Adizes.

The Adizes process began in the North America Division in the summer of 1983. Profits in its core business, lending to large corporations outside California, were declining. The inspiration that drove the unit during the 1970s was gone. Bank of America's calling officers were considered undertrained and poorly informed. And an annual survey of treasurers by a respected marketing research firm suggested the bank's reputation was sliding fast. More successful corporate banks, like Citicorp, Morgan, and even cross-state rival Security Pacific, were pulling away from Bank of America.

The North America Division was headed by Mont McMillen, a bank veteran who had succeeded Armacost in London. He and his staff met with Adizes for three days at the Westwood Marquis, a four-star hotel just off the campus of the University of California in Los Angeles, where Adizes teaches.

The session opened as do all Adizes meetings. Ichak explained how he felt about what he was going to do that day. Then he turned to the others in the group. One by one they answered the same question. It's a technique that Adizes calls "defreezing," and it has a single, effective point. Everyone must talk, at least once, early in the meeting. They must focus on the session, not on the work piled up back at the office. To keep everyone's attention, Adizes levies fines for lateness and for other infractions. "It sounds foolish until you're there," says one participant. "He sort of mesmerizes you. It's like mass hypnosis."

Adizes delights in creating acronyms. Virtually every part of his process is described with one. They provide a new language for discussing old problems, one of the standard gimmicks of consultants. The McMillen group was a POC, which stands for a Participative Organizational Conduit, a name no more helpful than the acronym. But the group, roughly, is a high-level team that identifies problems and suggests solutions. Each member is also in other groups and serves as the conduit for information to and from those other committees. The POC's first responsibility is to draft a list of PIPs, Potential Improvement Points, better known to most as problems.

In the three days that McMillen's group met, it defined over four hundred PIPs. Adizes filled page after page of easel paper with notes in a scrawl that was almost indecipherable. By the time the group was done, the list of problems stretched across all four walls of the conference room. Many were minor items, others were multimillion-dollar problems, but Adizes listed them all. A former colleague says at this stage Adizes is like a Talmudic scholar, intrigued with concepts but obsessed with detail. Once the problems were identified, the next step was more complex. Adizes asked the committee to categorize every problem by who in the company needed to help solve it.

This step took seven days. When it was done, McMillen had a blueprint of what was wrong with the North America Division and what he needed to make it function better. After categorizing all those problems, McMillen had two large groups: those that the North America Division could solve by itself and those that required help from other divisions. Of the four hundred problems, the division could handle only forty by itself.

In August, Mont McMillen presented his findings to the managing committee. This produced action at the top of Bank-America. In mid-October, fifteen of the company's highest ranking executives met to form the corporate POC, the top layer in the Adizes hierarchy. The process began all over again, defining PIPs, categorizing problems, looking for ways to reorganize the company. Over the next two years, this group spent weeks in meetings, discussing problems. One of the most vocal members was Lee Prussia, who pushed the bank to diversify into new businesses, especially those involving the application of computers to bank problems. Sam Armacost remained quiet most of the time, simply watching as Adizes helped him develop a consensus and build a team spirit.

Almost every unit looked for ways to speed up the Adizes process. Though the theory was fine, the day-to-day activity was drudgery. The people running BankAmerica expected a steady string of meetings—that was one of the curses of a big company—but they were also used to getting things done. And week after week, meeting after endless meeting, nothing seemed to happen.

Charles Schwab invited Adizes over to his offices for a day, apparently feeling duty-bound, since he was responsible for recommending Adizes to Armacost as a speaker for the management retreat. The session was well attended. At the end of the day, Adizes wanted to arrange a second meeting. Schwab and his team hedged, then agreed to sit down alone later and discuss the next step. When Adizes left, they voted unanimously to go it alone. "We decided that what he wanted us to do was turn over control of the company to him," said one senior officer. "We weren't interested."

Max Hopper found Adizes difficult to work with, so after roughing out a restructuring plan, Adizes let Hopper work with one of his associates, Jerry Faust, who worried less about detail and as a result helped make decisions faster. With Faust's help, BASE, another Adizes acronym, this time for BankAmerica Systems Engineering, became the first product of the Adizes process.

By the end of 1984, the Adizes process had brought forth BASE, BARE, and BAPS. BARE was BankAmerica Real Estate, a unit that combined the real estate specialists from around the company, and BAPS was BankAmerica Payment Systems, a collection of all the people who processed checks, worked on new ways to use plastic cards, and provided services to corporate bill payers. Jim Wiesler's retail bank also reorganized into Global Consumer Markets.

A spirit of enthusiasm emerged out of the long meetings. "It got people talking," said Max Hopper, "It developed more of a team spirit." Adizes sensed the confidence, as well. "I remember how we would sit down and how proud we were of ourselves, of the changes we'd made, how everything was becoming better. People were more accountable, good people were staying, morale was high," he said.

At the lower levels of BankAmerica, Ichak Adizes and his process drew derisive comments. Decisions that many thought could have taken an hour, dragged on over weeks and months, never getting resolved, never seeming to get even close to resolution. "He never understood what a joke it was to people at lower levels," says a former member of the managing committee.

But Armacost stood by Adizes. In a two-page Sam-O-Gram to senior executives in April 1985, shortly before Armacost admitted Adizes was too great a liability to keep around any longer, Armacost said that "while you do not necessarily have to be enamored of the method, you must understand it and the reasons we use it, if it is to remain an effective tool." He bragged about BASE, BAPS, and Global Consumer Markets, which he described as "successes." The heart of the message came a little later. "Implementation takes time and will require your continued commitment and dedication to getting things done the right way. As I have said before, we cannot tolerate anything less."

Outsiders, detached from the internal strife, wondered what was going on. The decisions that Armacost was reaching were neither brilliant nor inspired. They were no more exciting than something drawn up on the back of an envelope by two people during a coffee break.

The problem, they argued, was that the wrong people stayed in top jobs too long. Adizes didn't believe in firing people. "You cannot tell whether the truck is not moving because the driver is bad until you repair the truck." he said. Those comments reinforced Armacost's timidity about changing executives.

Long before the Adizes process ended, evidence was abundant that things were going wrong, vital things that needed Armacost's attention. It seemed he was spending far too much time in meetings with Adizes and not enough repairing the damage inflicted on the bank.

Chapter Nineteen

Banking is largely a matter of credit. The successful banker must be an experienced and keen credit man. Besides, he must know conditions.

A. P. Giannini, 1928

Jim Nelson was a group vice-president at Bank of America who didn't fit the mold. In a bank full of lending officers with refined selling skills, gracious manners, and controlled emotions, Nelson was a wild man. With a thick head of blond hair and a full red beard, he roared through the streets of London on a Harley-Davidson motorcycle. His laughter exploded with maniacal energy, his wry observations revealed an inherent distrust of big organizations and their executives.

Nelson had joined BankAmerica in 1977 from Citicorp. He was an expert in the Middle East, construction, and real estate, joining Bank of America as head of a unit based in London that made loans for international construction projects. When he arrived, Nelson suffered culture shock. He found that the bank was woefully behind Citicorp in all the basics of international lending. "I had to write my own credit manuals," he says. "I developed my own information system for tracking loans. The bank just didn't have anything like that, so I did it. I just thought it was normal."

By 1981 Nelson was in San Francisco, in charge of marketing for the World Banking Division, which meant deciding where and how that division should be lending. During his training at Citicorp, Nelson had absorbed that company's views and standards on credit. He decided something was terribly wrong at BankAmerica. He felt he knew how to make loans that would eventually be repaid, but he worried that few others at Bank of America had the same skill.

Nelson began arguing, passionately, that the bank was out of control. "The people on the line didn't have a clue as to what they were supposed to do," he says.

In August 1981, just four months after Sam Armacost became president of BankAmerica, Nelson prepared an analysis of the "Account Officer Problems" for his bosses at the World Banking Division. The report spent thirty-five pages arguing that Bank of America's lending officers—the ones who were making those huge loans to governments and corporations all over the world—didn't stack up to their competitors.

Nelson relied on interviews with corporate treasurers from an annual survey by Greenwich Research Associates, a highly respected market research firm. Greenwich annually samples opinions of top financial executives at the nation's biggest corporations, and the ratings change with glacial slowness, lagging behind reality by several years. What Nelson found was startling. Corporate treasurers thought Bank of America's lenders were the worst-equipped officers at the nation's five largest commercial banks. From 1976 to 1980, the bank's rating had been sliding at an alarming pace.

Nelson was frantic. Good lenders were leaving because of low pay, turnover was far too high, and training was inadequate. Yet a push was on, had been on, for the past five years to increase loans by at least 10 percent a year.

"I spent most of my time in the last two years trying to explain the severity of the situation without sounding like Chicken Little," he says. "They didn't want to hear it. And if they heard it, they didn't know what to do about it."

By late 1981 and into 1982, Nelson remembers, "I was getting pretty shrill." Within a year, he had left Bank of America in frustration.

Others saw the same thing. A senior credit examiner transferred to London in the early 1980s to clean up a problem found that, under pressure to build the loan portfolio, bank officers had begun dispersing money before all the financial analysis and documentation was complete—a classic violation of good banking practices. But that was only part of the problem. The credit officer also found inexperienced lenders, sloppy documentation, and a raft of loans that should never have been made.

The increase in loan problems supported their concern, even way back in 1981, when losses rose from $51 million the year before to $340 million, an increase of almost 700 percent. Staff memos had begun to fly in which executives tried to explain what was going wrong. Some of them asked the right questions, about the training of loan officers and the dwindling ranks of credit specialists.

In the years since 1977, Clausen and Armacost had tightened the purse strings. Money flowed to the people making loans and increasing profits, or to sexier investments in computers. One of the areas hit hardest by cost controls was the audit and examining function, the group that came along "once the barn door was open and tried to shut it." Credit administration, the unit that reviewed loans before they were made, also felt the knife. Clausen and Armacost were confident these units were doing a good job and didn't need big investments.

But the bank's lending had swollen so much that its top credit men were drowning in paperwork. Each night they would leave the bank carrying stacks of homework, new loans to review for a meeting the next day. "There was no way they could evaluate all of that material," says one sympathetic former Bank of America lender.

Moreover, the systems needed to monitor the bank's bad loans were not up to the task. During the late 1970s, national bank examiners sharply criticized the bank because when they asked for reports on problem loans the material was way out of date. No central system existed to collect information on problem loans; that data was kept at the branches. As a result of the criticism, the credit examination staff began sending out quarterly requests for information on problem loans, though most banks require monthly updates. Each office, worldwide, would compile and send back a list of problems. This was all done on paper and not until two weeks after the quarter ended did the bank have current information on its losses and loan problems.

The system was unchanged in late 1986, even though most well-run major banks had by then put their systems on computer. Max Hopper, Armacost's technology guru for three years, summed up the problem, "It had never been brought forward as a critical need of the bank."

Someone had missed the point. "The crash was inevitable by 1981. It was just a question of how severe the damage would be when it happened," says Nelson. "Management should have put the bank into a panic mode, a crash mode. Fasten your seat belts. Start behaving like the company is in trouble. Management didn't do that. As a result, the crash became that much worse when it happened."

The message that Armacost had been broadcasting since 1980 was not one of panic. He wanted innovation, he wanted boldness. He told people to produce, not to worry about the process. "I'd like us to be oriented toward getting things done, not toward how something was done or what was done," he said. The credit people heard another, subtler message. They were standing in the way of growth. In his first year at the bank, Armacost pushed for more decentralization of lending authority. Just as Clausen had, he wanted more decisions made in the field, to reduce the influence of the bureaucracy back home. In 1983 and 1984, the process continued. Says one credit specialist, "It was like the Red Guard—especially in the North America Division. There was more pressure on the loan committee than I had ever seen before."

Who was out in the field, making the decisions delegated by Armacost? The poorly trained, rapidly moving lenders that Nelson worried so much about. With each passing month they were getting more authority and more pressure to produce.

BankAmerica's problems grew steadily from 1981 to 1986. Actual losses increased from $345 million in 1981 to over $1 billion in 1984. Internal studies that year found that the bulk of the loans that went bad had been made in a surge of lending between 1978 and the end of 1980. Many of the loans never should have been made; they were simply bad credit decisions. Others were marginal loans that no one watched after they were made, as in one case where, according to a former credit officer, the bank gave away its right to collateral at a company that shortly went bankrupt. Lenders were too busy filling the demands for new loans from the head office to worry about the quality of loans made by somebody else two years earlier.

Top management responded to the deterioration with disbelief. "They saw these numbers and they simply could not believe this was happening to BankAmerica," says one former executive vice-president. Adds a former government bank examiner, "They weren't stupid. They were as bright as senior management in other places. They thought they were insulated from problems. They thought that if things got this bad, warning bells would flash and sirens would go off."

Instead, management got a sickening string of reports, each with numbers worse than the last. The steel needed to tackle these problems was missing. Pete Talbott, recruited in 1983 as a senior vice-president in retail banking, remembers attending one of his first meetings with other top executives in the division. They heard a fifteen-minute presentation on the problems in the agricultural loan portfolio, where loan problems totaled over $1 billion. "Nobody said a word, no questions, nothing," he says. "They started to move on to the next subject. I raised my hand meekly and said 'Don't those numbers just scare you to death? I've never seen anything like that in my life.' They said, no, the loans are classified [as problems]. 'That's not good, but we have a handle on it. We know where they all are.' " But they didn't know how bad the losses would be.

Many of the loan problems were inescapable. In certain industries—agriculture, real estate, shipping, and oil and gas—the change in the world economy after 1982 doomed loans to default.

In some of these industries, Bank of America felt a moral obligation to lend. "The agricultural lending business was never very profitable," says the former head of agricultural lending for the bank. "But we had to make those loans to show our commitment to the community. If you didn't make those loans, then the rest of the area, the merchants and other businessmen who borrowed from the bank, would have turned their back on us."

But BankAmerica's problems were widespread. At other banks that faced serious trouble, the losses came in one or two industries. Oil, real estate, or agriculture created the problems. At BankAmerica, however, the losses came throughout the bank. No one door had been left open. No single department nor individual was at fault. "It was not like Continental, where you could pinpoint a single source," says a former bank examiner. "Here it was diffuse."

The bank lost millions on loans to Greek shippers and Mexican brewers. It lost millions on loans to farmers in Fresno, food processors in Paraguay, and geothermal energy projects in southern California. It lost millions on pulp and paper companies in Asia, coal mines in Canada, and commercial banks in Colombia.

In retrospect, the loans appear foolish or wrongheaded. A cautious lender would have thought twice, might never have made the loans, at least not on the terms accepted by the bank, but BankAmerica was reaching for business, associating with dubious characters, allowing loan officers to take actions that showed limited understanding of the risks they were assuming.

If there was an embarrassing concentration, one that the bank never should have permitted, it was the losses in commercial real estate. In shipping, or mining, or Latin American lending, the bank could explain away the mistakes. Everyone else was making the same loans—Citicorp, Morgan, and Chase—and there was no way anyone could have foreseen the losses. In commercial real estate, that wasn't true. BankAmerica had been making such loans for decades. It knew the pitfalls and should have understood the difference between sound, established borrowers and those who represented a special risk.

Yet the losses on commercial real estate rose to more than $500 million. Many of the bad loans were made before Sam Armacost took office, but hundreds of millions more were added under his management in a reckless, uncontrolled surge of lending by a few senior officers in the North America Division.

One of the bank's most colorful losses involved a lantern-jawed, six-foot-four-inch Texan, named Melvin Lane Powers. Powers made a fortune building real estate in Houston, a town that created and broke real estate speculators overnight. But Powers was a special character, even by the tall standards set in Houston.

He first came to the world's attention as the defendant in a widely publicized society murder trial, accused, along with his aunt, of murdering her husband. Powers's aunt was Candace Mossler, a forty-five-year-old platinum blond, the mother of six children, and the wife of Jacques Mossler. Jacques had made millions in oil, then spread his money into banking and finance.

Candace grew up poor, ran away from home at fifteen, started earning money modeling shoes and toothpaste, and within a short time owned a modeling agency in New Orleans. In 1948 she met and married Mossler, her third husband. Sixteen years later, on June 30, 1964, at 1:30 A.M., Candace piled three of the couple's four adopted children into a red convertible and drove aimlessly through the streets near their house in Key Biscayne, Florida. She later explained she had been suffering from a migraine headache and stopped at a hospital emergency room.

At 4:30 A.M. she returned home and discovered the mutilated body of her husband, who had been stabbed thirty-nine times and struck on the head with a large blunt object. On the sink was a palm print, which police said matched the hand print of Mel Powers. The police also said they found a note from Jacques Mossler: "If Mel and Candace don't kill me first, I'll kill them."

The trial sketched the lurid details of Candace Mossler's personal life. Powers, only twenty-four, appeared to be her lover and the prosecution produced evidence of motel room trysts, as well as love letters in which Candace told Powers, "Darlin' I love you. I want you in my arms." Candace, an effusive individual, apparently well aware of her personal charms, dismissed the letters. "I say the same thing to my lawyer. It doesn't mean I really love him."

The defense attorney portrayed her husband as a sexual deviant, a possible homosexual who regularly picked up strangers, brought them home, and may have been slain by one of his lovers. In one of the many interviews she granted during the trial, Candace told the noted psychologist Dr. Joyce Brothers, "He [Jacques] would waltz into the house with strangers by the half-dozen. He would tell people that we were wealthy and important and owned a chain of banks and then say, 'Come on over and have a drink any time!'"

A jury eventually acquitted Mossler and Powers. She inherited a banking empire worth $33 million and he moved to Houston and quickly built a real estate construction company. Within a few years he was a multimillionaire.

Bank of America didn't get to know Melvin Powers until the mid-1970s. By then he had all the trappings of success: the largest yacht in America, 166 feet long and worth $8 million; several vacation homes including one in Aspen and two condominiums at Las Hadas, an exclusive Mexican resort; a collection of airplanes and helicopters; a Cadillac limousine and a small fleet of American-made sedans; and a half-dozen trucks.

Bank of America helped Powers build a nineteen-story office tower in a Houston suburb, on top of which he lived in a luxurious two-story penthouse. Houston's *Home and Garden Magazine* said in 1983 that his suite contained a fireplace covered in leather, enough exercise equipment to fill a small health club, and a two-story wooden sculpture. Powers began each day with a jog around his AstroTurf track and a plunge into his twenty-five-meter pool.

Most bankers are cautious people. When they see a businessman living lavishly, they grow nervous about where the money comes from—and where their money might go. Yellow lights flash. But BankAmerica had not been cautious. The company financed the building of Arena I, as the tower was called, lending Powers more than $40 million and getting a lien on his office building and penthouse in return.

In 1984, after the oil price plunge threw the Houston economy into a tailspin, Mel Powers filed for Chapter 11 protection against his creditors. At the time, he had outstanding debts of more than $420 million. By mid-1985, Powers had managed to repay $320 million and won the forbearance of his lenders, emerging from Chapter 11.

One of his unpaid loans was to Bank of America. The bank still held the mortgage on Arena I, which now represented the bulk of what was left of the Powers empire. The rest was a twin building called Arena II, which had been built with the help of another California bank, Crocker National, with a lending record as bad as that of Bank of America. Powers apparently hoped to repay both mortgages by quickly leasing the buildings, but he couldn't pull it off.

In early 1986, Bank of America seized his building. A few months later it tried to evict Powers from his penthouse for not paying rent of $129,000. In September of 1986, Powers filed a pauper's affidavit with the court, arguing that he didn't have the substance to provide a $129,000 bond. In December, Powers moved out, and Bank of America took possession of the penthouse and everything in it.

Builders more conservative than Mel Powers lost everything in the Houston real estate market in the mid-1980s. Commercial banks have the scars to prove it. But conservative lenders argue that Mel Powers was a disaster waiting to happen. Bank of America was not the only bank to lend him money, or the only bank to lose money. It's just that Bank of America seemed to find more borrowers like Mel Powers than other banks, in more markets all over the world. These were borrowers who looked good on paper, but whose character flaws might have discouraged more cautious lenders. Bank of America had a host of reasons for saying "no" to these customers. It didn't and it paid a price.

Just as dubious was a decision to lend money on Heritage Plaza, a high-rise office building in Houston constructed long after the oil price collapsed. By the time construction of the 1.2 million-square-foot building began in 1985, the downtown office market had stagnated, vacancy rates were running at over 20 percent, and rents were plummeting.

BankAmerica helped finance the $250 million project anyway. The original builders went bankrupt in 1987. Other investors took over the property, leaving BankAmerica to wait, perhaps for years to come, until the building is rented and can begin to repay the money owed the bank—money that could have been invested elsewhere in the interim.

In at least two other cases, Bank of America managed to turn small potential loan losses into whopping legal problems. In mid-1985, a California court awarded a $37 million judgment for a lawsuit by several farmers that grew out of a loan of under $2 million. And in a real estate case in Philadelphia, it cost Bank of America nearly $60 million to settle a suit involving a $39 million loan.

The first suit involved the Jewell family, which owned orchards in Sonoma County, north of San Francisco. The family had spent more than thirty years growing Gravenstein and Red Delicious apples, relying on Bank of America for money and advice. In 1976, Bank of America asked the Jewells to bail out a troubled local apple drier and the family agreed, not knowing, the family later argued in court, how badly run the company had been.

The Jewells had to borrow heavily from Bank of America to prop up the apple drier, but went along, they alleged, because they were encouraged by Bank of America's branch manager, a friend of the family. By 1980 they had a total of around $2 million outstanding from the bank. That's when the apple market was squeezed and a competing apple drier, which owed Bank of America around $20 million, ran into serious trouble. Customers of that firm, a cooperative run by the local apple growers, began to shift business to the Jewells and other independent apple driers. About then, Bank of America cut off credit to the Jewells, they charged. In January 1981 George Jewell filed for bankruptcy protection and a few months later, his son Shorty, who had been buying the ranch, also went bankrupt.

Bank of America countered that it didn't encourage the Jewells to borrow, as they had argued, but the jury sided with the family. The initial judgment for the plaintiffs came to $37 million, after which both sides appealed—the Jewells arguing the judgment was too small, the bank arguing it was too large. A California appeals court overturned the judgment in May 1988, though the Jewells planned to challenge that decision.

Another loan, in Philadelphia, cost the bank even more. Bank of America lent money for the construction of a hotel complex on Rittenhouse Square, an expensive address in center-city Philadelphia. The loan was originally made in the late 1970s for $39 million to Jack Wolgin, a Philadelphia developer, even though, Wolgin claims, he told the bank the building would cost at least $60 million. The bank, Wolgin argues, assured him more money would follow, but then it changed account officers.

Wolgin's loan fell to a young lending officer with little real estate experience. She reviewed the progress of the hotel, decided that the building could not be completed, and sought to foreclose.

Wolgin fought back. He filed suit against Bank of America for breach of contract and fraud, arguing that the lending officer didn't understand her business.

During a difficult trial, Bank of America kept control of the partially completed hotel, which turned out to be a mistake. The bank never got clear title to the building, so it refused to spend the money to seal it off. Pigeons began to roost in the ventilating systems, creating a health hazard and an expensive cleanup problem. The building had brand-new thermal windows, still carrying the original labels. After a few weeks, the lettering on the labels transferred to the glass, so the windows had to be replaced. In the first rain the building got damp; after the first freeze, marble in the lobby popped off the wall and shattered. The repairs mounted to millions of dollars.

The lawsuit went against the bank, so in 1985 it settled out of court, bringing its loss to $64 million, before it sold the building for about $18 million. As an added insult, Wolgin pursued a claim against an insurer, winning a $6 million verdict after BankAmerica waived its rights to collect.

Throughout the bank, there were pockets of losses. One of the most exotic came in Paraguay, where the bank reported a loss of $60 million. Paraguay is so remote and small that one competing banker wondered how Bank of America could have made loans of $60 million, let alone lost that much. Bank of America appears to have cornered the market there on loans to businesses that canned fruits, tanned hides, and processed other commodities. It lent to these businesses, expecting repayment once the processed goods were sold. When the commodity markets collapsed, the loans fizzled. The bank later charged that it was misled by employees, sued its own insurer to collect, and won reimbursement, though it won't say how much.

Other losses were inexplicable. In 1984, the bank rolled out a new program for consumers, a large personal line of credit backed by nothing but the borrower's signature. The bank put together an incentive system, providing bonuses to employees who added new loans. The incentive program worked like a charm; loans came pouring in.

The problem was that the credits weren't all carefully screened. Each borrower was reviewed, analyzed, and given a credit score under a standard credit scoring system. The local loan officers dutifully calculated these credit scores for almost every borrower. But instead of using the scores as intended, they seemed to ignore them. Says Pete Talbott, who headed the effort, "I don't know if they were ignoring the credit score, but they weren't using it. The branches were making $10,000 to $25,000 loans to almost anybody that walked in the door." The snafu cost the bank millions of dollars in loan losses.

Also hard to explain were the losses in the bank's "private banking" unit. In the early 1980s, private banking was a fad among commercial bankers. The banks created special units that catered to the whims of the wealthy, meeting them at their homes or in special bank offices, providing special personal services. To head the marketing effort, the bank recruited John Farnsworth from Chemical Bank. Farnsworth built a strong program. "The private banking system probably outdid any other program on the West Coast," says an admiring former Bank of America executive. But in the midst of a drive to lend money to these customers, weaknesses in the credit staff appeared. The bank transferred private banking's credit officer and began looking for a successor. It took almost six months to find a replacement. Meanwhile, Farnsworth got specific instructions: Don't stop the flow of loans and don't worry about the credit judgments; that is not your job.

An uncomfortably large percentage of the loans made in that period eventually went bad. But the problems, at least $18 million of questionable debt, didn't surface until early 1986 when the bank finally brought in a new team of auditors and credit examiners, who scrutinized the retail loan portfolio. By then, private banking had a new credit officer. But the bad loans were already on the books. It was too late. The disaster that Jim Nelson had foreseen was a reality.

Chapter Twenty

The long established policy of the bank of "sitting tight". . . particularly with regard to controversies . . . actual or threatened, has . . . proven most safe and advantageous in our case.

A. P. Giannini, 1914

The events that finally forced Sam Armacost to face BankAmerica's loan problems began in Chicago, in the headquarters of Continental Illinois Corp., a hulking granite skyscraper that consumes an entire block of downtown Chicago and is a monument to the wrongheadedness of bank regulation.

When Armacost was named president of BankAmerica in 1981, Continental Illinois was considered one of the best-run banking companies in America. It wasn't as big as Bank of America, but then it was hemmed in by regulation. In Illinois, independent bankers had long ago banded together to inhibit the kind of aggressive banking practiced by A. P. Giannini. Illinois didn't allow branch banking. In fact, in 1981, the state allowed only one location per bank.

That made life more difficult for Chicago's biggest banks. Unlike banks in New York and California, which were free to gather deposits anywhere in the state, Continental and other big Chicago banks bought money from large investors—corporate treasurers, money fund managers, insurance companies. The banks issued large certificates of deposit, borrowed in the Euromarket, and sold commercial paper. But despite the restrictions, they grew. In 1981, Continental Illinois was the nation's sixth largest commercial bank and rival First Chicago was the nation's tenth largest.

Continental's huge physical headquarters is, oddly enough,

199

symbolic of those restraints. The bank built a massive business on a tiny foundation. Unlike BankAmerica, which was built on millions of small accounts in hundreds of branches, Continental Illinois was a bank with little local business and few deposits from consumers. A bank is only as safe as its foundations, and in 1982 word began to leak out that Continental was dangerously weak.

Public disclosures of the troubles came in mid-1982, after Penn Square collapsed, leaving Continental's management with more than $1 billion in bad loans bought from the tiny storefront Oklahoma lender. Continental argued that the Penn Square loans were an aberration, a pocket of bad business in a loan portfolio of otherwise very high quality.

Bankers knew better. In the late 1970s Continental had set off on a lending binge. It already had solid relationships with many of the biggest and best-known oil companies; now it went after the smaller companies, offering interest rates one or two percentage points below competitors and using generous assumptions on the value of oil reserves hidden under the ground.

It rushed in where others feared to lend. Knowing that big corporations rarely change banks, Continental reasoned that the best time to gain a new account was when a company was in trouble. Within days of the nuclear accident at Three Mile Island, near Harrisburg, Pennsylvania, Continental Illinois was there offering to lend money to its owner, General Public Utilities. When Firestone Tire and Rubber Co. lost money because of foreign competition, Continental was there. Almost anywhere there was an eager borrower, in Latin America, in Europe, in the United States, Continental Illinois was on the spot.

The collapse of Penn Square crippled Continental by making it hard for the big bank to raise money. Corporations and other large depositors, like money market mutual funds, lost faith. Some closed accounts, but most simply scaled back their relationship. New deposits went to other banks, and the money that stayed switched to deposits of shorter maturities, so that if a crisis struck, corporate treasurers could pull their money within a few days.

By early 1984, Continental Illinois maintained a precarious balance in the markets. It raised enough deposits each day to replace the money leaving the bank, but it had to pay a premium— as much as two percentage points above the rates paid by other banks—in order to keep the money rolling in.

Then the rumors began. In the first week of May, word spread that Continental Illinois was about to go bankrupt. The rumors became so virulent that a Reuters reporter asked management about them. When Reuters printed the denial, it only fueled speculation. In Japan, then in Europe, panic spread. Institutional depositors began to freeze out Continental Illinois.

On May 10, Todd Conover, Comptroller of the Currency, denied reports that the big Chicago bank was failing. He took the unprecedented step of guaranteeing that the government would protect all the depositors of any of the ten largest banks. But even then, the run didn't stop. Within hours Continental borrowed $4 billion from the Federal Reserve to cover the deposit drain. Over the next few days a group of fourteen banks arranged a "safety net," a $4.5 billion line of credit that Continental could use to cover the loss of its deposits. A few days later the banks increased their line to $5.5 billion, with twenty-eight banks participating.

Continental announced it was looking for a merger partner, but it was too big and too troubled to be bought. On July 25 the Federal Deposit Insurance Corp. seized control of Continental Illinois. It acquired 80 percent of the company's stock, leaving the remaining 20 percent with the public, but under the terms of a bailout that almost assured shareholders would lose their entire investments.

The reverberations from Continental's collapse spread throughout the banking industry. At one point a run began at Manufacturers Hanover Trust Co., the nation's fourth largest bank, which had serious loan problems, including a surprisingly large pocket of loans to Argentina. Other banks and financial institutions with shaky balance sheets felt the pain as depositors demanded higher interest rates to calm their jittery nerves.

The most far-reaching effects of Continental's fall came at the Office of the Comptroller of the Currency. In the days following the Continental Illinois takeover (in effect, the nationalization of a bank) fingers pointed at the agency, which had the primary responsibility for watching over Continental Illinois. The Comptroller had believed, as had so many outsiders, that big banks, with their well-trained, highly paid executives had an edge over the examiners. If a dispute arose, the Comptroller's staff tended to knuckle under.

Not any more.

In the aftermath of the nationalization of Continental Illinois, a new spirit of vigilance filled the Comptroller's office. "For a long time the big banks were held pretty much in awe," says Michael Patriarca, former Deputy Comptroller for Multinational Banking, "They had MBAs everywhere, they had people who earned five or ten times what the examiners earned. This created an arrogance, a sense of 'Who are you, you government clerks, to come in here and tell me how to do this?' Unfortunately, the bankers proved that they are not so goddam smart after all. After Continental Illinois, the whole relationship changed. We realized after all that examiners are not so stupid and bankers are not so smart." (Patriarca refused to discuss BankAmerica specifically.)

The Comptroller's office also changed its approach to auditing big banks. Instead of flying in once a year with a team of examiners, the agency kept men on site all year round. "We learned that a lot can go wrong in twelve months," says Patriarca.

Armed with renewed skepticism, bank examiners began to take big bankers to task in 1984. One of the victims was Bank of America.

A full review was begun in the spring. By mid-year, the preliminary results had been sent to management. The result, says one former board member, was "a scathing report."

"They hit all the right points," says a former senior vice-president, "but often for the wrong reasons."

Most directors bore the criticism in silence, but Robert McNamara, the former Secretary of Defense, launched an attack. After the regulators forced the bank to add to the reserve against possible loan losses in the second quarter, McNamara complained that he didn't like learning about the condition of the bank from examiners. Later McNamara suggested that Armacost could use help, that he needed a chief operating officer. A former BankAmerica executive who heard McNamara make that suggestion twice at board sessions in 1984, says that each time, "The room went totally silent. No one else spoke." Then Armacost would deflect the question and the board would move on.

Armacost took the Comptroller's reports as a personal affront. What seemed to irritate him most was that the Comptroller's office wrote two separate reviews. The first one, developed by the examiners in San Francisco, included a few pats on the back and was only mildly critical. The second was harsh, incorporating changes made after the local staff finished its review and sent its conclusions to Washington, where senior regulators, comparing the BankAmerica report to others from large banks, cut out many positive comments and intensified the negatives.

Armacost turned petulant. The arrogance that emerged back in the early 1960s when working on the Bougainville loan surfaced once more. "The message from Sam was 'I'm not going to allow Washington to run this bank!' " says a member of his managing committee. "He decided to take the bastards on."

Armacost challenged the examiners on almost every point. Instead of responding cordially, taking a cooperative attitude, he treated the report as an unjust attack. He and Prussia sat in long meetings with the examiners in which they argued and bullied, trying to soften the report's conclusions. Across the table sat Patriarca, for whom Armacost made no attempt to disguise his contempt. Patriarca stiffened. "The two personalities clashed almost immediately. That made it more difficult," says one person who attended several meetings.

But the personality clash was only a minor part of the problem. Armacost had decided that the Comptroller's office was off-base, that it had singled out Bank of America for unusually harsh treatment. The rest of Bank of America's top executives shared the sentiment, though they urged him to cooperate. "They needed to make an example of us after Continental Illinois," said a former member of the managing committee.

The examiners didn't see it that way. "We couldn't believe what we were finding," says one. "Everyone bent over backwards because of who we were dealing with." The deeper the examiners dug, the worse it got.

The examiners worried most about the bank's loan problems. The bad loans were growing too rapidly, the loan loss reserve was not large enough. The bank's computer systems were in disarray. Many of the basic systems for gathering information were antiquated.

For every commercial bank, regulators develop what they call a CAMEL rating. The rating is granted on a five-point scale, with one being highest and five lowest. The letters of the acronym stand for *C*apital Adequacy, *A*sset Quality, *M*anagement, *E*arnings, and *L*iquidity. (Liquidity is the ability to pay off depositors quickly, either by raising deposits elsewhere or by selling short-term investments.) Regulators don't disclose CAMEL ratings, even to the banks they have rated, but bankers get a sense of their rating from the language in examination reports and the actions regulators take.

If the regulators are displeased, management hears about it. The examiners review their findings with top executives, listing problems and discussing ways to improve the bank's condition. Then the examiners present the material to the board of directors. A rating of 1, 2, or 3 under the CAMEL system is a passing grade. (Before 1984, insiders figure, Bank of America probably had a 2 rating, and a downgrading of one notch to 3 was thought likely.) If the rating drops to 4, the regulators almost automatically ask the management and the board to sign a letter of agreement, which lays out exactly what the Comptroller's office expects from the bank. The examiners sometimes request a similar letter from a bank on the low end of the 3 rating. This letter is the mildest enforcement action the Comptroller can take against a bank, next to a private tongue-lashing. If the bank fails to comply, the Comptroller can file a cease and desist order, begin levying civil fines, and eventually go to court.

In November of 1984, after Armacost got tough with the Comptroller's office, Bank of America announced it had signed a letter of agreement with the Comptroller's office that required the bank to raise its primary capital—a combination of equity capital, the loan loss reserve, and debt that can be converted into equity—to 6 percent of assets by the end of 1986. (At the end of 1984, primary capital stood at 5.85 percent of assets.)

The bank also agreed to study the adequacy of its loan loss reserve and to improve the job it was doing managing problem loans.

Buried as a footnote to the Comptroller's agreement was a vague reference to a fouled computer system in the bank's securities trading operation. Compared with the bank's loan problems, a computer snarl seemed an inconsequential event. But within a tiny circle of Bank of America watchers, the event held special significance. As these former officers watched from a distance, they noticed a troubling pattern. Obviously, the bank's profits were falling and, as they knew from sources inside the bank, the profits always fell far short of the projections by management. Now in bank outposts around the world, in tiny enclaves of the empire, things seemed to be going wrong with increasing frequency. This added to their dismay. It was nothing they could put their finger on, nothing certain, but they had begun to sense that, as one put it, the wheels were falling off.

The computer snarl that worried the Comptroller's examiners was hushed up as tightly as possible, because it involved one of Bank of America's most vital computer systems. Almost a year earlier, the system had failed, leaving billions of dollars of tangled securities sales. The system was the heart of what the bank calls its BankAmerica Investment Securities Division (BISD). Through that unit, housed in New York and San Francisco, pumped billions of dollars of securities purchases and sales every day.

In late 1983, Bank of America was preparing to install a new computer system for handling the heavy volume flooding through BISD. It was a simple computer conversion, but it required Bank of America to switch to new accounting and bookkeeping systems. Many other banks had converted to this system with success, so after a short experiment, the bank switched over entirely. The new system worked, but not perfectly. Thousands of transactions were improperly recorded, so that the bank might know it had bought $1 million of municipal bonds, but it couldn't be sure where it bought the securities—whether from another unit of Bank of America or from an outsider.

The installation had been botched. Instead of running the new system and the old system in parallel until all the bugs were worked out, executives had switched directly to the new system without any backup.

Only a small percentage of the system's total trades got snarled, but the bank couldn't tell which were good and which were bad. Teams of auditors were flown in from San Francisco to sort out the paperwork, trying to reconcile the orders for buying and selling securities.

By the time the Comptroller's office came in to review the problem in 1984, Bank of America's audit staff was already in the midst of the cleanup, which took months to complete. The auditors had to sort through all the transactions by hand, checking both sides of every trade.

In the process, the morale of the bank's audit staff plunged. Not only did they need to review transactions done before they arrived, but BISD kept adding new transactions. Unable to shut off the flow of business entirely, the bank continued to make trades, but at a slower pace, and the unit's managers, ignoring advice from higher up, regularly made exceptions to the slowdown if they thought they could get a higher profit.

The failure created huge risks. "If somebody had missed a dividend or interest payment, there was no way for us to know," says a former insider, "unless somebody sat down with a card file and checked every transaction."

"We were very lucky that word never leaked out," says one of the specialists charged with cleaning up the mess. "There was no telling what might have happened if the street had known we couldn't handle our transactions." In the end, the mistakes involving outsiders—money inadvertently paid to the wrong customers or customers never properly billed—turned out to be minimal and the losses were minor.

The dollar amount wasn't important, but the loss of control was. Other systems were crashing too. The bank switched to a new system for sending out statements to corporate clients, which also failed. A system for trading foreign exchange collapsed and traders ended up working on notepads for weeks while the new snarl was cleaned up. At another trust unit in New York, the bank's mutual fund unit grew overburdened with business and paperwork, worrying management.

None of these events was catastrophic. Minor dislocations happen in a big company. Rarely, though, do the errors occur in such bunches. The trend was symptomatic of a loss of management control more frightening than the events themselves, made even more ominous by Armacost's resistance to firing any of the senior executives responsible for the foul-ups.

Chapter Twenty-one

There is only one way to do a thing, and that is the honest, fair, and straightforward way. Everybody likes a square deal, and it doesn't take really worthwhile folks long to distinguish the wheat from the chaff.

A. P. Giannini, 1927

Among the mistakes that Sam Armacost made in his five years as president of BankAmerica, none came at a more inopportune moment than his attempt in late 1984 and early 1985 to hush up an embarrassing $95 million problem at a single branch of Bank of America in Inglewood, a suburb of Los Angeles.

Compared with the bank's critical problems—falling profits, mountains of bad loans, angry confrontations with the Comptroller, even the snarl in handling securities—this scandal should have passed as an inconsequential glitch. Instead, it became a focus of concern for board members and a public reminder of what was wrong at Bank of America.

This nightmare began in October 1984. The bank got a call from Seamen's Bank for Savings in New York City, which was having trouble collecting interest on a $19.5 million investment in mortgage-backed securities. Since Bank of America was the trustee and escrow agent for the notes, Seamen's thought the bank might be able to speed up collection.

The phone call triggered an investigation by Bank of America's legal and financial staff that lasted more than six months. The bank slowly uncovered an elaborate mortgage scheme, masterminded by a small group of businessmen that included two felons. The trail led through worthless insurance companies, highly inflated real estate appraisals, and bogus financial statements, which the men had used to raise millions of dollars from unsuspecting investors.

Bank of America's branch in Inglewood had become a willing, if unwitting, accomplice in this scheme. Responding to Armacost's encouragement to "think it, try it, fix it," a few officers in Inglewood did just that. Using a little initiative, they agreed to place Bank of America's name, as trustee and escrow agent, behind more than $133 million of mortgage-backed securities. In the end, the securities proved to be nearly worthless. The bank's protection—the insurance companies that backed the paper—proved bankrupt. Bank of America ended up on the hook for $95 million.

What shocked outsiders was that Bank of America's staff had either criminally or negligently failed to check the collateral on many of these loans. As trustee and escrow agent, that was part of its job. In one instance, a 310-unit apartment house in northwest Houston was so run-down no one could live there. The swimming pool—Olympic-sized—was filled with mud and debris and the rest of the property lay vandalized and vacant.

Fraud losses happen often at big commercial banks, which are regular targets for con men and speculators. Almost every major commercial bank has suffered at least one or two scandals. But Sam Armacost didn't need this embarrassment right now. Bank of America had just signed its accord with the Comptroller; its overhang of problem loans seemed to swell each day; McNamara and other board members were expressing open concern. And now there was more evidence that the bank was slipping out of control. If just one branch could lose $95 million in a matter of months, what was happening at other branches? Just how deep did the problems run?

Within the bank the trouble in Inglewood quickly became known as the NMEC (pronounced NEE-meck) scandal, after the initials of National Mortgage Equity Corp., the company at the center of the controversy. NMEC created mortgage-backed securities. It found mortgages, bundled them together, and then sold securities to investors, who expected to be paid as NMEC collected on the mortgages.

BankAmerica's problems involved three entities: NMEC, which created the mortgage securities; Glacier Assurance Co., in Missoula, Montana, which insured those securities; and a group of companies, controlled by Kent R. Rogers, that borrowed heavily from NMEC, bought properties from Glacier, and, later, opened an insurance company that guaranteed repayment of NMEC securities. Rogers had been convicted of bankruptcy fraud in 1982. An officer of NMEC, David A. Feldman, had been convicted of mail and wire fraud against his employer, Merrill Lynch & Co., in the same year.

The story of the NMEC scheme began in 1982 with Glacier Assurance. A start-up company run by a sixty-year-old California businessman, Glacier had gotten into trouble early in life. It had only one major customer, Sierra Realty and Investment Co., and when Sierra went bankrupt, Glacier lost heavily. Of $56 million in insurance that Glacier wrote through mid-1982, $42 million went to guarantee the repayment of securities created by Sierra. By the end of the summer of 1982 virtually every loan from Sierra Realty insured by Glacier was in default, leaving Glacier facing $45 million in claims, even though the insurance company had collected only $2 million in premiums with which to cover its losses.

Glacier should have disappeared, but was rescued by NMEC, a joint venture of Feldman, the former employee of Merrill Lynch, and a cousin. NMEC had been in business for just two years, and it was not doing well. Insurance companies refused to guarantee its mortgage securities because they didn't like the quality of NMEC's mortgages. In order to stay in business, NMEC had to find a more open-minded insurer. Where better to find reasonable men than at a company with one foot in the grave?

The mutual needs of National Mortgage and Glacier, Bank-America's investigators later decided, gave birth to an elaborate Ponzi scheme—a sort of financial pyramid in which money raised from later investors is used to pay off early investors. NMEC agreed to buy some of Glacier's bankrupt properties. Where did it get the money? It sold securities to investors. Where did it get the insurance that had proved so elusive just weeks before? From Glacier.

The first hitch developed when NMEC had to pay interest on its securities. The mortgages it had bought from Glacier were not being paid on time or were in default. So to pay interest on the first securities, NMEC sold a second round of securities.

This scheme should have quickly collapsed, but for more than two years Glacier and NMEC kept afloat by steadily increasing the reported value of their real estate—and borrowing more and more money against it. Between 1983 and 1984, Glacier guaranteed $92.6 million of securities created by NMEC.

This was about when the scheme was joined by Kent Rogers, a muscular, young entrepreneur with a family of companies doing insurance and real estate work. Rogers was busy arranging real estate tax shelters for private investors. He needed insurance and found a helpful insurer in Glacier. It agreed to back his securities and he, in turn, bought real estate from Glacier.

Over the next three years, Rogers borrowed nearly $49 million through NMEC on close to a thousand loans. Another of his companies, Pacific American Insurance Co., guaranteed the repayment of securities that NMEC was selling to investors. Some of Rogers's borrowing ostensibly went to finance improvements on his property, which were never made, as at the vacant Houston apartment building.

After 1982, the trustee and escrow agent for NMEC's securities was BankAmerica's Inglewood branch. Normally, the trustee's role in a securities transaction is a paper-shuffling function, making sure that all the documents are on hand, ascertaining that everyone is dealing in good faith, and seeing to it that checks get delivered on time. But as trustee and escrow agent, BankAmerica was doing a little more than these functions implied. It was, in effect, assuring that the collateral behind the mortgages was solid.

However, because the volume of trust and escrow business moving through the Inglewood branch was so high, its staff took appraisal reports at face value.

By the time BankAmerica began to investigate, the NMEC scheme had whirled completely out of control. There was virtually no collateral to back up the securities that BankAmerica had indirectly guaranteed. At first, the legal staff responded coolly. The bank was not at fault for any losses; its only obligation was to protect its good name by buying back the securities.

In October of 1984, long before the details of the tangled mortgage scheme were clear, BankAmerica called together representatives of the nineteen financial institutions that had bought NMEC's securities. It offered to buy back their $133 million of securities for fifty cents on the dollar. The idea didn't fly. The representatives began to discuss lawsuits and criminal charges. BankAmerica's legal and financial representatives huddled and came to a discomforting conclusion. After reviewing the escrow and trust documents, they decided BankAmerica was liable for a lot more than a few cents on the dollar. It might be liable for the full value of the securities.

In late October, the bank bought back the NMEC securities at one hundred cents on the dollar. A task force involving dozens of bank employees began sifting through the mountains of material related to the mortgages to determine just how bad the damage might be.

By late November, the task force thought it had a fix on the losses. Though the real estate was turning out to be worth less than its face value, the insurance on the securities appeared to cover the bank. As BankAmerica's board of directors sat down for their December board meeting, Sam Armacost knew he faced a loss, but he didn't know how large it would be.

"Most successful corporate presidents that I know of," says a former BankAmerica executive, "remain successful because they share information with the board. They like to be a little pessimistic even, so that the board doesn't have any negative surprises. Sam's bias was to tell the board as little as he could."

The board was already upset about the lack of information coming from Armacost. McNamara was the only one speaking out at board meetings, but other directors grumbled about being kept in the dark.

Armacost tended to be secretive. He seldom informed aides of all his plans, doling out information carefully. He hadn't even told the board about buying Schwab & Co. until after it was in the newspapers. He had kept the securities computer snarl quiet and he had hushed up several other operating problems.

Now he opted not to tell the full board about the NMEC scandal. He gave some details to the auditing and examining committee, but glossed over the problem.

At the December board meeting, the task force still believed that the losses on the mortgages would be minor, not more than $10 or $15 million. But as December passed into January, the bank got more bad news. The task force discovered that one of the insurance companies, Pacific American, faced a lawsuit—brought on Bank of America's behalf—regarding its refusal to honor insurance on four mortgaged properties.

Bank of America's board did not have a scheduled meeting in January and Armacost decided not to call the directors with information about the deepening loss on NMEC.

In early January the task force determined that the losses would run more than $20 million. On January 21, when the company announced its fourth-quarter profits, the news announcement included a cryptic mention of a $27 million special charge against earnings in the fourth quarter. There was no explanation, no more detail. Sam Armacost overrode the advice of aides and decided to give out minimal information.

The news release set off a frenzied search by the press for details. Stories quickly appeared in the *Wall Street Journal* and local papers. For days the bank was besieged with calls and criticisms for mishandling the announcement of the reserve and for attempting to cover up what was happening inside the bank.

For Armacost the problems of the NMEC scandal were only beginning. His decision not to brief the board in December put him in an awkward spot. Many of the board members learned of the special reserve in the newspapers and were sputtering with indignation.

At the February board meeting, Armacost once again glossed over details, but provoked no cries of outrage from the board. He described the mortgage problem, mentioned what the task force had found, and then suggested that the $27 million charge would be sufficient to cover all losses. Armacost was either being optimistic or lying to the board. Charles Schwab, who was already a critic of Armacost, had picked up rumors through the bank grapevine that the $27 million figure was too low: the task force had finally caught up with Glacier and Pacific American, and found nothing but a black hole. Suspecting the rumors were true, Schwab asked Armacost whether there was any chance that the bank might lose more than $27 million. Faced with a direct question, Armacost acknowledged that there was some risk that the loss might be higher—but once again, except for Schwab and McNamara, the board seemed to miss or ignore the omission.

Three days later, Armacost announced that the reserve needed to be more than tripled, to $95 million.

These events did not disturb the remarkable quiet at the February board meeting. McNamara, Schwab, and at least three other directors—Najeeb Halaby, sixty-nine, the former chairman of Pan Am; Walter Haas, also sixty-nine, retired head of

Levi Strauss; and Dick Cooley, sixty-one, head of Seafirst—had misgivings about Armacost, based on all the evidence suggesting the company was out of control. But there were others on the board who argued that Armacost was handling events properly. Two of the most important were Thomas McDaniel, sixty-eight, former president of Southern California Edison and the chairman of the audit and examining committee, and Franklin Murphy, sixty-nine, former president of UCLA and now head of the executive committee at Times Mirror. McDaniel quieted the discontent at the audit and examining committee over Armacost's tardiness in giving information to the board, while Murphy championed Armacost's cause with the full board.

In this atmosphere of eerie calm, the board in February voted itself a raise, a $250 increase in daily expense allowances, which raised the per diem of each director to $750. Over the course of the next twelve months, that would amount to about $4,800 per director, or an increase of around 20 percent in their compensation.

On March 1, BankAmerica announced that it had fired five employees, including a senior vice-president. The bank also announced that it would pursue two lawsuits. The first was a standard suit, seeking payment from the companies that had insured or created the bogus securities.

The second was against BankAmerica's fired employees, charging negligence and seeking payment from BankAmerica's insurance company under the bank's directors and officers liability insurance. The suit attempted to stretch the coverage of directors and officers insurance to cover hundreds of officers at a bank, even though, traditionally, such policies cover only a handful of senior executives, those in danger of suits from irate shareholders.

It was, in the overly dramatic language of the legal profession, "a proactive strike," a decision, like the beginning of a nuclear war, in which one side hopes to gain an advantage by attacking first, knowing it will incur tremendous damage—in this case at least the loss of its insurance—even if its suit is successful.

BankAmerica's board almost immediately felt the pain of retaliation. BankAmerica's insurers, Employers Insurance of Wasau and First State Insurance Co., of Boston, canceled the policies that covered the company's directors and officers. At a moment when BankAmerica Corp. was drowning in problem loans, suffering from steadily falling profits, and just starting a legal battle over the negligence of its employees, the directors had to go naked, to make reasonable businesslike decisions, all the while risking their entire net worth.

The discussion at the next board meeting was "animated," as one participant remembers. For the first time, members of the board other than McNamara expressed strong concerns. This time, Armacost's actions had struck home, costing the board its insurance. John Beckett, the former chairman of Transamerica Corp., a strong-willed, mercurial man who peers out from behind thick glasses that give him an owlish look, spoke up loudly, as did McNamara and others.

With a deftness that was becoming expected, Armacost diffused the issue. Using the speaking skills that had helped catapult him to the presidency, Armacost outlined a program of self-insurance. BankAmerica would invest $40 million in an insurance subsidiary in the Bahamas, which would then provide $50 million of coverage to the board, enough to protect against all but the most devastating legal judgments. Armacost's parry and thrust left dissenters on the board in a quiet minority. No one else seemed disturbed that $40 million of shareholders' money was at risk. All that mattered, it appeared, was that the directors were protected.

Chapter Twenty-two

Apparently the guiding principle of the bank's present leadership is that banking is no longer a people's business, but a private arena for the power plays of the few who are more and more reluctant to be held accountable for their actions.

Claire Giannini Hoffman, 1985

O ther executives marveled at BankAmerica's board. Despite four years of declining profits the directors stuck by Armacost with world-class obstinance. Outsiders gave the credit to Armacost. Says one investment banker, "Sam was superb at managing the board of directors."

Armacost continued to have help from board members such as Franklin Murphy, chairman of the executive committee at Times Mirror, the publisher of the *Los Angeles Times*, who regularly reminded the directors that he and the board at Ford Motor Co. had stuck with Donald Peterson, its chairman, through five rough years. In the end, Ford emerged as the most competitive car company in America.

Armacost was also helped by the desire of many directors not to rock the boat. Of "The Over-the-Hill Gang," five members, including Murphy, planned to retire in 1986 because they were almost seventy years old, the mandatory retirement age. One captured their thinking when he declared, "There'll be no changes on my watch."

All but a few directors may simply have been lost in the world of commercial banking. McNamara, because of his stint at the World Bank; Andrew Brimmer, who had once been a governor of the Federal Reserve; Roy Ash, who had once been an accountant at Bank of America; and John R. Beckett, who ran an

215

insurance company, understood the financial statements well. The other directors had run manufacturing companies. Every few months the financial staff would trot in to explain the difference between a loan loss provision, the loan reserve, and a loan write-off, but some directors never quite seemed to get the hang of it.

This was not unusual for major corporations. A few hours a month these men dealt seriously with the problems of Bank-America. The rest of the time they relied on the chief executive, whom they had chosen to run day-to-day affairs.

Armacost fed these men a steady diet of reports on the bank's progress, always reflecting his own, optimistic bias. In December 1984, he produced a revised strategy for the bank. A persuasive study, it was a modification, a polishing, of plans the directors had seen before.

In the four years since Armacost had become president, the bank's strategy had slowly evolved. Both Boston Consulting Group and Adizes were still at work in 1984, which meant almost every unit of the bank had been refining BCG's work while simultaneously reorganizing.

Armacost's road map was clearer now, sharpened by the company's shortage of capital. BankAmerica could no longer afford to be all things to all people. Nationwide expansion was out, as was retail and small business lending overseas.

BankAmerica would become a large, regional bank with a small number of overseas offices. It would concentrate on serving consumers and small businesses in the western United States. It would pursue only those large corporate customers who did enough business with the bank to generate a clear profit for the bank.

That was the message to the board, delivered carefully and emphatically. The strategy was unarguably solid, but it was a long way from reality. The document on which Armacost briefed the board came from one or two trusted lieutenants, led by Steve McLin. McLin appeared to be growing closer to Armacost, his name regularly appeared in the press, making him an unofficial spokesman for Armacost and earning him the distrust of many in the bank, especially on the retail side, where he was often perceived as one of the enemy.

The rest of senior management was in the dark about Armacost's strategy, or only slowly gaining insight. Adizes and many top executives were still operating under the old vision of BankAmerica. As Armacost spoke to the board, Jim Wiesler, now a vice-chairman and still head of the retail bank, was drawing up a list of properties he hoped to buy overseas. A careful plan for nationwide expansion into retail and small business lending was still very much alive. Max Hopper, Armacost's technology expert, planned to announce that BankAmerica would spend at least $5 billion to improve its computer systems over the next few years. And overseas the bank was still courting any corporate customer that walked and talked. Even McLin was still thinking growth. He had struck a deal to buy troubled Orbanco Corp., Oregon's largest bank holding company, and applied to open twelve small consumer banks in other states.

This dichotomy between plans and action was largely out of the board's sight. The plans sounded good and the directors wanted to believe in Armacost. When they asked tough questions, which was rare, Armacost answered knowledgeably. He understood the problem, had thought it through, and was working on a solution.

Armacost's answers left an indelible impression. They were fluent, persuasive responses. But almost no one remembers anything memorable that Armacost said. His persuasive ability is captured in these excerpts from an unpublished interview with *Fortune* in the spring of 1985, in which he parried questions as deftly as at board meetings:

Why isn't the bank laying off people?
We just laid off eighty people in Hong Kong. We've done it quietly. . . . We've been able to use attrition along with a much more rigid performance appraisal process to get most of the job done. It's pretty impressive in terms of the people taken out of the [branches]. . . .

I can cut my costs. I can lay off 10,000 people tomorrow. But who's going to process the work? I don't have my technology yet in place to stand in their stead. Why should I be frantic about destroying a lot of inherently good parts of the cultural values of this company to achieve some short-term gains, to destroy my quality of service, to drive most of my customers away?

When will profits improve?
The big driver at the moment is credit quality. There is a pill one can take for that, but it's a disaster pill and it's not worth taking. If you're an industrial company, you see these guys, they do $700–800 million write-offs of obsolete plants. They hammer a year and then move on.

You don't do that to a loan portfolio at a financial institution. There is a grave risk that it will be misunderstood by the public. They don't like banks to take these gigantic write-offs. It's a precarious part of being a highly leveraged institution requiring a lot of public confidence.

What about the bank's future profits?
The company has so much fundamental earnings power, but it can only be captured over the long term. There is no sixty-to-ninety-day wonder pill you can take to get rid of $6–7 billion of old mortgages. If we didn't have [the] Wellenkamp [decision] we'd have rolled through most of those old mortgages or at least another couple of billion, which is another $2 billion you could not put back in the marketplace.

Why was the Comptroller's office so tough on the bank?
We were chosen as a target vehicle for making a statement and the statement has been made. . . . We want to get rid of the Comptroller as an issue in our lives.

One director unimpressed by Sam Armacost was Claire Giannini Hoffman. Since 1949, Claire Hoffman had held her father's seat on the board at BankAmerica. In 1974, when she turned seventy, the mandatory retirement age, she had become an honorary director.

Claire Hoffman had kept a vigil for more than thirty years. She fought for and protected the ideals of her father. In her eyes, though, she was losing ground, the battle was getting tougher all the time. Since the 1960s, when Rudolph Peterson became president, Claire Hoffman worried about the shift away from her father's vision, a drift away from serving the little people, a loss of values. Those on the fortieth floor dismissed Claire Hoffman as a crackpot, someone with quaint, old-fashioned ideas. But to many in the ranks, those who believed in the genius of A. P. Giannini, Claire Hoffman was the keeper of the flame.

On March 7, 1985, Claire Hoffman resigned from the board of BankAmerica, making front-page news in Los Angeles and San Francisco. Her decision was a milestone in the company's history. For the first time since the founding of the Bank of Italy, the Giannini family had severed its ties with management.

Claire did not leave in silence. "It's just killing me to see what they are doing with that bank," she said in the weeks that followed. "They are ruining the foundation. They've stopped all of the things that made us great."

What triggered her resignation was the board's decision to sell BankAmerica's headquarters, the tower of carnelian marble. To the board, the sale was simply a financial transaction, not something it wanted to do, but a necessary evil. If the Comptroller demanded more capital, this was one quick way to get it. To Claire Hoffman the sale was the violation of her father's memory. She saw the tower as a monument to the genius of A. P. Giannini, a symbol of the enduring values of the bank. Selling the building was like selling her birthright. "This is an appalling decision," she said, "truly unpardonable particularly for a bank that chose to honor the memory of its founder by naming the large [square] that surrounds its magnificent fifty-two-story tower the A. P. Giannini Plaza."

Claire Giannini understood the economics of the sale of the Bank of America building. She understood that management was looking for a quick fix for its earnings problems at the expense of the future. After it sold the building, BankAmerica would lease back its office space, trading today's profit for a stream of expenses paid out over decades.

At eighty, in 1985, Claire Hoffman was still an imposing presence. Her face is a mirror of her personality, strong, sharply etched features, heavy dark eyebrows, gray hair pulled back in a bun, and the unmistakable, strong profile of an Italian American. Since the mid-1950s, when her husband died, Claire Hoffman has lived alone in Seven Oaks, the home that A. P. Giannini bought for his family in the year before Claire was born. It is a large, two-story house in a modified

Tudor style that sits in downtown San Mateo, a twenty-minute drive south of San Francisco. Just a few blocks off the main commercial drag, the El Camino Real, the house is now nearly overwhelmed by apartment buildings and commercial properties—another sign of the times.

What Claire Giannini regretted most was the disappearance of the family spirit at BankAmerica. She had grown up as a part of Bank of America. It was not simply a company, it was the center of her family's life. She was born in the same year that the Bank of Italy was established, and as she grew, her father immersed himself in the affairs of his company. He would rise early, work long hours, and return home to ruminate about the future. On occasion he would fall asleep over his meal. Throughout her life, from the time she was a child, Claire traveled with her father. By seventeen she had become his "girl Friday." She wrote letters for him, accompanied him on visits to heads of state, ventured into business meetings with such luminaries as Thomas Watson, the genius behind IBM, or J. C. Penney.

Claire Giannini grew up in comfort. At twelve she was sent to boarding school on the East Coast. Her parents expected her to go to Bryn Mawr, but she rebelled and ended up at Mills College, back on the West Coast. Photographs of her as a young lady show a stylish, attractive woman, usually on her way overseas or on vacation. Though her father never built a fortune, he always had a large drawing account at Bank of America.

By the standards of A. P.'s parents, life was elegant, but nowhere near what Giannini might have enjoyed. Claire related her envy when she visited the home of Charles Crocker, an equally famous San Francisco banker, who kept a staff of fifty servants and threw lavish parties. The Giannini household had a single servant, with meals served family style, and furnishings that she described as "early Grand Rapids."

When she complained to her father, she later told a reporter, he asked, "Don't you have a happy home? Well, Claire, you might not have that happy home if I kept that money. I would probably have a mistress and a yacht."

In 1930, she married Clifford P. "Biff" Hoffman, a onetime football star at Stanford. Hoffman became a stockbroker in San Francisco, and Claire and he moved into a home not far from Seven Oaks. Claire wanted to establish an independent life. She

encouraged Biff not to trade shares in any of her father's companies. In the Depression, she sometimes had no more than $5 in
her checking account at Bank of America.

She lived as a middle-class housewife, joining the Junior
League and doing volunteer work. But in 1941, after her mother
died, she and her family moved to Seven Oaks to keep her father
company.

In 1949, after A. P.'s death, Claire assumed a role that A. P.
had relished, visiting the branches and meeting the bank's employees, the people he had called "my boys and girls." She became a roving ambassador for management. At annual meetings
of the American Bankers Association, she and the management
of Bank of America would stand in separate receiving lines,
greeting bankers at the company's cocktail parties.

Though she was an articulate and powerful presence on the
board, she never became part of the inner circle of management.
For years she appeared a potentially dangerous force to insiders.
None of them could forget the support that A. P. had received
from shareholders in the proxy fight of 1930. Claire now became
the rallying point for those shareholders, the old-timers who had
benefited from A. P.'s success. Management knew that it had a
Giannini watching over its shoulder, just as when A. P. was alive.
The threat that a member of the Giannini clan would challenge
management was just as real after his death as when he told senior executives in the late 1940s, "I've retired, I'm through. I'm
leaving it to you fellows to run the bank. But by God if you don't
run it right, I'll get somebody who will."

When A. P. was alive he encouraged loyalty by refusing to
lay off employees during the Great Depression, making it easy
for small children to open accounts at the bank, eschewing great
wealth for himself, giving much of his personal fortune away, and
donating much of his estate to a foundation to support the education of the families of BankAmerica employees.

Claire Giannini tried to preserve that spirit. Times had
changed and, as a single voice, she lost regularly. The disappearance of the school savings program still stung her deeply. It was a
Giannini tradition that had taught a generation of children how
to save. It was so controversial that A. P. had to defend it before a
congressional subcommittee, some of whose members appeared
to consider the practice akin to stealing money from babes.

Claire knew that the program didn't make money, that it was a headache and a nuisance. But to A. P., and his brother Doc, who had first championed the program, it was a service with a big pay-off. As they grew, the children kept coming back. Their parents came to the local branch and left as customers. "Not only customers, but friends," Claire said. "When you cut off service, you lose friends. That's the thing that happened in our bank. Our customers had a loyalty that no one had. That loyalty isn't something that you build overnight."

Claire had reason to wonder about the bank's loss of value. She looked around and saw a new generation of immigrants in California, including hundreds of thousands of Vietnamese and Cambodian refugees, who had become the state's fastest-growing minority groups. These were the kind of people A. P. had created his bank to serve. In the old days, Bank of America might have opened special units with officers who spoke the language of the newcomers. It had done that for Italians and Slavs and the Spanish-speaking.

But the bank had lost that interest. It now argued that these were people who could not pay their way. By 1985, when Claire resigned, BankAmerica was discouraging small depositors. It charged large fees for handling small accounts. It had canceled the school savings plan. It had begun to provide special services for the wealthy. The sense of democratic values that had guided the institution had slipped away.

She summed up her distress in a statement accompanying her resignation:

> The bank's decision [to sell the headquarters] is just the latest item in a sad chronology of corporate myopia and thoughtlessness. For the past fifteen years or so, I have watched three successive administrations stray further and further from the policies and practices that were such a vital part of my father's leadership: clear thinking, a willingness to place the human needs of ordinary people above private ambition, and a realization that the bank was less a place of work for its thousands of employees than an extended family of fellow workers.
>
> Never in the long and remarkable history of the bank has the concept of public welfare meant less. Never has cor-

porate self-interest, insincerity, and insensitivity been more conspicuous. Apparently, the guiding principle of the bank's present leadership is that banking is no longer a people's business, but a private arena for the power plays of the few who are more and more reluctant to be held accountable for their actions.

Chapter Twenty-three

I will never allow Washington to manage this bank.

Sam Armacost, 1985

Claire Hoffman was not alone in her anger and bewilderment. In Washington, the Office of the Comptroller of the Currency was beginning to feel a sense of outrage.

Largely unnoticed in the furor over BankAmerica's scandal with NMEC and the publicity that surrounded Claire's resignation, were a series of equally dubious decisions by Armacost's management team—and BankAmerica's board.

In October of the previous year, when the Comptroller's staff wrangled with management over its examination reports, one message ought to have been clear. The examiners worried about the bank's loan portfolio. They didn't think the reserve against possible loan losses was high enough.

BankAmerica argued that its reserve was slightly above average for large commercial banks. The trouble was that BankAmerica's problem loans—as a percentage of total loans—were twice the average for big banks and seemed to be growing, suggesting the need to double the reserve.

The directors on the audit and examining committee knew how bad the loans were. They had been receiving quarterly reports from the credit examination group, and with each report the figures grew worse. Every quarter, the bank wrote off millions of dollars of loans, thus dumping some of its troubles overboard. But every quarter the bank found more problems than it wrote off, so the total kept growing. In 1984, Bank of America jettisoned more than $900 million of bad loans. Yet at year's end, its total of nonperforming loans had declined by $200 million from a year earlier. That meant it had discovered more than $700 million of new problem loans in 1984—an alarming amount.

At the final review of the credit portfolio in 1984, the credit examination staff urged the board to increase the reserve against problem loans. With the numbers going in the wrong direction, that was only prudent.

But the directors listened to Armacost, who argued that the worst of the bank's loan problems were over. In the coming year, he argued, the bad loans would begin to decline. Thus, instead of increasing the reserve, the board allowed it to drop. As a direct result, profits in 1984 rose slightly for the first time since 1981. (That increase was later eliminated by the $95 million reserve for the losses tied to the NMEC mortgage problem.) "Our plan for 1984 was to start the up-track," Armacost said a few weeks after the NMEC scandal began. "But for this debacle down in Inglewood, we would have achieved that. The earnings at that level would have been unsatisfactory in my mind, but they would have started the positive track."

Sam Armacost was determined to show progress. Despite write-offs in 1984 that equaled 90 percent of its reserve against possible loan losses and despite the pressure from the Comptroller, Armacost let the reserve decline, permitting profits to rise. Even though problem loans were up sharply, even though the company's reserve—as a percentage of its problem loan total—was now the lowest for any commercial banking company among the fifteen largest in the United States, Armacost allowed the reserve to inch lower, just as he had four years before while helping Tom Clausen report record profits in his last year as president.

The Comptroller was not pleased. "If you see that a bank hasn't been adequately providing for the loan loss reserve or hasn't been taking proper write-offs, you get very critical," says a former bank examiner. "It all smacks of these guys manipulating their numbers. They are managing their earnings. They are trying to keep the stock price up. They are in essence deceiving the people about their true condition, because they are understating the losses and the loan loss reserve."

The regulators were equally mystified by the bank's dividend policy. One of the more arcane parts of banking is the difference between banks and bank holding companies. The Comptroller regulates the bank, not the holding company. So when it demanded more capital, it wanted to see more capital at the bank. Armacost moved quickly. He stopped paying dividends from the bank to the holding company.

But in the first quarter of 1985, BankAmerica reversed itself and reinstated the dividend from the bank to the holding company. Why? The holding company faced a cash shortage, and without cash, Armacost could not keep dividends flowing to shareholders. After the bank stopped paying dividends, the holding company's income dropped sharply. In 1983, Bank of America paid $251 million in dividends to BankAmerica Corp. BankAmerica Corp. then turned around and paid $229 million in dividends to its shareholders. In 1984, Bank of America paid no dividend to BankAmerica Corp., but BankAmerica Corp. paid the same $229 million to its stockholders.

As BankAmerica laid plans to sell its headquarters building and other assets, the motivation seemed obvious to some regulators. Armacost wanted to avoid the embarrassment of cutting his dividend. Rather than acknowledge the severity of the company's problems, he preferred to liquidate the company, selling assets at whatever price he could get, in order to keep shareholders happy.

This raised temperatures in Washington.

In March 1985, the Comptroller of the Currency began a new audit of the Bank of America. The agency flew in a team of examiners from the East Coast, headed by Michael LaRusso, an experienced examiner who struck bank executives as a refugee from professional football who had somehow wandered into banking. LaRusso had a reputation for being tough and thorough, he was one of the agency's best. And he was heading a team of examiners who had worked on problems at some of the largest commercial banks in New York. "We were outsiders," says one of the men on that team. "We were not close to the problem. If you work with something too long, you get too close to the problem. We had worked with Chase, Marine Midland, even Citicorp. We knew that these guys all put their pants on one leg at a time."

BankAmerica's decisions in late 1984 may have lent a messianic zeal to the team conducting the 1985 examination. Also adding to the pressure on the examiners were newspaper and magazine articles detailing BankAmerica's plight. Chris Welles, a respected financial writer, then with the *Los Angeles Times*, produced a long, critical article in December 1984, raising all the right questions. In March 1985, *Fortune* ran a piece that suggested the institution was veering out of control.

After Continental Illinois, the Comptroller did not want any surprises at big banks. As the examination started, the message got through to Armacost. This review would be more critical than the last. Instead of accepting management's good intentions, the examiners were looking for evidence that steps had been taken to improve the bank's position and that management was complying with the letter of agreement signed in October, the letter that complained about the adequacy of the loan loss reserve.

The economy didn't cooperate. A new spate of commodity price declines was pushing borrowers over the brink. Cotton growers and cattle farmers, who the bank had been trying to keep afloat, now looked more doubtful. Shippers in Greece and Hong Kong struggled under the renewed slump in oil prices. The examiners took samples of loans outside the bank's list of problem credits. They found that too many of these were going bad, not only in farming and shipping, but in real estate. "They got very tough on the real estate portfolio," says a former senior vice-president.

Armacost and Prussia met regularly with LaRusso's team. What Sam heard he didn't like. Armacost kept pointing to the 1984 examination report. "That's last year," LaRusso would reply, "This is this year."

Prussia seemed to feel vindicated. He had been warning since 1981 about the risks that could not be foreseen. Now was his moment to say "I told you so." While Armacost fumed about the report, Prussia agreed with its conclusions.

Armacost complained again that the examiners were treating the bank unfairly. He wanted to meet with LaRusso's boss. In late 1984, C. Todd Conover had resigned as Comptroller, replaced by H. Joe Selby, a career employee, a difficult, strongwilled man with the mind-set of an examiner. Selby agreed to meet with Armacost and Prussia in Phoenix during an annual conference for his agency's senior staff scheduled for June.

Within Armacost's management team, a few voices once again encouraged conciliation. On the finance staff, in some other quarters of the bank, pragmatists argued that no matter how rough the regulators were, the only way to win was to cooperate.

Armacost didn't want to hear it. He wanted to get tough, to take them on.

Armacost went to Phoenix prepared to talk with Selby, man-to-man. When he arrived he found a half-dozen regulators waiting for him, and a tough, uncompromising Selby. "It was a very candid meeting," said one of the participants.

Armacost repeated his point that this report was far tougher than last year's examination. It seemed to him that the examiners were going out of their way to find new problems.

Selby backed up LaRusso. As for the 1984 report, he told Armacost, "Forget it."

The examiners made it clear that they were not optimistic about the latest review. LaRusso said there would be some additional write-downs in the quarter.

"Like what?" Armacost asked.

"I don't know yet," LaRusso responded.

"Can't you give us some feel?"

LaRusso provided some specifics about the problems in shipping where hundreds of millions of dollars of loans had gone bad, in agriculture, in real estate, and elsewhere, but he had no single, magic number to give Armacost. He could only warn him that there were big problems and that he would give him a better feel for the total in a few weeks.

LaRusso kept his word. After BankAmerica's reports filtered in from various branches, LaRusso met again with management. They discussed the portfolio in more detail. When the question came up of how much to set aside, LaRusso backpedaled.

"It's management's responsibility to run the bank," he told Armacost and Prussia. "If I were you I would err on the conservative side." That meant, given the figures LaRusso was sharing with the two men, an increase of at least $500 million in the reserve, a jump of more than 50 percent.

In early June, Armacost announced that BankAmerica would break even in the second quarter, after a meeting with Chuck Schwab in which Schwab encouraged Armacost to be specific about how bad the problem would be.

At the July board meeting, Armacost discussed the examination report. The company had written off over $400 million of loans in the quarter, so in order to increase the reserve by $500 million BankAmerica would need to add $900 million. Some board members felt uncomfortable with the Comptroller's request. It seemed excessive. Armacost agreed. He argued, persuasively, that the bank probably could get by with much less. But he also acknowledged that it was best to go along with the regulators.

The debate was almost entirely one-sided. The only strong voice for prudence came from Dick Cooley. Cooley had lived through countless nightmares at Seafirst. He had watched closely the run at Continental Illinois. What he knew, now, was that the problems are always worse than one imagines. He suggested, as LaRusso had, that Armacost err on the side of caution. "I think you should be conservative," he said, then he encouraged Armacost to add "$800 million, maybe even $1 billion" to the reserve—which would have increased the loss for the quarter to between $600 million and $800 million. The board ignored him. It added the minimum requested by the examiners, producing a loss of $338 million for the second quarter of 1985.

Chapter Twenty-four

Courage implies the willingness to back your judgment to the limit. Often it takes more real courage to do that than it does to face physical danger.

A. P. Giannini, 1926

By mid-1985, the discomfort of two BankAmerica executives propelled them to action. One was Charles Schwab. The other was a newcomer to BankAmerica, a former Methodist minister from Philadelphia, Thomas A. Cooper.

Sam Armacost hired Tom Cooper in March of 1985 to run the BankAmerica Payment Systems unit designed by Ichak Adizes. Cooper looked overqualified, having been president and chief operating officer of Girard Bank, a $4 billion institution and vice-chairman of Mellon Bank, a $25 billion company based in Pittsburgh. Many suspected that Cooper was Armacost's choice for chief operating officer and that BAPS would be his proving ground.

Cooper quickly become the most controversial member of management. One senior executive summed it up by saying, "You either loved him or you hated him."

Cooper is a blunt, combative individual, who challenges people and their ideas. "He is extremely strong," said Adizes, "Seldom right but never in doubt." Said one former member of the managing committee, "He attacked everybody. He came in and created a lot of dissension. He was very divisive." A second top executive adds, "He says one thing and then does another."

He also engenders tremendous loyalty. "He is a very capable businessman," said a former executive vice-president. "He is very decisive." A senior vice-president who worked for Cooper

230

goes further, saying, "He's the only reason I regretted leaving the bank."

Those who don't like Cooper consider him political, devious, simplistic. Those who like him find him honest, clearheaded, loyal. Defenders heap praise, calling him a superb manager and communicator. Everyone agrees he is hardworking, dedicated, and determined to do what he thinks is right.

Tom Cooper's personality is one part street fighter, one part minister, one part self-made man. There is in Tom Cooper a sense of solidity, a strain of strong middle-class values. Even his appearance, his hair, his glasses, suggest an earlier time—the 1950s, perhaps, and a clean-cut, virtuous middle America. Cooper grew up in a lower-middle-class section of Philadelphia. By the age of twelve he was working as much as sixty hours a week. He was a good student, the first member of his family to go to college, working his way through school, first at Haverford College in Pennsylvania, and then at Drew University, a Methodist school in Madison, New Jersey, where he took more psychology courses than courses in religion or the Bible.

After two years as a minister, Cooper left the calling. He took odd jobs, knocked on doors, and finally found a position at the Girard Bank, Philadelphia's third largest. Girard was one of the bluest of Philadelphia's blue-blood banks. The management was stuffy and patrician and mingled well with its customers, an upper-crust corporate clientele.

Cooper didn't exactly fit the bank's mold, but then again, the bank was changing. Cooper spent more than twenty turbulent years at Girard. Unlike California, whose large, diverse economy provided insulation from the recessions of the seventies, the East Coast was hit hard. In spite of the difficult times, Girard transformed itself from a corporate lender into a broader, more diversified institution. It wooed consumers, installed a network of automated teller machines, branched out into new communities.

One of the guiding forces behind that transition was Tom Cooper, who first came to attention by restoring order to the back office. In the late 1960s, as the bull market roared on Wall Street, the stampede of buying swamped the back rooms of the biggest stockbrokers. Their computers couldn't process all the paper. Trading hours on the New York Stock Exchange were reduced to give member firms an extra two hours a day to clear up their paperwork, but still firms drowned in paper, and failed.

Girard had an active trust department, which bought and sold stock for wealthy clients, pension funds, and other large investors. When volume surged on the stock exchange, Girard suffered the same fate as firms on Wall Street. It didn't have the computing power to handle high volume.

Management brought in Cooper, who had earned a reputation for getting things done in the branches. He restored order quickly and, in the process, got to know Girard's top executives. He began to rise, heading the retail side, then corporate lending, and finally becoming president, where he oversaw Girard's push into retail banking and its huge investment in automated teller machines. Some insiders credit him with building a solid, reliable computer system in the mid-1970s for organizing the data on the bank's customers—a data base management system similar to the one that Max Hopper was working on for BankAmerica in 1985.

Tom Cooper was not one to brag about his role at the bank. Friends in and around Philadelphia knew he worked for Girard, but they didn't know just what he did. Many were surprised when the serious young man became president of a bank with a pedigree that stretched back more than a hundred years.

In 1984, after a change in Pennsylvania law allowed mergers between banks throughout the state, Mellon swallowed Girard and Cooper became vice-chairman at Mellon. Within six months, he was gone after a clash with Mellon management.

In 1985 Cooper came to BankAmerica to run the new payment systems unit, BAPS. In his first few months at the company, he immersed himself in that job, bringing together the units that processed checks, credit card purchases, and the like. Cooper thought BankAmerica was one of the few banks with enough size, capital, and business to build a payments system network, drive down costs, and capture a large share of the market. Armacost wanted a slimmer, more competitive unit, and he quickly got it. Cooper set aggressive targets for cutting staff, laid out plans for building a big business, and, within a few months, produced profits.

Nights and weekends, Cooper read the bank's financial statements. His family was still in Philadelphia, finishing out the school year, so he shut himself up with the reports. He understood the reams of numbers that commercial banks produce and he knew these numbers could tell him a lot about BankAmerica. As an outsider—a banker from the East Coast, who had lived in the shadow of institutions that were failing and who had survived recessions, loan problems, and funding crises—Cooper found BankAmerica's numbers deeply disturbing.

After four years under Sam Armacost, the statistics on BankAmerica simply didn't look very good. Compared with other big banks, BankAmerica was a bloated, inefficient company, saddled with bad loans, short on capital, unfocused, and apparently unaware of just how severe its problems might be.

Confirmation of the lack of awareness came a few weeks after Cooper arrived, when the company announced its new retail banking organization—another structure created through the Adizes process. At a mass meeting for branch managers in Los Angeles, the company threw a pep rally with all the hoopla it could muster, including an appearance by opera diva Beverly Sills and a barn-burning speech from John Madden, a former coach of the Oakland Raiders and an advertising spokesman for Miller Lite beer. One executive remembers Cooper turning and remarking, "This bank is losing money and they are doing things like this. It doesn't make sense."

Mostly Cooper kept his mouth shut and did his job. He won plaudits for his directness and the flurry of activity that seemed to emanate out of BAPS. But by the middle of the second quarter, Armacost grew concerned. The profits he expected weren't coming. The drumbeat of pressure from McNamara about a chief operating officer had begun to build. Jim Wiesler had volunteered for the job, but Armacost told him in no uncertain terms that he was the wrong man. Armacost thought Wiesler should take the fall for the NMEC foul-up. He was putting subtle pressure on Wiesler to take early retirement.

Faced with mounting bad news, Armacost decided to try something different. He appointed a five man committee, which quickly became known as the Group of Five. It had no chairman or coordinator. It included Jim Wiesler, head of the retail bank; Robert Frick, head of World Banking; Max Hopper, head of BankAmerica Systems Engineering; Robert Beck, head of personnel; and Cooper. These men ran the divisions that employed 95 percent of BankAmerica's employees. If any group could agree on the best way to cut costs or change the organization, they could.

Its goals were several: to pare expenses, find assets to sell, and forge a consensus on operations. The committee was also a testing ground. Sam Armacost was putting his top executives in a room and locking the door. Whoever emerged was likely to become the chief operating officer.

Cooper's bluntness set him apart, allowing him to dominate the meetings. "Cooper was very pessimistic," said a member of the Group of Five. "He was much more pessimistic than anyone else." Cooper argued that the bank desperately needed to take steps to rein in costs, sell unnecessary businesses, and bring its financial ratios into line with the rest of the industry.

This was not what others on the Group of Five wanted to hear. Jim Wiesler described the meetings as unproductive, disorganized, and wasteful. He told aides he had more important things to do. "Max Hopper was in shock," said one of the members. "He had one of the biggest budgets in the bank, and it was the budget most likely to get cut if the bank was in trouble. If Cooper was right, Hopper probably wouldn't get another dollar to spend for the next decade."

The Group of Five set priorities, drawing a list of expense cuts, offices to close, and operations to sell. Consensus came slowly. Frick resisted making cuts, Wiesler rarely came to meetings, Hopper seemed out of touch with the problems of the bank, and Cooper sounded overly pessimistic. Then, before the Group of Five presented its findings, Armacost announced that the second quarter would be break-even. A few weeks later, Bank of America announced a loss of $338 million for the second quarter.

Tom Cooper's pessimism had been confirmed. Within a few weeks, Armacost decided to make Cooper the president and chief operating officer of Bank of America. But it would take Armacost more than seven months to move Cooper into that spot, and then the change would come only under pressure from directors and from the outside.

By the spring of 1985, Chuck Schwab was a disenchanted man. He had joined BankAmerica Corp. with a spirit of enthusiasm, but his dreams were never realized.

By nature Chuck Schwab is an optimist. He dreams big. Joining forces with BankAmerica seemed to fulfill his destiny. It was not just the merger, it was the opportunity to join the board, to move into the highest circles of American finance. Schwab relished the idea of rubbing shoulders with the men who ran the nation's biggest companies.

By early 1985, the glamour had worn off. Schwab's stock in BankAmerica, worth $19 million when the deal closed, was worth far less by May 1985. After the company announced break-even results for the second quarter, the shares nose-dived.

Ever since he was a kid, growing up in Woodland, California, a farm community northwest of Sacramento, Schwab wanted to make money. He sold magazine subscriptions and raised chickens, starting to invest in the stock market when he was thirteen. Money was important to Chuck Schwab then, and it was important to him now. He owned part of a duck hunting club in the Sacramento Valley, part of a ranch for fly-fishing in Montana, and a vacation home in Hawaii. But from 1983 to 1985, Chuck Schwab had lost big on BankAmerica stock—at one point more than $9 million, or about half his investment. During that same time, the bull market carried most stocks straight up. The Dow Jones Industrial Average had more than quadrupled since August 1982. Chuck Schwab found that distressing.

Schwab played four different roles at BankAmerica. He was a director, the company's largest individual shareholder, a member of the company's management team, and the chief executive of Schwab & Co. In the latter role, Schwab had few complaints. Armacost was leaving him alone. His other roles were the problem.

Schwab is a gifted marketing executive, with an innate sense of what people will buy and a natural ability to package products so they will sell. He suggested products and services to Bank-America, but they were ignored or lost in committee meetings. Even simple joint ventures between Schwab & Co. and Bank-America never worked: BankAmerica's computers couldn't handle the product; the bank's marketing people wanted hundreds of modifications; it couldn't be done on time; or it wasn't a high priority.

Schwab grew so frustrated that he eventually offered to surrender his position as chairman of Schwab & Co. to head the marketing division at BankAmerica. Armacost turned him down. "Chuck felt his talents weren't being used," said a former Bank-America executive.

Schwab's relationship with Armacost also grew strained,

partly because of a clash of styles. Schwab is open, almost to a fault. He says what is on his mind. From the minute he joined BankAmerica, Schwab started prodding Armacost to get the company moving. Even in mid-1982, before the merger, Schwab urged Armacost to treat BankAmerica like a "turnaround," perhaps by bringing in a hired gun specializing in restoring companies to profitability. He also urged him to fire several executives.

At first Armacost listened politely, charmed to have a free, innovative spirit on board. But soon Schwab's questions grew irritating. As he had with others, Armacost spent less time with Schwab, and listened less closely to what he was offering. Schwab told his staff that Armacost was growing "arrogant." Armacost let his staff know that Schwab was "emotional" and didn't understand the complexities of BankAmerica. When Schwab suggested tough steps, like cutting the dividend or firing people who appeared incompetent, Armacost responded, as he did to others, "What do you want to do, blow this place apart?"

The split was irreparable by 1985. The catalyst, for Schwab, was a combination of the Comptroller's report and the NMEC mortgage scandal. The Comptroller's report increased his concerns about the loan losses at BankAmerica; the mortgage scandal raised questions about Armacost's candor, suggesting he was trying to hide the bank's true condition from the directors and the public.

As his discomfort grew, Schwab reviewed his options with friends and associates. Because of his unique position, Schwab could express his discontent in various ways. He could play the good executive, urging Sam to take bolder steps. He could disagree more openly at board meetings. He could use his power as a shareholder. He could resign as a director, or he could quit entirely.

Schwab didn't yet share Cooper's dark misgivings. He thought BankAmerica's problem was sluggish management, not serious internal problems. He urged Armacost, during the spring of 1985, to find a way to grow out of the bank's problems. He wanted to unleash the bank's marketing power, unlike Cooper, who felt the bank needed to trim its sails and prepare to ride out the gale.

In late May, a few days before BankAmerica announced that it would break even in the second quarter, Chuck Schwab went to see Sam Armacost. The two talked about the bank's profit problem. Schwab came away aghast. He had known the loan problems were serious, but had not known how serious.

What surprised him most was that Armacost was prepared to announce a drop in earnings, but in tepid language, not making clear the company would probably break even for the quarter. Schwab fumed, pushing Armacost to issue a clear statement of how bad things were going to be, to make it plain that the company was going to show no profit in the second quarter.

After Armacost made that announcement, Schwab started to sell his BankAmerica stock. The price of the shares had slumped. Stock worth $21 when BankAmerica bought Schwab was selling at around $19 a share when Armacost announced the break-even quarter. It quickly dropped below $14. In the biggest deal of his life, Schwab had lost big, and now he was selling his stock to show how little faith he had in BankAmerica's management.

Schwab had reason to be angry. He had agreed to sell his company to BankAmerica for $53 million, even though many in the company urged him to back out. Now he was forced to admit they had been right.

In fall 1982, Schwab might have had a chance to break his deal with BankAmerica. Although he had agreed to sell his company in late 1981, the Federal Reserve did not approve the purchase until late 1982. At one point in mid-1982, Schwab & Co.'s profits had plunged so drastically that Schwab worried BankAmerica would pull out. The letter of intent gave BankAmerica the right to walk away if Schwab's profits fell below $1.2 million in the twelve months before the merger took place, which looked possible.

Schwab's senior executives met with McLin and Armacost seeking assurances, and they got them. BankAmerica was not going to walk away.

Then came August. With a roar, the bulls began stampeding on Wall Street. The Dow Jones Industrial Average, spurred by the drop in interest rates that followed the crisis in Mexico and the collapse of Penn Square, raced skyward. Stocks began to trade in record volume and Schwab & Co.'s profits, which had looked so anemic weeks before, roared louder than the bulls. In September, the company netted over $1.25 million before taxes—enough in one month to meet the profit goal for the entire year. In October, pre-tax profits jumped to more than $3 million. They stayed at that level through November and December.

During the last five months of 1982, Schwab & Co. earned

more than it had in its entire previous existence. Profits were running at a rate of $36 million a year, or close to two thirds the total purchase price offered by BankAmerica—a bargain that was making McLin, who negotiated the Schwab contract, look like a genius, at Schwab's expense.

With a definitive contract still not signed, Schwab could demand a higher price. He could argue that the fortunes of his company had changed so dramatically that the price in the letter of intent was just not high enough.

But Schwab refused to budge. In effect, he told his executives, "A deal is a deal." Peter Moss, the man who had brought Schwab and Armacost together, couldn't understand Schwab's hesitation. Under other circumstances he might have accepted this Edwardian logic, but not when the value of Schwab had changed so abruptly. In the first week of November, Moss asked Schwab to have an outside consultant review the merger to ensure that the price was fair. Schwab at first agreed, then talked with his legal counsel and decided a fairness opinion was not necessary.

On November 19, 1982, Chuck Schwab signed the final contract. Instead of a specific price, the deal set a range of prices running up to $59 million, depending on how well Bank-America's stock performed. On December 7, BankAmerica and Schwab made the appropriate filings with the Securities and Exchange Commission.

The same day Peter Moss sent a letter to Schwab's directors. "It is my personal and moral duty to inform you that I formally oppose the merger," Moss wrote. With the rally in the stock market, Schwab might have been worth closer to $110 million than $55 million. In the year since the letter of intent was signed, the value of Merrill Lynch and Paine Webber had nearly doubled. The value of BankAmerica's stock had declined by 11 percent.

Moss, acting as a minority shareholder, demanded that the board obtain an outside appraisal of the value of the company, but once again Schwab refused.

Moss was stumped. It wasn't only the money that bothered him. Since the merger was first proposed, Moss had begun to work closely with Armacost and McLin and he was beginning to have second thoughts about the marriage. Moss struggled to understand Armacost's vision of the bank, but could not pin him down. The longer they talked, the more certain Moss became that Armacost had no vision of where BankAmerica was headed. In the year after the letter of intent was signed, the Latin American debt crisis had exploded, BankAmerica's problem loans had more than tripled, and its stock had sunk during a bull market. Moss had expected a sense of direction and urgency. He didn't see it.

He was equally concerned with the company's reported profits. He didn't exactly suspect wrongdoing, but having formerly worked with Ernst & Whinney, the firm that audited BankAmerica's books, Moss knew just how "flexible" bank holding company profits can be. He wondered if the company's condition might be worse than it appeared.

Without Schwab's approval, Moss sent a wire, criticizing the deal, to the branch managers of Schwab & Co., who were all shareholders. When Schwab heard about the telex, he flew into a rage. Normally even-tempered and easygoing, he confronted Moss and fired him on the spot.

Moss hired an attorney, and, on December 16, sent a letter to Schwab & Co.'s board informing the directors that he was prepared to file a class action suit.

Though Moss never actually filed the suit, months later it surfaced in a separate court hearing as evidence, detailing charges that help explain Schwab's growing frustration in 1985.

The lawsuit argued that BankAmerica was trying to mislead shareholders about the merger with Schwab & Co. Moss contended that Bank of America was being cavalier about what it reported and excluded from financial statements—a sentiment not unlike Schwab's in mid-1985. The SEC filing on the merger understated the turnaround in Schwab's profits. It didn't mention that during 1981 Schwab & Co. had lost over $500,000 in an effort to start an insurance business. Partly as a result, in the two months before Schwab agreed to sell to BankAmerica in November 1981, Schwab & Co. had lost more than $130,000, leaving it in no position to bargain hard with BankAmerica.

The public filing also minimized the surge in Schwab's profits in late 1982. It noted that in the three months ending in December 1982, Schwab & Co. would earn more than in any prior quarter. In fact, as Moss pointed out, the company was likely to earn more in one quarter than it had in the two previous years combined.

More intriguing were charges that hint at why Schwab didn't fight for a higher price. Moss alleged that during 1982, well before the bank and Schwab reached an agreement on the final terms of the sale, Chuck Schwab had compromised himself. He had agreed to vote his shares for the merger, an arrangement called a "lock-up" by investment bankers. He had also negotiated a lucrative employment contract and a seat on BankAmerica's board. Bank-America would pay Schwab a minimum salary equal to twice what he had earned at Schwab two years before.

Finally, Schwab arranged a bonus plan for his executives that allowed them to split 10 to 15 percent of Schwab & Co.'s pre-tax profits if Schwab & Co. was successful. Moss pointed out that the plan was never described in the offering circular. He called the bonus pool a scheme under which the company's top executives would reap profits at the expense of other shareholders.

On December 22, six days after Moss and his attorney sent their critique to BankAmerica and Schwab, BankAmerica was forced to file an amendment to its original offering circular, es-sentially admitting that Moss was right on almost all counts.

BankAmerica also, coincidentally, increased its bid for Schwab & Co. from 2.1 million shares to 2.6 million shares, rais-ing the offering price to about $53 million and leading Moss to drop his suit.

Despite the proposed suit, despite the enormous changes in the marketplace, Chuck Schwab had sold his company for an amount equal to about two years of expected pre-tax profits. It may have been one of the worst deals ever made by an entrepreneur.

In exchange, Chuck Schwab got a seat on the BankAmerica board and a share in the Schwab & Co. bonus pool, which even-tually paid him more than $4 million.

The unfairness of this deal gnawed at Chuck Schwab. He wondered whether he had been misled, whether Armacost knew more than he told him in the fall of 1982, whether the bank had failed to disclose how much was wrong with the company.

Watching Armacost's decisions in 1984 and 1985 on NMEC, on the Comptroller's report, on the directors and offi-cers insurance program, Schwab's doubts grew. When Armacost hesitated in May 1985 to announce the poor results in the second quarter, Schwab moved into action. He hired Deloitte Haskins & Sells to analyze the published financial statements of Bank-America—paying the costs out of his own pocket. He wanted to know whether Armacost had covered up the company's loan problems.

The Deloitte study proved highly critical. Relying on information available to any analyst, it covered all the familiar ground, the high costs, low capital, and poor loans. But the heart of the report was an analysis of three items: the bank's total of problem loans, its actual loan losses, and the size of its reserve against loan losses.

In 1981, for every dollar of problem loans on its books, BankAmerica had about fifty cents set aside as a reserve. By the end of 1982, the reserve had dropped to about twenty-five cents per dollar of loan problems—well below average for major banks. The reserve stayed at that level until mid-1985, when the Comptroller forced the bank to add $500 million to the reserve.

Analysts and regulators know that banking companies can manipulate their profits by keeping the loan loss reserve too low and thus passing on more earnings to shareholders. That is what so infuriated the Comptroller's office in 1984.

The numbers suggested that BankAmerica had been manipulating its reserve since 1982 and that when BankAmerica bought Charles Schwab & Co. in late 1982, it may already have been knowingly overstating its profits.

Deloitte completed its study just before the August 1985 board meeting. Schwab had no time to brief other board members. He rushed to copy the findings and handed them to board members during the meeting. He asked for a special committee to review the company's policies on disclosing loan problems and establishing reserves.

John Beckett, the former president of Transamerica Corp. and then head of the audit committee, dismissed Schwab's report. He and the audit committee had reviewed these numbers every quarter. Schwab's motion died without a second. "They didn't even listen," said another board member sympathetic to Schwab, but whose sympathy did not extend to seconding the motion himself.

Like Peter Moss, Chuck Schwab found himself faced with an inexplicable action. It was obvious that BankAmerica's management was not being aggressive enough in building its loan loss reserves. It was obvious that news of loan problems was coming much later than warranted. But the board was not willing to assert itself. It stood behind Armacost. As Schwab told an associate, "I felt like the Lone Ranger."

Chapter Twenty-five

In the event that a [run] should start at your branch keep a stiff upper lip and let every man wear a big smile. Do business in the *usual* manner and honor all legitimate demands . . . without asking questions. . . .

James A. Bacigalupi, 1921
President, BancItaly Corp.

On June 4, 1985, when BankAmerica announced it would break even in the second quarter, control of the company shifted out of the hands of management. The company was put on the defensive, forced to respond to outsiders. First it was confronted by a loss of faith among its customers, then by overtures from investment bankers eager to put BankAmerica into the hands of a new owner.

One of its toughest battles, virtually unheralded because it was successful, came in the war to keep depositors. And one of the men who made life difficult for the bank was Greg Root, a thirty-six-year-old executive at a New York firm virtually unknown outside the banking industry. Root rates the debt of commercial banks, leading a small team of analysts at Keefe, Bruyette & Woods, an investment bank.

In this corner of the financial markets, Greg Root is one of the most influential men in America—overshadowing counterparts at better-known companies like Moody's Investor Services and Standard & Poor's. The ratings Root generates are gospel to more than five hundred of the most important depositors in the country—corporate treasurers, money fund managers, commercial bankers, and city treasurers, that is, people with millions of dollars to deposit.

The offices of Keefe, Bruyette are on the eighty-fifth floor of the World Trade Center in New York. On a clear day, like June 4, Root can watch the smoke rise from the factories across the Hudson River in New Jersey.

Early that morning Root got a call from BankAmerica. The call was not unusual; he and his team talked regularly with top executives at each of the companies they rate. But the announcement of a break-even quarter came as a surprise. Root and a half-dozen top rating specialists spent more than thirty minutes talking with Lee Prussia, BankAmerica's chairman, and Harvey Gillis, the bank's top financial officer.

Like other analysts in New York, Root had been watching the fall of BankAmerica with increasing dismay. Keefe, Bruyette rates banks on a scale from A to E. Eighteen months before, Keefe had lowered BankAmerica from a B/C to a C. The company's falling profits, increasing loan problems, and basic condition all encouraged the change.

Keefe's clients noted the change with more than passing interest. BankAmerica moved into a gray area. A C rating by Keefe is at the bottom of the "acceptable" list for many depositors. If a bank drops below C, guidelines at many companies—sometimes set by the board of directors—force the treasurer to start closing accounts or to explain to the board why the accounts should not be closed.

Just after BankAmerica signed its letter of agreement with the Comptroller, in late 1984, Keefe, Bruyette issued a two-page memorandum to clients saying the bank was "vulnerable to further deterioration." In the weeks before the telephone call of June 4, Root and his colleagues grew even more concerned, writing, "If there are signs of any further deterioration in asset quality or earnings fundamentals, then a rating change would be forthcoming."

Prussia and Gillis realized their call would give Keefe Bruyette its reason to lower the bank's rating below a C. Though Prussia tried to put the best light on the announcement, he wasn't convincing.

After the call, Root and his colleagues moved to a glass-walled internal conference room, where they met whenever bad news broke. The entire team of fifteen analysts assembled as an informal committee. Although they had no hint that the quarter would be worse than break-even, their instincts told them to be cautious.

They discussed the "big bath" theory of bank management. If a quarter is turning bad, bank managers invariably dump as many problems into one quarter as they can, trying to take a big loss and then move on. Looking at BankAmerica's financial statements, it was clear the bank could use a much higher reserve for loan losses, if only to reach the industry average. It was possible, Root speculated, that BankAmerica would end up adding as much as $500 million to the reserve. If it did that, there would be no break-even quarter.

After a brief debate, the majority agreed to drop Bank-America's rating from C to C/D. They quickly called the bank to let it know the change was coming and to give its executives another opportunity to muster counterarguments. Then word of the downgrading went out in telexes, by phone, and through the mail.

The firm's final memo on the downgrading only hinted at Root's uneasiness. "This latest announcement represents another setback which increases our concern about asset quality." he wrote. "While we recognize the progress that has been made in controlling staff expenses and maintaining strong net interest margins, these latest developments offset the areas of improvement. . . . BankAmerica Corp. no longer meets the standards of our major 'C' rated banking organizations."

With that memo, BankAmerica fell from grace in the eyes of many institutional depositors. Nothing was automatic, the markets did not suddenly close, but the bank's market specialists could almost feel the chill descend.

Corporate treasurers and others who manage large banking relationships rarely panic, nor do they agree on actions to be taken. Many of BankAmerica's biggest corporate depositors, both in the United States and elsewhere, had been leaving Bank-America for months. Bob Frick, the head of the World Banking Division, knew that best. He had spent long hours on the phone with his people in London and with customers all over the world trying to reassure them about the company's wealth.

Now it was only going to be tougher. Some customers, those that had been with the bank for years, would never budge, but others were already headed for the exit. An assistant corporate treasurer at a Fortune 500 company in the Midwest found no reason to stay loyal to Bank of America. He accepted "hand-holding" calls from San Francisco, but he declined to have the bank fly in one of its top executives. He knew it wouldn't change

*Samuel H. Armacost, chief executive, BankAmerica Corp.
(1981–1986)*

*Leland S. Prussia, chairman of the board, BankAmerica Corp.
(1981–1986)*

Robert S. McNamara (photo by William Smith, Stanford University Visual Art Services)

Charles Schwab, founder and chairman, Charles Schwab & Co., the nation's largest discount stock broker (Courtesy Charles Schwab & Co.)

Stephen T. McLin, architect of BankAmerica's acquisitions of Charles Schwab & Co. and Seafirst Corp.

Ichak Adizes, consultant to BankAmerica

Michael Patriarca, former Deputy Comptroller of the Currency

H. Joe Selby, former Comptroller of the Currency

Thomas Cooper

Sanford I. Weill

John Gutfreund

Joseph J. Pinola

Philip Hawley (photo by Richard Kelsey; © 1987 Los Angeles Times)

his mind. He began to pull accounts from Bank of America, and as he did the pressure for him to accept a visit from Bank of America's top brass built.

The treasurer relied on Bank of America for what bankers call "a lock-box." At certain points throughout California the company needed to collect checks every night. Bank of America handled the paperwork, so that on any given day, it held company checks worth several million dollars.

The money didn't stay at Bank of America very long, but was transferred to accounts at other banks. Even though the money was in Bank of America for only a few hours, the treasurer had to worry. Every dollar of that cash was committed to be somewhere else. What if a crisis hit? What if the money were frozen overnight? Operating problems could occur, payrolls might be harder to meet, the company could be forced to borrow.

Though that event was probably less likely than his being struck by lightning, it was too big a risk to take. The company quietly moved its lock-box business to a Bank of America competitor. It sent word to its subsidiaries, many of which had independent treasury operations, that they should review their relationships with the bank as well. If Bank of America had the only branch in town, or the best lock-box in town, stick with it. Otherwise it was time to move elsewhere.

Other big clients were being just as thorough. A large oil company based in London directed deposits to other banks. A big automobile finance company slowed the flow of new deposits to Bank of America to a trickle. (Despite the wisdom of their decisions these firms prefer to remain anonymous.)

The quickest to leave were the nation's money market mutual funds. At the end of June, the ten largest money funds had about $1 billion on deposit at BankAmerica. After the downgrading by Keefe, the money evaporated. Instead of "rolling over" their deposits, money fund managers pulled the money out when their accounts matured. Within a quarter, the fund holdings had dropped to $300 million. By the end of the first quarter of 1986, not one of the nation's largest money funds had any money on deposit.

Large depositors overseas grew wary as well. Internal bank documents show that many of those depositors moved rapidly to shorten the maturity of their deposits at BankAmerica, letting those of four to six months expire, and transferring the money to accounts of only a few days or a few weeks. As the deposits dwindled, the bank had to offer a premium over other large banks to attract money, not the bank-breaking two percentage points paid by Continental Illinois, but a premium of as much as a half percentage point at times. Unlike Continental, BankAmerica had enough consumer deposits so that it could stop raising money elsewhere for a short time if the premium got too large.

But in California the same steady erosion of confidence occurred. The branch managers all felt it. Says a former senior executive in the retail division, "For two weeks after every announcement of bad news, we'd work overtime trying to convince customers to keep their deposits in place."

Some of the worst outflows came in branches that were close to retirement communities. Retired people, many of whom relied on the interest from their deposits to eat and pay the rent, responded quickly to bad news. "You'd see the little gray-haired ladies come in. They'd withdraw their deposits and then you could literally watch them walk across the parking lot to the Security Pacific or Wells branch," says a retail banker.

It was not a panic; there was no run, no rush of depositors into branches to pull accounts. But a squeeze was occurring, just as it had at Continental Illinois. Confidential internal reports of BankAmerica show that its share of consumer deposits in California would shrink from more than 13 percent in mid-1985 to less than 12 percent in mid-1986. The bank lost more than $1 billion in deposits, but since the deposits at other banks grew, its lost market share totaled $3.4 billion—over 10 percent of its consumer deposit base. The bank's strong core of business seemed to make it immune to a crisis, but within BankAmerica, top executives prepared for the worst.

Beginning in late 1985, the bank stepped up its program of sending top executives to call on corporate customers. At the first sign of a defection, they flew or drove to see major depositors. Competitors marveled at the effort. Armacost, Prussia, and others called regularly and on almost any pretext. "The president of the company was out making cash management calls," one competitor recalled later in amazement.

"It was a very successful program," says a former member of the managing committee. "We found after a while that we were creating concern with some customers. They wanted to know why we were there—was something wrong? So we cut back."

As the bank's deposit problems stabilized, top executives worried about another pressing problem at the holding company. BankAmerica owned FinanceAmerica Corp., a consumer finance company with over 250 offices in forty-two states. Although consumer finance companies operate much like banks, lending money to businesses and consumers, they do not take deposits, so they are not considered commercial banks and are free to branch across state lines. Clausen had bought the company in the 1970s, hoping that when interstate banking laws changed, he could convert its offices into branches of the Bank of America.

Since FinanceAmerica could not raise deposits, BankAmerica sold long-term debt and issued commercial paper, then advanced the money to its subsidiary. Like large depositors, the investors who bought BankAmerica's paper tended to be a nervous lot. At the first whiff of trouble many cut and ran.

Steve McLin was one of the first to worry about whether the holding company would have trouble borrowing in credit markets. As a strategic planner, McLin worked for both the holding company and the bank, and part of his job was to watch the holding company's finances. In late 1984, when the bank stopped paying a dividend to the holding company, McLin knew he faced trouble. The holding company had enough cash to pay dividends to its shareholders for a few quarters, but at some point its hoard was going to give out.

The sale of the company's headquarters in San Francisco had been planned to ease the cash crunch. It would be completed in the third quarter of 1985. Now McLin also wanted to sell FinanceAmerica. It no longer fit the company's strategy, and selling it would have a double benefit. The cash would help, but more important, selling the subsidiary would eliminate the need for the holding company to raise $2 billion in the commercial paper market and the need to regularly sell long-term debt.

Long before he knew how bad the second quarter would be, McLin had begun to press Armacost to sell FinanceAmerica. But he got nowhere. Armacost remained certain that a turnaround was imminent. He didn't see any reason to sell a profitable asset.

So McLin called Lee Kimmel, the Salomon Brothers investment banker who had represented Seafirst when it was sold to BankAmerica. Maybe he could help convince Armacost to sell FinanceAmerica.

Kimmel and two key associates—Ken Wilson and Richard Barrett—prepared an analysis of the FinanceAmerica sale, then flew to San Francisco to make the pitch to Armacost on May 31.

The market for finance companies was excellent. Not only were big commercial banks interested in buying, but industrial companies were eager as well. And they had little to buy, as few large finance companies were on the market. Kimmel told Armacost he could get a top price.

Armacost demurred. "I could see how you might come in here as blind entrepreneurs, proposing this deal," Armacost told the Salomon team. "But you don't understand the value of FinanceAmerica."

Salomon's bankers flew home feeling thwarted.

In early July, after Armacost realized the bank would lose more than $300 million in the second quarter, he turned to McLin. "How long will it take you to sell FinanceAmerica?" he asked. Then Armacost called Kimmel and asked the same question.

Now he grasped the wisdom of selling FinanceAmerica. The loss meant Bank of America could not pay any dividends to the holding company for at least a year. The sale of Finance-America would provide the cash to keep dividends flowing to shareholders until the turnaround came.

BankAmerica announced quickly that FinanceAmerica was up for sale, hoping to drum up bidders. Chrysler Corp., Chase Manhattan, and three or four other large corporations lined up.

Salomon hoped for a price of $300 million, but as its specialists and McLin pored over the numbers, they found a huge hidden asset. In the late 1970s, FinanceAmerica, like Bank of America, had bet heavily on interest rates. Even though its loans ran for five years, ten years, or longer, FinanceAmerica had borrowed for much shorter periods.

It had won its bet. As interest rates declined, it paid lower and lower rates on its short-term borrowings, instead of the double-digit interest rates paid by other finance companies that had issued long-term debt in 1981 or 1982. A company that decided to buy FinanceAmerica now could issue long-term debt at low, attractive rates and lock in profits. This "discovery" helped push the price of FinanceAmerica up by $100 million.

The sale looked like a snap, but McLin and Salomon Brothers faced a tight deadline. The bond rating agencies, led by Standard & Poor's, were studying their rating of BankAmerica's debt.

It was obvious that the rating would go down, perhaps making it impossible for BankAmerica to sell commercial paper or long-term debt in large amounts—at least at prices the company could afford.

BankAmerica probably would have found a way through such a crunch, but within the bank, "We chose to operate as though a crisis was imminent," says a former executive vice-president. McLin and Salomon pushed to get FinanceAmerica sold.

On October 8, BankAmerica announced that it had signed a deal to sell FinanceAmerica to Chrysler for $405 million. One month later, Standard & Poor's lowered its rating of the company's debt by a notch, enough to worry already skittish commercial paper investors. The sale had come just in time.

Chapter Twenty-six

*Many a brilliant idea has been lost because the man who dreamed it
lacked the spunk or the spine to put it across.*

A. P. Giannini, 1921

By June 4, 1985, the day BankAmerica announced that the
second quarter would be break-even and long before the sale of
FinanceAmerica, a small team of professional bank watchers were
hatching plans that would affect the fate of BankAmerica and Sam
Armacost. From offices in the Transamerica pyramid, the famous
tower two blocks from the bank's San Francisco headquarters,
they sought a way to put BankAmerica "in play," Wall Street jar-
gon for putting a company on the sale block.

J. Richard Fredericks and Robert Huret form the nucleus of
a brain trust on commercial banks at Montgomery Securities,
one of the few investment banks on the West Coast that special-
ize in serving large, institutional investors. Montgomery is a
high-energy, high-pressure firm, a New York brokerage house
transported to Montgomery Street. Traders dominate the company, fast-talking, fast-moving salesmen who buy and sell securities in large blocks from the minute the markets open on the
East Coast until long after they close. Their world is intense,
highly charged, usually profitable, and largely male. They relax
with the same intensity with which they work, throwing lavish
parties and celebrating birthdays by hiring strippers to perform
on the trading floor.

Fredericks and Huret remained separate from this world.
Fredericks, an analyst and partner in Montgomery Securities,
has a full auburn beard, a thick head of hair, and a taste for fine
California wines. Though he can make more than a half-million

dollars a year, Fredericks seems as solid and unpretentious as the Midwest, where he grew up. Only when he talks banking does he lose that common touch, slipping into a language of ratios and percentages incomprehensible to the uninitiated.

Huret, who is five feet five inches tall, with a thick black beard and tortoiseshell glasses, has the look and the mind of a scholar. "He is simply brilliant," says one banker. While Fredericks clarifies with numbers and ratios, Huret searches for analogies and images. Formerly a strategic planner for First Chicago Corp. (he was McLin's boss), and BanCal Tri-State, the company that owned Bank of California, the state's tenth largest bank, Huret earned a reputation as a thoughtful, sometimes bold, strategist. When other commercial banks were talking about someday selling branches, Huret did it. He laid plans, which management followed, to rebuild Bank of California, shrink it, redefine its business. Then, in late 1984, after a Japanese bank bought Bank of California, Huret formed his own firm and became a consultant to Montgomery.

In mid-1985, Huret and Fredericks championed their thesis of "Darwinian banking," arguing that deregulation had so reduced the margin for error in banking that only the strong would survive. Badly managed banks would disappear, while the well-managed would build "fortress balance sheets," strengthening their reserves and their capital.

BankAmerica did not make their list of the fittest, and they suspected that more bad news would follow the announcement of a break-even quarter. "What NMEC showed was a company that was very widespread—and that had always been overcontrolled—was now out of control," said Huret. "There was no telling what else was out there. But it was likely that the next news would be bad news."

On June 26, Huret was in Washington, D.C., on business with a third member of Montgomery's team, Jim Hale, a gregarious Harvard MBA who had worked as a strategic planner for McLin at BankAmerica. On a cab ride to the airport, the two began to discuss BankAmerica. "It was stream of consciousness," said Huret, "talking about a leveraged buyout of Bank of America, why you couldn't do that."

Huret and Hale, like other investment bankers who follow regulated industries, shared a sense of discontent. In the last half of the 1970s and the first half of the 1980s, a wave of unthinkably large mergers and acquisitions had shaken the U.S. corporate world. Whenever a management team stumbled in the oil industry or in half a dozen other fields, it would find a buyer knocking on the door. Whereas once big corporations had seemed immune from takeover, size was no longer any protection. Waiting to snatch weak companies were a group of corporate raiders, investors with deep pockets who bought, then dismantled, companies and made huge amounts of money. Equally hungry were the leveraged buyout firms, investment bankers, and former corporate executives who borrowed massive sums from banks to buy and dismantle firms.

What these sophisticated investors realized was that many large companies were worth more dead than alive. Buy a company, break it into pieces, sell the pieces, and come out way ahead—if a buyer was smart enough he could even finance the purchase with money in the target's cash drawer. Alternatively a buyer could take over a company, fire people, close offices, and trim it to a more manageable and profitable size.

Regulation protected commercial banks from the schemes of the corporate takeover artists. Governments consider banks special. Not only are bank deposits insured by government agencies, but the information they collect on borrowers is considered too sensitive to fall into the hands of unscrupulous, greedy people.

As long as a commercial bank is healthy, it is virtually impervious to an unwanted takeover. The rules passed by regulators to protect depositors also protect entrenched managers. Regulators take months to review proposed acquisitions, long enough for the target bank to mount strong defenses.

What made Huret and Hale speculate about BankAmerica was its weakness. Like Continental Illinois and Seafirst, BankAmerica was now very ill. No one knew how sick, but if "Darwinian banking" was the rule, if only the strong would survive in this new deregulated world, then BankAmerica was a company in danger of extinction.

A leveraged buyout might have made sense: borrow enough money to buy BankAmerica, sell some of its most attractive assets, and hack away at the overhead—salaries and other expenses—until the profits begin to revive. But BankAmerica's size represented an obstacle. In order to buy BankAmerica, the purchaser would need at least $3 billion—a huge, though not insurmountable obstacle in these days of mega-mergers.

The real problem was banking law. The Bank Holding Company Act barred big corporations, like Ford or General Electric, from owning both banks and industrial operations. Despite their deep pockets, regulations kept them from buying BankAmerica. Wealthy investors might want to buy, but the Federal Reserve had never permitted a bank this big to fall under the control of a small group of wealthy men.

On their flight home from Washington, Huret and Hale examined BankAmerica's options. With his intimate knowledge of BankAmerica, Hale was able to give Huret a sense of how the company might break into pieces. "We didn't reach a specific conclusion, but we had a tremendous feeling of excitement," Huret says. "We knew we ought to do something."

They realized that this something meant finding a banking company interested in merging with BankAmerica. Since BankAmerica was the nation's second largest banking company, only a few banks were big enough to consider swallowing it. The logical choices were all in New York, which presented another legal problem. The McFadden Act and the Bank Holding Company Act had been passed to keep A. P. Giannini from branching beyond California. Now those laws kept others from coming in. None of the New York banks could buy BankAmerica without a change in state or federal law, and that wasn't likely unless BankAmerica was in deathly serious trouble.

Foreign banks could buy smaller banks, but not one this big. Although the Japanese and many Europeans had plenty of money, Congress wasn't happy about foreign banks buying major U.S. banks. In the late 1970s, regulators permitted a few rescues by foreigners—Franklin National in 1974, Marine Midland in 1979, Crocker National in 1981. But the Marine Midland purchase so upset Congress that it slapped a brief moratorium on further purchases of U.S. banks by foreigners. At the time Marine Midland was the nation's thirteenth largest commercial bank. Neither the Federal Reserve nor the Comptroller was likely to want to test the will of Congress by approving the sale of the nation's second largest bank to the Japanese.

Huret and Hale, working now with Fredericks, quickly narrowed the prospects to two large banks in California. The larger was Security Pacific Corp., based in Los Angeles. Headed by Richard Flamson, a tough, profit-minded executive, Security Pa-

cific was trying to get out of the banking business. It had diversified into a range of related businesses, such as bond trading,
equipment leasing, and investment banking, because it thought
profits in the commercial banking business were meager. So buying BankAmerica would be a step back for them.

The second was First Interstate Bancorporation in Los Angeles, the other banking child of A. P. Giannini, created in the
1950s, when the government forced Giannini's holding company, Transamerica Corp., to divest the banks it owned. By 1985,
First Interstate had assets of $45 billion and banks in thirteen
states. It was one third the size of BankAmerica.

At the helm of First Interstate was Joseph J. Pinola, Clausen's former deputy. A onetime high school basketball star, the
son of a Pennsylvania coal miner, Pinola seems descended from
Giannini's style of banker. Muscular, thick-necked, with thinning
white hair, Joe Pinola has never shaken his working-class heritage. His speech is simple and blunt, which permits him to talk
just as comfortably with the man on the street as with another
bank executive, and even though Pinola's $800 suits are precise-
ly tailored, they seem somehow ill-fitted, as though he is out of
place in them.

Joe Pinola possesses a natural sense of the dramatic. He
speaks slowly, emphatically in a rumbling bass voice. As he leans
forward to emphasize a point, light from a single spotlight above
his desk catches his face, throwing into relief his strong, Italian
features. Then he sits back in the darkness of his chair, the only
thing visible the silhouette of his hands, large, rough, virile,
holding the arms of the chair.

Invariably, journalists liken Pinola to a football coach. He
has gathered around him a team of young executives, most of
whom once worked at BankAmerica, who protect him, support
him, and carry out his wishes.

The investment team from Montgomery knew some of
Pinola's history, how he had left BankAmerica when it became
clear that he was unlikely to be president, then transformed a
stuffy, unprofitable confederation of banks into a tightly knit
holding company. When that was complete, he launched a
campaign to sell franchises to banks in all fifty states, a sort of
McDonald's of banking that skirted regulations against owning
banks in other states and brought Giannini's dream of nationwide banking closer to reality. This man, with a commitment
to A. P. Giannini's vision of banking, was their target.

On Friday morning, July 12, Huret met in Los Angeles with Don Griffith, Joe Pinola's chief financial officer. Huret suggested that First Interstate take a run at BankAmerica.

On and off for the last several years Griffith had speculated about a merger with the giant of California banking. He remembers staring at BankAmerica's San Francisco headquarters in the spring of 1983 and musing aloud, "There ought to be a way." Months later, one of the most aggressive investment banks on Wall Street, First Boston Corp., proposed a merger of the two companies, but Griffith thought the odds were stacked against it.

Now there might be a chance. If BankAmerica was in deep trouble, regulators would encourage a merger. If not, Bank-America might see the combination as a positive step. He told Huret that it would be better if BankAmerica approached First Interstate, as they were the bigger company. "Why don't you think about it some more and give us a call," Griffith said as the meeting ended.

Huret and Fredericks talked over the weekend. On Monday they began their analysis. They met with Alan Stein, a grizzled veteran of Goldman Sachs, who heads Montgomery's investment banking unit. Stein was skeptical, but polite. "He didn't throw us out," Fredericks said, "although he may have thought about it." Why would anyone think that First Interstate, a company with $45 billion in assets, could acquire BankAmerica, which had more than $110 billion in assets? On its face, it seemed unlikely.

Huret and Fredericks spent more time with the numbers and decided it was not that crazy. Together BankAmerica and First Interstate would be stronger than either alone. United they might be victors in this competitive new world. Without a merger, they would both survive, but perhaps never rise above mediocrity.

Huret arranged another meeting with Griffith. On the plane to Los Angeles on July 16, he and Fredericks penciled out their ideas again, reworking the proposed offer. When they arrived at First Interstate's sixty-story black-and-white tower, they asked for a conference room and a chalkboard.

Griffith sent them into "The War Room," a conference room closed off from prying eyes on the fifty-ninth floor. Griffith and Bill Sudmann, a young lawyer and merger expert, listened for more than an hour. When it was over, Montgomery had permission to explore the idea. "Operation Snowflake" was born.

The next day BankAmerica announced that its second quarter had been worse than break-even; it had lost $338 million. The problems were deeper than Montgomery Securities had suspected. The bank's big bath had come overseas, in shipping loans and other bad credits, and the loss was much bigger than anyone had anticipated. For Pinola that meant things were looking up—the weaker BankAmerica became, the more likely a deal.

In the first week of August, Huret and Fredericks flew to Los Angeles again, meeting other clients, and then driving to Pinola's home late in the afternoon. When they arrived, Pinola, who was waiting downstairs in his wine cellar, was irritated. He didn't like to be kept waiting and the pair from Montgomery were late. Pinola had his coat off, but he made it uncomfortable enough for Huret and Fredericks that they kept theirs on.

The meeting lasted just long enough for Pinola, who had already discussed the idea with Griffith, Sudmann, and others in management, to ask key questions and bless their efforts. The next step was a meeting with BankAmerica.

Huret knew McLin well. Not only had they worked together, but over the years they had worked for competing institutions only a block apart. Huret called McLin and said he had an idea to discuss with Armacost. McLin set an appointment for August 12.

A half hour before the scheduled meeting, Huret met privately with McLin and briefed him on the idea. Then Huret, Fredericks, and Stein, the head of Montgomery's investment banking group, joined McLin and Armacost in "The Corner Office."

The Montgomery team knew their quarry. They emphasized the strategic importance of the merger. It was a bold move, a way for BankAmerica to secure its place as the unquestioned leader in the western United States. "It would recreate the Giannini dream of a national empire," Huret told Armacost. It might also save Armacost's job, a message that was clear, but never specifically stated. In one bold stroke, Armacost could quiet his critics, as Huret put it, "drawing a chain link fence west of the Rockies."

Montgomery emphasized that the transaction was its idea, but said it had talked with First Interstate and Pinola was willing to merge. Armacost seemed interested. He asked a few questions about the possible roadblocks. He asked about the regulators, the chance of completing the deal, and about specifics of how the deal might be structured. He worried about a price that would satisfy shareholders.

The team from Montgomery came away enthusiastic. Armacost sounded positive. They had even raised the sticky question of who would be chief executive, and Armacost seemed comfortable with Pinola, who was only a few years short of retirement, as CEO of the combined company.

At his first meeting with Montgomery, Griffith had told Huret and Fredericks that if negotiations got serious he would call in Goldman Sachs & Co., First Interstate's investment banking firm in New York. Although Montgomery had developed the idea, and would earn a whopping fee if the deal went through, Goldman Sachs was a veteran of many takeover battles. In a deal this size, First Interstate wanted Goldman on its side.

In mid-September, Goldman's top merger and acquisition specialist, Geoffrey Boisi, flew to San Francisco to talk with Armacost. Boisi had represented BankAmerica in its purchase of Seafirst and knew Armacost well. He came away just as optimistic as Montgomery. "It has to make sense for the shareholders," Armacost cautioned Boisi.

Negotiations began to move rapidly. On September 26, McLin and Griffith met alone at the Fairmont Hotel, where they jumped into structural issues. The two banks had large areas of clear duplication. In California and Washington many of their branches were on the same street corner. They both had teams that served corporate customers, but only one would be necessary. The two walked through a host of other issues: would the Federal Reserve approve the merger? Were there serious accounting problems? What was the likely route for succession as chief executive? Which executives would stay and which would go? "It was clear that McLin was interested in doing something," says Griffith.

What emerged from the talks was a plan for an exchange of shares that would give BankAmerica shareholders about 60 percent ownership in the combined company. After the merger, it looked likely that First Interstate's banks in Washington and California would be sold, but nothing was settled. This was all preliminary.

The meeting ended with a sense of increasing momentum, but then progress abruptly stopped. BankAmerica faced the end of the third quarter, and profits did not look good. It had sold the San Francisco headquarters for $600 million, a high price, mitigated by the fact that the bank had provided 80 percent of the fi-

nancing and agreed to pay rent that was above the market price
for comparable office space in San Francisco. The gain from that
sale was eaten up by loan losses in the third quarter. The sale of
FinanceAmerica had not been completed by the end of the third
quarter and it was still taking up much of McLin's time. Bank-
America's stock had settled below $16 a share, well under the
company's book value of $26 a share. At that price, First Inter-
state's proposed exchange of shares would give its shareholders
over half the merged company, even though BankAmerica was
contributing the bulk of the assets. McLin was having a hard time
swallowing those numbers.

     Armacost faced other pressures. In August a few directors,
led by McNamara, had tried to eliminate the quarterly dividend
to shareholders. Key executives recruited by Armacost started to
defect. Pete Talbott, a rising star in the retail bank, left to join
First Boston, and Max Hopper, Armacost's technology guru,
faced with stiff budget cuts, returned to American Airlines.

     BankAmerica's legal department also came back with a neg-
ative response. They replied as they had to the proposed acquisition of Schwab & Co., arguing there was almost no chance to pull
off the First Interstate merger.

     By late October, the merger was on hold. Armacost men-
tioned it to the board at the November board meeting, but he did
so only in passing. The numbers for the fourth quarter of 1985
had begun to trickle in and they looked just as bad as the third
quarter. BankAmerica was spending more time trying to keep
depositors than worrying about a merger. Although First Interstate disliked the stalling, it was willing to be patient. Bank-
America's fortunes were likely to get worse before they got better. The worse they got, the more pressure Armacost would face;
the more pressure on him, the better the chances for the merger.

Chapter Twenty-seven

Fighting was a mistake of my competitors. . . . We might have become careless, but so many attacks were launched against us that we watched every move we made . . . so that no one could ever get anything on us.

A. P. Giannini, 1928

In the last half of 1985, in private conversations with senior managers, Sam Armacost groused about his board. Armacost didn't doubt that his strategy for BankAmerica was working or that he was on the right track and would prevail. But these seventy-year-olds were losing their nerve. The Comptroller's staff was putting pressure on them. The newspapers and shareholders were crying for blood.

One man worried him more than any other. "I never should have let McNamara on the board," he told one executive.

Robert McNamara had gradually become the leader of a small, vocal group of dissidents. They were a minority that included Cooley, Schwab, Halaby, Haas, and on occasion others, like Rudolph Peterson, the retired president of BankAmerica and an honorary board member.

The dissidents were making life hard for Sam Armacost. They didn't win battles, but they challenged Armacost at inopportune moments. At the August board meeting in 1985, the dissidents led a fight to at least cut and preferably eliminate BankAmerica's dividend. That put them on the side of the Comptroller's office, Armacost's self-defined enemy, which since 1984 had been pointedly explaining to the board and to management that Bank of America was dreadfully short of capital. The Comptroller's office had pointed out back in 1984 that the common stock dividend of $229 million a year and the preferred stock dividend of $78 million exceeded 85 percent of the company's profits. With the loss in the second quarter of 1985, paying a dividend looked ludicrous.

Despite the Comptroller's attack, the board had refused to change the dividend prior to August 1985, arguing that it had an obligation to shareholders and that profits were about to turn around. At the August board meeting, the examiners showed up again. Once more they explained their concern with the bank's capital, heightened by the recent loss. The examiners did not recommend an action, they simply made a compelling case for stopping all dividend payments. It was an impressive show by the regulators, who reviewed the company's loan problems, its capital and financial position, and then zeroed in on the problem of management. One board member later praised the review as being "like a McKinsey study," referring to one of the nation's most respected management consulting firms.

The decision on the dividend should have been simple. After the second quarter loss, logic demanded that the board stop paying dividends until it had profits once more. Sam Armacost, however, had vowed not to allow Washington to dictate the policies of the BankAmerica Corp. He countered the arguments from the regulators by asserting that the board had a different responsibility. "Regulators do not approach our business from a shareholder point of view. We're still paying out too much of our capital, but because we can see the fundamental turn and we can see the basics flowing through, we're not inclined to disadvantage our investing public relative to others," he said more than once, in vintage BankAmerispeak.

McNamara led the push to eliminate the dividend. Armacost first contended there was no need even to cut the dividend, then responded to critics by agreeing the dividend could be cut in half.

McNamara's continuing criticism had begun to take a toll. Although Armacost remained firmly in control, backed by most of the directors, McNamara's arguments were too cogent to ignore. As one insider said, "He really understood the numbers better than anyone on the board."

Board members had watched McNamara's outrage grow. He asked questions of Armacost, seeking precise, detailed information. Armacost, instead of turning to another executive for the data, plunged in, tackling the subject at an angle, veering off into another area, never answering. "You could see Bob getting angrier and angrier as the months went on," says one source.

McNamara joined the Comptroller on Armacost's blacklist. "Sam thought LaRusso [the Comptroller's senior examiner] was out to get him fired," says a former executive vice-president.

Before 1985 ended, the Comptroller and McNamara gained an ally: the Federal Reserve. The two agencies issued a joint policy statement, saying they would frown on any banking company that used the cash from a sale of assets to pay a dividend. Dividends, they argued, should come from a bank's profits, not from the slow liquidation of the company. In certain circles on Wall Street, the ruling was known as "the BankAmerica decision." (It had an effect. At the January board meeting, the directors would finally eliminate the dividend.)

Armacost's personal style also began to work against him. Instead of hunkering down in his office, Armacost appeared at golf tournaments, regularly attended social events, and rarely missed a meeting of the boards on which he served as director. Despite the bank's staggering problems, he became chairman of the Bay Area United Way, a potentially time-consuming obligation. Within the San Francisco financial community, Armacost's working ethic became a joke. "He'd stop by for the opening of an envelope," one investment banker observed. One bank president told a senior BankAmerica official, "Sam's problem is that he's too visible on the golf course." Another bank CEO reportedly told Armacost during a social event, "You're either the smartest banker I've ever seen, or the laziest. I'm not sure which."

In December, H. Joe Selby, acting Comptroller, flew to San Francisco for the monthly board meeting of BankAmerica. It was not a friendly visit. The board's actions had mystified the Comptroller's staff. Despite warnings, tough examination reports, even a year-old letter of agreement, the board didn't seem energized. As hard as the Comptroller pushed for realistic, conservative change, it got no reaction. The board continued to side with Armacost.

BankAmerica finally was about to sell FinanceAmerica and it appeared obvious the proceeds would go to pay the dividend on the company's stock—a direct violation of the spirit of the policy just announced by the Comptroller and the Fed.

In executive session, after the board meeting, senior staff of

the Comptroller of the Currency met privately with the outside
directors. Over the past year, the examiners had reached an inescapable conclusion. The loan problems, the computer snarls, the
slowness to set aside reserves all pointed to a larger cancer.
BankAmerica's management was not in control of the bank. It
was time for a change.

The Comptroller's problem was that he didn't have the
power to remove management. The Comptroller can remove a
president for specific and very limited cause, such as doing
something illegal, like dipping into the till or lending huge sums
to his neighbors. But a case of mismanagement, botched decisions, ineptitude, or plain stupidity, isn't cause enough for action. "When it comes right down to it," says a former national
bank examiner, "unless you've got a case to remove management under the removal statute, the decision is up to the board."

The regulators can't force the board to act, all they can do is
step up their pressure. First come the critical examination reports, like those filed in 1984 and 1985. If management does not
respond, there is the letter of agreement, like the one Bank-
America's board signed in late 1984. By December 1985, the
Comptroller's staff thought it had put the critical question
squarely in front of the board. "The sum total of the disasters
was only a symptom of a bigger problem," one of BankAmerica's
former examiners says. "They needed a management that would
give them direction." If a board ignores all the signals, the
Comptroller's office goes one step further. It puts the question
directly to the outside directors, those not also part of management.

"You go into an executive session and you ask them what
they think about management," another former examiner says.
"This is the big issue here, should you change the management
or shouldn't you?"

That was why H. Joe Selby had flown to San Francisco. But
the response was not what he might have expected. A few weeks
later, in the midst of a sudden public battle with one of the
best-known figures on Wall Street, BankAmerica's board stood
unwaveringly behind Sam Armacost.

The Armacost
Years
1986

Chapter Twenty-eight

Wall Street's mind is never open to suggestion and I have noticed many a moth escape a politely raised silk hat along its thoroughfares. It is my contention that these moths lived in the hair—and not the hats—of Wall Street's citizens.

A. P. Giannini, undated

BankAmerica's board refused to accept any ideas from outsiders.

Investment Banker, 1987

On January 31, 1986, Sanford Weill made an unprecedented offer to BankAmerica. He volunteered to become its chief executive—even though it already had Sam Armacost. He made the offer, not in a direct appeal to the board, but in a letter to Armacost, an approach one director later described as "among the craziest things I've ever seen."

Weill was not a corporate raider or a leveraged buyout specialist, but a builder of companies, one of the best-known men on Wall Street. With a full head of curly black hair, graying at the temples, and a big, easy grin, Weill at fifty-two resembled one of those character actors always cast as morally outraged defense attorneys from the big city. His success allowed him to own a seventeen-acre estate in Connecticut and a Manhattan townhouse. He donated $2.5 million to help rebuild Carnegie Hall.

The money came from twenty-five years in the securities business, in which Weill helped transform a tiny brokerage house into the second largest firm on Wall Street. In the process he earned a reputation as a tough boss, but also as a man who wanted to be accepted and liked. Hostile takeovers did not fit his style.

Sandy Weill's biggest deal had come in 1981 when he sold his firm, which has since become Shearson Lehman Brothers, to American Express Co., a giant financial conglomerate built around the ubiquitous plastic card. Weill joined American Express as the number two man. He lasted almost five years before leaving to find his own company to run once again. In his last two years at American Express, Weill managed the turnaround of Fireman's Fund, American Express's troubled insurance subsidiary. When James Robinson, the number one man at American Express, decided to sell Fireman's, Weill offered to buy it. Robinson, said no—selling to an executive represented sticky legal problems. But then Robinson offered Weill a lucrative contract—potentially worth tens of millions of dollars—to stay on as chief executive at Fireman's Fund after American Express sold it to the public. The two couldn't agree on final terms, so Weill walked away.

After a long vacation in the summer of 1985, Sandy Weill searched eagerly for a company to buy, to run, or, perhaps, to revive. What bigger challenge than BankAmerica?

Here was a huge company in trouble, perhaps the most visible, demanding challenge in American business. During his tenure at Fireman's Fund, Weill had met Sam Armacost briefly, asking him for a donation to Carnegie Hall. The two sat down in the spring of 1985, as the publicity about NMEC was swirling around the bank, but before the big second-quarter loss. Armacost kept Weill waiting for nearly forty minutes, and then apologized, saying he had been talking with bank regulators and hadn't been able to break away. Based on his experience with Fireman's Fund, Weill suggested the bad publicity was likely to encourage regulators to get tough, but Armacost disagreed.

When BankAmerica announced a few months later its second-quarter loss—forced on the bank by regulators—Weill concluded Armacost was either naive or disingenuous. That's when he realized that BankAmerica might be a company in need of help.

By December, Weill's enthusiasm had increased. He called Martin Lipton, a senior partner in Wachtell, Lipton, Rosen & Katz and the principal architect of dozens of successful corporate takeovers and takeover defenses. Weill outlined his objective. It was obvious that BankAmerica was on the ropes. What the company needed was a hard-driving chief executive, someone who, either as a replacement for Sam Armacost or teamed with him, could take tough steps to turn the company around. Weill liked San Francisco, he liked a challenge, and he wanted a chance to run BankAmerica.

Lipton was skeptical. He knew enough about the inbred crowd that ruled big San Francisco companies to know they would not welcome an outsider, particularly someone from Wall Street. As with businessmen in all large cities, San Francisco executives, at least those at the top of the ladder, respected, envied, and feared businessmen who had made money in New York City. One of the lessons BankAmerica's board seemed to draw from A. P. Giannini was that outsiders were not to be trusted, especially those from Wall Street.

Despite his skepticism, Lipton recommended that Weill talk with Warren Hellman, who had once been president of Lehman Brothers, a company Weill and American Express bought in 1984. Before the merger, Hellman quit to return to San Francisco, where his family had played an influential role since the days when his great-grandfather Isaias Hellman helped run A. P. Giannini out of the Columbus Savings Bank. The Hellmans then helped build Wells Fargo Corp. into a huge banking company.

Warren Hellman had set up his own investment banking firm in San Francisco with Tully Friedman, formerly the senior West Coast officer for Salomon Brothers. They had engineered the leveraged buyout of Levi Strauss & Co., making the big jeans maker a private company and putting it once again under the control of the Haas family, one of whose members sat on the BankAmerica board.

Hellman had been brooding about San Francisco's future. Committed to living and working there, he found the financial community's lack of vitality dismaying. There was a link, though he wasn't sure how direct, between the disastrous performance of BankAmerica and the steady decline in San Francisco's status. Over the past ten years, the financial center of the West Coast had shifted inexorably to Los Angeles. Not only was Los Angeles larger, it was more vibrant.

The city's corporations also seemed inexcusably mediocre. A host of once well known San Francisco companies, Crown Zellerbach, Del Monte, Castle & Cooke, Southern Pacific, and others, had disappeared, gobbled up in the takeover wars started by raiders and leveraged buyout specialists. San Francisco's companies always seemed to end up as victims, never victors.

Warren Hellman welcomed the call from Weill. The two met in mid-January in San Francisco and then again in Pebble Beach, eighty miles south of the city, where Weill was scheduled to play in the AT&T National, a major pro-am golf tournament.

Weill had also talked with bankers (including Walter Wriston, Clausen's old nemesis, the retired former chief executive of Citicorp), bank regulators, and a few board members, including Robert McNamara and Chuck Schwab. They all encouraged him to take his ideas to BankAmerica's board.

What Weill offered, and what McNamara seemed to find especially interesting, was capital. At Pebble Beach, Weill obtained a signed commitment to raise $1 billion from Shearson Lehman's president, Peter Cohen, who had once been Weill's aide at Shearson.

Hellman, Cohen, and a small group of other advisers discussed his options. They had the capital to attempt a hostile bid, but they could just as easily walk away and do nothing. Winning control, coming away with anything, would be difficult. Rick Wolf, Shearson's commercial banking specialist, gave Weill only a 20 percent chance of getting more than his foot in the door.

Weill remained calm and assertive. He wanted the bid to be friendly. He wanted to sit down with Armacost and discuss some way of working together. He wanted the chance to turn Bank-America around. "There was no way that I would think about doing this at all without the complete blessing of the board and the community, because this was really a hard job, a big, big job," Weill said later.

He realized that even $1 billion of capital might not be enough to work any miracles at BankAmerica. Weill planned to use the capital as his nest egg, a cushion to allow him to write off many of the problem loans sitting on the balance sheet. Though $1 billion was a huge amount, his advisers had wondered aloud whether the losses might eventually require $2 billion or more of new capital.

Throughout his career on Wall Street, Weill was a fiscal conservative. In a world full of gunslingers and risk takers, he focused on the basics, keeping risk to a minimum, anticipating problems, and reserving for them early. The $1 billion in capital from Shearson would allow him to bring a new conservatism to BankAmerica.

Weill thought he could slash overhead, reorganize, sell some parts of the business. Then he would hire a new generation of managers who understood consumer and investment banking and start the bank growing again.

Weill returned to San Francisco at mid-week. He drafted a letter to Armacost, but hoped never to send it. Without a letter, McNamara had counseled, Weill's idea would never reach the board. If Weill sent a letter, McNamara assured him that the board would give his ideas a fair hearing.

On the Friday before the AT&T tournament ended, Warren Hellman called Sam Armacost. They arranged for Armacost and Weill to meet in Armacost's office. Hellman dangled the $1 billion of capital and Armacost bit.

Steve McLin, Armacost's strategic planner, was preparing to spend the weekend in Pebble Beach watching golf. But on Friday he sensed that Armacost had something on his mind, and with a board meeting on Monday in Los Angeles (the board met alternate months in San Francisco and Los Angeles), McLin offered to cancel his plans and stay in San Francisco to help handle any problems. Armacost told him to go to Pebble Beach, and then asked, "What could the bank do with $1 billion of capital?" McLin responded, "I gave up believing in Santa Claus a long time ago."

A few hours later, after Armacost had talked with his legal staff and others at the bank, he called Warren Hellman to cancel the meeting. Perhaps at first, Armacost had focused on the capital rather than Weill's interest in a top spot at the company. He had a strong opinion about Weill, despite their brief encounter. Armacost had once remarked to an aide that Jim Robinson, Weill's former boss at American Express, thought Weill was a "tough son-of-a-bitch." Armacost also realized, after talking to his advisers, that this might be the first step in a takeover attempt. If Weill was coming after BankAmerica, the best thing Armacost could do was to avoid him.

"He was abrupt to the point of being nasty," says Hellman. Armacost said that if Weill wanted to meet they could talk in the days after the board meeting, but it was clear to Hellman that Armacost had already decided this was a hostile bid.

With the urging of McNamara, Weill sent his letter, knowing two of McNamara's allies on the board, Walter Haas and Najeeb Halaby, were retiring at the shareholders meetings in April, only two months away. If he wanted their votes, he had to hurry.

Weill volunteered in a cover letter to meet Armacost over the weekend. Attached was the two-page commitment from Shearson. Weill's offer, which he had wanted to present informally, was now on paper, making it somehow more formal, more ominous than intended.

Armacost panicked. At first, he wouldn't open the letter. He seemed to believe that if he didn't open it, he could argue that he had never received it. But he immediately prepared to repel Weill, reaching out for assistance. McLin, who had driven to Pebble Beach on Friday night, got an urgent call on Saturday morning. Armacost described the bid in general terms, but didn't tell him the offer came from Weill. He wanted McLin's advice on which investment banker to hire. McLin suggested that he sit tight.

McLin was more worried about legal counsel. From his motel near Pebble Beach he called Wachtell, Lipton, which had worked with the bank on some smaller mergers. But when McLin reached Edward Herlihy, the attorney he had worked with on Orbanco, he got a chilling response. Herlihy knew about the bid, he knew it was from Weill and couldn't help, he had a conflict of interest. McLin started to worry. If Weill had already lined up Wachtell, Lipton, this might be serious. He called Armacost to tell him about the problem, suggesting that the bank enlist Skadden, Arps, Flom and Meagher, Wachtell, Lipton's top competitor.

While McLin hopped on a plane for San Francisco, Armacost, ignoring McLin's advice to sit tight, phoned First Boston Corp. in New York, one of the most highly respected merger and acquisition advisers on Wall Street. Their top specialist was Joseph Perella, who agreed to fly out for the board meeting.

Once he was back in San Francisco, McLin urged Armacost to talk with Weill, but it was too late. Armacost had already hired First Boston, and, to McLin's horror, Skadden, Arps also had a conflict of interest, although Armacost wasn't worried. He told McLin he had met George Coombe, the bank's general counsel, on the golf course that morning, and Coombe had hired the local law firm of Morrison & Foerster, with little experience in the takeover wars. Now it was McLin's turn to panic.

On Sunday, February 2, Armacost called together his advisers in a conference room on the fortieth floor of the Bank-America building. The most imposing hired gun was Perella, flanked by Robert Smelick, the firm's managing partner in the San Francisco office.

Also present were McLin and Lee Prussia. As chief financial officer, Prussia should have played a major role in this debate, but since mid-1985, he had grown so pessimistic about the future of BankAmerica—and so distant from other executives—that he seemed almost isolated. Other executives worried about his health, while complaining about his gloominess. In the midst of one of the sessions, as Armacost, McLin, and the First Boston team drafted numbers that needed to be reviewed elsewhere, Prussia, who had played a minor role in the discussions, volunteered to act as a messenger, taking the figures to other analysts for their perusal. The offer showed Prussia had not grown arrogant in his new post, but it would have made him, at $420,000 a year, one of the highest paid messengers in the country.

Over the next three hours, this team fashioned a response to Weill's proposal. Perella summed the offer up as "a joke." "This is nothing more than a job application from Sandy Weill and a solicitation for new business from Shearson Lehman." One of the points in Shearson's letter, despite its confident tone, was that it would not sell securities until after it had investigated the financial position of BankAmerica thoroughly, done its "due diligence" work. In the eyes of BankAmerica's management, that meant the securities would probably never be issued.

Calmed by Perella's assessment, Armacost decided to treat the bid as just that, a joke, "a twenty-two-cent job application," with nothing behind it but the postage stamp. He explained Weill's offer to the board in terms similar to those used by Perella, giving them little information, maintaining his control over the aging men on the board. McNamara moved that the board create a special committee to review the proposal, but after Armacost's analysis, the rest of the directors remained silent. McNamara's motion died without a second.

Late Monday evening, after the board meeting, Sam Armacost called Warren Hellman. The board wasn't interested in the proposal. Sandy Weill thought about moving on to other things, the first of which was a vacation in the Caribbean.

Chapter Twenty-nine

When you are blocked, that's when you have to learn to find your
way around whatever is stopping you.

A. P. Giannini, undated

For the next two weeks, until mid-February 1986, an ominous
quiet surrounded Sandy Weill's offer to BankAmerica. Although
dozens of lawyers and bankers knew about the bid, nothing
leaked to the press. The calm allowed time for Sam Armacost to
reconsider his position. Armacost knew Weill only by reputation—as someone who got what he wanted. He worried that
Weill might attempt a hostile takeover, but he hoped that the silence meant this battle was over.

Armacost took heart from the January profits. In just one
month, the company showed a $50 million gain, a good sign, the
sort of sign that might ease doubts on the board. From deep
within BankAmerica, word trickled out to analysts that the company's profits looked very strong. A hint that the company could
earn about $500 million a year slipped into discussions. The *Wall
Street Journal* mentioned the figure in an article in mid-February,
leading one skeptical insider to describe the story as part of a
"disinformation campaign," aimed more at "The Over-the-Hill
Gang" on the board than at the public.

As the February figures rolled in, though, Armacost must
have realized that January had been an illusion. The budget for
1986 called for an addition to the reserve of $1 billion, or more
than $80 million a month. This would be offset by the sale of the
southern California headquarters and other assets, so the effect
was a drain on profits of about $50 million a month. Because
loan losses in January are usually low, that $50 million drain was
not reflected in the monthly figures. If it had been, January

would have been break-even. February would be much worse; profits were well below budget. In mid-February the bank adjusted its forecast for the year, dropping it from $450 million to about $360 million.

Morale was slipping almost as quickly as the profit projections. Rumors that the board would fire Armacost kept spreading. Under pressure from Armacost, Wiesler, now a vice-chairman and still head of the retail bank, had agreed to take early retirement. (Armacost's aides say he was pressured to leave, Wiesler's aides say he left in disgust at what Armacost was doing to the bank.) Robert Frick, vice-chairman and head of World Banking, confided to colleagues at times that he could no longer communicate with Armacost. Chuck Schwab and Dick Cooley, the chief executive at Seafirst, told associates they wanted to buy their companies back from BankAmerica, news that quickly appeared in articles in *Fortune*.

Despite the pressure, Sam Armacost didn't change his routine. He took a short business trip in early February to play in the Hawaiian Open, a pro-am tournament sponsored by United Airlines.

As Armacost worried about his putting, Robert McNamara brooded about the bank's future. McNamara had assured Weill that he would get a hearing from the board. With the pressure from the Comptroller's office, that only seemed logical.

He was furious when the board ignored Weill's bid. McNamara wanted the directors to discuss the bank's weak capital. In mid-February, he put his thoughts on paper, writing the first of a series of letters to both Armacost and the board, urging them to reconsider the Weill proposal. He encouraged Armacost to create a special committee to review Weill's offer and the entire question of how to raise capital.

McNamara also told Weill there were enough votes on the board to assure him a fair hearing now. With that encouragement, Weill agreed to try again, feeling dissatisfied with the brush-off at the February board meeting. It was incomprehensible that a bank in this much trouble would ignore an offer to raise $1 billion in capital. What was the board thinking?

On February 20, as Weill discussed a possible second try, the Reuters wire service made public some details of his first offer to run BankAmerica, although the story mysteriously linked Weill with Carl Icahn, a corporate raider whom Weill had never met. With the news that BankAmerica was "in play" and Armacost's job was in jeopardy, the stock market voiced its enthusiasm. Shares of BankAmerica stock rose more than $3 to over $17 a share, an increase in value for shareholders, as a group, of almost $500 million.

Weill sent a second letter, containing a few more details about his plans for the company, emphasizing that Shearson was promising to raise $1 billion in capital, even if the public refused to buy BankAmerica securities. Shearson would swallow the securities itself if need be—although the matter of due diligence remained.

Armacost, under attack again, began to build his defenses. It was not clear what Weill might do, and it was not at all clear where the board stood. McNamara was certain to get support from the dissidents—Haas, Halaby, Schwab, and Cooley. With twenty-one people on the board, that was still a minority. But a few directors, Andrew Brimmer, the former Fed governor; David Lewis of General Dynamics; Ruben Mettler of TRW; and Philip Hawley of Carter Hawley Hale, might side with McNamara under the right circumstances. Armacost could count on support from Franklin Murphy of Times Mirror, John Beckett of Transamerica, Jack Grey, the former president of Standard Oil, and Ray Dahl, former chairman of Crown Zellerbach. And those votes tended to sway other directors.

Armacost again reached out to Wall Street. He talked with the team at First Boston, called Nicholas Brady, chairman of Dillon Read & Co. (Brady is an influential Wall Street executive, who often provided counsel to Armacost.) He checked with Morrison & Foerster, the law firm in San Francisco. Then he began to pull together a comprehensive review of management's performance over the past five years, a review that would show how much the bank had accomplished under his leadership.

Armacost began work on a new, five-year forecast. This would be the heart of his defense, an aggressive, upbeat look at the future, a projection that showed what the company could expect from the changes made during the Armacost presidency. The board wanted proof that Armacost was in control; Armacost would give it to them.

He turned to Steve McLin and his small group in the strategic planning department. This was not going to be a "bottoms-up" analysis, taking the estimates of each line manager and adding them up, which was how the bank produced its annual budget. This was going to be a plan developed by senior management, "top-down," setting aggressive targets and defining how to achieve them. McLin and his team began by comparing BankAmerica with other large banks, looking closely at the relationship between stock price and profits. Their goal was to restore profits, raise capital, and satisfy the board.

They began with a target of $1 billion in pre-tax profits in 1990. With those profits, the stock market would open to BankAmerica. At any lower level, its shares would very likely remain unpopular.

Setting the goal was easy, getting there wouldn't be. Armacost and McLin enlisted Tom Cooper. In the months since he had taken over BAPS and asserted his leadership as head of the Group of Five, Cooper had won respect as BankAmerica's cost-cutter. He didn't enjoy the Friday afternoons when management met to discuss layoffs, but Cooper talked tough about firing people and had the sense of urgency that Armacost sought. Cooper would find a way to reach that $1 billion target.

Cooper already had a basic blueprint, drawn up by the Group of Five back in mid-1985. But he also had something more. For the first time in Sam Armacost's presidency, a spirit of crisis permeated the executive suite. It might be too late to keep the company independent, with Sandy Weill prowling around, but BankAmerica's management was finally committed to change.

Cooper checked with each of the key units, asking how much they could cut, what was realistic. Their responses convinced him that BankAmerica could attain that goal. It wouldn't be easy, the target was aggressive, leaving little room for error. But if each major division of the bank operated at a level comparable to "the best of breed" in its business, the target was attainable.

What bothered many executives was the incentive for the changed attitude. After watching the bank drift through four years of inaction, they questioned Sam Armacost's motivation. Cynics in McLin's team began to refer to the entire effort as "Project SSJ," for "Save Sam's job."

As Armacost prepared his defenses, someone else took aim at BankAmerica. In the second week of February, a few days before the Reuters story broke, rumors about Weill had spread through the investment banking world. They were amorphous, incomplete: Weill had talked to the board. Weill had talked to Armacost. Weill wanted a job. Weill was ready to mount a takeover.

One of the first to have heard the rumors was Gene Fife, a partner at Goldman Sachs in San Francisco. Fife called Armacost, offering his help against Weill. Armacost knew and liked the Goldman bankers, they had worked on the Seafirst purchase. He told Fife that with Weill snooping around, Goldman could probably be of more help representing First Interstate than doing anything else. Whether or not Armacost intended to encourage First Interstate, Fife got the message that Armacost wanted a "white knight."

Geoffrey Boisi and Joseph Wender, the Goldman bankers working with First Interstate, called McLin, seeking a meeting between Armacost and Joe Pinola, First Interstate's chief executive. First Interstate was preparing a bid, they told him. Before Weill appeared, BankAmerica's stock had dropped to $12 a share; now it was over $17. Pinola and Goldman had been looking at an offer of around $17 a share, $19 tops. McLin responded that Armacost was caught up with Sandy Weill's offer, that it wasn't a good time to talk. Boisi told him First Interstate was eager enough that if Sam and Joe didn't talk soon, First Interstate would probably send an offer by mail.

McLin reached Armacost and recommended they meet with Goldman. It was better to negotiate now than to walk into the March board meeting with two unsolicited offers on the table. He and Pinola might reach an understanding. Then if the board decided that Weill's proposal had some merit or if Weill launched a hostile takeover, Pinola could serve as a "white knight," riding in to save BankAmerica—and Armacost.

Armacost expected to beat Weill in the boardroom. He counted enough votes to win, but he couldn't be certain. Pressure was building on the board. Not only were the regulators bearing down, but the press, stockholders, even friends of the directors, were putting pressure on the board to do something. Though Armacost prided himself on his ability to keep the board in line, there was always a chance that something unexpected might happen, that the board might assert itself.

Armacost agreed to call Pinola to arrange a meeting, but first he wanted his own investment bank advisers. With Goldman representing First Interstate, Armacost phoned Jay Higgins, then head of mergers and acquisitions at Salomon Brothers. Salomon would analyze First Interstate's bid, First Boston would handle the defense against Weill. Higgins flew out to San Francisco on February 21, the day after Reuters ran its story on Sandy Weill.

The merger with First Interstate looked far less attractive now than it had in late 1985. When Armacost first considered the proposal, BankAmerica's stock was selling at around $20 a share. BankAmerica's shareholders would have ended up with about 60 percent of the combined company, which meant they would have received 60 percent of the profits. Since then BankAmerica's stock price had dropped and First Interstate's price had risen. With First Interstate offering to pay about $17 a share, BankAmerica's shareholders would end up with about 40 percent of the new company.

First Interstate faced its own problem. Buying BankAmerica was not unlike buying a nuclear power plant after an accident. Everyone knows the reactor is damaged, but no one has been inside to assess the damage. Pinola knew enough about BankAmerica's loans to estimate the total loss, but he couldn't be certain how much of the portfolio was contaminated. To be fair to his own shareholders, he had to build in protection. The only thing certain, at least to those who had bought troubled banks in the past, was that the loan losses were likely to be worse than anybody on the outside expected.

By now, Montgomery Securities' "Project Snowflake" had become Goldman's "Project GoldCoast." Huret and Fredericks still provided advice to First Interstate, but they were on the sidelines. Goldman was leading the negotiations and had arranged to meet Armacost on February 27. But as that date approached, the stories broke about the Weill bid and BankAmerica's stock rose to more than $17 a share, making First Interstate's bid look meager.

On Thursday, February 27, four days before the March board meeting, Sam Armacost met with the representatives of Goldman Sachs. In a little less than a week, Goldman had pieced together a forty-four-page analysis of the largest, and perhaps most audacious, merger ever proposed in the banking industry. Prepared in haste, the study was flawed. If two of the ten largest banking companies in America were to merge, a welter of complex financial and accounting questions needed to be solved.

The companies had to convince the regulators, iron out potential operating problems, and ensure that the institution that emerged from the combination would be a survivor. Goldman's rushed projections skimmed over the most difficult problems.

Its figures did show, though, that the merger was no panacea. Whether BankAmerica merged or not, its recovery would come slowly. Combined with First Interstate it had more options, deeper management, and better odds of surviving as an independent company, but there was no reason for jubilation.

The combined company could shed perhaps $15 billion of assets, leaving it with more than $150 billion in assets, operations in thirteen states, and a strong international branch network. Earnings would be high enough to pay a dividend to BankAmerica stockholders, but the underlying financial position of the company—its capital and its ability to raise money in the markets—would still be shaky.

Goldman didn't need to dwell on the numbers, though. This was a merger driven by other considerations. Although no one was certain the numbers made sense, the promise of the combined company tantalized everyone. Together, BankAmerica and First Interstate would reunite the Giannini empire. With banks in fifteen western states, they would dominate banking in half the country. Pinola knew how much mileage there was in the Bank of America name. He had visions of capitalizing on that name to breathe new life into his franchising program. It would open the way for a worldwide effort, attracting bigger and healthier banks. If there was magic left in Giannini's vision, this merger would tap it.

Goldman was swept along in this enthusiasm. Its investment bankers had prepared a list of major issues, on which they briefed Armacost. Geoffrey Boisi and Joe Wender, the two senior advisers from Goldman, offered their ideas on which directors would remain on the board, plus some ideas on which executives would stay and what posts they might hold in the new organization. Goldman mentioned regulatory problems, but both sides agreed the regulators would probably go along.

Armacost expressed misgivings. He thought the bid was very low, since he remained confident that BankAmerica was about to revive and show a strong increase in profits. When the recovery came, the stock would soar. He didn't want to give away a rich franchise in a hasty merger.

There was also the question of the chief executive. It was obvious to everyone that Pinola, sixty-one, expected to emerge as chief executive. He was older than Armacost, Armacost had once worked for him at BankAmerica, and BankAmerica was in trouble, not First Interstate. Armacost worried about his chances of succeeding Pinola. He was willing to wait for Pinola to retire, but he wanted assurances that he would run the merged company after Pinola left.

While Armacost, McLin, and Goldman's senior investment bankers met for more than three hours on the fortieth floor of the BankAmerica headquarters, executives from First Interstate waited on the thirty-third floor in Goldman Sachs's office, eating pizza and drinking Anchor Steam beer. Occasionally questions would filter out from the meeting upstairs. The one that provoked the most interest was perhaps the simplest: "How old is Joe Pinola?" It was important to Sam Armacost that he know exactly when Joe Pinola would retire.

Among the senior staff at Goldman, a sense of enthusiasm was building again. They had discussed key issues with Armacost and he was agreeing with their findings. It was obvious that he had some doubts, but it was also obvious that Sam Armacost wanted this deal to go ahead. Armacost agreed with Goldman that it was best to have lawyers standing by over the weekend to draft a merger agreement. "It was clear to us," says Joe Wender, a managing director of Goldman Sachs and specialist in bank finance, "that this deal had a chance of being completed before the weekend was over."

The only question left was whether Pinola and Armacost would feel comfortable with one another. A meeting was set for Saturday morning. Goldman's Boisi wanted to serve as a "referee" when Pinola and Armacost met. He knew both and they felt comfortable with him. He felt he could ensure the talks would progress. McLin and Salomon balked. If anybody was going to be in the room with the two, it ought to be someone from Salomon *and* someone from Goldman Sachs.

Where would the two meet? Pinola wanted a neutral setting, someplace outside the BankAmerica building, but he finally agreed to meet in a conference room in Goldman's offices—in the BankAmerica building, but not in a BankAmerica office. Joe and Sam would meet alone. If the meeting went well, Armacost would have a merger to take to the board on Monday morning.

Chapter Thirty

The bank . . . was launched and has had its remarkable record of
growth on a policy of conservative yet energetic and enthusiastic
optimism. The institution has never known the word "failure" in
any matter, large or small.

A. P. Giannini, 1914

The next day, Friday, February 28, 1986, Sam Armacost spent building his defenses against Sandy Weill's unwanted
offer. He reviewed his presentation to the board and his five-year
forecast, making changes throughout the day. Working with Ken
Wilson, then a senior investment banker with Salomon Brothers,
he analyzed the proposal from First Interstate, the "white
knight" bid, and prepared for his meeting with Joe Pinola.

Armacost had also obtained the backing of three of the nation's largest investment banks. They agreed that BankAmerica
did not need Sandy Weill's help to raise $1 billion. Salomon
Brothers, Merrill Lynch, and First Boston each offered to help
raise the money, without Weill's presence, if BankAmerica decided to sell securities.

The final element in Armacost's defense of his job was the
decision to appoint Tom Cooper chief operating officer. Armacost had been planning this appointment since the middle of the
previous year, under pressure from the board. Now, in order to
make his five-year forecast more believable, he would install
Cooper, whom the board accepted as a cost-cutter.

Late Friday afternoon, Armacost sat down with McLin, Wilson, and Dick Barrett, one of Salomon's top investment bankers
on the West Coast. They reviewed their assessment of the First
Interstate bid and the company's forecast of earnings. Armacost

objected strongly to McLin's five-year earnings projections. "You've got to make the numbers look better," he told him.

Throughout the evening, the reviews continued. Armacost, along with Cooper and Lee Prussia, chairman and chief financial officer, stayed until after 10:00 P.M., refining projections. The numbers began to look better as the cost-cutting went deeper. But not until after midnight did the last of the staff leave the office.

On Saturday morning, the entire BankAmerica team arrived at World Headquarters before 10:00 A.M. For days the press had been speculating about what would happen at the board meeting. Word had leaked out about the letters of support from First Boston, Merrill Lynch, and Salomon Brothers. That morning the *New York Times* carried a disquieting story. Robert Cole, the *Times* business writer who covers mergers and acquisitions, described the pledges to help raise $1 billion, and then carefully pointed out that Goldman Sachs, one of BankAmerica's main advisers in the past, had not returned his calls. Insiders at BankAmerica knew that if Cole dug further, the talks with First Interstate would become public, something no one wanted right now.

At 11:00 A.M., McLin called Goldman's offices. Armacost was too busy to come downstairs, he told them. Pinola would have to come to Sam's office. Boisi and others at Goldman were furious. Merger negotiations are a form of psychological warfare. The question of which party is in control, which has more negotiating power, changes depending on the mood of negotiations, even the surroundings. Goldman's office was a neutral setting, Armacost's office was not. Armacost would be at home, in control. Pinola would be the visitor, the supplicant.

Pinola didn't have much choice, having already flown from Los Angeles for the meeting. He and Boisi took the elevators to the fortieth floor where Pinola and Armacost met in Armacost's office for an hour. The result was not good.

Armacost still didn't like the price. He thought BankAmerica was worth at least $25 a share, its book value, and First Interstate seemed willing to offer no more than $19 a share. He expressed concern about his own role, seeking answers to the question of succession, but Pinola refused to put him at ease. There would be no guarantee that Armacost would become chief executive once Pinola retired.

Armacost let Pinola scan the examination reports from the Comptroller of the Currency and then told him that he was plan-

ning to make Cooper chief operating officer. Pinola advised
against it. Though Armacost certainly could use help, Pinola told
him it was a "lose-lose situation." If Cooper carried out Armacost's plan and the bank turned around, Cooper would get the
credit. If Cooper failed, people would blame Armacost for picking Cooper.

The meeting broke inconclusively. Armacost was uneasy
with Pinola's stance, but he appeared optimistic that a deal could
be struck. He liked the long-term outlook for the combined company. Over a lunch of Whoppers brought in from a nearby Bur-
ger King, Armacost shared some of his concerns with McLin and
Salomon's Wilson.

At 3:00 P.M. Boisi from Goldman Sachs called to suggest another brief meeting between Armacost and Pinola, who was
downstairs in Goldman's office and was staying in San Francisco
that evening. McLin said it couldn't be done. Armacost was preparing for the board meeting and was conferring with John Gutfreund, Salomon's top executive, who had flown out from New
York for the occasion.

That evening the entire Salomon team joined McLin and
Armacost for dinner in the executive dining room. Armacost
raised a series of questions, but one was particularly intriguing.
The directors had proposed establishing a special committee to
review Sandy Weill's suggestion. What did Gutfreund think?

John Gutfreund emanates a calm, quiet self-assurance.
With his round face, heavy lids, and stocky build, he draws to
mind images of a Buddha, albeit a cigar-smoking, Jewish incar-
nation. Armacost and McLin wanted Gutfreund's advice in part
because he was a master at board politics. (In 1983 he had per-
suaded Salomon's board to oust its former chief executive, leaving him in sole control.) Gutfreund's skill in manipulating a
board was what Armacost was seeking.

Gutfreund thought the special committee was a terrible
idea. The question of capital was clearly the prerogative of management. If Armacost set up a special committee to review
Weill's proposal, he would be asking the directors to do management's job, opening the door for them to take a greater role in
day-to-day management. It was better to confront the problem at
once and get it out of the way, rather than resorting to a committee, which would drag out the decision for months.

After dinner, in a quiet moment with his staff, Gutfreund

wondered aloud about Armacost as a manager. Why didn't he have more people with him? Where was his team? This was probably the most important weekend of his career. Why was there only one person, McLin, with him at dinner? Where was the rest of management?

BankAmerica's board met on Sunday afternoon in Los Angeles. Early that morning, Armacost headed south, but before leaving San Francisco, he called Pinola promising they would talk again after the board meeting.

Once in Los Angeles, Armacost met with the executive committee, emerging unsettled. The numbers for the presentation at the board meeting on Monday were not good enough; they had to be higher. Armacost found McLin and told him to work up new projections. Over the next eighteen hours, McLin, Cooper, and a small team of McLin's aides dug to find another $100 million of expense cuts or sources of potential revenue. Armacost's earlier projection had been aggressive, the revised one, said an onlooker, was "unbelievable."

The bankers from Salomon Brothers, including Gutfreund, had arrived in Los Angeles in the late morning. There was nothing to do but wait. Armacost thought Gutfreund might join him at the committee meetings, but he wanted to get a sense of the board first. He wanted Gutfreund to stand by; at the least Gutfreund would join the board and Armacost for dinner.

As the day wore on, Gutfreund's good humor faded. He was upset by the scurrying around to manufacture higher profits. And he didn't like waiting.

Near the end of the day, after the committee meetings ended, George Coombe, BankAmerica's general counsel, asked Gutfreund to come upstairs for a briefing with the company's other investment bankers. Coombe, who sometimes irritates his staff by lecturing them like schoolchildren, managed to incense Gutfreund. No one had told Gutfreund that First Boston, one of Salomon's arch-rivals in the mergers and acquisition business, had also been brought out for the board meeting. He declined to head upstairs, where First Boston was waiting, and started wondering what else he might not have been told.

Sensing Gutfreund's anger, Coombe started to brief Salomon's team alone. He reeled off a list of questions that he expected Salomon to answer. The board wanted an analysis of the various alternatives for raising capital. Coombe asked Gutfreund to offer prices and terms for various securities the company might sell. "This was ludicrous," said one of the investment bankers who saw the meeting. "We had been asked to come out a week before. What Coombe wanted requires weeks of analysis. And we would never commit to specific prices before a security went to market."

Gutfreund barked, "That's not what we came here to do." Then he explained his mission to Coombe. He had come to review the bid from First Interstate and to help convince the board that it didn't need Sandy Weill's help to raise $1 billion.

As a final injury, Coombe showed Gutfreund a draft of several motions he had prepared for the board meeting. Near the top of the pile was a motion to create a special committee to review the Weill proposal. "You could see the smoke coming out of John's ears," says one source. This was the same proposal that Gutfreund had dismissed as terrible at dinner the night before. It was obvious that Armacost and Coombe weren't talking, or that Armacost was ignoring Gutfreund's advice.

"If you want to do this, go ahead, but you can do it without us," Gutfreund said. "Come on, let's get out of here." Gutfreund turned to leave, but then thought better of it. He huddled with his staff and decided to stay for the dinner. That evening he told the board that BankAmerica did not need Sandy Weill or his help to raise $1 billion in capital.

The first day of the March board meeting was over. Armacost thought he was ahead. After dinner, he met again with McLin to review the projections, which finally worked. They made a few more adjustments. At 2:30 A.M. they finished their last-minute additions in Armacost's hotel room at the Bonaventure Hotel.

On Monday morning, the full board meeting began as usual, at 10:00 A.M. Armacost had been over the presentation a dozen times in various forms. He was as prepared as he would ever be.

The report began with a review of Armacost's entire tenure. This was not a balanced, objective view of the world; it was a sales document. No one who heard Sam Armacost's March speech to the board would have guessed that he led a company in deep trouble.

Armacost reminded the board of where BankAmerica had

been when he took office. Although it was highly profitable, it was weaker than it appeared. Its share of the California market had been dwindling steadily. Customers were complaining about poor-quality service—a poll by the bank showed that some one third of all people in California had once banked at Bank of America and swore they never would again. Computer systems were archaic and overhead was swelling.

In the last five years, Armacost went on, the company had made tremendous strides. He had reduced the interest rate mismatch from more than $7 billion to less than $2 billion. He had increased primary capital from under 4 percent to more than 6 percent. He had installed the automated teller network, closed more than 230 branches, reorganized the rest, and cut more than seven thousand employees from the payroll. Those were not minor accomplishments. "You're not going to be able to find too many other institutions that have reduced employment more than us," he said.

He did not tell the board that the mismatch had cost the company as much as $3.5 billion. He glossed over the point that the major reason primary capital had risen was that the loan loss reserve—part of primary capital—had been increased under pressure from bank regulators. He played down the fact that many jobs had been cut by selling subsidiaries. And he didn't mention that despite his cuts the bank's expenses were still far too high.

Armacost turned instead to his strategy, the document that had grown out of painstaking meetings with Adizes, countless studies by Boston Consulting Group, and an equal number by McLin's strategic planning group. BankAmerica would no longer serve all markets, all around the world. It was going to become a West Coast bank. It would serve some large corporations elsewhere in the United States, but not many. Its attention would focus on California and Washington.

Then came the heart of the presentation, the projections of profits. The company had been forecasting a profit of $360 million in 1986. The new plan—the Project SSJ plan—called for a profit of $415 million. Cooper, McLin, and their staff had found $100 million of cost savings and increased revenues, but that was reduced by an increase in the annual provision for loan losses and a rise in income taxes. It was a brash prediction, suggesting a swing in profits of more than $750 million from the previous year's loss of $337 million.

No bank in history had come close to such a rebound. Just breaking even in 1986 would have been a major accomplishment. But under pressure from board members, Armacost promised that he could deliver what no other bank CEO had delivered.

With that heart-stopping turnaround, BankAmerica would be on its way to a superb decade. The steady rise in profits after 1986 would lower its funding costs and restore its debt ratings. It would be able to sell common stock to raise capital. By 1990 the company would earn more than $1 billion and its shares would be selling for over $40.

Despite the record of management, the directors accepted this plan with only mild questioning. Despite the fact that Armacost had proven unable to push costs down rapidly, they accepted his pledge to slash spending throughout the bank. Although revenues looked anemic, they accepted his assertion that a sharply focused strategy would produce immediate results. And despite the fierce competition in all BankAmerica's markets, they accepted that Armacost could attract wealthy consumers, small businesses, and medium-size and large corporations based in California and Washington.

A few board members listened with skepticism, knowing that Armacost had missed every one of his budget projections for the last five years. They knew expenses were still too high and that every major bank in California was lusting after the same customers that Armacost wanted to serve—devoting so much effort to the market that profits were growing skimpy.

But Armacost's message was what most of the directors wanted to hear so they could reject Sandy Weill and keep Bank-America independent.

What seemed to make Armacost's case more convincing was his decision, after months of pressure from McNamara and other directors, to appoint a chief operating officer. Though not all the board members thought Tom Cooper was the right man—some would have preferred a banker with experience at something larger than a $4 billion Philadelphia bank—it was possible Cooper might get the job done.

Now Armacost was prepared to discuss the Weill proposal. Without mentioning the potential offer from First Interstate, BankAmerica's executives presented the Weill offer as two separate proposals. One was a job application. The other was a new business proposal from an investment banking firm with which BankAmerica did very little business.

Described that way, it seemed obvious that the proposal had remarkably little merit—if one believed Armacost's forecast for the future. The idea of a special committee to review the Weill bid died once more. Armacost had diffused the issue—almost.

At the end of the day, the outside directors moved into executive session. They asked representatives of Salomon and First Boston to stay, so they could solicit answers to a couple of critical questions. But bank management left the boardroom.

One of the directors asked whether hiring a new CEO, not necessarily Weill, would make it easier to raise capital. This was the sort of question that might have triggered a rebellion, since the answer was obvious. First Boston's Dave Batten hesitated, so Gutfreund jumped in. Yes, it would be easier to raise capital with new management, he said, but that's not the real question. The question is, do you want to change management? You have a management team. They have a plan. If you think they can deliver on that plan you should give them a chance. If not, then you should think about changing management. Sandy Weill, he reminded them, was not the right guy.

Whatever rebellion might have occurred, died. The dissidents on the board, still in the minority, had been outmaneuvered. They had lost their chance to use the threat of Sandy Weill to force a reexamination of Armacost's tenure.

John Beckett, an influential board member, asked a question that hinted at a latent machismo among BankAmerica's directors. "If they don't make their plan, then we will have grounds for removing management, right?" he asked. After five years of inaction, as Armacost missed budget after budget, that question offered an ironic commentary on the board's vision of itself.

Despite Beckett's posturing, John Gutfreund had served Sam Armacost's purpose—he had saved Sam's job. The board had agreed to wait.

Days later Sandy Weill received two letters. One, from director Franklin Murphy, rejected his offer. The second, from Sam Armacost, said that the bank's advisers raised "serious questions as to whether such a financing program would be in the best interests of stockholders under the present circumstances." Armacost also asked Weill to send him a copy of any plans he had for the bank, noting that he and the board would consider the ideas in their efforts to revive the company. Weill bristled at the suggestion and never shared his thoughts. "Their whole reaction was idiotic," says an adviser to Weill.

Armacost also called Joe Pinola to say he was still interested in a merger and wanted to meet a week later in Los Angeles, when they could discuss the offer in more detail.

On Wednesday morning, Bob Cole of the *New York Times*, who had continued to dig, broke the story of the First Interstate merger talks. When he learned the story was running, Sam Armacost had brought his chief legal counsel, his top public relations person, and McLin to his office to draft a response to the *New York Times* story. Armacost wanted to say the two companies had never talked and were not talking now, even though he had scheduled another session a week later. McLin fumed. He thought the wording violated securities laws regarding takeover bids and might send them to jail. The attorney and p.r. man disagreed, although it was not clear to McLin that they realized how close the bank had come to a merger with First Interstate. Armacost wouldn't budge, so McLin ended up stalking from the room. The denial was softened when Armacost made a courtesy call to Pinola, read him the release, and changed the statement at the request of Paul Minch, Pinola's public relations man.

On Wednesday afternoon, BankAmerica issued its denial: "We are not negotiating with First Interstate or anyone else."

Sandy Weill shortly announced that he would not pursue a hostile takeover. With that, Sam Armacost heaved a great sigh of relief. The pressure was gone, Weill would not try again, so there was no reason to see Joe Pinola. Their scheduled meeting in Los Angeles never took place.

Chapter Thirty-one

It doesn't matter if you don't always hit the exact bull's-eye. The other rings in the targets score points too.

A. P. Giannini, 1921

During the board's tense meeting in Los Angeles, Tom Cooper remained at his desk in San Francisco. He knew that Armacost planned to appoint him president and chief operating officer of Bank of America, but he had been hearing that for nearly seven months. He couldn't be sure the board would go along. When Armacost finally phoned to tell him it was official, Cooper's first response was to call his wife.

A few minutes later, congratulations began to flood in. For months it had been clear that Cooper was on the rise, his influence growing. Just as when Sam Armacost became president in 1981, BankAmerica's managers were prepared to charge any hill Cooper might decide to take. They hoped one man could painlessly restore direction to BankAmerica.

Cooper continued his long hours, arriving at 5:30 A.M., and staying late. Customers' nerves had to be soothed, budgets reexamined, and costs cut. Just four days after becoming president of the bank, Cooper sat down with his top aides to review their program for cutting expenses. Each knew about Armacost's aggressive new budget; their job was to achieve it.

Cooper had his list of priorities. Little had changed since a year earlier—costs were still out of control, capital was still low, and problem loans were too high. One of his most pressing jobs was the sale of major subsidiaries. Armacost had hesitated to close offices overseas or sell large lines of business because he expected a rebound. Cooper saw these business units as a way to

289

raise capital—the capital the bank needed if it was to survive. Beginning with the list of salable properties drawn up a year before, Cooper, working quietly with McLin and others, began to search for buyers. He tried to put a price on the bank's Italian subsidiary, its branches in Argentina, and any other operation that did not fit in with the new, leaner vision of Bank of America. The retail bank in Germany, the credit card operation in the Netherlands, and the bank in Spain all would be sold by early 1987. Other assets had already been sold, including, fittingly, a subsidiary in Guam that seemed a tribute to the bank's excesses, with a lobby in its one office that stretched the length of half a football field and stations for fifty tellers—on an island that barely justified a storefront branch and an automated teller machine.

The biggest piece of BankAmerica's overseas empire was the Banca d'America e d'Italia, large, independent, and profitable, which put it at the top of the list of assets to sell. The only pieces of the company that were not for sale, aside from the core banking business in California, were Seafirst and Charles Schwab & Co., companies that Sam Armacost had acquired. They were valuable and untouchable, because Armacost refused to sell them.

BankAmerica set its investment bankers to work developing plans for selling its car loans and real estate mortgages. Selling those loans would reduce the size of the bank. Since the bank also earned a fee by making and selling each loan, loan sales might become a source of profits in the future. This was already a fashionable business for other banks, though not a highly profitable one.

Parceling up the bank and finding buyers for the pieces was the easy part. The hard part was forcing managers to fire people. The one vivid point Cooper and McLin had made to Armacost prior to the March board meeting was that bodies had to be eliminated in order to save money. Not only did they earn salaries, but they took trips, used paper clips, and took up office space. Unless he shrank the work force, he could not hope to get costs under control.

Firing employees required the help of hundreds of line managers, which made it perhaps Cooper's hardest challenge. Armacost had found out how difficult it was to force tough decisions on these people; now it was Cooper's turn to learn that lesson. If he couldn't force the cuts, BankAmerica would never revive as Armacost had promised.

Cooper found places to save quickly, mostly in the back office, where checks were sorted and data entered into computers. The bank had cut costs by moving these functions from the branches to regional centers. To shrink costs further the bank could reduce the number of regional centers. Cooper did just that, and with each closed office he lowered the body count, driving down costs.

But most managers resisted laying off people. For years they had been compensated on the basis of how big their branch was and how many people they employed. Instinctively, branch managers fought Cooper's efforts. They stalled, claimed cuts that proved overstated, and only reluctantly fired anyone. When layoffs eventually did come, severance pay and related expenses seemed to gobble up months of expected savings.

Cooper won admiration for pushing the executives under him to attack the right problems. He sat down with them at least once a month and discussed their loan losses, their expenses, the items that needed to be brought under control. Yes, it was important to make new loans; yes, it was important to sell, but right now the company needed an intense, all-absorbing focus on expenses. And it needed to build a new awareness of the importance of credit quality, a message Cooper continually drove home.

As chief operating officer, Cooper oversaw all the major business units. The staff functions—the legal, finance, and personnel departments—reported to Armacost or Prussia. Inevitably this led to friction. Cooper tackled his own units first, hacking away at overhead, while the staff functions, many of which Cooper considered bloated and unnecessary, remained virtually untouched—or so it seemed to those under Cooper.

Morale never improved. In the branches, the continuing flux of changes and reorganizations left branch managers and regional branch managers dispirited. A few weeks after Cooper became president, Jim Wiesler, head of the retail bank, agreed to take his previously announced early retirement. Wiesler had encouraged branch managers to innovate. Some did so successfully, developing new ways of doing business, trying to keep the quality of service from deteriorating. But as the branches closed, that was difficult. Each time the bank closed one branch, it gave an edict to the regional office to retain 80 to 90 percent of the customers at the closed branch. Customers were transferred to neighboring offices, which overloaded tellers there. In order to handle the higher volume, the branch managers added more people, defeating the attempts at cost-cutting and bringing rebukes from the head office. But even with the extra tellers, customers moaned about the poor service.

Although regional offices now processed loans and checking statements, customers still brought their problems to the branches. But now the information on a misfiled check or the application for a loan was in a regional office ten, twenty, perhaps even a hundred miles away. The branch called the regional office, but it wasn't equipped to handle complaints. When branch managers groused to the head office, Cooper put the burden on them. "If it's your customer and he's got a problem, it's up to you to fix it. Even if it means driving out to the service center at midnight," he told them.

This was not what branch managers wanted to hear. Faced with customer complaints, firings, constant reorganizations from above, branch managers grew mutinous. To many, Cooper became a symbol of the callousness of the new regime. Those who remembered the bank's history compared him to Elisha Walker, the broker from Wall Street who had fired staff and tried to dismantle A. P. Giannini's empire in 1931.

Cooper also faced resistance on the fortieth floor. Although Sam Armacost wanted Cooper's assistance, he hesitated to relinquish authority. Armacost expected to continue to make decisions and be involved in day-to-day operations. Cooper assumed he had a job to do and a mandate to get it done. He made decisions quickly, without consulting Armacost. Armacost decided Cooper was overstepping his authority, which created a constant, low-voltage friction between the two.

Perhaps Cooper's most dedicated opponent was Lee Prussia. Prussia had played only a peripheral role in the effort to cut costs in March. The board's promotion of Cooper had stripped him of some of his responsibilities, but that didn't seem to bother Prussia as much as his continuing dread about the dark side of the economy, Third World debt, and the likelihood of a recession. Cost-cutting by Armacost and Cooper, at least in Prussia's mind, was sapping the bank's strength. The bank was prepared to sell profitable subsidiaries and reduce employees, but that would reduce revenues.

Prussia saw a danger that outsiders called "the death spiral." In the past, whenever a commercial bank got in serious trouble it grew its way out. It wrote loans in a controlled frenzy, increasing its income, and covering part of the drain from its loan losses. As the bank grew, the loan problems shrank as a percentage of the bank's total business.

But since 1984, bank regulators had demanded that banks keep a minimum level of capital. That meant that if a bank wanted to grow, it needed to first add capital. BankAmerica didn't have the capital, and couldn't raise it cheaply, so its growth was constrained. Its only option was to shrink, get its expenses in line, and hope its troubled customers would get healthier.

Could a commercial bank shrink its way to health? No one knew for sure. The bank ran the risk of entering a never-ending downward gyre.

BankAmerica had already started to shrink. It was selling profitable subsidiaries, such as FinanceAmerica and Banca d'Italia. The sales brought in money, but this was quickly eaten up by loan losses. The sales also lowered the bank's overall revenues, because the profits from the subsidiaries no longer belonged to the bank.

If the death spiral analogy was correct, the bank would remain in danger, with too little capital. Its bad loans would represent a larger percentage of its total assets. So the company would be forced to slash overhead, close branches. That would reduce income even more. The bank would continue to lose money, its thin base of capital would shrink further, and it would be forced to sell more assets, starting the cycle again.

Prussia and Cooper both realized they were fighting a difficult battle. Cooper stressed that the only way out was to cut costs and sell assets. Prussia emphasized the need to generate higher revenues, since that was the only way to ride out a recession, which would bring more loan problems. Without more capital and higher revenues, the bank would teeter constantly at the edge of disaster.

However, they both grasped the fundamental problem. There were too many banks chasing too few good loans. Large corporations rarely borrowed from banks anymore and many smaller corporations didn't either. They could raise money by selling securities directly to the public through the "junk bond" market or by issuing commercial paper. When corporations did borrow, they were pursued by banks from the United States, Europe, and Japan, all of which were desperate to lend money to high-quality borrowers. The competition for good credits had driven profits on corporate lending down to unacceptable levels for most U.S. banks.

So banks courted consumers, throwing money at less credit-worthy borrowers and cutting rates on loans to high-quality borrowers. That was making consumer lending a riskier, less profitable business. Even if BankAmerica could find a way to begin growing, the borrowers it was likely to find would represent greater risks than in the past.

Prussia's realistic concern about the death spiral, unfortunately, didn't offer a solution for BankAmerica. The only way to get BankAmerica growing again was to arrange an infusion of capital from outside the bank. Prussia thought that was the only option, if he was right about how desperate things were. It meant a merger or a large investment from some outside source. Cooper dismissed Prussia's alternative, figuring that if Prussia were right there was little he could do about it in the short run and whether he was right or not, BankAmerica still had to trim costs and sell subsidiaries to survive. Prussia was worried about how the bank would survive an economic downturn in 1988 or 1989; Cooper was worried about next quarter and the quarter after that.

The 1986 annual meeting of shareholders took place on April 29, six weeks after Cooper became president and began searching for ways to slash costs. The Masonic Auditorium atop San Francisco's Nob Hill was packed with more than fifteen hundred shareholders and employees, a noisy and obstreperous group. "It was like hell night at a fraternity," says a former bank regulator. Both Lee Prussia and Sam Armacost spoke. Prussia explained what had happened in 1985, Armacost talked about what would happen in 1986.

Armacost boasted about the company's $63 million profit in the first quarter. He didn't mention that after a $50 million profit in January, the earnings had tailed off sharply. He wanted to sound confident, and he did. Despite the jeers and boos, Armacost put the best possible face on the bank's performance.

"There is no magic strategy to solve our problems, no secret formula for success" he acknowledged. "I can describe our activities over the past year with two four-letter words—hard work.

"Hard work hammers at our loan problems, improving our loan portfolio.

"Hard work shapes our operations to meet the demands of tough competition.

"Hard work serves our customers.

"Hard work will result in returns to you, our shareholders, at the bottom line."

Armacost finished his remarks with one of the messages that went over well in meetings with employees: "As I tell Bank-Americans, this is no time for the faint of heart. It's going to take courage, competence, and confidence to get to the top again. . . . But we will."

Armacost took the same message to New York, selling his rosy vision to the analysts who followed BankAmerica's stock. As he did on most business trips, he spent the flight out reviewing file cards on the customers and analysts he would meet. He took the red-eye, started his meetings early in the morning, and continued through dinner. The next day began with a breakfast meeting, followed by a morning of meetings with analysts, after which he caught a plane back to San Francisco for an evening event.

His message throughout this whirl of meetings was as optimistic as his presentation to the board. He saw tremendous progress at the bank and was certain that costs were coming under control. He was not as specific with analysts as he had been with the board, but he made it clear the bank could show a sizable profit in 1986. In the days after his visit, a few stock analysts who had fallen victim to Armacost's persuasion wrote of the turnaround that was coming at BankAmerica.

One of the promises that Armacost had made was that the operating costs of the company would not rise during 1986—the same claim he had made to the board in March. Armacost also asserted that the bank understood its loan loss problems, that there would be no more surprises.

On that last point he was to be quickly proven wrong. Early in the year, a complete review of Bank of America's loan portfolio had started. The bank's international loans had been thoroughly examined with the help of the Comptroller in earlier years, prompting the large loan write-offs. But the retail bank, with its nearly nine hundred branches in California, had not shown the same weakness. Its loans had been reviewed with normal diligence. Now, BankAmerica's senior credit officer, Glenhall Taylor, who had worked previously for Wells Fargo Bank and Seattle First National Bank, wanted a thorough review of the retail loans. Even though money was tight elsewhere, he got the cash to upgrade the credit examination staff and send them into the branches.

In the past, examiners had reviewed a sample of loans, just to check for possible problems. Taylor's new team broadened the sample. Taylor wanted to be sure that the bad loans were behind BankAmerica. Before 1986, Taylor's review might have run into resistance from branch managers, but not now. With the centralization of the lending activities, the responsibility for bad loans had shifted from branch managers to regional offices. The regional staff didn't want to be saddled with bad loans made at the branches. They wanted every piece of bad paper identified and cleaned up.

Pockets of bad loans showed up immediately. Customers who had once banked at branches with indulgent managers who looked the other way when borrowers missed a payment, now faced curmudgeons at the regional office. Any spirit of forbearance was gone.

As May drifted into June, the sense of accomplishment at the bank grew. Cooper felt he was getting costs in line; senior credit officers expressed more confidence about the loan problems. The losses at the California branches would be higher, but there was nothing to alarm anyone.

In mid-June, Sam Armacost left San Francisco for a long-scheduled trip to review the Asian operations of BankAmerica. In the folklore that has emerged since mid-1986, Armacost is said to have ignored entreaties from his executives to stay home. Actually, no one tried to stop him. Although Glenhall Taylor's group was turning up bad loans here and there, no one had any reason to delay Armacost's trip.

In the days that followed, the bad news increased, the review team found more problem credits. In the cashiers office, a new specialist, Barbara Otto, had been brought in to examine the bank's techniques for forecasting problem loans. Each quarter the bank obtained three forecasts of possible loan problems. One was the view from the branch managers, who tended to be optimistic. Another was an economic model, which varied in reliability depending on how good the economics department's forecast was. The third was a statistical analysis done by cashiers.

Barbara Otto inherited that model and decided to make it more conservative. Based on information from Taylor and some additional sampling, she advised that the bank take a huge addition to the reserve for possible loan losses, increasing it by about $900 million.

Sam Armacost had consistently fought draconian additions to the reserve and won. He had kept the reserve down in 1984 and kept the second quarter 1985 increase in the loan loss reserve to $500 million, the minimum demanded by the Comptroller's office. Now Sam Armacost was in Asia, out of touch, and the case for a huge addition to the reserve gained support in his absence. Glenhall Taylor was new, Tom Cooper was new, Barbara Otto was new. Their bias was to take the biggest hit possible to clean the slate. In early July, with their conviction about the reserve growing, Tom Cooper called Sam Armacost, reaching him at 3:00 A.M. in China, and asked him to return. Armacost was scheduled to fly to Tokyo that morning to speak on a panel, but he canceled his speech and flew home, stopping in Tokyo only long enough to allow the corporate jet's crew to rest.

At a weekend session in San Francisco, Sam Armacost reviewed the loan problems. He had been blindsided again and was furious. But the case was irrefutable. Just four months before, he had promised the board that the bank would make more than $400 million in 1986. Just three months ago he had promised analysts that the bank would at least break even. Now he faced a loss of $600 million for the second quarter, and nothing could be done about it.

In the late evening, after the painful meeting on the loans and the inevitable discussion of profits, Armacost paused outside his office and observed wistfully, "It was fun while it lasted."

Chapter Thirty-two

It is my belief that [men who have been executives here in the bank] are better qualified to sit [as directors of Bank of America] than businessmen who drop their own intimate business affairs for an hour once a month to attend such meetings.

A. P. Giannini, 1924

Two days later, on Tuesday, July 15, 1986, Sam Armacost met with the board in special session and informed them of the loss for the second quarter. "It was a complete surprise," one of the directors said. Now the pressure to oust Armacost would build.

Just minutes before the hastily called July board meeting, Salomon's Jay Higgins took a few moments to prepare Armacost. Higgins explained that the board might ask him to leave.

"I've got my resignation in my pocket," Armacost said. "I've been prepared for this for two years."

But the board did not ask Armacost to resign. In fact, it took the loss with remarkable calm. Since March some board members had been quietly discussing among themselves whether to ask Armacost to leave. Some thought it was time in March, but others were so close to mandatory retirement that they hesitated. At the April board meeting five directors had stepped down: Walter Haas, former chief executive of Levi Strauss; Franklin Murphy, head of the executive committee of the Times Mirror Corp.; C. B. Branch, the former chairman of Dow Chemical; Najeeb Halaby, former head of Pan Am; and T. M. McDaniel, former president of Southern California Edison. A sixth director, Peter O'Malley, president of the Los Angeles Dodgers, quietly left the board, even though he was just forty-nine, nowhere near the mandatory retirement age of seventy. He gave no explanation for his resignation.

In July the directors faced the same hurdle that had stopped many of them in March. Just as Armacost worried about the public's confidence in the bank, so did they. They worried that if they began to search for a new chief executive, confidence in the bank might falter. It was better, they decided, to stick with Armacost than to risk the possibility of destabilizing rumors.

The July meeting did not change their minds, but between mid-July and the end of September, the pressure on the board intensified.

The forces of opposition to Sam Armacost were gaining strength. In the weeks between the July meeting and the regularly scheduled session in August, the few dissenters, Schwab, Cooley, former BankAmerica president Rudolph Peterson (an honorary director), and Robert McNamara, grew angrier. One of their gripes had been the structure of the board sessions themselves. At almost no time, except in executive session of the full board, did directors have an opportunity to meet alone. At almost all other times there was a member of the bank's management present, discouraging frank discussions. Even the audit and examining committee, which is supposed to serve as the most vigilant watchdog of management, rarely met without a senior executive present.

The dissidents were also upset with the lack of information from management on the company's mounting problems. It seemed that Armacost had been glossing over difficulties, disguising their severity. He had done that with the loan losses since 1982 and he had consistently done that with operating problems such as the NMEC mortgage scandal and the computer snarls.

As August approached, a few dissident directors pushed for change. On the Sunday afternoon of the August meeting, the executive committee of BankAmerica's board finally exerted its independence. It requested additional reports from management on everything from loan problems to cost-cutting efforts. It wanted the right for any board committee or the board as a whole to meet without executives of the company present. This was the initial step toward wresting control of BankAmerica away from management. The change didn't come easily, says one insider, but was forced by the threat that one of the dissident directors would resign, probably McNamara—an event that would have provoked too much negative publicity.

The board had also begun to worry about a possible take-over. First Interstate had not gone away. In various meetings since March, Joe Pinola had repeated his desire to merge with BankAmerica. Now, with the stock trading at $10–12 a share and drifting lower, Pinola might be in a position to come after the company again.

The board, acting in its role as the guardian of shareholder rights and using money from the shareholders, hired Martin Lipton—the senior partner at Wachtell, Lipton who had counseled Sandy Weill—to create defenses against a takeover. It also re-tained Salomon Brothers—working for the board rather than management—as its investment banker and approved "golden parachutes" for seven of the company's top executives. Covered by the plans were Armacost, Cooper, and McLin, as well as Bob Frick, head of the World Banking Division; Glenhall Taylor, the bank's top credit specialist; and George Coombe, the company's general counsel.

If BankAmerica were taken over by another company and its executives fired, they would be entitled to three years' salary. Coombe stood to earn the least under the parachutes, just $667,828, while Armacost would float to earth with more than $1.7 million. The parachutes were designed to make Bank-America's executives more objective in their evaluation of take-over bids. Their own income would not be affected by the change in control. But the move struck outsiders as strange. It came less than fifteen days after BankAmerica announced that the management team it was hoping to protect had generated a loss for the second quarter of $640 million.

One disbelieving investment banker, assuming Bank-America would never stay independent, groused at the time, "They aren't parachutes, they are severance packages." The company defended them as normal procedure for large busi-nesses, even though few other businesses had lost more than $1 billion in the year before their executives were handed golden parachutes.

The board dispatched Salomon Brothers to review the busi-ness plan of BankAmerica, assess the bank's capital position, and offer guidance to the board on the company's direction.

Of the fifteen directors left on the board, Philip Hawley had become the swing vote. The sixty-one-year-old chairman of Carter Hawley Hale Stores ran one of the nation's largest department store chains, descended from the company that Prentis C. Hale had operated when A. P. Giannini opened his first branch in San Jose. Hawley, who is invariably described by journalists as having "movie star good looks," was a veteran of boardroom battles, having suffered through a takeover war as a director of Walt Disney Productions and having survived attempts by outsiders to gain control of Carter Hawley Hale.

Hawley knew the rules of combat and he knew the potential costs. In recent weeks, he had hired an attorney to advise him on his legal responsibilities as a director of a troubled company—a company that might soon face an unwanted takeover bid.

He was wavering in his support of Armacost, although he had always seemed somewhat ambivalent about the chief executive. Outside the boardroom he sympathized with dissident directors, but once inside, he voted with Armacost.

The pressure on Hawley, and other directors, built in the days after the August board meeting. That Tuesday Armacost canceled a trip to New York to visit stock analysts. He and his chief financial officer, John Poelker, had decided months earlier to go to New York each quarter, good news or bad. The canceled trip set off predictable rumors on Wall Street about Armacost having been asked to step down during the board meeting, forcing BankAmerica to announce belatedly that it was Poelker, not Armacost, who had resigned. (Poelker had joined the bank days before the March board meeting and had never moved his family from Atlanta to San Francisco. He had flown back each weekend to be with them, finally deciding not to stay.)

The following Monday a writer from *Fortune* phoned Charles Schwab & Co. and talked with Hugo Quackenbush, a Schwab & Co. spokesman.

"A source that I trust tells me that Chuck has resigned."

"I don't know anything about that," Quackenbush said. "He's talked about it in the past, but I don't think he's taken any action."

"This source has never been wrong. Could you check with Chuck for me?"

"I don't think it will do any good. He's in Hawaii. If I have to call him about something else, I'll ask about it."

Two days later, the *Fortune* writer called again.

"You were right," Quackenbush said. "I talked to the bank and they are going to put out a statement this afternoon."

Several board members, worried about how Schwab's resignation might look to the public, tried to persuade him to stay, but in vain.

At the August board meeting, Schwab had given a presentation on the performance of his company. Profits were up, revenues were growing steadily. His company was doing extremely well, but Schwab was growing anxious to regain control of the firm. It was not just the mismanagement of BankAmerica, it was more. Schwab & Co. was hemmed in as part of a bank holding company. It was forbidden by the Glass-Steagall Act from offering many products that bordered on investment banking, and faced lawsuits every time it proposed an idea that investment bankers didn't like. Growth, which was so important to Chuck Schwab, was harder to come by. The board was not taking his advice, his company was fettered, and he was potentially on the hook for millions of dollars in class action lawsuits. Staying on the board seemed futile. So after a sleepless night, Schwab finally decided to leave the board, devoting himself to running Schwab & Co., and perhaps buying it back from BankAmerica.

With Schwab's resignation, speculation about the firing of Armacost built. The press was growing peevish about the board's inaction. The $640 million loss in the second quarter seemed to cry out for decisive change. As Beckett had observed in March, this was grounds for removing management. Yet the board hesitated in August and seemed to be no closer to a decision as the September board meeting drew near. The catalyst for board action, however, was brewing in the BankAmerica executive suite.

For three days in mid-August, Salomon Brothers' investment banking team met with executives from BankAmerica. They reviewed the bank's options for raising capital and its prospects for meeting its five-year plan.

Sam Armacost was still a believer. He still believed, despite setback after setback, that the strategy he was putting in place was destined to work. He told the *San Francisco Examiner* in mid-July, just after the latest loss was announced, "I've got to tell you—most people who are coming in new are saying, 'You know, without this credit problem, you guys could be treated as heroes for your strategy.' And I think that someday that's going to manifest itself. I still think the analysts are going to give us grudging, grudging acceptance.

"The effects of the people reductions this year have a minimum impact next year of $180 million. That shows the magnitude in a big company when you start getting expenses moving in a positive momentum."

As he met with Salomon Brothers, Armacost was trapped by his earlier profit forecast. In March he had promised to generate net income of $415 million in 1986. That was obviously not going to happen. But he had also promised that by 1990 the company's profit would reach $1 billion. That goal was one that he felt he could not give up.

Armacost wanted to develop a forecast for the next five years that would bring the company to the same profitable spot it would have been in without the second-quarter loss.

As analysts from Salomon and BankAmerica reviewed Armacost's numbers, neither wanted responsibility for the forecast. These were Armacost's goals, and the analysts realized they were foolishly optimistic.

The forecasts brought disagreements among Armacost, Prussia, and Cooper. Cooper's split with Prussia had by now gone beyond philosophical differences. In his quest for efficiency, Cooper was encouraging Armacost to get rid of Prussia, just as he was encouraging him to fire a half-dozen other executives who seemed to contribute little to the company. Cooper saw Prussia's role as superfluous. He earned $420,000, but nobody seemed to know what he did. With the appointment of Cooper as chief operating officer, Armacost had assumed many of Prussia's functions. And Prussia's unrelenting pessimism was dismaying.

With Cooper and others in management growing impatient, Armacost pushed Prussia into agreeing to retire early. On the surface, the decision seemed motivated in part by humanitarian concern. Prussia's gloom was taking a toll on his health. He looked old and tired, and he had often said he aspired to move into other work after retiring from the bank. He had spent thirty years with BankAmerica, which guaranteed him a comfortable retirement income. Prussia saw other motives, though. He felt that Armacost was looking for a scapegoat, one more person to jettison in order to save his job. Reluctantly, he agreed to retire later in the year.

In the week before the September board meeting, Prussia and Cooper argued over the need to present additional information to the board. Prussia wanted to alert the board to the dangers of a recession. He had the Cashiers Division draft alternative economic outlooks for the next five years. Cooper, Salomon Brothers, and Armacost all argued that the additional forecasts would simply be confusing.

Prussia stuck stubbornly to his objective. In desperation, Armacost called one of the officers in the Cashiers Division and told him not to prepare the forecasts.

"You're telling me to refuse to do what my boss asks?" he remembers saying to Armacost.

"That's right," Armacost said.

"What if the next time he calls I tell him to talk to you?" he responded.

Armacost didn't answer. The executive finished his work, arming Lee Prussia with three economic scenarios for the board meeting in Los Angeles. During the informal sessions on the Sunday before the board meeting, Prussia once again asked questions about the profit forecast, and got the same response as before.

On Sunday afternoon John Gutfreund and Jay Higgins, the top Salomon Brothers executives who had flown out from New York for the board meeting, counseled Armacost again that the board might ask him to resign and that he should think about helping to pick a successor.

On Monday morning, September 8, nearly seven months after Robert McNamara had encouraged Sanford Weill to bring his ideas to BankAmerica, the directors finally were prepared to discuss the issue of capital. Salomon Brothers had prepared a forty-six-page report on the company's options for selling securities or raising capital in other ways.

And then Lee Prussia took his stand. He presented his economic scenarios, arguing that, in effect, Armacost's forecasts for the company would not be attainable.

Salomon Brothers presented its grim assessment of the markets. Big investors had no appetite for BankAmerica common stock, private investors might be willing to put as much as $500 million into the company, but they would want a degree of control in return. David Lewis of General Dynamic asked an obvious question, wondering why Salomon had said it could raise $1 billion in capital in March, but now seemed unable to raise any capital in the market except at extremely high prices. The answer, that the second-quarter loss had changed the world, was just as obvious.

Salomon sketched other alternatives in detail, providing estimates of how much could be raised by selling various assets. Salomon presented the board with the list of sales that Cooper and McLin had been investigating—the Italian bank, a mortgage bank in England, a bank in Germany, operations in Thailand, and the like.

The investment bankers also presented a quick review of a merger with First Interstate. Although the talk of a merger had died, Salomon wanted to familiarize the board with the numbers and prepare them in case talks should start again.

With Prussia's challenge to Armacost and Salomon's gloomy outlook for raising capital, the board of BankAmerica finally realized that it had a serious management problem. After Robert McNamara summed up the doubts and uncertainties about the future, savoring his moment of vindication, "The Over-the-Hill Gang" moved into executive session—where it found itself impotent. Despite all that had gone wrong over the past five years it did not have a successor to Sam Armacost. If it had, Sam Armacost would not have survived the informal poll on whether he should stay, which he won by only a single vote.

Throughout September, the directors remained mum about Armacost's one-vote victory. BankAmerica's executives marveled at the board's inaction. All they knew was that Armacost was still in charge. They thought the board had somehow overlooked Lee Prussia's challenge, Robert McNamara's tirade, even the overall spectacle of a management falling apart. The board's failure to act seemed to confirm that Armacost was unassailable.

But the bad news didn't end. In mid-September, the fence sitters on BankAmerica's board got a push. After the September board meeting, some directors had discreetly asked others on the board and close friends for suggestions on who might succeed Sam Armacost.

In the second week of September, the rumors started. In Europe, in Japan, and in the United States, the story spread that

BankAmerica Corp. was in danger of failing. Rumors circulated that senior executives were talking with the Federal Reserve about a bailout. BankAmerica's stock sank to $10.50. The U.S. dollar fell skittishly, too, as concern about the nation's second largest bank produced nervousness about the entire U.S. financial system.

On September 18, Sam Armacost responded. He asked the Securities and Exchange Commission, the New York Stock Exchange, the Chicago Board of Options Exchange, and banking authorities in London and Tokyo to investigate the rumors and punish the guilty. He told the press, "We are extremely angry at the parties responsible for spreading these rumors, which have the potential of harming thousands of shareholders and placing the integrity of the market at risk."

Though the agencies never investigated, the rumors stopped almost as quickly as they had begun. BankAmerica found it harder to roll over deposits in Europe and Asia, but there was no panic after September 18. Nevertheless, the bank lost deposits steadily, at a faster pace than at any time since the slow erosion had begun in 1984.

News stories about the rumors spread confusion in California, where consumers began to pull accounts. On September 24, Armacost went on the radio to tell California consumers the bank was healthy. In a one-minute advertisement, Armacost introduced himself as president of the company, then reassured depositors that the bank was sound, that it had plenty of capital, and more deposits than any other bank in California, in fact, so much on deposit that it was lending money to other banks.

The radio spots helped ease the sense of nervousness. But the slow loss of deposits continued, and the rumors cost BankAmerica at least $2 billion in deposits.

The rumors, and the edginess of depositors, ended the reticence of some board members to dump Armacost. Their fear of shaking customer confidence—which had kept them from removing Armacost—was no longer a restraint. In fact, it appeared they needed to change management in order to reassure the markets.

As the board's support for Armacost weakened, some directors got a strong message from a potential replacement. Using intermediaries, Tom Clausen, who had not been asked back for a second term as president of the World Bank and had left that post in July, let board members know that he was ready to help if they needed him.

Throughout the past five years, as BankAmerica's profits plunged, Armacost's team blamed Clausen, who remained quiet, circumspect. Not until January 1986, in a seventy-five-minute interview with the *Los Angeles Times*, had Clausen finally responded to the critics.

"The managers of the bank now were managers when I was there," Clausen said. "They shared in those decisions. I rest my case.

"I'd say my record is there. It's very visible. I left the West Glendale branch as assistant manager in 1956, and ten years later they were still charging off loans in my name. I've been out of the bank for five years now. So be it."

Clausen accepted some blame. He even admitted that he had focused too heavily on the short term.

He also stated that he was following the company very closely. "I bleed a little with each story," he said.

In the summer of 1986, Tom Clausen sent a message to the board. It was not a loud message, it was not done directly, but he let them know that he was waiting, just waiting for a chance to serve.

Chapter Thirty-three

Good banking is the result of good management; and good management comes from hiring the best men that can be had in any particular field. That is the secret of success of the bank . . . picking the best talent and paying what it is worth.

A. P. Giannini, 1927

In mid-afternoon on Friday, October 3, Sam Armacost's secretary received a call from Geoffrey Boisi of Goldman Sachs. Was Sam in? No, he's not in today. Well, a letter is on its way; it should arrive late this afternoon.

At just about 4:00 P.M., a young officer from Goldman Sachs arrived on the fortieth floor of the BankAmerica tower. She handed an envelope to Armacost's secretary.

"Wouldn't you know it," the secretary said. "Everything always happens on Friday afternoon."

Inside the envelope was a neatly typed, double-spaced three-page letter from Joe Pinola. It was an offer by First Interstate Bancorp to acquire BankAmerica. The deal was complicated; First Interstate would trade BankAmerica shareholders four different securities for each share of BankAmerica stock. First Interstate was offering securities worth about $18 a share, but the letter was only the opening volley in what Goldman hoped would be a brief, dramatic war.

The investment bankers at Goldman Sachs had learned over the course of the past year that Sam Armacost respected the letter. Putting a business proposal in writing made it seem much more concrete and, in this case, more threatening.

Boisi had planned to negotiate, not to send a letter. On September 17, he had met BankAmerica's adviser, John Gutfreund

308

of Salomon Brothers, for breakfast at the Plaza Athenee, a luxurious Manhattan hotel. Goldman's investment bankers had described Joe Pinola's continuing interest in acquiring BankAmerica, but Gutfreund remained noncommittal, saying, somewhat cryptically, "There's a lot going on here."

Goldman and First Interstate spent the next week and a half developing the details of a bid for BankAmerica. With its stock selling at around $10 a share, an offer worth $18 seemed likely to win shareholder support. The major concern for First Interstate was the "nuclear reactor" problem—what if they got inside and found that the bank had suffered immense damage?

Goldman had designed a series of securities, similar in concept to the preferred stock used in the Seafirst acquisition. If BankAmerica was profitable after the merger, these preferred shares would pay a nice dividend. If BankAmerica was not profitable, if the core had melted, if too many loans had gone bad, then the dividend would be quite low or might never be paid.

Pinola thought he had BankAmerica cornered. The board was growing uncomfortable with Armacost. That much anyone could see. Pinola knew little about the September board meeting, but he understood the panic inspired by rumors and lost deposits. He was also getting word, indirectly, that some BankAmerica directors would welcome a bid from First Interstate.

Pinola knew the board faced a difficult decision. Finding a chief executive to replace Armacost would be tough. No one inside the bank was a likely choice. The only person with enough experience was Dick Cooley, the boss at Seafirst. But the BankAmerica board considered Cooley an outsider. They rarely listened to him at board meetings and even less frequently turned to him for advice.

Anyone from another bank presented a risk. It might take a newcomer months to dig in and understand BankAmerica's problems. If the board had acted in March, or at some point in 1985, the list of potential candidates might have been longer. But now, with depositors scared and time short, the list was not long. The newspaper stories carried some likely candidates: Frank Cahouet, the former president of Crocker National Corp.; William Simon, a former bond salesman and Secretary of the Treasury who had made millions buying and selling companies; and Thomas Theobald, the top corporate lender at Citicorp, who had been passed over for the presidency there. None of these people knew BankAmerica well. None had ever run a bank as big as BankAmerica. Each presented a risk—to a board that did not like outsiders or undue risk. Pinola doubted the board would turn to anyone unfamiliar with BankAmerica for help.

First Interstate was a logical alternative. Its management knew BankAmerica. Pinola had spent twenty-three years at the company and had spent his entire career as a California banker. On his team he had more than a dozen young executives recruited from his alma mater.

Pinola had expected a merger in March. With Sandy Weill on the attack, he thought Armacost would try something bold to protect his position at the bank. But the timing proved wrong and his sense of Armacost had been wrong. "Armacost never seemed to understand how much danger he was in," said a First Interstate insider. The timing now looked far better.

As expected, the delivery of the letter set off alarm bells on the fortieth floor. Sam Armacost was not in his office on October 3, he was in Los Angeles playing golf at a tournament for retired professional football players. His foursome included Daryl Lamonica, a former quarterback of the Oakland Raiders, and two former Los Angeles Rams, Danny Villanueva and Jon Arnett. George Coombe, BankAmerica's corporate counsel, accepted the letter. He discussed it with Cooper, Prussia, and others; then they found Armacost.

The board meeting was only three days away. Salomon Brothers drew up an analysis of the offer from First Interstate. In addition, it reviewed a proposal that had quietly been made by Drexel Burnham Lambert, an old-line investment banking firm that had recently become a major source of innovation in the field. Led spiritually by the young king of the junk bond market, Michael Milken, Drexel was known for trying to find creative solutions to corporate problems.

Drexel reasoned that America's bankers—at least most of them—didn't realize how fundamentally deregulation had changed the rules in banking. In order to stay competitive, Drexel argued, banks had to rid themselves of the bad loans on their books and use the money tied up in those bad loans to go after business with higher returns.

Drexel's unsolicited plan for BankAmerica called for it to dump $4 billion worth of bad debt into a new company, a "bad bank." That would strip away the lousy loans from BankAmerica, leaving a "good bank." The good bank would immediately be profitable, would be able to raise capital in the marketplace, and would begin to grow. The bad bank, run by people who understood problem loans, would concentrate on turning sows' ears into silk purses. With the right prices, with the right people, it might work—the problem was making sure that the good bank and the bad bank were completely separate companies.

On the warm, sunny Sunday morning of October 5, Sam Armacost met with his key advisers in a conference room on the forty-eighth floor of the San Francisco headquarters. The meeting involved a few bank insiders, plus senior executives from Salomon Brothers and Wachtell, Lipton. It began at 10:00 A.M.

"I assume the other directors know about this letter?" John Gutfreund asked, referring to the First Interstate proposal. They did.

This was Gutfreund's first chance to sit down with Armacost since the letter had arrived. He outlined the situation. The board could stick with management's plan, hoping to ride out the current storm and stay independent. But the danger was increasing. In addition to the proposals from First Interstate and Drexel, other investors were circling, prepared to make a bid. A group led by Stanley Hiller, a longtime customer of BankAmerica who had revived a score of troubled companies, including Bekins Corp., had offered to inject capital and strengthen the board but had been rebuffed.

Gutfreund offered a chilling conclusion, "You are close to having other people in control of this bank."

Armacost wanted Gutfreund's advice on procedure. "How do we decide which of these proposals we pursue?" he asked. "What percentage of equity are we going to have to give up for a specific infusion?"

Gutfreund knew the board was considering asking Armacost to step down. He responded, "What do you want to do, Sam? You've got to decide what you want to do."

The group began to discuss the First Interstate proposal. What the board, and Sam, needed to know was what the bid would actually be worth to a shareholder. According to First Interstate's investment bankers, Goldman Sachs, the price was $18 a share. But Salomon Brothers didn't think the bid was that high. Although it had not been able to review the offer thoroughly, it was obvious the two sides would spend time negotiating over the value of these securities—if talks proceeded.

It was hard to put a value on the preferred stock included in the First Interstate offer, since it was tied to BankAmerica's profits. So many variables affected BankAmerica's profits that it was possible to imagine circumstances where the preferred would be virtually worthless.

Lipton advised caution. "Look, you've got to take at least three to six weeks to go through this." Lipton knew the legal problems. The bank had to study this offer, analyze it, and consider the alternatives. The board had the right under the "business judgment rule" to turn down the bid, even if it was a fair price, as long as the board decided the price was not high enough. Once the board decided to sell the company, though, it had to make sure that it got top dollar. The board's primary responsibility was to its shareholders, not to management or to some amorphous concept of the company as an institution. They had an obligation to review any formal proposal. Lipton concluded, "It is the obligation of the board to thoroughly explore all the options."

Despite the pressure and the tension that everyone else felt, Armacost remained composed, apparently self-controlled. "We'd have a real fracas if we dismissed any of these opportunities out of hand," he said. "Maybe I should convene a California-based subset of the executive committee to deal with these issues. In three to six weeks we would have something definitive."

As the meeting ended Armacost left to join the executive committee of the board for its Sunday meeting, which was to be followed later by dinner.

Gutfreund and Lipton stepped in to talk with the board's executive compensation committee. Alarmed by the events of the previous board meeting, it was discussing names of possible replacements for Armacost.

On the following day, Monday, October 6, BankAmerica's monthly directors meeting convened at the company's San Francisco headquarters, a smaller and less imposing boardroom than in Los Angeles, but with a far more dramatic backdrop. The fifty-second floor of the BankAmerica building is a corporate aerie, a safe, protected spot, far above the problems of the city street.

With the stock price dropping and with Joe Pinola's public

statements of interest, the directors had been expecting the First Interstate bid. They realized that as a bank, they could probably repel any attack from outside because of bank regulations that guaranteed them enough time to build defenses.

BankAmerica would have months to analyze the bid and respond. Regulators would have to review the merger, which would take at least six months. In the meantime, the bank could argue the legal merits of the bid, lobby regulators, and build public support against the opposing company. In other industries, a corporate raider could sweep in, seize control, and oust both the management and the board in a matter of weeks. But the market's bracing winds did not blow in the banking industry.

In the weeks since the September board meeting, the control of the board had shifted perceptibly. Management was no longer dominant. The power to make decisions rested with perhaps four directors. John Beckett, the former chairman of Transamerica Corp. (the descendant of A. P.'s holding company); Rudolph Peterson, at eighty, an honorary board member; Philip Hawley; and Robert McNamara.

Except for McNamara, these men represented the nucleus of a West Coast group that had the most influence at the company. Anyone from east of the Sierras was in an outer circle, including two executives still active in running companies—Ruben Mettler of TRW and David Lewis of General Dynamics. The board's inner circle met more often with management, socialized with top bank executives in San Francisco and Los Angeles, and knew more about the company.

Compared to the September meeting in Los Angeles, the October board meeting proceeded with order and calm. Marty Lipton, who now represented the board, opened the proceedings. "We can't immediately refuse the First Interstate offer," Lipton said. "We have to consider other possibilities. We've got a range of alternatives, from an infusion of capital to a liquidation."

Some members were ready to move faster. Roy Ash, one of the founders of AM International, said, "If the price is too low, we should reject it." And Lewis of General Dynamics worried, "If we start talking with First Interstate, the game is over. It's just a question of who will win."

Lipton counseled against hasty decisions. "No one is suggesting that we begin to negotiate," he said. "The best course is to explore the proposal, review it, then reach a decision."

The First Interstate bid demanded more analysis. How much was the preferred stock worth? Salomon offered a range of prices, but its analysis was not complete. How much was Bank-America likely to earn over the next five years? What was First Interstate likely to earn? If the merger occurred, what would the effect be on the combined profits? First Interstate had included a range of profit projections—high, medium, and low—of its own performance and BankAmerica's. Even its highest projections for BankAmerica fell below Armacost's forecast. First Interstate assumed that BankAmerica might make $200 million to $1 billion in 1990. BankAmerica's projections showed a profit of more than $1.1 billion, period.

After the debate in September over BankAmerica's profit forecast, the board knew not to trust the projections from either BankAmerica or First Interstate. In order to assess the bid, the board would need a review of both forecasts, after which it could decide what to do.

After more than five hours of presentations and discussion, the review of the merger and the Drexel plan was complete. Philip Hawley of Carter Hawley Hale, took charge. As chairman of the executive compensation committee, which was responsible for hiring, firing, and paying top executives (including handing out golden parachutes), Hawley had an important role to play in the closed-door session that followed.

"Let's not be in a rush to arrive at a decision today," he said. "The board is under a harsh public spotlight. There are strict legal constraints on how to proceed. It's important to act calmly and with a lot of thought." A few moments later he said, "Let's have a session with Marty [Lipton] and John [Gutfreund], then let's meet alone."

The board asked Gutfreund and Lipton to stay as it moved into executive session. The rest of the advisers and members of management stepped into an adjoining conference room for a buffet of slightly soggy finger sandwiches.

Hawley and Beckett, chairman of the executive committee, dominated the private discussion. The two asked Lipton and Gutfreund about the financial markets. How were they responding to the bank's problems? What would happen if Armacost was replaced?

Then one of the directors asked how Wall Street would respond if the board selected Tom Clausen as the new chief executive. Gutfreund asked, "Why would you want to do that?" (He thought it was such an appalling idea that he bragged the next day to aides at Salomon Brothers that he had stopped an effort to draft Clausen—only to learn a few hours later that his advice had been ignored.)

The board listened politely, then moved into a brief executive session with no outsiders. It was clear now that the company needed new management. Hawley proposed Clausen, knowing that he was prepared to come back. Rudy Peterson and others also had received the same message. No other name received serious consideration. Anthony Frank, the head of First Nationwide Savings, a large San Francisco savings and loan, was mentioned, as was Dick Cooley.

None of the board members thought Clausen was a brilliant choice, but of the names available he made the board most comfortable. The directors were propelled by a sense of urgency. The loss of deposits in September had unnerved them. The First Interstate bid was frighteningly real now. They felt a need to restore order, to bring in someone who understood the bank and could bring stability. In Tom Clausen they saw a man who knew the bank, was a tireless worker, and commanded respect in financial circles. Their discussion lasted perhaps fifteen minutes, after which they gave permission to a small group of directors to ask Tom Clausen to come back.

Hawley and Beckett went with Rudolph Peterson to his office in the space set aside for retired executives, then on the forty-ninth floor of BankAmerica's world headquarters. At 4:30 P.M. they called Tom Clausen and asked him to return. He immediately said yes. Later he would deny that he had lobbied for the job, that he had sent word to the board that he was available. He was simply happy that his friends had called. He was glad to get the opportunity to return to BankAmerica.

The next morning, Tuesday, Armacost and Prussia were told of the decision. Prussia, who had been with the bank thirty years, was entitled to a generous early retirement package, plus two years of his salary of $575,000. Armacost was not eligible for the early retirement benefits, so the board agreed to pay him an amount equal to three years of his salary, a package that closely resembled the golden parachute—and which was later justified as being standard practice in the industry. In addition, he would receive options on BankAmerica stock worth $1.7 million, and when he reached age fifty-five would be entitled to retire on as much as $11,000 a month—rich rewards for someone whose tenure had been so dismally unsuccessful.

A few days later, as he was cleaning out his office, Armacost told a longtime BankAmerica watcher that the board had made a mistake. "It was like pulling a pitcher in the ninth inning, when the team is behind, but just before they are about to win the game," he said.

On Thursday afternoon, reporters from the *Wall Street Journal* began calling executives at BankAmerica. Was it true, they asked, that Tom Clausen had been selected to replace Armacost?

The next day, the *Journal* story, written by G. Christian Hill and Richard Schmitt, alerted the world to Clausen's return. The response on Wall Street was predictable. They ridiculed the board. "This is like bringing back Sam Insull to run the utilities," said the chairman of one industrial company, who was obviously overstating the case. (Insull had almost singlehandedly ruined the electric utility industry in the 1920s, defrauding thousands of investors by issuing bogus securities.)

Tom Clausen was the man who had chosen Sam Armacost to be president, the man who was blamed for creating many of the problems that Armacost inherited. This was the man criticized inside the bank as an autocrat, a harsh taskmaster with a shortage of people skills, who had built a huge bureaucracy, underinvested for the future, and put the men in place who wrote many of the bank's bad loans. A critic on the West Coast derided Clausen's return as "PU cronyism," referring to the Pacific Union Club, which for years was reputed to control all the top businesses in San Francisco.

On Saturday, BankAmerica's board met again in special session and appointed Tom Clausen the chairman and chief executive of BankAmerica Corp. Tom Clausen thanked his friends for asking him to come back.

Clausen
Revisited

Chapter Thirty-four

You better watch staff
You better watch costs.
Balance the books—
We've got a new boss!
Santa Clausen's coming to town!

He's making a list
And checking it twice.
Finding out who gave
Lousey [sic] advice.
Santa Clausen's coming to town!

Anonymous, 1986

T he next day, Sunday, October 12, 1986, Tom Clausen's first full day as chairman of BankAmerica, he spent sixteen hours at world headquarters. He had been gone five years, he had a lot to learn, and very little time in which to learn it.

In a series of meetings with top executives, Clausen began to assess where the bank stood—and his executives began to assess Clausen. They weren't impressed. Clausen had not done his homework. He had no idea how bad conditions were at the bank, or how much authority the board had vested in Tom Cooper. Cooper, who had been president of the bank since March, had received the title of president of the holding company at the Saturday board meeting. Clausen was chief executive, but he had not realized that both the retail and international banks reported directly to Cooper, which meant Clausen had only a few head-office functions, such as finance and personnel, reporting to him.

One former executive quipped that Clausen was twenty years out of date, even though he had only been away from the bank for five years. As key managers began to discuss issues,

Clausen offered solutions that would not work in a deregulated
world. He had lost his feel for the market, for competitors, for
the demands of regulators, for the basics of the bank. As head of
the World Bank in Washington, D.C., Clausen had been caught
up in a global nightmare, the forces that were pushing and pulling at debtors in Latin America, eastern Europe, and elsewhere.
Now he was back in the trenches, and the rules had changed.

Competition was far more vicious than it had been a few
years earlier, and one of the key culprits was the savings and loan
industry. After the S&Ls nearly went bankrupt in 1981 and 1982,
Congress and the S&L regulators allowed savings and loans to
operate with virtually no capital. Therefore, they could grow
rapidly, earning money on a higher volume of loans. They could
pay slightly higher interest on deposits, charge slightly less on
loans, and still produce bigger profits than BankAmerica.

Overseas, the Japanese, the French, and others had the
same edge. They were siphoning off top-quality credits by offering rates that American banks couldn't match. The business left
to big U.S. banks was of a lower quality, but the competition for
these credits was so fierce that it was driving down profits on
these low-quality loans as well.

BankAmerica, which needed to cover the losses on its problem loans and to help rebuild its capital, was caught. Intellectually, Clausen knew that. But his responses were based on ten years
of banking when the markets were not as harsh. It had not yet
sunk in how profoundly the banking world had changed. He
wanted to rev up the bank's retail branches, add loans, build revenues—but he couldn't do it.

Clausen also seemed lost in the midst of the takeover battle.
He was unfamiliar with this terrain, even though it had been a
central topic of discussion for corporate executives for much of
the past five years. Clausen relied on his advisers—Marty Lipton,
his legal adviser from Wachtell, Lipton, and the investment
bankers from Salomon Brothers. In addition, he turned to Frank
Newman, BankAmerica's chief financial officer, the last senior
executive hired by Sam Armacost, just a week before he was
fired. Steve McLin, Armacost's deal maker, was pushed into the
background, working on selling the company's Italian subsidiary
assets, and would leave in early January of 1987 to become president of a small investment banking firm.

What was more disturbing to those who listened closely was

that Tom Clausen had no vision of BankAmerica's future. He praised the strategy developed by Armacost, he embraced it, but he offered no special insight of his own. Clausen, the man who had run BankAmerica for a decade without altering its strategy, seemed ready to repeat that performance. He seemed most comfortable discussing only one goal for BankAmerica—restoring it to profitability. Beyond that he offered little.

What Clausen understood was expenses, budgets, and plans. BankAmerica was in the middle of its budget review for 1987, so Clausen dug in. In those numbers, Clausen seemed to find a familiar, comfortable world. He used them to restore his sense of BankAmerica. He used them to begin to shape an operating plan that would permit BankAmerica to return to profitability within twelve months and that would allow him to turn down the takeover bid from First Interstate.

On Tuesday, October 14, Clausen met with more than two hundred senior executives. He was not the glowering tyrant that many expected. He was low-keyed, modest. He even made a few jokes. "The board looked around for a new chief executive," he told the crowd of employees, "And it didn't see any tens. It didn't see any nines or eights." So it hired him instead.

Clausen admitted that the job they faced was tough. He told the executives that he expected every one of them to stick around for the battle.

A day later, he faced the press. Once again, he was self-effacing, good-humored. "Will Tom Clausen bring changes?" he asked rhetorically. "Of course, it's the nature of the situation and of my experience.

"I want you to know we recognize the difficulties the bank faces, but I also want you to realize the strengths of the bank and the corporation. I believe the direction set by the managing group and the board of directors is the right direction," he said. The only change would be "in degree and pace rather than in direction.

"Our focus is going to be on the future and to return the bank to preeminence in the financial services industry."

Clausen's presentation left lingering doubts for those who heard or read his remarks. One of the most disturbing signs, to those who had recently left the bank, was the choice of the word *preeminence*. Staunch supporters of Clausen thought this was a sign of overconfidence, a lack of understanding of the bank's

condition. Though BankAmerica had a chance to become profitable once more, to perhaps play a major role in banking on the
West Coast, it was unlikely to be preeminent. It was drifting now,
losing money, low on capital. Clausen's job was to patch the
holes, keep the vessel from sinking. If he truly believed that
BankAmerica was headed for preeminence, he was guilty of the
same overoptimism that had trapped Sam Armacost.

Others caught a disturbing glimpse of the old, autocratic
Clausen. A reporter asked whether he would consider selling
Charles Schwab & Co. "That question is completely out of order," Clausen snapped, then quickly added. "We need to look at
what our core business is . . . and those discussions and studies
have been under way." In fact, Schwab & Co. would shortly go
on sale.

The press conference also permitted Clausen the chance to
snub Tom Cooper. Throughout the long briefing, Cooper,
BankAmerica's number two man, stood in the shadows at the
back of the dais. Clausen didn't pass questions to Cooper, didn't
yield the floor. Just once did he ask Cooper to come forward.
That was when a reporter asked how Cooper was getting along
with Clausen. Cooper's answer was not an overwhelming en-
dorsement. "We've got a group of people here that are primarily
committed to the shareholder. We have our loyalty to the shareholder first and our responsibility to our marketplace second.
We are committed to work on behalf of our business plan and in
that spirit I told [Tom Clausen] he could expect 100 percent of
our support."

It was clear, almost from the moment that Clausen's appointment was announced, that Cooper and Clausen would
clash. Executives who had known both saw striking similarities—
they were no-nonsense, operating types, who wanted control.
Under Armacost, Cooper had asserted himself, acting as though
the chief executive's job was to think about strategy, give speeches, and call on outsiders. Everything else was the responsibility of
the chief operating officer. Since Armacost was under pressure
from outsiders, he accepted an arrangement that he didn't like.

Tom Clausen could redefine the roles any way he wanted.
Skeptics who knew Clausen predicted that Cooper would be
gone within a matter of months. They would be proved right.

Despite his good humor in public appearances, Clausen
had not really changed. Shortly after he retired, Lee Prussia visit-

ed Clausen, offering to help. Clausen, Prussia told friends later, essentially kicked him out of the office and off the executive floor. "I don't think I'll need your assistance," Clausen told him.

The day after Clausen's press conference, BankAmerica announced a loss for the third quarter of $23 million. The loss would have been bigger, but the bank had large gains from the sale of its Los Angeles headquarters and other assets, totaling $169 million. The operating loss—the real bottom line, excluding all those special items—was nearly $200 million. The sales of assets and the loss of deposits during the quarter had shrunk the bank by $4 billion. And its problem loans had increased.

BankAmerica's basic problem remained. Its income was shrinking faster than its expenses.

The number that captured this best was one of those simple equations that securities analysts love so much. At a well-run bank, the net interest income—all the interest earned on loans and investments minus the interest paid out on deposits—completely covers overhead expenses (salaries, office rental, and the like). Any profits the bank makes elsewhere—fees on credit cards, money from trading foreign exchange, or other income—flow directly to the bottom line.

Not at BankAmerica, where the net interest income was several hundred million dollars *less* than overhead. Even after all the cost-cutting that the bank had done, BankAmerica's expenses in 1986—excluding the amount set aside to cover possible losses on loans—still exceeded net interest income from lending and investing by more than $640 million.

Costs did seem to fall more rapidly over the next few months. But Cooper's aides say that almost all the drop in Clausen's first six months came from Cooper's actions between March and October 1986. As one said, Cooper and Armacost had "loaded up the pipeline." When Clausen arrived, the benefits finally started to spill out.

The drop in employee rolls in the third quarter was part of that effort. The sale in the fourth quarter of Banca d'America e d'Italia, the company's large Italian subsidiary, had been set before Clausen came, as had the sale of assets recorded in the third quarter. The company had already found a buyer for a securities subsidiary in New York, and it had quietly begun work on the sale of its trust operation in California, while approving the sale of a host of overseas retail businesses. The process began before Clausen's return, but the benefits came afterward.

The overriding challenge facing Tom Clausen was the take-over offer from First Interstate. On October 27, First Interstate raised its bid by $600 million to $3.4 billion, hoping to pressure Clausen into accepting its offer. The new bid increased the price per share from $18 to $22, more than 50 percent above the $14 per share market value of Bankamerica's stock.

After the November board meeting, BankAmerica issued a brief statement, asking First Interstate to table its bid until Bank-America's new management team had time to examine the company's plans and prospects. This was an unusual maneuver in the midst of a takeover battle, especially when the price being offered was much higher than the market.

Tom Clausen had already made it clear that he would do everything in his power to stop a merger with First Interstate. He was careful to stop short of outright rejection, but the message came across loud and clear. "I didn't come back to rearrange the deckchairs on the *Titanic*," he said at one point.

Chapter Thirty-five

I have told the stockholders many times that their destiny is in their own hands, but they must continue to exercise eternal vigilance to preserve their rights. . . . When the stockholders have right on their side they should not be too cowed to fight.

A. P. Giannini, 1932

Joe Pinola was not pleased with the return of Tom Clausen. "We were stunned," says one of Pinola's advisers. Pinola knew Clausen well, having worked for him at BankAmerica during much of his twenty-three years at the bank. The two claim they got along well before Clausen became president, but by the time Pinola left BankAmerica, the relationship was chilly.

Pinola didn't learn of Clausen's return until the story broke in the newspapers on the Friday after the October board meeting. When BankAmerica's board members met in San Francisco to consider the First Interstate bid, Joe Pinola was in Oklahoma City. In First Interstate's slow expansion across the country with franchises and acquisitions, Pinola had acquired the First National Bank and Trust Co. He had hoped to boost morale by visiting the bank and having dinner with its employees. At 8:00 P.M. on the day of the BankAmerica board meeting, Pinola was scheduled to deliver a speech. Just a half hour before, he had received a call from Los Angeles informing him that the letter that he had sent to BankAmerica was going to be made public.

Pinola had been furious. For weeks he had been trying to open negotiations with BankAmerica, to get a serious discussion started on a price. The letter was intended as an opening offer, a basis for negotiation. Now BankAmerica was taking it public, clearly a hostile response.

He finished dressing for dinner, went downstairs to the grand ballroom, delivered his speech, swapped stories with the bank's employees, and answered their questions, without a hint that his mind might be elsewhere.

After dinner he got back on the phone to Los Angeles. Was it important enough to fly back from Oklahoma City tonight? Nothing seemed to justify that. At 5:30 A.M. Tuesday, Pinola took the corporate jet home. He spent the day answering questions from the press and preparing for the next step in his siege on BankAmerica.

Three days later, when the *Wall Street Journal* broke the story that Clausen had returned, the tremors registered throughout the First Interstate organization. Now Pinola had a better sense of why BankAmerica had gone public.

Over the next three months, investment bankers for both sides met occasionally, but never went beyond the basics of exchanging information. The banks spent more time hurling charges at one another through the press. The leader of BankAmerica's counterattack on First Interstate was Frank Newman, the new chief financial officer. Newman is a tough-minded financial technician, a slender man with a bushy, light brown mustache. At Wells Fargo he had a reputation as "the consummate soldier." Tell him which direction to go and he would produce miracles.

As the leader of the forces against First Interstate, Newman launched an attack on the bid. In a long report to securities analysts in mid-November, he argued that the proposal was so flawed it had little chance of being approved by regulators. The report was marked confidential, but it quickly leaked to the press.

Newman focused on the disappearance of capital from the banking system. As a result of the merger, First Interstate would mark the assets of BankAmerica down to their salable, market price. Not only the bank's problem loans, but many of its loans to troubled Latin American debtors would shrink in value—perhaps by billions of dollars. That, Newman argued, would savage the capital base of the combined company, leaving it with less capital than if BankAmerica remained independent.

Newman didn't mention that BankAmerica's "capital" was a fiction, based on the assumption that all those bad loans were worth one hundred cents on the dollar. If BankAmerica had been forced to write down its loans to market value, the First Interstate deal would have strengthened the company.

As First Interstate and Newman both knew, the merger between BankAmerica and First Interstate was likely to create a company that was slightly stronger than BankAmerica, but weaker than First Interstate. The real problem, as Newman pointed out, was that the health of the combined company would depend on the profits of BankAmerica. BankAmerica was so much larger than First Interstate that its problems could overwhelm this now–$55-billion company.

Two basic questions should have dominated the public debate. The first was whether Pinola was better equipped to run BankAmerica than Clausen. Pinola did not have a record as a cost-cutter. His bank had expenses that were just as high as those of BankAmerica. His record of loan losses was not that much better—First Interstate had been burned in Latin America, agriculture, and real estate, just as BankAmerica had.

But Pinola had a vision of the future of banking and he was willing to innovate, to attempt something bold. The combined company would have more options than either company alone, plus deeper management.

The second question was whether the deal was better for BankAmerica's shareholders—not at some unnamed, future date, but at that moment, in that market. First Interstate and its investment bankers from Goldman Sachs said they would negotiate with BankAmerica's advisers at Salomon Brothers to ensure that BankAmerica's shareholders received securities worth at least $20 or whatever higher price the final agreement between the companies established.

In the war of words that followed, the initial bid and the potential benefit to shareholders appeared largely irrelevant. BankAmerica had no intention of bringing the bid to a vote and it never did. Even though shareholders could have received securities worth perhaps 50 percent more than the market price of BankAmerica stock or more than $20 a share, Clausen and Newman felt no compulsion to bring the offer to shareholders.

The directors were immediately impressed with Clausen's analysis, though it was little different from Armacost's. In reviewing First Interstate's bid, they invoked the "business judgment rule." Clausen argued, as Armacost did, that Pinola was "a bottom-fisher," unwilling to pay a decent price, and trying to steal control of BankAmerica. As part of the public battle, Clausen demeaned Pinola's management skills. "We may have taught them all *they* know, but we didn't teach them all that *we* know," he said at one point in the midst of the debate. An executive at First Interstate wondered whether Clausen's decision not to complete the education of Joe Pinola was the reason First Interstate was still profitable.

The figures on which the directors based their decision were similar to those presented to the board by Armacost in September. BankAmerica still believed that it could mount a turn-around of tremendous strength. Clausen promised that the bank would be profitable by the end of 1987. He blithely ignored the truth about its assets and capital, which was that the assets were overvalued and the capital was overstated. And the directors went along.

Throughout November, December, and January the two sides sparred and threatened. Pinola prepared to buy Bank-America's stock even if Clausen rebuffed him. BankAmerica charged that First Interstate had withheld information from the public, understating its own loan problems. Both chief executives flew around the state talking with the press, while Clausen held pep rallies at the bank and handed out T-shirts, lollipops, and white buttons emblazoned with B of A and FIB in a red circle with a line through it—the international symbol for no.

By January the cost of seeking BankAmerica had risen for Joe Pinola. After the attacks from BankAmerica and after discussions with regulators, First Interstate knew it needed to sell common stock, that is, raise its equity, before it could buy Bank-America. Goldman Sachs was urging Pinola to sell shares soon, to show that the market would buy First Interstate securities. Pinola faced a tough decision. If the sale of stock went through, but the merger didn't, he would have extra shares outstanding, but no new profits. Analysts already thought his profits per share were skimpy.

If Pinola hoped to push his deal through quickly, he had to solve another problem as well. Both BankAmerica and First Interstate owned large banks in Washington that could not be merged for six months—until the state's law against interstate banking changed in July 1987. If Pinola wanted to speed up the merger he had to sell his Washington subsidiary, which he didn't want to do—especially if there was a chance the merger with BankAmerica would never be completed.

Lawyers' fees were mounting, management's time was consumed by the effort to acquire BankAmerica. Pressure was building on Joe Pinola to escalate the battle or quit the field.

After BankAmerica's January board meeting, Tom Clausen phoned Joe Pinola. He asked him to drop his bid, which Pinola refused to do. This time BankAmerica's board had voted unanimously to reject First Interstate's offer. In a statement, the directors said the merged companies would be undercapitalized. They described the First Interstate offer as "highly conditional" and argued that the regulatory issues were "unprecedented." They also took a slap at Pinola and his team, arguing that First Interstate's management lacked "experience in managing an institution as large and complex as the combined company would be."

BankAmerica did not attempt to argue that the price offered by First Interstate was unfair to shareholders. The offer still represented a substantial premium to the price available in the stock market—a benchmark of fairness. Even Salomon Brothers, which had been hired to decide whether First Interstate was offering a fair price, could not bring itself to claim the price was too low. It had written a tepid opinion of the First Interstate offer, saying that if BankAmerica's analysis and forecast of the future were right then the board was safe in rejecting the offer. Based on an earnings projection that showed BankAmerica making profits by the end of 1987, the board rejected First Interstate.

On January 12, 1987, before Pinola could reassess his position, BankAmerica announced that it had agreed to sell Charles Schwab & Co. back to a management group headed by Chuck Schwab. If there was a final, critical factor in First Interstate's decision to quit its fight for control of BankAmerica, this was it.

Chuck Schwab had begun to discuss buying his company back from Tom Clausen during a luncheon meeting two and a half months earlier, on October 31, 1986, Halloween Day. At lunch he had explained why he was the logical buyer for his company. Tom Clausen listened politely. A few days later, at the November board meeting, he asked for and received the board's approval to sell Schwab & Co. Clausen turned to Salomon Brothers and asked its investment bankers to begin the time-consuming process of putting the company up for auction.

Chuck Schwab was not pleased. He hated the idea of his company being auctioned off to the highest bidder. After nearly four years as the subsidiary of a commercial bank, Schwab was leery of being owned by any big organization. He did not want to be tethered to another bank because of the regulatory problems. He ruled out securities firms and insurance companies because of their high-pressure selling. Schwab didn't market his own products and pay salesmen on commission, and he didn't want Schwab & Co. to be sold to an owner that would force him to push its products.

During November and early December, Schwab had prepared his own bid, offering to pay slightly less than $200 million and giving BankAmerica an ultimatum. Schwab would protect the character of his firm. If BankAmerica sold Schwab to an insurer or a securities firm, Chuck Schwab would not go with it.

His contract with BankAmerica ran out in less than a year. After that he was a free agent. And under that contract BankAmerica owned the rights to his name, but not the rights to transfer the name to someone else. If BankAmerica sold the company, Schwab argued, the rights to his name would revert to him and he would be free to leave and set up shop across the street under his own name.

Schwab didn't stop there. He said he was prepared to file a lawsuit arguing that BankAmerica had overstated its profits from 1982 to 1984. He felt the sale of Schwab & Co. to BankAmerica should be reversed because of the misleading statements put out by the bank.

The board didn't like Schwab's position. David Lewis, now retired as chairman of General Dynamics, summed up the feeling, "Where I come from," he said, "they call this blackmail. We shoot blackmailers."

But BankAmerica was in no position to shoot anyone.

Salomon Brothers had determined it could sell Schwab for $250–350 million. Since Schwab was the nation's largest discount broker, since it had a strong position in the West, especially in California, it was probable that BankAmerica could get a price at the upper end of that range. That was especially true given Schwab's surprisingly good year. In early 1986, the bank expected Schwab & Co. to earn around $30 million in pre-tax profits. By November it was clear the company would earn closer to $60 million because of the tremendous surge in stock trading.

One of BankAmerica's outside legal firms, Morrison & Foerster, argued that Schwab's legal action had no merit, that it would never hold up in court. But the lawyers at Wachtell, Lipton, BankAmerica's New York counsel, offered a different view. No buyer in his right mind would pay top dollar for Schwab & Co. if he thought a lawsuit would tie up the sale for years. Morrison & Foerster might be right that Schwab was not entitled to reclaim the use of his name. But it wouldn't matter much if Schwab could so entangle the proposed sale that no outsider would touch it.

The other overriding concern was the publicity that the suit might bring. With First Interstate beating at the door, the last thing Clausen and Newman needed was allegations that shareholders had been lied to and misled for at least three years. No matter how persuasive BankAmerica might be in defending its actions, in the end it would be the loser.

BankAmerica chose not to test Schwab. Although Salomon Brothers was asked to put Schwab & Co. on the block, it never got the chance. After Schwab's first bid, BankAmerica stopped looking for another offer. Just as BankAmerica had turned the screws on Schwab when buying his company, now Schwab had BankAmerica's management in a vise. Instead of hanging tough, Newman caved in. BankAmerica reviewed Schwab's proposal during early December. In mid-December, Newman sat down to negotiate. It took just one day to set a price, with Newman on one side and George Roberts, an old friend of Schwab's, on the other. Roberts was the president of Kohlberg, Kravis, Roberts, the nation's largest leveraged buyout specialist.

Roberts, who had worked on dozens of corporate acquisitions, wrung a bargain out of BankAmerica. In real, economic terms, Chuck Schwab paid no more than $190 million to buy his company—or about three times his profits in 1986.

The way the sale was designed, however, BankAmerica could brag that the price was higher. One newspaper put the price at $280 million, another at $230 million, but those prices, as one investment banker put it, reflected "the optics of the deal," appearances rather than reality.

Schwab agreed to pay $175 million in cash. Then it borrowed $105 million from BankAmerica at below-market rates. Total price: $280 million.

But BankAmerica also canceled a $50 million loan to

Schwab, which reduced the total price to $230 million. And the way the accountants look at it, BankAmerica's loans to Schwab at low interest rates represented a gift as well. The real economic value: less than $190 million.

The only potential gain for BankAmerica came from its right to share in 15 percent of the increase in the value of Schwab & Co. when it went public.

Instead of a price of $300 million for a company earning $30 million a year, BankAmerica got a price of $190 million for a company earning $60 million. Stock appreciation rights may some day bring the total price to more than $230 million. But even that falls at the bottom of the range that Salomon estimated as the company's worth in late 1986.

Once again Salomon Brothers' investment bankers were not happy about the price. They had agonized over their "fairness opinion" on the First Interstate offer. Now they faced another problem. Put on a $1 million-a-month retainer by Newman, Salomon had an obligation to assess the Schwab proposal. Salomon wrote a carefully worded fairness opinion. It said that given the circumstances surrounding the sale, the price was fair to shareholders, but the statement was so carefully worded that it made clear that Salomon was putting distance between itself and the decision.

The sale of Charles Schwab & Co. at a bargain price helped end Joe Pinola's pursuit of BankAmerica. By the first week of February, it was clear that the benefits of buying the company had shrunk. BankAmerica was still losing money. It had sold several of the properties Pinola had hoped to sell. It was reducing its work force faster, cutting expenses. These steps did not guarantee success for BankAmerica, but they reduced Pinola's flexibility if the merger went through.

Early on February 9, 1987, two of Pinola's key advisers, Don Griffith and Bill Sudmann, flew to San Francisco. In the Red Carpet Club of United Airlines they met with the president of the Federal Reserve Bank of San Francisco, Robert Parry, and two of his key aides. Griffith and Sudmann explained that First Interstate was withdrawing its bid for BankAmerica. Parry was concerned. No one knew what might happen if First Interstate withdrew its offer. There was a chance that the rumors that had dogged BankAmerica in September would recur. The Fed urged First Interstate to "be temperate in what you say."

That afternoon, after the New York stock market closed, First Interstate announced its decision. The press release was carefully worded, tinged with the bitterness of the battle that had gone before. "Every word in that press release has a meaning," Joe Pinola said later. "I drafted it myself."

"The current dismemberment of this institution no longer justifies our current offered price," Pinola wrote. "As profitable and strategic BankAmerica Corporation assets are sold, the remaining Latin American debt and other [less-developed country] debt, together with other substantial nonperforming assets, become an increasingly larger part of the smaller banking company. Further, the capital raised through sale of these assets is required to support the balance sheet and thus not available for asset growth.

"The BankAmerica shareholder has been denied . . . the right to vote for or against our proposal."

On the evening of February 9, in the corner office on the fortieth floor of the BankAmerica world headquarters, a bittersweet scene climaxed the tumultuous battle between First Interstate and BankAmerica. Tom Clausen asked Tom Cooper and his executive assistant to walk over to his office.

Clausen had a bottle of champagne on ice. In the stillness of late evening, Clausen proposed a victory celebration. He broke open the champagne, made a toast. The trio stood uncomfortably, Clausen relishing his victory. Cooper suggested that perhaps they should send the news out to the branches. Clausen responded, "No, we deserve this."

In the isolation of the executive suite, Clausen turned to a man who had played only a peripheral role in the defense against First Interstate. (Within a few months, Cooper and his executive assistant would both be gone.)

At the March board meeting, the directors responded to the withdrawal of First Interstate enthusiastically. Midway through the session, one director leaned over to another and observed, "We're on a roll now."

Chapter Thirty-six

It had always been my aim . . . to see to it that the faith and confidence placed in us by our stockholders is more than amply justified. For, after all is said and done, it is just by such faith and confidence that we have been able to accomplish what we have.

A. P. Giannini, 1927

The inevitable clash between Tom Clausen and Tom Cooper had begun in the fall of 1986 and ended before the annual shareholders meeting in May 1987. As similar as they were in some ways, these tough, dedicated executives differed dramatically in style. Perhaps because of his Methodist training or just personal temperament, Cooper eschewed the luxuries of his office. He never flew in the company's Gulfstream III if public flights were available. He drove himself to work. He resented wearing Clausen's anti-FIB buttons and often forgot them, prompting secretaries on the floor to keep a store of buttons for him to put on when meeting Clausen. Cooper declined to speak at several rallies against the bid. And he had resisted hiring an executive assistant, figuring that was one more layer of unnecessary management (though he relented after Clausen arrived).

Tom Clausen, on the other hand, enjoyed the efficiency of his limousine and the company plane. Though he bragged about laying off more than fifteen thousand people in his first year on the job, his personal salary totaled $575,000—equal to what Sam Armacost had earned the year before. He bought a million-dollar home in Hillsborough, a San Francisco suburb where the average house in 1987 sold for $850,000. His personal commitment to cutting costs was a decision to keep just one of the two executive assistants that Armacost left behind. Unlike A. P. Gian-

334

nini, who took no salary after the Great Depression began, Tom Clausen saw no compelling reason to reduce his own standard of living.

The first major disagreement between the two men came in early November 1986, just a month after Clausen took office. Cooper flew to London to deliver a speech and talk with Bank-America clients there. The speech was similar to one Cooper had delivered before Armacost was fired. It outlined BankAmerica's strategy—the strategy first defined in 1984. Cooper explained why BankAmerica was pulling out of some businesses around the world. He explained that BankAmerica found it harder to compete outside the United States for the business of small and medium-sized companies and consumers. Local banks had grown more competitive in the past decade, so BankAmerica had decided to devote itself to California and Washington, selectively serving large corporations and governments outside the western United States.

In responding to questions from reporters, Cooper added detail. He said the bank aimed to cut $450 million in annual expenses, reduce loan losses by half in 1987, and sell $12–13 billion of assets over the next several quarters. There was nothing new in the answers, nothing that had not been bouncing around the halls of BankAmerica for months.

But Clausen was furious. Cooper had overstepped his bounds, disclosing too much of the bank's strategy, and, perhaps, claiming too much credit for shaping that strategy. In his few major public speeches after November, Cooper carefully avoided discussing bank policies in detail.

The two disagreed on the budget. Twice management developed budgets for the company, once in late 1986, and then again in early 1987. But as the first results appeared in 1987, the figures didn't look good enough. Revenues were off sharply, costs seemed to drop with painful slowness. While Cooper was out of the office on business, Clausen and Newman issued a memorandum asking for additional cuts of 10 percent—a third budget with even lower expenses, a budget Cooper thought would hurt morale and the bank's chances for a recovery.

The search had also begun for a new head of the retail bank. The task fell to Cooper, but with strict instructions from Clausen: Don't hire someone from a bank on the East Coast. We've got enough of them around here already.

One of the prime candidates was Richard Rosenberg, who had worked for Dick Cooley at Wells Fargo, then jumped briefly to Crocker National Bank. Before Crocker was bought by Wells Fargo, Rosenberg took a job as president of Seafirst, working for Cooley once more.

Rosenberg balked at leaving Seafirst to come to Bank-America. He asked for a seat on the board, a long-term contract, and an arrangement in which he would report only to the chief executive.

Tom Clausen was forced to decide between Rosenberg and Cooper. If he accepted Rosenberg's conditions, Cooper was almost certain to quit. Rosenberg would assume control of the retail bank, leaving Cooper only one major division reporting to him, the World Banking Division, which already had a leader.

In April, BankAmerica announced that Richard Rosenberg would become vice-chairman of BankAmerica and head of the retail bank, reporting directly to Tom Clausen.

On May 11, Tom Cooper resigned as president of Bank-America. He found himself in a position that was of no real value to the company, a $520,000-a-year post, without a justification for being. Almost every responsibility of the position was duplicated by a job elsewhere.

Outsiders read Cooper's departure as vintage Clausen. Throughout his career at BankAmerica, he had eliminated those with too much power, or those too close to the throne. The pattern was repeating.

At the top of Nob Hill, just a few blocks away from two of San Francisco's best-known hotels, the Fairmont and the Mark Hopkins, lies the Masonic Temple, the site each year of the BankAmerica annual meeting of shareholders. In the years of Sam Armacost's presidency, the shareholders meeting had taken on a circus air. Only on this day did the shareholders, the people who owned BankAmerica, get a chance to ask questions of the men who managed the bank. The rest of the year, they had to suffer in silence or write letters of outrage that were met with polite, impersonal replies. The annual meeting was the day on which they could vent whatever righteous indignation they felt.

BankAmerica's shareholders are unlike those of most American corporations. Normally the shares of companies as large as BankAmerica are controlled almost exclusively by large institutions—other commercial banks, insurance companies, and pension funds. But at BankAmerica, the small shareholders remained, a heritage of A. P. Giannini. Thousands of stockholders owned just a few hundred or a few thousand shares. Each year at the annual meeting, some of them would rise and reminisce about A. P.—how they had met him as a child or how A. P. had helped their fathers or grandfathers in business. Then they would challenge current management, either to remember what Giannini had taught, or to get off the job.

The annual meeting of 1987 had been delayed by a month. In the midst of the fight with First Interstate, the bank had realized that it would be better off delaying the session until well after First Interstate's annual meeting. Assuming the takeover battle would still be on, management wanted distance between the two sessions.

The shareholders met on May 28, a warm spring day, the air clear, with sailboats dotting the bay. More than two thousand BankAmerica watchers, shareholders, and employees passed up the weather for a meeting they had been anticipating for months. This would be a spectacular shareholders meeting, the turbulence of the past year, the losses, the front-page stories, the fight with First Interstate, the firing of Sam Armacost, all bringing out the ferocity of the old-timers.

This meeting would test Tom Clausen, who had never faced hostile shareholders. When he had left BankAmerica, he rode out on a wave of good feelings. He had seemed to produce so well, done what was required of him. Profits had risen, shareholders had been happy, and the board had voted him a special $700,000 bonus for his extraordinary performance.

Now Clausen was preparing to face the most difficult shareholders meeting of his life. A former executive, who had worked closely with Clausen at BankAmerica, thought he knew what Tom Clausen was feeling, and he didn't envy Clausen his task. "A week before the meeting, Tom is going to start practicing his smile," he said. "And every day, he is going to practice smiling and make sure that smile is glued on. And on the day of the meeting, that smile will be there. But at some point, the smile will crack. His hands will shake, his face will turn red, he will lose control."

The Masonic auditorium is a huge, domed amphitheater.

The president of BankAmerica and his senior executives sat on a raised stage. At this annual meeting, Tom Clausen was joined by five other senior executives at a table behind a lectern. They would prove a supporting cast, answering only one brief question. This was, after all, Tom Clausen's bank and Tom Clausen's annual meeting. Perhaps Clausen was being kind, taking all the heat and criticism himself. But to the skeptics in the audience, it was just one more reminder of the old Clausen style. One person was in charge at BankAmerica, and that person was the only man to speak to the shareholders.

In years past, in good times, BankAmerica's shareholders saw a carefully prepared slide show and presentation, the kind of thing that builds enthusiasm among the staff in the retail branches. At the 1987 meeting, held in austere times, there was no such hoopla, no attempt to generate excitement. It would be enough to state the facts, as simply as possible.

The first signal of how tough the meeting would be came with the introductions. As Clausen went through the list of names of senior management and the board of directors, the crowd remained mutinously silent, not wanting to encourage any of them. Then Clausen asked for Claire Giannini Hoffman to stand and be recognized. The entire room burst into applause, loud thunderous approval. But Mrs. Hoffman was not present. She had chosen to boycott the annual meeting of BankAmerica.

Clausen's smile was there. It appeared, at moments, that the smile had indeed frozen on Tom Clausen's face, for his eyes showed no sign of good humor and the words offered nothing to prompt a smile. After dispensing with the routine matters of the annual meeting, the introductions, and a few administrative items, Tom Clausen offered his speech. The presentation had been carefully set. In front of him was a teleprompter, a piece of glass that looks clear to the audience. From the lectern, though, Clausen read the words of his speech reflected from his side of the glass. The teleprompter allowed him to appear to stare right into the eyes of shareholders while reading his speech. The substance of the speech was important, but just as important was the illusion that Tom Clausen was in control, didn't need to speak from notes, having so carefully prepared for this session.

"I have never had to stand before a meeting of Bank-America shareholders and acknowledge that the organization of which I have been, and still am, so very, very proud failed to produce earnings in the year just ended and couldn't afford to pay the holders of its common stock a regular dividend.

"Those of you who know me, know that I am not given to making excuses. I offer no excuses for the performance of this corporation. The record is what it is. It is there to be seen and interpreted by whomever cares to do so, using whatever measures they care to apply.

"The record speaks for itself."

Then he moved quickly to the future. "If you expect us to return this company to sustained profitability, we are going to live up to your expectations," Clausen vowed.

From somewhere, deep in the audience, a woman asked, "When?" Clausen either didn't hear or chose to ignore her.

"If you expect us to restore the common stock dividend, we are going to live up to your expectations, not this year, and maybe not even next, but as soon as possible."

Groans from the audience.

"If you question the credibility of this statement—and on the basis of the corporation's past performance, you have every right to do so—let me remind you, you've not heard it from me before."

This was the rhetoric of battle. Tom Clausen was setting a pact with the shareholders, promising nothing specific, but in turn asking for their restraint and support.

He laid out two corporate objectives. "We will be the dominant provider of premier retail and wholesale banking services in the western United States, and we will be a preeminent wholesale bank offering a wide range of financial services in the United States and world markets. . . . Our conscious goal is to be a smaller company, a much more focused company, and most important, to become once again a *very* profitable company."

Clausen almost avoided criticizing previous management, making only one obviously barbed comment, aimed at Sam Armacost. "I want you to know that we are well aware that one of the chief casualties of recent years has been the credibility of the corporation with many of our constituencies. Excessive optimism that creates unrealistic expectations in the short term only leads to shattered confidence when performance does not match the promise." That excessive optimist could only have been Sam Armacost.

As the speech wound down, Tom Clausen once again found

refuge in a word that appeared oddly out of place. In a short, impassioned plea for support, not only from shareholders but from the many employees who packed the audience, Clausen said that "only as a team will we return to profitability and preeminence."

Clausen was stating his goal: to restore the glory of BankAmerica, to return it to its rightful place in the pantheon of financial companies. He had bragged back in 1977 when BankAmerica regained its position as the largest and most profitable company in the nation; now he was promising to regain that lost title.

During the meeting he chose largely to ignore a crushing development in New York. A week before, Citicorp, the nation's largest banking company, had added $3 billion to a reserve against possible losses on its loans to troubled debtors in Latin America and elsewhere in the less-developed world. Tom Clausen told shareholders only that the action was an unnecessary step, one BankAmerica would not have to follow.

The shareholders were unimpressed by Clausen's optimism. When Clausen opened the floor to questions, the first shareholder to speak, Ralph Pedrini, asked him to resign.

The audience exploded with applause.

The second shareholder suggested that management hire a specialist in turnarounds, maybe Lee Iacocca, who had restored health to Chrysler in the early eighties. Once again, the applause was thunderous.

It went on.

Why don't you cut your salary to $50,000 a year until the dividend is restored? How can you justify paying Sam Armacost $1.7 million in severance pay? The crowd booed when Clausen responded that the pay package was "normal for large companies."

Who do these directors think they work for? How can you nominate the same directors year after year after year when the performance is so miserable?

Clausen handled the questioning with aplomb. Only one question, from a young shareholder who accused him of sidestepping questions from others, seemed to draw out Clausen's inner thoughts. After repeating his summary of the bank's strategy, his voice displayed a hint of emotion. There was in this response an echo of the young calling officer who had just lost big money on a loan and was so devastated by his failure. His tone was almost plaintive.

"We have to reduce our expenses. There is no choice," he

said. "We can't have a third year of operating losses, a third year of reported losses. So therefore we can't keep doing 'things' the way we used to. There have to be changes."

With that, the mask slipped back on, the response became bland, impersonal. But in the moment that the mask had slipped, it revealed how little Tom Clausen had changed. What was being done at BankAmerica was being done to restore the profits of the bank as quickly as possible—the future was a long time off. He might as well have responded, "You're talking about tomorrow, I'm talking about this afternoon."

Eleven days after meeting shareholders, promising profits by the end of 1987, and promising that he would do something about the excessive optimism that led to "shattered confidence," Tom Clausen announced that BankAmerica would lose more than $1 billion in the second quarter—the largest loss in the company's history and nearly twice what it had lost in its worst quarter under Sam Armacost.

Those who attended the annual meeting may have felt outrage building, for Tom Clausen had misled them. As he was telling shareholders, "Confidence is one of the most important assets of a financial institution. We live and die at the hands of public trust," he must have known already that this loss was coming, but he did not share that knowledge with stockholders.

On May 19, nine days before Clausen met with shareholders, Citicorp had announced its decision to establish a special Latin American debt reserve in the second quarter. The market had cheered, sending Citicorp's stock higher.

Securities analysts knew immediately that other banks, including BankAmerica, would be forced to follow Citicorp's lead. What the analysts could not fathom was why Clausen denied the inevitable, becoming the only chief executive at a major commercial bank to state that he thought his bank's reserve was adequate—even though almost no financial analyst in America believed this was the case. It appeared he was trying to take pressure off himself at the shareholders meeting. Critics bristled. "He just stepped all over himself," said an investment banker. "He goes up to the shareholders and complains about 'excessive optimism' and then he does shit like this. The guy is an embarrassment."

Then Clausen chose an extremely aggressive course in creating a special reserve. Citicorp's announcement had been straightforward. Because of the tremendous risks and uncertainties related to the debt of Latin American borrowers, Citicorp would set aside $3 billion, bringing its total reserve for the debt of governments and businesses in Latin American and other less-developed countries to about $3.5 billion, almost exactly 25 percent of its shaky debts.

The reserve was not excessive. If Citicorp had been forced to sell its Latin American debt in mid-May 1987, the company would have received no more than fifty cents on the dollar, and probably less. A 25 percent reserve was a first step in providing for future losses.

Eleven days after its annual shareholders meeting, Bank-America announced it would set aside a similar reserve, suggesting that its cushion would approximate 25 percent of its shaky debts. The company claimed less debt outstanding to troubled less-developed countries than Citicorp—$10 billion versus Citicorp's $14 billion. But that still meant BankAmerica needed a special reserve of $2.5 billion.

Yet BankAmerica set aside just $1.1 billion in the second quarter, some $1–1.5 billion less than analysts expected. Ingenuity had been used to transform that $1.1 billion into a $2.5 billion cushion. First, Clausen had assumed that all the bank's "unallocated reserve," a sum of about $700 million, would be available to cover losses on bad LDC debt. The unallocated reserve is a portion of the loan loss reserve set aside as a general buffer. The rest of the reserve is earmarked for specific industries or specific loans. Since BankAmerica still had mountains of bad debt on its books, Clausen appeared to be double-counting, trying to use one dollar of reserves to cover two dollars of problem loans. But that was not his most puzzling decision.

Clausen also sanctioned a maneuver similar to what Chicago politicians used to do when they arranged for the dead to vote. In calculating its reserve, BankAmerica totaled the loans it had written off in those countries—loans already wiped off the books. It argued that the reserve wiped out by those losses should be counted as part of its current reserve against Latin American debt—even though it provided no cushion against possible loans. Using that argument, BankAmerica claimed some $700 million of nonexistent reserves as part of its special reserve against loan losses. The decision mystified most analysts, many of whom wondered how

Ernst & Whinney, its outside auditors, could be comfortable with the figures. But by making those adjustments, BankAmerica could claim a reserve equal to $2.5 billion, or 25 percent of its troubled debt, even though its actual reserve was far less, $1.8 billion at most—or 18 percent of the company's troubled LDC debt.

Robert Albertson, an analyst then with Smith, Barney, Harris, & Upham and now with Goldman Sachs, summed up the decision with kindness, saying, "I don't expect them to do what Citicorp did. But I don't want people to think they did, either."

Just seven months after returning to BankAmerica, Tom Clausen had proven that very little had changed. After bemoaning the "loss of credibility of the company" at the shareholders meeting, he stuck to a tradition of more than twenty years, massaging the financial reports of BankAmerica until it was nearly impossible for investors to assess the company's true condition. In 1980 he and Sam Armacost had created more than $85 million of dubious profits, an act that laid the foundation for years of mismanagement. From 1980 to 1984, the bank had consistently understated the effect of its loan problems on profits. In 1985 and 1986 regulators had forced a semblance of reality in the financial statements. Now the illusions were back.

In the months that followed the annual meeting, BankAmerica's management repeated its goal of returning to preeminence. It minimized its problems, and by the end of 1987 the company was encouraging the press to write stories about the powerful turnaround that was coming at the company.

Perhaps from the upper reaches of the BankAmerica tower perspective is distorted. The problems may have appeared distant, like storm clouds far over the Pacific Ocean. There must have been, after all, a suspension of disbelief in the executive suite in order to justify the continued payment of six-figure salaries to management. Perhaps these men took comfort because the board was still in place and BankAmerica was still a $93 billion company with offices around the world.

What they missed, apparently, was the accumulated damage wrought over two decades, made huge by the misguided wagers of management that were responsible for breaking the bank. The interest rate mismatch, one former insider estimates, cost the bank more than $3.5 billion. Since 1982, the company had written off more than $6 billion of bad loans, yet as 1988 began it had almost $5 billion in bad debt still on its books, plus at

least $8 billion of loans to shaky Latin American governments
and other less-developed countries, loans that might someday
be written off entirely. The total damage: almost $23 billion—six
times the bank's equity capital at its peak in the early 1980s.

BankAmerica was not the robust, muscular company that
Tom Clausen inherited in 1970. As 1988 began it was an anemic,
bloated firm that would suffer from the slightest economic down-
draft. It had survived as an independent company because of the
web of government regulations that support commercial banks. If
regulators were to force it to report its problem loans at their market value, instead of carrying many at face value, BankAmerica's
equity would likely disappear, the company would be bankrupt.

The men who oversaw the decline of BankAmerica have
suffered little. All earned six-figure salaries in 1987. Tom Clausen made $775,000 as chairman of BankAmerica, including a
$200,000 performance bonus. Sam Armacost and Lee Prussia
were guaranteed the same salaries they had earned at the bank,
$575,000 and $420,000, respectively. And BankAmerica's directors did not forfeit any of their annual fees, which run as high as
$35,000 or slightly more, for a few hours' work a month.

But BankAmerica's shareholders had paid dearly. The actual value of their stock declined by almost $3.3 billion from 1981
to 1987. Had shareholders switched from BankAmerica shares
to an index of the stock market in 1981, the value of their investment would have at least doubled by 1987. This lost value is what
economists call the opportunity cost of an investment. That puts
the price tag on the losses of BankAmerica's shareholders, including the opportunity cost of $4.4 billion, at almost $7.7 billion.

After Tom Clausen returned, in the period between the
time BankAmerica rejected First Interstate's bid and 1988 began—a period of just eleven months—shareholders saw their
wealth decline by half, or $1.1 billion, while the rest of the stock
market showed virtually no change.

As 1988 opened, BankAmerica was struggling to recover
from the accumulated damage of two decades of mismanagement. It was not in the midst of a turnaround. Management
boasted about the company's operating profits, yet those figures
overstated its improvement. The company remained undercapitalized, with about $1 billion less capital than it needed. It also
had a loan loss reserve that was at the low end of the spectrum for

major banks, when measured as a percentage of its problem loans. To reach the average for the industry, BankAmerica needed to add about $1 billion to its reserve. To reach a position of "preeminence," it needed to add more than $3 billion—once again, an amount that would wipe out its equity, in effect bankrupting the company. Despite the sorry state of its reserve, BankAmerica had decided, after setting aside $1.1 billion for LDC debt in mid-1987, not to build the reserve further, in effect diverting money from building the reserve in order to show higher profits in the last half of the year.

Perhaps the weakness of the company was why senior executives of BankAmerica Corp. preferred not to be totally candid. Perhaps this was why they had spent 1987 emphasizing the improvement in the bank's condition and minimizing the challenges that lay ahead.

It was obvious that the principles that had guided A. P. Giannini as he built the world's largest bank had fallen into disuse long before the end of 1987. Gone was the spirit of openness that Giannini had fostered. Gone was the sense that "bankers have nothing to hide." Gone was the commitment to the little fellow. Gone was the special spirit that had separated BankAmerica from the thousands of other commercial banks in the world.

In its place was the legacy of two decades of lost opportunities and misplaced priorities.

As 1987 ended two truths had clearly emerged. The bank that A. P. Giannini had built was dead. It was Tom Clausen's bank now.

Epilogue

No bank ever met disaster through the legitimate losses of a sane banker.

A. P. Giannini, 1928

Nineteen eighty-seven turned out to be the worst year in the banking industry since the Great Depression. The nation's fifteen largest banks lost almost $8 billion as they set aside reserves to cover potential losses on loans in Latin America. Smaller banks failed in near-record numbers, more than at any time since 1933, and the savings and loan industry as a whole lost $7 billion.

Throughout the nation, bankers found themselves facing the same disturbing problems that had plagued BankAmerica. In order to raise capital and restore profits, they were forced to sell buildings, jettison once-prized divisions, and fire employees. Even the industry's best-managed companies, such as Citicorp and J. P. Morgan & Co., suffered through a traumatic year.

By early 1988 the outlines of a dramatic restructuring of the entire banking industry were clear. A group of nearly two dozen large regional banks had emerged from 1987 with strong balance sheets and high profits. They were buying banks in neighboring states and growing larger and more powerful, establishing their claim to a position of leadership in the banking industry in the 1990s. New York City's major banks and other money center banks, which had led the banking industry since before the turn of the century, were in decline. Perhaps three banks—Citicorp, J. P. Morgan, and Bankers Trust—appeared destined to remain leaders in the industry. A second tier of banks, including Chase Manhattan and Chemical Bank, seemed destined to play a major, although perhaps less dominant, role in the industry,

347

while a third tier, including Manufacturers Hanover and Bank-
America, appeared so burdened by loan problems that their survival as independent companies remained uncertain.

Third-tier banks faced a bleak future. As valiantly as their
managements might proclaim that a recovery was underway, the
banks were saddled with too many loan problems and too little
capital. While they convalesced, their competitors grew stronger. And as their competitors grew stronger the chances increased
that one of them would acquire these weakened larger banks. No
matter what strategy a troubled institution followed it would remain vulnerable to a takeover through much of the next decade.

As 1988 began, BankAmerica was firmly anchored in the
third tier of the banking industry. Its management sounded increasingly confident that they were, as one senior executive told
a news service in early 1988, "mounting the most dramatic turnaround in the industry's history." Yet at the moment he made
that claim, BankAmerica had the weakest balance sheet of any
large commercial bank in the United States—a tremendous
handicap in a battle for survival.

Insiders at BankAmerica feel they have strong justification
for their optimism. Their financial reports during the last half of
1987 and the first half of 1988 suggest that the company is recov-
ering. Some investors apparently agree. A stock analyst at a major Wall Street firm proclaimed in late 1987 that BankAmerica's
stock offered a "golden buying opportunity."

Outsiders can only wonder. It remains almost impossible
for an outsider to test the validity of BankAmerica's claim of a recovery. Its profits in 1987 and 1988 came largely from a decrease
in write-offs of bad loans. The quality of BankAmerica's loan
portfolio did improve in 1987. Agriculture, real estate, and other
sectors of California's economy recovered some vigor. But without access to a fairly complete list of BankAmerica's borrowers it
is impossible to know whether BankAmerica's write-offs are an
accurate reflection of the health of the loan portfolio or simply
wishful thinking by management. Though the problem loans on
the company's books declined during 1987 and 1988, the bank
had more loan problems as a percentage of total loans than any
other major bank as 1988 began. Given BankAmerica's poor record of predicting loan losses prior to 1987, it was hard for investors to accept management's claims of improvement at face
value.

BankAmerica appears destined to be acquired by another company—probably in 1991 or shortly thereafter, when California law will permit banks outside the state to buy California banks. The exact timing of any acquisition will depend on the speed with which potential acquirors recover from 1987's losses. Very few banks had the financial strength to buy BankAmerica at the end of 1987 and fewer still would have been willing to take on its loan problems. The likely buyers for the company after 1991 would include major banks in New York and several of the strongest regional banks. It is unlikely that they will reward shareholders of BankAmerica for their patience. The company's liquidation, or book, value in 1988 was about $15 a share. In today's market, a purchaser might be willing to pay somewhere between $18 and $22 a share for BankAmerica stock—if BankAmerica's management had already cleaned up problems with its LDC debt and other troubled loans. The price is unlikely to be higher than the offer made by First Interstate in 1986.

Other, less likely alternatives remain as well. BankAmerica could be broken up and sold in pieces. Some portions of BankAmerica's business, most notably its basic franchises in California and Washington, are attractive and quite profitable. But other portions, including its Latin American debt and bad loans, could not be sold without recognizing huge losses. A breakup probably could only be done by bank regulators and they would not step in unless the company faced collapse. If regulators did intervene, shareholders would be virtually wiped out.

Another option for federal regulators is to force BankAmerica to shrink, hoping that a smaller institution would be easier to save or sell than a large one. BankAmerica has been shrinking since 1985, dropping from a high of about $120 billion in assets to $93 billion in assets at the end of 1987. Could it shrink further? Obviously, the answer is yes. Under minimum capital guidelines proposed by federal regulators, BankAmerica has enough equity capital to justify only about $60 billion in assets. Since it is unlikely that the bank can raise capital in the open market at prices acceptable to shareholders, some shrinkage must come. If federal regulators should force the bank to simultaneously boost its reserve against Latin American debt and meet minimum capital requirements, BankAmerica could be forced to shrink to less than $50 billion in assets. This downsizing would not necessarily solve its problems, and regulators realize that. BankAmerica's bad loans would not go away, nor would its high overhead. Although the company has trimmed some fifteen thousand people from its rolls since early 1986, if it were forced to shrink further it might need to lay off between fifteen and thirty thousand more simply to reduce overhead expenses to the average for the industry.

No one can rule out the possibility that BankAmerica will survive as an independent company. If the economy recovers briskly, if management makes no serious missteps, BankAmerica could struggle back to some form of anemic good health by the middle of the next decade. Given the changes occurring in the rest of the industry, BankAmerica would most likely end up as a relatively small player by world standards, a California bank with a solid consumer business. It is hard to imagine the company ever regaining the swagger and dominance that it had prior to 1980.

One of the most disturbing conclusions others have drawn from BankAmerica's fall is, in effect, that management does not matter much in banking, that it is luck, geography, and size that determine a company's fate, not the intelligence and foresight of its leaders. The *New York Times Magazine* intoned in early 1987, "There are no black hats at Bank of America: it's just that in organizations of a certain size unforeseen problems seem to become unrecognized difficulties and then unmanagable losses. Perhaps the populists (of both parties) are right, and the time has come to resume the crusade against bigness itself."

Yet the same article pointed out the difference in performance between BankAmerica and Citicorp in the 1980s—a telling example of the difference that management can make. In 1980, just before Tom Clausen stepped down as president of BankAmerica, Citicorp and BankAmerica were almost the same size, with about $115 billion in assets. The stock market thought they were each worth just under $3.2 billion. Seven years later Citicorp was nearly twice as big as BankAmerica, it was worth four times as much in the stock market, and employed nearly thirty thousand more people. Although Citicorp's decision to build a large reserve against its loans to less-developed countries produced a $1 billion loss in 1987, the company's pre-tax profit before the special reserve totaled over $2 billion, ten times the comparable figure for BankAmerica.

Just before the end of the 1970s Citicorp had made a major strategic investment in retail banking, betting that lending money to consumers would be a profitable, fast-growing business in the next decade. Management won its bet, in the process reshaping Citicorp to take advantage of opportunities in new markets.

BankAmerica's management, board, and outside advisers failed to prepare the company to compete in the 1980s. It made mistakes right out of management textbooks: decentralizing without proper controls, losing touch with customers and markets, spending lavishly on technology (more than $2 billion over five years, only to end up with a system still considered antiquated by the industry), and failing to find appropriate ways to measure and reward the performance of executives. BankAmerica grew too large for the management systems it had, but that does not excuse the men who managed the company. They failed to repair the company's management systems and seemed to miss the strains placed on the company by the inflation of the 1970s. By the time prices fell in the 1980s it was too late to make many of the repairs, but management still failed to move swiftly to minimize the damage.

There were black hats at BankAmerica, men who sat idle for too long at the highest levels of one of the nation's best-known companies, men who accepted large salaries and tremendous responsibility for running a corporation and failed in their duties. They have gone on to other high-paying posts or retired with generous benefits. The people who paid most dearly for these mistakes are the shareholders and employees of BankAmerica who lost their income, jobs, and, in many cases, their pride. Those losses cannot be regained.

Author's Notes

The foundation of this book is a series of taped interviews with close to two hundred executives, former executives, directors, former directors, and other individuals knowledgeable about Bank of America. Most of these people asked not to be identified because of their loyalty to others still working at Bank of America.

The sections of the book on the last twenty years at Bank of America draw heavily on these interviews, notes of participants, personal diaries, bank and board documents, court filings, annual reports, and newspaper and magazine articles.

Most direct quotes in this book come from interviews between the author and the individual cited. In some sequences, however, especially in boardroom scenes, the dialogue is drawn from notes of participants as well as interviews with at least two and in some cases more than a dozen who attended the session. Since some participants declined to be interviewed, the appearance of a quote from an individual does not assure that I have interviewed that person.

In some chapters, particularly in historical matter, I have relied heavily on previously published sources. The first section of the book, "The Giannini Years," is based almost exclusively on the many books and articles that have appeared on the life of A. P. Giannini. Some of this material comes from Bank of America's archives, and was provided by the bank, though the archives are largely closed to the public because of budget cuts. Among the sources of information used are the following:

Books

James, Marquis and Bessie. *Biography of a Bank: The Story of Bank of America.* New York: Harper and Brothers, 1954.
Dana, Julian. *Giant in the West.* New York: Prentice-Hall, 1947.
Dillon, Richard H. *North Beach: The Italian Heart of San Francisco.*

Novato, Calif.: Presidio Press, 1985.

Starr, Kevin. *Inventing the Dream: California through the Progressive Era.* New York: Oxford University Press, 1985

Yeates, Fred. *The Gentle Giant.* San Francisco: Wallace Kibbee and Son, 1954.

Articles

Clarke, Dwight. "The Gianninis—Men of the Renaissance." *California Historical Society Quarterly* 49 (September and December 1970). Two-part series.

Dowrie, George. "History of the Bank of Italy in California." *Journal of Economic and Business History* 2 (February 1930).

Giovinco, Joseph. "Democracy in Banking: The Bank of Italy and California's Italians." *California Historical Society Quarterly* 47 (September 1968).

Hayes, Reed. "The Story of the Bank of Italy and A. P. Giannini." Seventy-two-part series in the *San Francisco News,* 1928.

Jacobson, Pauline. "How I Began My Life: Amadeo P. Giannini Tells Pauline Jacobson the Story of His Early Struggles." *San Francisco Call*, 1921.

Josephson, Matthew. 'Big Bull of the West." Four-part series in the *Saturday Evening Post*, September-October 1947.

Articles in other publications, ranging from *Time* and *Sunset* magazines to various BankAmerica employee publications provided additional information.

Quotations from A. P. Giannini that precede each chapter are drawn from a 118-page collection compiled by BankAmerica in the mid-1960s.

Material in "The Clausen Decade," "The Armacost Years," and "Clausen Revisited" is based largely on interviews between the author and those involved in the bank's activities, supported by material from magazines and publications including *Fortune, Business Week, Forbes,* the *Los Angeles Times,* the *San Francisco Chronicle,* the *San Francisco Examiner,* the *New York Times, American Banker,* and the *Wall Street Journal.*

Sections of the book that draw more heavily on articles by others include the portion of chapter 12 on Samuel Armacost's youth, which is derived in part from articles in *Business Week* and the *Los Angeles Times.* The chapter recounting Seafirst Corporation's problems and merger with BankAmerica draws on sections of both *Behind Closed Doors* by Hope Lampert and *Belly Up* by Phillip Zweig. Facts on Melvin Powers's murder trial in chapter 19 are drawn from a book by Jay Nash, *Murder among the Mighty*, and from articles in Houston newspapers. Details of the Rittenhouse Square and Sebastopol grower cases come from court documents and news reports, as does the material on the National Mortgage Equity Corporation mortgage scandal.

Index